SECRETS of TEACHING ESL GRAMMAR

Carl W. Hart

Secrets of Teaching ESL Grammar:
A Fun, Easy-to-Understand, Fast-Paced, Intensive,
Step-by-Step Manual on How to Teach ESL Grammar

Copyright © 2015 Carl W. Hart
All rights reserved.
ISBN-13: 978-0-692-32976-4
LCCN: 2014920463

back cover photo: Stephen Barkley

RIVERWOODS PRESS

P.O. Box 424
Hobart, Indiana 46342
USA
info@riverwoodspress.com

<u>Table of Contents</u>

Introduction. xvii

Chapter 1: Advice, Heresy and Random Musings. 1

   1.1 Why teach grammar at all?. 1
   1.2 Boring grammar or boring teachers?. 1
   1.3 Only grammar in a grammar class?. 1
   1.4 Asking questions 2
   1.5 Vocabulary. 2
   1.6 Why no preposition chapter?. 2
   1.7 Variables 3
   1.8 Detailed lesson plans?. 3
   1.9 Tell them why you're doing what you're doing. 3
  1.10 Go with the flow. 4
  1.11 Textbooks aren't etched in stone. 4
  1.12 Motivation 5
  1.13 Be more than a teacher. 5
  1.14 Be a covert teacher. 6
  1.15 Watch your language. 6
  1.16 Repeat, repeat, repeat!. 6
  1.17 Whoa!. 6
  1.18 One step at a time. 7
  1.19 Game theory. 7
  1.20 Keep 'em talking. 7
  1.21 Error correction. 8
  1.22 Deductive/inductive 8
  1.23 i+1 9
  1.24 Interference 9
  1.25 Collocations 9
  1.26 Heresy. 10
  1.27 Alphabet soup. 10
  1.28 AE or BE? 10
  1.29 Jargon alert! 11
  1.30 Leave 'em with a tease. 11

Chapter 2: *Be*. 13

   2.1 Focus on form and function will follow. 13
   2.2 Tense/aspect/mood?. 13
   2.3 *be = am, is, are, was, were*. 13
   2.4 Uses of *be*. 13
   2.5 Start with *be* + nouns, *be* + adjectives and *be* + prepositional phrases. . 14
   2.6 *be* + continuous (and naughty grammar bits) 14
   2.7 *you*—singular/plural 14
   2.8 Don't be active with the passive. 14
   2.9 *be* + adverbs—not as simple as you think 14
  2.10 Suggested sequence and sample 15
      ▶ Present 15
         ▷ Present contractions 16
         ▷ Present negative contractions. 16
         ▷ Present *yes/no* questions 17

    ▶ Past 18
       ▷ Past negative and contractions 18
       ▷ Past *yes/no* questions 19
    ▶ Present and past short answers with *be* 20
  2.11 Ellipsis 20
  2.12 Listening practice 21
  2.13 Three-way speaking practice with *be* 21

Chapter 3: Present Continuous and Past Continuous 23
  3.1 Relatively easy 23
  3.2 Continuous used only for now? 23
  3.3 The *-ing* form 23
  3.4 Some verbs are never continuous (except when they are) 23
  3.5 Simple independent clauses at first 23
  3.6 Suggested sequence and sample exercises 24
  3.7 Mixed review exercises 25
  3.8 Speaking practice—*yes/no* questions 26
  3.9 Speaking practice—information questions 26
  3.10 Future continuous? 27

Chapter 4: *Do, Does* and *Did* 29
  4.1 *do, does* and *did*—vitally important and hard as hell 29
  4.2 Present simple 29
  4.3 Start with *do* 30
  4.4 Questions with *do* 30
  4.5 Negatives with *do* 30
  4.6 Contractions with *do* 31
  4.7 Short answers with *do* 31
  4.8 Speaking practice with *do* 31
  4.9 The accursed *-s* form 31
    ▶ Irregular *-s* forms 32
  4.10 *does* 32
  4.11 Speaking practice with *does* 33
  4.12 *did* 33
    ▶ *did* with regular verbs 33
    ▶ *did* with irregular verbs 33
  4.13 Speaking practice with *do, does* and *did* 34
  4.14 Strain their brains 34
  4.15 Ellipsis with *do, does* and *did* 35
  4.16 Alas 36
  4.17 Three more things 37
    ▶ One for now: *Have you a…?* 37
    ▶ And two for later 37
       ▷ Two, the emphatic *do* 37
       ▷ Three, *do* is an auxiliary verb and a main verb 38

Chapter 5: Future 41
  5.1 Two stages 41
  5.2 *will* and *be going to* 41
  5.3 *will* for willingness 41
    ▶ With *will* no *do*, no *does*, no *did*, no *s*, no *ed*, no *ing* 42
  5.4 Questions with *will* 42
  5.5 Negative contractions of will 43
  5.6 *be going to* 44
  5.7 *be going to* and *will* used for predictions and plans 44
    ▶ Predictions 44

    ▶ Plans 44
      ▷ Leave past plans for later. 44
  5.8 *go* overload 44
  5.9 *shall*? 44
  5.10 *gonna* 46
  5.11 Listening practice 46
  5.12 Speaking practice 46
  5.13 Present continuous for future plans 47
    ▶ More *go* overload. 48
    ▶ Practice present continuous for future plans. 48
  5.14 Present simple for scheduled future events 48
  5.15 *be about to* 49
  5.16 *be to* 49
  5.17 Ellipsis with the future 49

Chapter 6: Nouns and Pronouns 53
  6.1 Subject pronouns and object pronouns 53
    ▶ Speaking practice 54
  6.2 Possessive adjectives 54
    ▶ More speaking practice 55
  6.3 Possessive pronouns 55
  6.4 Possessive nouns 56
    ▶ Even more speaking practice 57
  6.5 Indirect objects 57
    ▶ Slight AE/BE difference 58
  6.6 It's easy to get ahead of yourself. 59
  6.7 Articles 59
  6.8 *any* and *some* 60
  6.9 Indefinite pronouns and indefinite adverbs 60
    ▶ Indefinite pronouns 61
    ▶ Indefinite adverbs 61
    ▶ Indefinite pronouns and indefinite adverbs: two negative patterns 62
  6.10 Count nouns, noncount nouns and quantifiers 62
  6.11 Reflexive pronouns 64
    ▶ Mistakes that native speakers make with reflexive pronouns (and that might include yourself) 64
    ▶ Three uses of reflexive pronouns 65
  6.12 Listening practice 65

Chapter 7: Asking Questions 67
  7.1 Why an entire chapter about asking questions? 68
  7.2 Two kinds of verbs 68
  7.3 Inversion 68
    ▶ *be* 68
    ▶ *have* 68
    ▶ Modal auxiliary verbs 68
    ▶ *do* 69
  7.4 *do*, a word about nothing 69
  7.5 *yes/no* question inversion practice 70
  7.6 Question words and information questions 70
  7.7 *who* 71
  7.8 *what* 71
  7.9 *when* 71
  7.10 *what time* 72
  7.11 *where* 72
  7.12 *why* 72
  7.13 *what kind of* 73

7.14 *which* 73
7.15 *whose* 73
7.16 *how much*. 73
7.17 *how many*. 74
7.18 *how often* (and adverbs of frequency). 74
7.19 *how far is/was it* (*from* + location) *to* + location 74
7.20 *how*. 75
7.21 *how* with adverbs 75
7.22 *how* with adjectives. 76
7.23 *how long* for lengths of time 76
7.24 *how long* + modal/a form of *do* + *it take* (someone) *to* 76
7.25 *what* + a form of *do* used when the answer to a question is a verb. . . . 77
7.26 *who* and *what* used when the answer to a question is the subject 77
7.27 *whom* 78
7.28 Negative questions—three functions. 79
   ▸ To start a conversation 79
   ▸ To confirm information that we already think is correct 79
   ▸ To make a point 79
7.29 Tag questions 80
   ▸ Making tag question 80
     ▹ *be* 80
     ▹ Modals/*do, does, did* 80
     ▹ Perfect tenses. 80
     ▹ *this, that, these, those* 80
     ▹ *there is, there are* 81
     ▹ *everybody, something*, etc. 81
   ▸ Two functions of tag questions 81
     ▹ To confirm information that the speaker thinks is probably true (and sometimes to also make a point) . . . 81
     ▹ To learn the answer to something we're really not sure about 81
7.30 *aren't I?* NO!!! 81
7.31 Listening practice. 81
   ▸ Reduced *yes/no* questions. 82
   ▸ Reduced information questions 82

Chapter 8: Phrasal Verbs 83
8.1 Phrasal verbs are verbs! 83
8.2 Phrasal verbs are everywhere.. 83
8.3 Separable or inseparable? 83
8.4 Nouns made from phrasal verbs. 84
8.5 Adjectives made from phrasal verbs 84

Chapter 9: *Have Got* and *Have Got To* 87
9.1 Why an entire chapter on *have got* and *have got to*? 87
9.2 So what does *got* mean? 87
9.3 Bewilder your students (for a good cause). 87
9.4 Listening practice. 88
9.5 Grammar stuff. 88
9.6 Negative with *have got*. 89
9.7 Questions with *have got*. 89
9.8 *have to* = *have got to* 90
9.9 Negative with *have got to* 91
9.10 Questions with *have got*. 91
9.11 Bad but sadly common grammar 91
9.12 Listening practice. 92
9.13 Ellipsis with *have got*. 92
9.14 Ellipsis with *have got to* 92

Chapter 10: Perfect Tenses 95
  10.1 *have*: auxiliary verb and main verb 95
  10.2 Three types of perfect sentences 95
  10.3 Past participles. 96
  10.4 Focus on the present perfect (especially) and the past perfect. 96
  10.5 Three uses of the present perfect 96
      ▶ One, to connect a past time and the present. 96
      ▶ Two, to connect two or more past times and the present 97
      ▶ Three, to connect a continuous time which started in the past and the present 97
  10.6 Mechanics and memorization 98
  10.7 Contractions and short answers 98
  10.8 Present perfect contractions 98
  10.9 Three ways to use the past perfect. 100
      ▶ One, to connect an earlier past time with a more recent time in the past. 100
      ▶ Two, to connect two or more past times and a more recent time in the past. 100
      ▶ Three, to connect a continuous time and a more recent time in the past 101
  10.10 Past perfect contractions 101
  10.11 Past perfect used to show causality 102
  10.12 Three uses of the future perfect (in case your students aren't totally confused already) 102
      ▶ One, to connect an earlier time in the future with a later past time in the future. . . . 103
      ▶ Two, to connect two or more times in the future and a later past time in the future. . . . 103
      ▶ Three, to connect a continuous time in the future and a later time in the future 103
  10.13 Future perfect contractions. 103
  10.14 Past perfect and future perfect tenses and reversible clauses. 103
  10.15 Continuous perfect sentences 104
      ▶ Present perfect continuous. 104
      ▶ Past perfect continuous. 104
      ▶ Future perfect continuous 104
  10.16 *for* and *since* 104
  10.17 *just, yet* and *already* 105
      ▶ *just*. 105
      ▶ *yet* 105
        ▷ Simple sentence 105
        ▷ Compound sentence (two independent clauses joined by a conjunction) 105
        ▷ Complex sentence
          (an independent clause and a dependent clause joined by a subordinating conjunction) 105
      ▶ *already* 105
  10.18 *ever*. 106
  10.19 *been to*. 107
  10.20 *not* vs. *never* 107
  10.21 Listening 107
  10.22 Ellipsis with perfect tenses 107

Chapter 11: Adjectives 109
  11.1 Two basic patterns of adjective use 109
  11.2 Before a noun109
  11.3 After a linking verb (aka copular verb). 109
  11.4 Comparative and superlative forms. 111
  11.5 Opposites of comparative and superlative forms 111
  11.6 Comparative forms. 111
      ▶ Comparative adjective forms 112
  11.7 Superlative forms 112
      ▶ Superlative adjective forms. 113
  11.8 Modifying comparative forms of adjectives. 113
  11.9 Using superlatives 114

11.10 Participle adjectives 114
11.11 Adjective + preposition combinations 115
11.12 *get* used with adjectives 115
11.13 *get used to* and *be used to*. 116
11.14 *-ing/-ed* participle adjectives 117
11.15 Nouns used as adjectives (aka compound nouns) 118
11.16 Most common mistake with nouns used as adjectives (aka compound nouns). . 119
11.17 Two words?, hyphenate?, one word? 119
11.18 Compound adjectives 119
11.19 Common compound adjective mistakes 121
11.20 Adverbs and compound adjectives 121
11.21 Making comparisons with *same, similar, different, like* and *alike*. 122
    ▶ *same*. 122
    ▶ *similar* 122
    ▶ *different*. 122
    ▶ *like/alike* 122
11.22 Adjectives modified by adverbs 123
    ▶ Grading adverbs modify gradable adjectives 123
    ▶ Non-grading adverbs modify non-gradable adjectives. 124
    ▶ Staying out of trouble with the grammar police (not your students, you!) . 124

Chapter 12: Modals and Phrasal Modals 127
12.1 Go beyond the basics 127
12.2 Terminology. 127
12.3 Easy and not easy. 127
12.4 Meaning and functions 127
12.5 Asking for permission with *may, could* and *can* 129
12.6 Asking for permission with *would you mind* and *do you mind* 129
12.7 Asking people to do something with *would, could, will* and *can* 130
12.8 Asking people to do something with *would you mind* 131
12.9 *borrow* and *lend* 131
12.10 Saying something was necessary in the past with *had to* 133
12.11 Saying something is not necessary with *have to* or is not allowed with *must* . . 133
12.12 Saying something is a good idea or a bad idea in the present or future with should, ought to and had better . 134
    ▶ *should*. 134
    ▶ *ought to*. 134
    ▶ *had better*. 134
12.13 Saying something was a good idea or a bad idea in the past with *should*. 135
12.14 Talking about ability in the past, present and future with *can, could* and *be able to* . . . 136
    ▶ *can* and *be able to* for present ability. 136
    ▶ *could* and *be able to* for past ability. 136
    ▶ *could* and *will be able to* for future ability. 136
12.15 Talking about repeated past actions and past situations with *used to* and *would* . . . 137
12.16 Using modals with the phrasal modals *have to* and *be able to*. 138
12.17 *would rather* 138
12.18 Certainty, predictions and expectations 140
12.19 Degrees of certainty about the present with *must, have to, have got to, may, might, can* and *could* 140
    ▶ + 100% sure (no modal or phrasal modal). 140
    ▶ + Very certain (*must, have to* or *have got to*) 140
    ▶ + Maybe (*might, may* or *could*) 141
    ▶ – Maybe not (*might not* or *may not*) 141
    ▶ – Very certain with emphasis on the negative (*must not*) 141
    ▶ – Almost 100% sure with emphasis on the negative (*cannot* or *could not*) . 141
    ▶ – 100% sure with emphasis on the negative (no modal or phrasal modal) . 141
12.20 Degrees of certainty about the past with *must, have to, have got to, may, might, can* and *could* . . . 142

▶ + 100% sure (no modal or phrasal modal) 142
▶ + Very certain (*must have*) 142
▶ + Maybe (*might have, may have* or *could have*) 142
▶ − Maybe not (*might not have* or *may not have*) 142
▶ − Very certain with emphasis on the negative (*must not have*) 142
▶ − Almost 100% sure with emphasis on the negative (*cannot have* or *could not*) . . 142
▶ − 100% sure with emphasis on the negative (no modal or phrasal modal) 143
12.21 *may have* and *might have*: slightly different 143
12.22 Degrees of certainty about the future, part 1, with *will, be going to, might, may* and *could* 144
▶ + 100% sure (*will* or *be going to*) 144
▶ + Somewhat certain (will *probably* or *be probably going to*) 144
▶ + Maybe (*might, may* or *could*) 144
▶ − Maybe not (*might not* or *may not*) 144
▶ − Momewhat certain with emphasis on the negative (*probably will not* or *be probably not going to*) 144
▶ − 100% sure with emphasis on negative (*will not* or *be not going to*) 144
12.23 Degrees of certainty about the future, part 2, with *will, be going to* and a bunch of adverbs 145
12.24 Certainty: talking about expectations based on previous knowledge or experience with *should* and *ought to* . . 146
12.25 Plans: talking about past plans with *be going to* 147
12.26 Talking about expectations with *be supposed to* 148
12.27 *be to* 149
12.28 Headlinese 151
12.29 Ellipsis with modals and phrasal modals 152

Chapter 13: Adjective Clauses and Adjective Phrases 155
13.1 Adjective clauses do the same job as adjectives 155
13.2 Subject adjective clauses 156
13.3 Object adjective clauses 157
13.4 Object adjective clauses with verb + preposition combinations 159
13.5 Amazing additional info on verb + preposition combinations 160
13.6 *whose* in subject adjective clauses 160
13.7 Relative adverbs *where* and *when* used in adjective clauses 161
13.8 Relative adverb *why* used in adjective clauses 161
13.9 Punctuation of adjective clauses—restrictive and nonrestrictive 162
13.10 Nonrestrictive adjective clauses and quantifiers 163
13.11 Nonrestrictive adjective clauses and superlatives 164
13.12 Adjective clauses reduced to restrictive adjective phrases 165
▶ Restrictive present participle phrases 165
▶ Restrictive past participle phrases 167
▶ Restrictive adjective phrases with actual adjectives 168
▶ Restrictive adjective phrases made with prepositional phrases 168
13.13 Adjective clauses reduced to nonrestrictive adjective phrases 169
▶ Nonrestrictive present participle phrases (fronted and extraposed) 169
▶ Nonrestrictive adjective phrases with actual adjectives (fronted and extraposed) . . 170
13.14 Appositives 171
▶ Nonrestrictive appositives 171
▶ Restrictive appositives 172
▶ Nonrestrictive appositives (fronted and extraposed) 172
13.15 *which* used to modify an entire sentence 173

Chapter 14: Noun Clauses 175
14.1 Definition of noun clause 175
14.2 Embedded questions: noun clauses beginning with a question word 175
14.3 Noun clauses beginning with *if* or *whether (or not)* 177
14.4 Noun clauses with question words and infinitives 178
14.5 Object noun clauses beginning with *that* 178
14.6 Subject noun clauses beginning with *that* 179

14.7 Noun clauses in reported speech 179
14.8 Quoted and reported speech. 181
14.9 Plans: talking about past plans with noun clauses with *would* and *be going to* 181
  ▶ Direct speech about future plans. 181
  ▶ Direct speech about past plans 181
      (which may have already happened or which may be unrealized or unconfirmed) 181
  ▶ Reported (indirect) speech about past plans
      (which may already have happened or which may be unrealized or unconfirmed) 181

Chapter 15: The Passive 183
15.1 The passive voice 183
15.2 A lot of baloney is believed by some people about the passive.. 183
15.3 Review past participles. 183
15.4 Start with mechanics. 183
15.5 *why* and *when* 186
  ▶ To emphasize the receiver of the action of the verb rather than the doer . . . 186
  ▶ When the doer of the verb's action is unknown. 186
  ▶ When the doer of the verb's action is obvious or not important 186
  ▶ When we want to avoid revealing the doer of the action of the verb. 187
15.6 Not always simple SVO. 187
15.7 Passive modals. 188
  ▶ Present/future: modal/semi-modal + *be* + past participle 188
  ▶ Past passive: modal/semi-modal + *have been* + past participle 188
15.8 Passives with *get*. 189

Chapter 16: Adverbs, Adverb Clauses, Adverb Phrases and More 191
16.1 Adverbs—an oddball grab bag. 191
16.2 Adverbs of manner 191
  ▶ Comparative and superlative forms 192
  ▶ Irregular adverbs 192
  ▶ *well* 192
  ▶ Adjectives: *well/bad* 192
  ▶ Adverbs: *well/badly*. 192
  ▶ *fast, hard* and *late*. 193
  ▶ *lately* and *hardly* 193
16.3 Adverbs of place. 194
16.4 Adverbs of time. 194
  ▶ Adverbs of (indefinite) frequency 195
    ▷ *almost never/hardly ever*. 195
    ▷ *almost always* 195
16.5 Adverbs of purpose. 196
16.6 Adverbs modifying adjectives and other adverbs 196
16.7 Adverbs of degree. 196
  ▶ Intensifiers. 197
  ▶ Emphasizers. 197
    ▷ Emphasizer + verb 197
    ▷ Emphasizer + gradable adjective. 197
    ▷ Emphasizer + adverb 197
  ▶ Amplifiers 197
    ▷ Amplifier + absolute (aka non-gradable) adjective. 197
    ▷ Amplifier + verb 197
  ▶ Downtoners 197
    ▷ Downtoner + adjective. 197
    ▷ Downtoner + verb 197
    ▷ Downtoner + adverb 197

16.8   Placement of adverbs 198
16.9   Midsentence adverbs. 199
16.10 Adverb phrases and adverb clauses 199
16.11 Adverb phrases 199
    ▶ Prepositional phrase adverb phrases 200
    ▶ Infinitive phrase adverb phrases 200
16.12 Adverb clauses. 201
16.13 Conjunctions 201
16.14 Types of conjunctions 202
16.15 Coordinating conjunctions. 203
16.16 Connecting sentences with *and* and *but*. 204
16.17 Conjunctive adverbs 207
    ▶ To talk about the reason for something—that something is the reason, or cause, of something else 208
       ▷ *as a result* (= *because of that*). 208
       ▷ *consequently* (= *because of that*) 208
       ▷ *therefore* (= *because of that*) 208
       ▷ *thus* (= *in this way, because of that, for example*) 209
    ▶ To talk about the time relationship between two things—
          something happened before, at the same time or after something else 209
       ▷ *in the meantime* (= *at the same time*) 209
       ▷ *meanwhile* (= *at the same time*) 209
       ▷ *subsequently* (= *later*) 209
    ▶ To talk about things that happen in a different place 209
       ▷ *elsewhere* (= *in another place/= in other places*) 209
    ▶ To help explain how we feel about something. 209
       ▷ *after all* (= *you need to understand/= the truth is*) 209
    ▶ To help explain something further 209
       ▷ *in other words*. 209
    ▶ To give additional information that supports (makes stronger) what was just said 209
       ▷ *besides* (= *also*) 209
       ▷ *furthermore* (= *also*) 209
       ▷ *in addition* (= *also*) 209
       ▷ *moreover* (= *also*). 209
    ▶ To give additional information that does not support (makes weaker) something that was just said 209
       ▷ *on the contrary* (= *the opposite is true*) 209
    ▶ To give additional information that is opposite or different from what people expect 209
       ▷ *however* (= even though that is true) 209
       ▷ *nevertheless* (= even though that is true) 210
       ▷ *nonetheless* (= even though that is true). 210
       ▷ *on the other hand* (= *but it is true that*) 210
    ▶ To predict a different result 210
       ▷ *otherwise* (= *if this is not done/= if this does not happen*) 210
16.18 Punctuation and conjunctive adverbs 210
    ▶ Beginning of clause 210
       ▷ With a semi-colon 210
       ▷ With a period 210
    ▶ Middle of a clause 210
       ▷ After *be* 210
       ▷ Before main verbs. 210
       ▷ After an auxiliary verb 210
    ▶ End of a sentence 211
16.19 Subordinating conjunctions and adverb clauses 211
16.20 Adverb clauses and clause reversal 212
16.21 What are subordinating conjunctions? 212

16.22 Adverb clauses about time 213
  ▸ *after* 213
  ▸ *as* (= *while*) 213
  ▸ *as long as* 213
  ▸ *as soon as* (= *immediately after*) 213
  ▸ *before* 213
  ▸ *by the time (that)* (= *when*) 213
  ▸ *every time (that)*. 213
  ▸ *once* (= *when, after*) 213
  ▸ *since* (= *from the time*) 213
  ▸ *the first time (that)/the next time (that)/the last time (that)*, etc. 213
  ▸ *until/till*. 213
  ▸ *when* (sometimes = *while*) 214
  ▸ *whenever* (= *any time*) 214
  ▸ *while* 214
16.23 Adverb clauses about reasons (aka cause and effect) 214
  ▸ *as* (= *because*) 215
  ▸ *because* 215
  ▸ *now that* (= *because it is now true that*) 215
  ▸ *since* (= *because*). 215
  ▸ *so (that)*. 215
    ▷ *so (that)* somebody *can/could* 215
    ▷ *so (that)* somebody *will/would* 215
    ▷ *so (that)* somebody *don't/doesn't*. 215
16.24 Adverb clauses about opposites (aka contrast/concession). 216
  ▸ *although* 216
  ▸ *despite the fact that* 216
  ▸ *even though* 216
  ▸ *in spite of the fact that* 216
  ▸ *though*. 216
  ▸ *whereas* (= *even though it is true that*) 216
  ▸ *while* (= *even though it is true that*) 216
16.25 *although, even though* and *though* 216
16.26 *despite the fact that* and *in spite of the fact that* 217
16.27 *while* and *whereas*. 217
16.28 Adverb clauses about place 217
  ▸ *where* 217
  ▸ *wherever* 217
16.29 Adverbs of condition. 217
  ▸ Tense of the clauses 217
  ▸ *even if* (= *in the unlikely event that, regardless of the fact that*) 218
    ▷ Meaning of *even if* 218
  ▸ *if*. 218
    ▷ A common student mistake with *if*. 218
  ▸ *whether or not*. 218
  ▸ *unless* 218
16.30 Adverb clauses reduced to adverb phrases. 218
16.31 Time adverb clauses reduced to adverb phrases 219
  ▸ Adverb clauses about time with *be* reduced to adverb phrases. 219
  ▸ Adverb clauses about time with other verbs reduced to adverb phrases . . 219
  ▸ Past perfect or present perfect adverb clauses about time with *after* reduced to adverb phrases 220
16.32 Reason (cause and effect, etc.) adverb clauses reduced to adverb phrases . . 220
16.33 Adverb clauses about opposites (contrast/concession)
       with *despite the fact that* and *in spite of the fact that* reduced to adverb phrases. 222

16.34 Present participle adverb phrases of manner with prepositional phrase time and place expressions 223

16.35 Correlative conjunctions 224

   ▶ *as/as* 224

    ▷ Adjectives 224

    ▷ Adverbs 224

   ▶ *both/and* 224

    ▷ Subjects 224

    ▷ Objects 224

    ▷ Verbs 224

    ▷ Nouns 225

    ▷ Adjectives 225

    ▷ Adverbs 225

    ▷ Prepositional phrases 225

   ▶ *either/or* 225

    ▷ Subjects 225

    ▷ Objects 225

    ▷ Verbs 225

    ▷ Nouns 225

    ▷ Adjectives 225

    ▷ Adverbs 225

    ▷ Prepositional phrases 225

    ▷ Independent clauses 225

   ▶ *neither/nor* 226

    ▷ Subjects 226

    ▷ Objects 226

    ▷ Verbs 226

    ▷ Nouns 226

    ▷ Adjectives 226

    ▷ Adverbs 226

    ▷ Prepositional phrases 226

    ▷ Independent clauses 226

   ▶ *not only/but* 226

    ▷ Subjects 227

    ▷ Objects 227

    ▷ Verbs 227

    ▷ Nouns 227

    ▷ Adjectives 227

    ▷ Adverbs 227

    ▷ Prepositional phrases 227

    ▷ Independent clauses 227

   ▶ *would rather/than* 228

    ▷ Objects 228

    ▷ Verbs 228

    ▷ Independent clauses 228

Chapter 17: Gerunds, Gerund Phrases and Infinitives 229

17.1 What is a gerund? 229

17.2 Gerunds as objects 229

17.3 Gerunds as subjects 230

17.4 Other things to point out 230

   ▶ Negative gerunds 230

   ▶ *being* as a gerund 230

   ▶ Gerund objects of continuous verbs 230

17.5 Gerunds as subject complements 231

17.6 Gerunds as objects of prepositions 232

17.7   Verb + noun/noun phrase + preposition + gerund/gerund phrase 232
17.8   *be* + adjective + preposition + gerund/gerund phrase 233
17.9   *have* + noun/noun phrase + (sometimes a preposition) gerund/gerund phrase 233
17.10   Verb + time or money expression + gerund/gerund phrase 234
17.11   *go* + gerund/gerund phrase 235
17.12   Other words and expressions used with gerunds 236
        ▸ *get used to* 236
        ▸ *in addition to* 236
        ▸ *instead of* 236
        ▸ *look forward to* 236
        ▸ *take advantage of* 236
        ▸ *take care of* 236
17.13   Possessives used with gerunds 237
17.14   *by* + gerund/gerund phrase used for explaining how to do something 237
17.15   Past forms of gerunds 238
17.16   Verbs followed by gerunds and infinitives with the same meaning 239
17.17   Gerunds and infinitives with a different meaning 239
        ▸ *remember* and *forget* 239
        ▸ *regret* 239
        ▸ *try* 240
17.18   Subject gerund/gerund phrases = *it* + infinitives 240
17.19   Verb + infinitive direct object 240
17.20   Verb + indirect object + infinitive direct object 241
17.21   Verb + (indirect object) + infinitive direct object 241
17.22   *be* + adjective + infinitive 241
17.23   *be* + adjective + present perfect infinitive 242
17.24   Infinitives as adjectives 243
17.25   Infinitives as adverbs of purpose, *(in order) to* and *so (that)* 243
17.26   Causative verbs 244
        ▸ *make* 244
        ▸ *have* 244
        ▸ *help* 244
        ▸ *let* 244
        ▸ *get (someone) to* 245
17.27   *too* and *enough* used with infinitives 245
        ▸ *too* 245
          ▹ *be* + *too* + adjective + (*for* someone) + infinitive 245
          ▹ Verb + *too* + adverb + (*for* someone) + infinitive 246
        ▸ *enough* 246
          ▹ Verb + *enough* + noun + infinitive 246
          ▹ *be* + adjective + *enough* + infinitive 246
          ▹ Verb + adverb + *enough* + (*for* someone) + infinitive 246

Chapter 18: Conditionals 247
18.1   Introduction 247
18.2   Important concepts 247
        ▸ Important concept 1: possible, etc., vs. impossible, etc. 247
        ▸ Important concept 2: present = future 247
        ▸ Important concept 3: the past is not the past 247
        ▸ Important concept 4: familiar sentence structure 247
        ▸ Important concept 5: one clause tense doesn't determine the tense of another 248
        ▸ Important concept 6: meanings of *condition* and *conditional* 248
18.3   Zero conditionals: always true 248
18.4   First conditional: true in the present or in the future 249
18.5   Second conditional: not true in the present or in the future 250

18.6 Second conditional with past result clauses 251
18.7 *were to* used for hypothetical future events 252
18.8 Third conditional: not true in the past 253
18.9 Third conditional with present result clauses 254
18.10 Implied conditionals 255
18.11 Conditional sentence pattern practice 256
   ▶ Continuous, passive, interrogative, imperative conditional sentences 256
     ▷ Continuous 256
     ▷ Passive 256
     ▷ Interrogative 257
     ▷ Imperative 257
   ▶ Negative conditional sentence practice 257
     ▷ Negative zero conditional 257
     ▷ Negative first conditional 257
     ▷ Negative second conditional 257
     ▷ Negative third conditional 258
18.12 *wish* 258
   ▶ *wish* in the past 258
   ▶ *wish* in the present 259
   ▶ *wish* in the future 259
   ▶ *wish* with *would* and *could* 259
18.13 Canceling *if* in conditional sentences 260
   ▶ *had* 260
   ▶ *were* 260
   ▶ *should* 260
     ▷ *should* before the verb 260
     ▷ *should* before the subject 260
18.14 *would rather* in conditional sentences 261
18.15 *would you mind* in conditional sentences 262
   ▶ *would you mind* in the present/future 262
   ▶ *would you mind* in the past 262
18.16 *it's (about) time* in conditional sentences 263
18.17 Ellipsis with the conditional 263

Appendix A: Irregular Verbs 267

Appendix B: Verb + Preposition Combinations 269

Appendix C: Adjective + Preposition Combinations 271

Appendix D: Noun + Preposition Combinations 273

Appendix E: Sentence Structure 275
   ▸ A brief lesson in sentence structure—three basic patterns 275
   ▸ Simple sentence (aka independent clause) 275
   ▸ Compound subject 275
   ▸ Compound verb 275
   ▸ Compound sentence 275
   ▸ Complex sentence 275

Appendix F: Main Verb Forms 277
   ▸ Form Overlap 277
   ▸ Infinitives, the present simple and verb 1: an easy way to sidestep grammatical quicksand 278
   ▸ Oversimplification for a good cause 278
     ▷ One, use verb 1 any time a verb is used with any auxiliary verb. 278
     ▷ Two, use verb 1 any time a verb follows *to*. 279

Answer Key 281

Index 301

Introduction

Are you an ESL teacher (or would-be ESL teacher) who doesn't know (or know enough) English grammar? Do you tell your students that grammar isn't important or that grammar can be learned from games and conversation in order to hide the fact that you don't know much about grammar? Saying that grammar isn't important to ESL students makes about as much sense as saying that equations aren't important to algebra students or that formulas aren't important to chemistry students. Of course grammar is important, and if you want to get ahead in the ESL profession, if you want to be taken seriously by your boss, by your colleagues and by your students, and more than anything, if you want to be a good ESL teacher, you need to know grammar—what it is and how to teach it.

So what should you do? Well, you could go to graduate school and spend a ton of money and a year or two or three getting an M.A. in linguistics and learning virtually nothing useful about how to actually *teach* ESL grammar. That's what I did. In my grad school ESL grammar class, I learned all about transformational grammar and affix hopping—both interesting but about as useless as anything can be in an ESL classroom—but about how to teach English grammar to ESL students, I learned very little. If my grammar professor had ever set foot in an ESL classroom, I saw no sign of it. Good or bad, any M.A. program is going to be a long and expensive process.

Or you could tackle some scholarly English grammar reference books that will teach you a lot about English grammar if you have loads of time to study them but will teach you nothing about how to actually teach grammar to ESL students.

Or you can read *Secrets of Teaching ESL Grammar,* a thorough, intensive, practical, easy-to-understand manual on ESL grammar—from very basic to very advanced—for teachers like you who don't have a lot of time and need to quickly and easily get up to speed with the English grammar that ESL students need and how to teach it to them.

Secrets of Teaching ESL Grammar explains each grammar point in depth—in plain, simple language—so that *you* will really understand it and be able to explain it to your students so that *they* really understand it. I'll give you advice about how to teach it. I'll give you examples to put on the board, I'll give you sample exercises that you can do with your students and use as a template for writing more.

And that's not all. *Secrets of Teaching ESL Grammar* is bursting with advice on teaching techniques, classroom management, how to answer the questions that your students will ask (or should ask) and how to address (or anticipate) the errors they will make.

And along the way I'll dish out generous servings of frank and irreverent commentary regarding a lot of the mythology and lamebrained ideas that plague the ESL profession. I do this not because I'm full of myself but in hopes that it will make you a better teacher. You'll learn what took me years to learn—that what works in the classroom (aka reality) often has little to do with the half-baked and unproven theories floating around the ivory tower or the boss's office. I'll tell you what works and what doesn't work in the trenches.

Some grad school professors might gasp at some of my opinions and suggestions. I make no apologies. What is my goal—to train my students to be grammarians? No! To train them to teach English to native-speaking English majors? No! My goal—and your goal—is to teach ESL students the grammar they need to speak, write, read and understand English—as much as possible as quickly as possible. You don't have forever and neither do they. I teach you techniques and strategies that work—they're all classroom-tested. They'll make you a better teacher by not wasting your time and confusing your students with unimportant info, ineffective methods, confusing jargon, irrelevant grammar points and useless baloney (as opposed to useful baloney).

And when we're finished, you'll know what you're doing. You'll know your grammar, you'll know how to teach it and you'll know a lot of the concepts, buzzwords and jargon that, if you didn't, would give you away as a poorly-trained amateur.

So who am I? If I learned little about how to teach ESL grammar in grad school, where did I learn it? By studying grammar on my own and by teaching it for more than 25 years in the USA, Mexico, Equatorial Guinea, Saudi Arabia and the United Arab Emirates and by having written eight book related to English language learning and instruction. *Secrets of Teaching ESL Grammar* is the distillation of that experience.

Secrets of Teaching ESL Grammar is written for the real word, not the fantasy world of some ESL teacher training books which assume perfect students, perfect bosses, perfect jobs, perfect classrooms and wonderfully effective techniques and methodologies. None of that is reality, I'm sorry to tell you. I write from the perspective of the real world where some students don't give a you-know-what, where some bosses don't know what the you-know-what they're doing, where some jobs suck, where some classrooms suck, where some books you're forced to use suck and where some goofy ideas about how to teach ESL just don't work. I'll tell you what does work, or at least what has worked for me. Is my way the only way? Of course not. Is it the best way? Who knows? Teaching ESL isn't a hard science. There are as many opinions about how to teach ESL as there are people doing it. But I've had great success in the classroom teaching grammar and all aspects of ESL. My way works pretty well for me, and I'm confident it will for you too.

Did I mention my books? My most recent book prior to *Secrets of Teaching ESL Grammar* was *Rocket English Grammar**, an intensive, fast-paced, fun, student-friendly, one-volume basic-to-advanced comprehensive ESL grammar book (or at least that's what the blurb on the back cover says). *Secrets of Teaching ESL Grammar* isn't meant to be a companion book to *Rocket English Grammar,* but it sort of is anyway. You don't need to have *Rocket English Grammar* to benefit from *Secrets of Teaching ESL Grammar,* but they work well together. The sequence of topics is parallel, and many of the sample exercises in *Secrets of Teaching ESL Grammar* are drawn from *Rocket English Grammar.*

Secrets of Teaching ESL Grammar is meant to teach you how to teach English grammar to students ranging from absolute beginners, to (jargon alert!) *false beginners* (students who have had a bit of English instruction but need to start over at the lowest level—very common) to very advanced students. The topic sequence I've followed is not random—each chapter builds upon topics discussed in previous chapters—so if possible, I recommend studying the chapters in sequence. In general, in each chapter the grammar discussed early on can be considered more essential than what follows, so depending on time, your students' level and both your and their needs, you can start at the beginning of a chapter and, if you get only halfway through, be confident that you've covered what is most important. In your teaching job, you'll often be required to follow a syllabus given to you, and therefore you won't have the freedom to organize your grammar instruction in the same sequence as it is covered in *Secrets of Teaching ESL Grammar*. In this case, it should be easy to scan through the sections listed in the table of contents to find what you need.

I consider a thorough knowledge of the basic grammar in *Secrets of Teaching ESL Grammar,* an extensive knowledge of the intermediate level grammar in *Secrets of Teaching ESL Grammar* and at least a solid familiarity with the advanced grammar in *Secrets of Teaching ESL Grammar* to be the least a competent, professional ESL teacher should have. If you have that, you won't get nervous when your colleagues start talking about *phrasal modals* or *cloze exercise* or *zero conditionals* or *dependent clauses* or *subordinating conjunctions* or *the subjunctive.*

I've tried to make *Secrets of Teaching ESL Grammar* as easy-to-understand and useful as possible. I really want you to make fast progress, so I've tried to write in a breezy, informal and accessible style. I welcome suggestions and comments. Good luck!

Carl W. Hart
carl@carlwhart.com

*available from Amazon.com or in PDF format from www.drmz.net/re/catalog

Chapter 1
Advice, Heresy and Random Musings

1.1 Why teach grammar at all?

Why teach grammar at all if, as some in the ESL field contend, students can absorb grammar passively by playing games, by looking at pictures, by studying the anemic grammar lessons sneaked almost apologetically into integrated skills books, by writing journals and by engaging in communicative, student-centered (whatever that means) activities? I'll tell you why: because to a large extent students <u>don't</u> learn grammar in these ways. Yes, they can certainly improve basic and some intermediate grammar somewhat by engaging in nongrammarcentric (a word I just made up) activities, but even then, sparing time to actually focus on grammar will greatly improve their ability to understand English and to use English accurately and effectively. And as for more advanced English grammar, there is no way students can learn it without studying it. (What a radical concept.) Grammar is not everything, but it absolutely should be a component of an overall ESL program.

1.2 Boring grammar or boring teachers?

Despite grammar's importance, there is a reluctance to teach grammar, especially more advanced grammar. Why? Two reasons, I think: First, it's a plain and simple (and sad) fact that a lot of ESL teachers don't know much about it.

The other reason is the myth that grammar is borrrrrrrrrrrrrring, and God forbid we should torment our students with anything boring. If we want those students to keep paying to attend our school, everything must be fresh, peppy, bubbly, smiley, happy, lite and fun, fun, fun.

This attitude does a disservice to students. First of all, grammar is NOT boring. (And even if it were, in what other field of study do teachers avoid teaching students what they must know because it might bore them?) I feel very strongly that the reason for this silly claim is that it's not grammar that's boring but the teachers who are teaching it—they are boring. A good teacher can make a class engaging and entertaining no matter what the subject matter. I have a lot of fun in my grammar classes, and my students do too. This isn't anything I learned in grad school; it's who I am plus what I've learned in more than 25 years of teaching. That's about the best bit of advice I can give you—make your classes lively, entertaining and useful. If you do that, no one will complain that grammar is boring. And did you notice that I said "useful"? By useful I mean your students will actually learn something, not just play games and have a few laughs. I mean you'll make them work hard. I mean they'll leave your class feeling that they've gained something valuable. They'll have a solid foundation in English grammar and a clear mental framework to build upon. The way to do that is by not just being an engaging, lively, entertaining teacher, which you should be, but by knowing your stuff and knowing how to teach it too.

And besides, in my experience students crave grammar whether it's boring or not. No matter what silly ideas their teachers may have about its not being important, the students know better—that it's vitally important. Many a time I've heard students express frustration that the program they were in seemed to ignore grammar and worse yet, that their teachers could not answer their questions about grammar. Students can see through "grammar isn't important" to know what it really means: their teacher doesn't know much about grammar.

1.3 Only grammar in a grammar class?

Since this book is about how to teach ESL grammar, obviously all I'll ever discuss is English grammar, and all you should ever discuss in your grammar class is English grammar, right? Wrong. Although I'm ready to help students in any way I can, admittedly a grammar class isn't the ideal place to be focusing on speaking, writing and reading. But what about listening? I believe it makes perfect sense to discuss listening in a grammar class, and I do. Why listening? Your students don't need to just be able to use English grammar when they speak and write, i.e. (jargon alert!) *productive skills*; they need to understand the English grammar that they read and <u>hear</u>, i.e. (jargon alert!) *receptive skills*.

So do not overlook listening. Never forget that your students need to understand not just the generally somewhat slower, more clearly pronounced and simpler English that they hear from their ESL teachers but also the fast, (jargon alert!) *reduced*, casual and not always grammatically correct English that they hear outside of their classrooms. I have many times been told by students how frustrating it is that they can understand their ESL teachers easily but have great difficulty making sense out of the English they hear in movies, on TV or from native speakers they encounter outside the classroom (who are not ESL teachers and have no idea how to modify their language to help nonnative speakers understand them).

A grammar class is the perfect place to focus on how we native speakers pronounce particular words and phrases. In my classes, I frequently take time to (jargon alert!) *model* (say something so the students can notice *how* I am saying it) what I call "outside-the-classroom English" but always with the reminder that I'm doing it to help them with their listening, not speaking. They should not, I tell them, try to copy the reduced pronunciation they're hearing. In fact, I discourage this because it will very likely result in their pronunciation being *more* difficult to understand by native speakers. So at many points in this book, I will discuss (jargon alert!) *reductions* and how to teach them to your students. I don't believe this is something that most grammar teachers do—at least in a systematic and thorough way.

I do, and my students are grateful for it. If you do too, your students (and your boss) will be impressed with what a brilliant teacher you are. So do it!

And speaking of listening, do not fail to continually emphasize contractions (which are a kind of reduction). Native English speakers use contractions much of the time in writing and most of the time in speaking. My approach is to tell students that they never have to use contractions, but they absolutely must understand them, so to help your students become more familiar with contractions, frequently model them and frequently insist that your students use them. They will resist, so if you've insisted that they use contractions in a certain exercise, don't accept an answer as correct unless they do. We native speakers think of contractions as short cuts—less work for the mouth to say than the two words the contractions are made up of—so it will seem odd that ESL students avoid using contractions. It's all about what language learners learn first and are more comfortable with. Native English speakers actually learn contractions first. Only later in childhood do we learn the two-word version. With second language learners, it's the opposite, so they are often more comfortable with the two-word version and prefer to stick with that.

1.4 Asking questions

A large part of conversation is asking questions, so don't forget to emphasize proper question formation. You'll find a lot of that in *Secrets of Teaching ESL Grammar,* including an entire chapter which focuses on asking questions—how to form them, the meanings of question words and what I think is a really clever way of helping students learn to avoid making the most common mistake nonnative English speakers make when asking questions. (For example, *Where he went?* and *Where she is?*)

1.5 Vocabulary

How about vocabulary? How much focus on vocabulary should there be in a grammar class? If your answer is "not much", I agree—sort of. A grammar class isn't the ideal place to be learning new vocabulary. Actually, I believe very firmly that unfamiliar vocabulary, along with oddball personal and place names, should be avoided as much as possible in grammar instruction because it can distract students from the grammar that you want them to be focusing on. Many times I've had a grammar lesson come to a screeching halt by having to waste time explaining some difficult vocabulary in the book that contributed nothing to the understanding of the grammar point. I make sure to keep vocabulary simple, though as your students progress to more advanced grammar, the level of suitable vocabulary will increase as well. Inevitably, you'll still need to explain unfamiliar vocabulary sometimes, and you might even take advantage of opportunities to teach some new and useful vocabulary if you have time because, despite what I just said about avoiding distracting vocabulary in a grammar class, continually learning new vocabulary is extremely important to ESL students. In fact, the *higher* the student's level, the *less* he or she needs to be studying grammar and the *more* he or she needs to be working on (jargon alert!) *acquiring* vocabulary. Very often, what prevents students at higher levels from expressing what they are thinking or from understanding what they are hearing or reading is not that they haven't mastered the future perfect passive continuous, but that they don't know the words for what they're thinking or they don't understand the words they are reading or hearing. Strongly encourage your students to work hard to learn new vocabulary. (For more on this topic, I highly recommend *Vocabulary Myths* by Keith S. Folse, University of Michigan Press.)

Having just said that I avoid distracting vocabulary that contributes nothing to students' understanding of grammar, you'll find that many times in *Secrets of Teaching ESL Grammar* I actually advise you to treat a particular lesson more as a vocabulary lesson than a grammar lesson. Why this seeming contradiction? Because many grammar lessons in this book and others will explain that a particular grammar point is often used with certain words, and a list of those words will be provided. Very often many of those words will be unfamiliar to your students, and very often understanding the meanings of those words may be much more of a challenge to your students than the comparatively easy grammar those words plug into. So teach them! The grammar you're teaching won't be of much use to your students if they don't know the words it's used with.

1.6 Why no preposition chapter?

Why no preposition chapter? Mainly because I hate teaching prepositions, but that doesn't sound very intellectual, does it? I guess I need to come up with something better than that. Hmmmm, OK, how about this: What I find, and you will too, is that certain basic grammar is impossible to avoid using even before you actually get around to focusing on it. For example articles, subject pronouns, possessive pronouns, some question words, basic adjectives, simple noun phrases, some modals, gerunds and basic preposition use too. Students will already be familiar with these before it's time to make them the focus of a lesson.

As for prepositions, at some point you should have a lesson about prepositions of location: *on, under, in front of, behind,* etc. You can easily do that in a classroom using whatever is at hand. But so much about prepositions is random and idiomatic that I've never seen any point in trying to organize it in any systematic way. It just doesn't make sense (to me, anyway) to have a lesson on what *to* means or what *of* means or what logic explains <u>at night</u>, <u>in the morning</u> and <u>on</u> Friday or why we say *get out of the car* but not *get in of the car.* There are times when you will discuss a specific use of one or more prepositions with a particular grammatical structure, like *to* used with infinitives or *by* used with the passive. Also prepositional phrases and their uses as adjectives and adverbials belong in discussions of adjectives clauses and phrases and in adverb clauses and phrases, not in a separate preposition lesson. That's what makes sense to me.

But the good news is that much of what students need to learn about prepositions will be learned intuitively, passively and easily in conjunction with other grammar topics.

1.7 Variables
Your students will vary, but so will many other things: class size, the classroom itself, the book you're required to use, the level you're teaching, whether your students really belong in that level, how much time you have, what the goals of the program are, whether you're teaching in your students' native country or in an English-speaking country, whether your students all speak the same language or various languages (which can be a major factor) and how much, if anything, you speak of their native language. Despite these many variables, I'll attempt some general advice. Not all my advice will work in all situations, of course. You'll need to adapt and adjust and tweak and fine tune and figure out what works best for you and the situation you're in.

1.8 Detailed lesson plans?
First of all, I'm not a big believer in detailed lesson plans; therefore, I don't make detailed lesson plans (heresy!). I always have an idea of what I want to accomplish before I go to class, but it might be in my head, it might be a few notes written in the margin of a textbook page, it might be a few examples or explanatory language jotted down on paper that I want to put on the board when I get to class, but that's it. Obviously, if I'm teaching a complex grammar point for the first time, I'll want to take time to plan it out and maybe prepare materials, but never do I feel that a detailed lesson plan, complete with objectives and expected outcomes, is necessary. The most detailed I usually get is a list of things I want to do in the class—pages I want to cover, handouts I want to hand out, homework to assign or collect—just so I don't forget something.

Of course, that's easy for me to say. It makes sense, when you're inexperienced and unsure of yourself, to make sure that you thoroughly understand what you're going to be teaching and that you can do it in an organized and effective manner, but I think there is a real danger in overplanning and being too rigid in following a plan. No class ever goes exactly as you think it will: Either your students are completely blown away by something you think will be a breeze or they easily learn something that you think will be hard and take forever—leaving you with 20 minutes to fill before the bell. (Now what do you do?) You have to learn to think on your feet, to be flexible. With experience you'll learn ways to ensure that your lessons, amazingly, always conclude a minute before the bell. You'll learn how to stretch and condense when necessary. You'll develop a repertoire, a bag of tricks, that you keep adding to, refining and improving class after class, month after month, year after year. I mean ways to manage time, ways to teach certain points, answers to questions, useful advice, jokes, stories, techniques for dealing with plagiarism, laziness, confused students and problem students. I've been telling some jokes and stories for 26 years, and you know, they just keep getting better and better. And no need to let the facts get in the way of a good story—embellish!

Being unwilling to modify or even throw out a lesson plan is one of the main reasons why a grammar class (or any class) might be a boring and painful experience for student and teacher alike. *By God, I have a plan, and I'm going to stick to it no matter what!* That's no fun. Be flexible.

Now having said that I don't believe in detailed daily lesson plans, I do believe in having a master plan for the entire course. It might be that you have the freedom to create the course syllabus yourself, or it might just be a plan of your own for how you're going to execute the syllabus you have been given. Either way, you want to be sure to budget your time optimally— making sure you don't squander your time and have to rush to catch up with what you were supposed to cover in that course before the final exam. I'm always very careful to build in ample time for review before an exam. Not doing that and worse yet, having, near the end of the course, to zoom through the remainder of what you were to have covered in the course, will make you look like an amateur. But again, master plans aren't etched in stone.

1.9 Tell them why you're doing what you're doing.
Explain your rationale to students—why you're spending so much time on one thing and not much on another. Explain your plan or why you're changing your plan. I always find that students really appreciate that and respect you for it. They'll

---

see that you know what you're doing, that you're a pro. And by all means ask your students what they think. What are they having trouble with? What do they want to go back to and review? They'll appreciate your asking and appreciate your being willing to modify your plan to take what they say into account.

1.10 Go with the flow.
A good teacher must have a sense for the mood of the class—not just overall but as it changes day-by-day, period-by-period, minute-by-minute. Students who are bouncing off the ceiling with energy one day may be zombies the next.

I vary the pace—buckling down, forging ahead, backing off, tackling new material, reviewing past material, getting firm, having a laugh, taking a time out, etc., based upon what I sense will work best to achieve maximum results with those students in that class at that time. And remember, no matter how much you think all your students are keeping up with you, there will be some who are a bit behind, a bit confused, a bit lost. Taking a breather now and then will give them a chance to assimilate, to catch up, to ask a classmate for help. Keep this in mind.

Obviously, what you teach and how you teach it will vary according to your students—who they are, what their needs are, what their native language is, what their educational background is, how old they are, what level you're teaching. Not everything will work well for everybody. That's what experience teaches you. What fascinates one class will go over like a lead balloon in another. What works like a charm in one class will be an utter disaster in another. Trust me, I know. ESL is a vast spectrum. Students have different needs and abilities ranging from zero-level immigrants who need to quickly learn enough to survive in an English-speaking country (and may not even be fully literate in their native language) to students who already speak a good deal of English preparing for English-language university studies to already quite fluent businesspeople who want to take it to a higher level in order to wheel and deal in the world of international business.

1.11 Textbooks aren't etched in stone.
You've got to think on your feet and be flexible. That may include deviating from your textbook's intending use. Don't feel that you have to do each exercise in your textbook exactly as it was intended by the author. Very frequently, if I feel an exercise is not challenging enough, or if I just want to squeeze some more usefulness out of it, I'll modify it. That could be done in a number of ways, but the main thing I do is add a question formation and listening element to the grammar exercise. Let's say, for example, that the exercise instructions ask the students to change some sentences from present to past, and we're on number 3. The students are expected to change

> 3. Carlos goes to school every day. (yesterday)

to

> *Carlos went to school yesterday.*

Although the instructions are simply to change the sentences from present to past with the provided vocabulary, what I might do, rather than just calling on a student (Sarah, for example) and saying "Sarah, number 3", is say "Sarah, where did Carlos go yesterday?" Sarah's task hasn't changed. She still needs to change number 3 to past, just as instructed by the book, but now it's also the answer to my question; now she's getting some practice with listening and understanding questions as well.

At other times, the exercises will be a bit *too* challenging for the student, so rather than just give a stumped student the answer, I'll rephrase the question—maybe along with a little extra language designed to help the student figure it out. Into the extra language I might slip a few hints to help the student to understand an unfamiliar word or the grammar involved. Better to coax students to the right answers than to carry them; better to let them feel a sense of accomplishment than failure. This is some of the most useful advice I can pass along. Whether it's an entire book that's too easy or too difficult for your entire class or a particular exercise that's too easy or too difficult for a particular student, what I describe above is a way to make it work—to squeeze maximum effectiveness out of a textbook.

And regardless of what you or your boss may fantasize about not being chained to a textbook, you will be using textbooks, and you should be, but the book isn't the be all and end all of teaching ESL. The book is just raw material to work with. Often you will have no control over the choice of textbook, and whether you do or not, it won't always be just right—too easy or too advanced for the class as a whole or for a particular student. Even at the right level, it may not be suitable for other reasons, or it may just be a piece of crap. But a good teacher can be a good teacher even with a bad book. Often, I'll teach new material myself first—putting explanations and examples on the board—and only after that will I refer students to the corresponding lesson in their book. You should know your stuff well enough so that you can teach it without the aid of a book.

1.12 Motivation
Student motivation will vary considerably too. Get used to it. An almost universal mistake made by writers of books de-

signed to train ESL teachers is that they presuppose respectful, highly motivated students who listen with rapt attention, who are eager to answer questions, who are enthusiastic about participating in classroom activities, who are diligent about doing homework and completing projects. If only that were true. In my career I have at times been lucky enough to teach students like that—they hung on my every word and crowded around my desk after class asking questions. I've also had classes where virtually all the students were engaged in loud nonstop conversation with each other (in their native language, of course) throughout the entire class. I've even had classes where every single student was literally sound asleep, sprawled on his desk—some snoring, some drooling on the books they were using as pillows. I've had classes in which I thought, *Damn, if this classroom were on the tenth floor and not on the ground floor, I could jump out of that window and put an end to this horror.* That's the reality of teaching ESL. You do the best you can, and a skilled teacher can learn ways to counter negative behaviors, but only to a degree. It really can be overwhelming at times. My grad school linguistics program didn't prepare me for classes like that, but thankfully, it's not usually that bad.

So what about motivation? How to motivate students is something you'd better think about—not just because it's important but also because in every job interview you'll ever have, you'll be asked how you motivate students (along with "What is your teaching philosophy?"). You'd better have an answer! Here's mine: The key to motivating students is making the classroom experience lively and engaging. It should provide an opportunity for interesting, challenging activities, friendly competition and enjoyable social interaction. Students will want to come to class and participate in class because they don't want to miss the action. That's my job interview answer, and it's a good one, I think, but other student motivation factors are not wanting to let down a teacher who's busting his or her you-know-what for them, the rewards that passing the class (in the short term) and learning to speak English (in the long term) will bring and, along with those carrots, the sticks: the consequences of having their lack of effort reported to whomever they're afraid of catching hell from, the consequences of failing the class and the shame they ought to feel for letting down their teacher. All of that is true and all of it will sound good in a job interview (at least the carrot part will), but the truth is that throughout your ESL career, there will always be some students that you just can't light a fire under no matter how hard you try—they just don't care. You do the best you can, but that's the way it is. Don't blame yourself. There are many factors at work—the student's personality, family, culture—and there's nothing you can do about any of them. Get used to it.

1.13 Be more than a teacher.

No matter what kind of class you have, connecting with your students will make a world of difference. A good teacher is not just someone who knows and can teach his or her subject but someone who wants to help people. Try to develop a rapport with your students. Be sincere (even if you have to fake it). If you have classroom management issues (and even if you don't), try to make your students see you as an ally, not an adversary. Let them get a sense that you know their situation, you know how hard it is, you know the pressure they're under and the unreasonable demands that are being made of them. *We're all in this together, so let's make the best of it* is my approach. Never criticize the administration, other teachers, the boss, the country you're in (unless it's your own—then you can say whatever you want, but remember that your students aren't there to learn your political views) or say anything that will come back to haunt you, but nod your head sympathetically when your students air their gripes. If there is something you can do to make things easier for them, try, but often you'll be as powerless as they are to change anything. They might imagine otherwise—that you can just march into the director's office, the dean's office or somebody's office and demand action. Let them know that's not the case—that director, that dean, that somebody is your boss, and you have to go with the program (up to a point). Keep reminding them that their hard work and suffering will pay off in the long run. Remember that a good teacher is not just a teacher but a counselor as well. Just like you and me, behind your students' bright and determined faces, they're full of worries—personal, academic or career-related. Don't pry, but if a student seeks advice, or you see a need for some advice, do the best you can. Be supportive and encouraging; give them the benefit of your experience and wisdom. Just don't get too involved, and don't say anything that's going to get you into trouble. (Like *You should divorce that guy.*)

If you're lucky enough to have serious and motivated students, you will almost certainly be asked questions constantly—questions before, in and after class, questions about what you're currently working on, questions about something you covered long ago, questions about something you have yet to get to or may never get to, even questions about something language-related from another class entirely. A student in an academic setting might have English-related questions that arise from another class he or she is taking—maybe engineering, law or something science-related. And because you are good teacher, you will be more than happy to try to answer those questions. That's how I feel. I enjoy the challenge of tough questions, and I'm delighted, time willing, to help students as much as I can. That's how people who are natural teachers feel. The rewarding feeling and good karma that come from helping people and, *inshallah,* the respect and appreciation that you get in return is what gets ESL teachers out of bed in the morning. (It certainly isn't the money.)

A good teacher does, and is happy to do, a lot of one-on-one teaching—before class, after class, at another time by arrangement or in class by circulating among the students for miniconferences—often while the other students are doing (jargon alert!) *seatwork,* some work which keeps them quiet, in their seats and busy working independently. That's when you may be asked tough questions.

And it's nice to be able to answer those tough questions. It may be beyond the level of the class, and you'd better be prepared, or it may be about what you're working on in class that day. If it is, you'll be able to tailor your explanation to that student—perhaps simplifying what you presented to the class as a whole or, depending on the student, getting into the deep grammar involved in a way that is not appropriate for the entire class. It's nice to know that deep grammar even if you don't necessarily discuss it in class.

1.14 Be a covert teacher.
Always be aware of the language you use: not just when you're up at the board in the middle of your big presentation but in down time when you're talking about your students' weekend plans or why someone was absent yesterday or when the final exam is or why the air conditioner isn't working. Remember that you are *always* teaching. I like to use the terms *overt* and *covert* to explain this. Overt teaching is done when you are obviously doing what teachers do: explaining, asking questions, writing on the board. Covert teaching is modeling language for your students and listening for errors in what seems to the students to be down time—perhaps in class, perhaps outside of class. In class or out, don't resort to (jargon alert!) *teacher talk*—super simple, ungrammatical English—in order to help your students understand. You're not doing your students any good by modeling incorrect English. But do keep it at as comprehensible a level as possible.

1.15 Watch your language.
That's important. I believe that a major reason why some ESL teachers are ineffective in the classroom and have ongoing problems with students and therefore their bosses is that they don't know how to communicate effectively with their students. Why? Their (jargon alert!) *metalanguage,* language used to talk about language, is way over their students' heads, and they just don't know it. One way I can tell whether an ESL teacher has a clue or not is by listening to the language he or she uses when speaking to students. If I think to myself *If those students could understand what their teacher is saying, they wouldn't need to be studying English,* then I know that teacher just doesn't get it.

So be conscious of your grammar, vocabulary and pronunciation at all times. Be careful about (jargon alert!) *idioms* that may be unfamiliar to your students. Be conscious of using the passive voice or other grammar that may be way over their heads. Be conscious of using reductions. Yes, they absolutely need to learn idioms, advanced grammar and reduced pronunciation, but they won't learn anything if they never know what the hell you're talking about.

1.16 Repeat, repeat, repeat!
Whether you're presenting new material or just doing (jargon alert!) *housekeeping* (discussing classroom management stuff, discussing homework, taking attendance, etc.), repeat key language several times, and each time, make it a bit slower and clearer in terms of pronunciation and a bit simpler in terms of grammar and vocabulary. Often I'll use synonyms and stress them so the students understand that they *are* synonyms (*We won't, we will not go to lab tomorrow; You have to, you must turn in your project by Friday* or *Read the question and then pick out, then choose, then select the best answer.*) Go ahead and use language in class that you feel might be a bit challenging, but if need be, call attention to it, repeat it slowly and clearly, explain it.

1.17 Whoa!
One of the biggest dangers, when you introduce new material, is to just plunge right in and go for it full speed ahead. I'm guilty of that myself sometimes, especially when I'm full of coffee. Sometimes I need to remind myself to slow down. You really need to take things one step at a time and be sure you're following a logical progression and not jumping around. Teachers must give students a sense of what is most essential—what must be understood before progressing further—in order to construct a mental framework. Remember, your students' understanding will often be very tenuous and can be lost entirely if you're not careful. Constantly check for understanding and <u>never</u> assume that, because there are no question, there are no questions. Students can be very shy about admitting that they don't understand something in front of their classmates. Assume there are questions, and you'll almost always be right. Then answer those questions whether they've been asked or not. Remember that confused students sometimes can't even express just what they don't understand (unknown unknowns?). It's just a cloud. They're so confused that they don't even know what to ask.

So review, review, review. It could be what you covered a few minutes ago or, if you have some time to fill or see a need, something from yesterday, last week or last month. You can never really review enough. Amazingly, your presentation will be better the second (and third and fourth) time around. And sometimes that review is just a few seconds long—no more than a quick reminder or check to make sure the students remember something you discussed previously before continuing with the new material. It could be a word meaning or an irregular verb form or a reminder of the third person singular. I do this all the time, and you should too.

1.18 One step at a time.
Almost always, whatever grammar you're introducing builds upon something covered previously: The passive requires an understanding of past participles, which you may not have discussed since you worked on perfect tenses. The conditional requires an understanding of dependent and independent clauses, which you may not have discussed since you worked on adverb clauses. It's easy to assume that since you've covered something already, there's no need to review it. Wrong! Always go back further than you think is necessary; always review more than you think is necessary. Remember what I said: Just because there are no questions doesn't mean there are no question!

Inevitably, some students will be stronger than others. Use this to your advantage when you call on students to answer questions by starting with the stronger students. This will give the weaker students more time to catch on. But don't be too obvious about it! You don't want to embarrass anyone. Ask stronger students to help the weaker ones. Call on students at random. Worrying that they might be next keeps them alert. If you see a student daydreaming or nodding off, call on him or her. One way I have a little fun in class sometimes is to startle a student who's lost in the ozone by suddenly demanding that he or she answer an exercise question that we're not doing, maybe on a page that we're not on (and maybe in a book that we're not using). As the daydreaming student scrambles and panics, you and the rest of the class can look on in amusement.

A great way to liven up a class (and eat up the clock if you're stretching) is to have students come to the board. Depending on what you're doing, you can stay in control or let that student take over and call on his or her classmates. But always insist that the rest of the students work too, not just watch the student at the board.

Speaking of boards, I like to use chalk or markers of various colors and use those different colors to focus students on key elements in my presentation. You can use every color of the rainbow if you're unfortunate enough to have to use a smart board (a solution in search of a problem if ever there were one).

1.19 Game theory
More than once I've mentioned keeping the class lively and entertaining, so obviously I must frequently make use of games and group activities. No, I don't (heresy!), and here's why: The main reason is that I think games and activities usually generate more heat than light—a lot of activity but not much learning. Another is time management. Time is often so precious that I want to make the most of what little time I have. Games and other activities can easily eat up an entire period without accomplishing much. Also, depending on your students, games and group activities can be an invitation to chaos (not to mention bedlam and pandemonium). If you have serious classroom management issues, maintaining control of your class is difficult enough when your students are in their seats facing you. Once they get up and start moving around, you can lose control entirely. Your students may half-heartedly pretend to be doing what you just laboriously explained, and as soon as you turn your back, start yakking in their native language. That's the worst case scenario, but obviously it depends on a number of variables, so if you have enough time, cooperative students and a class small enough to manage effectively, go for it. In no way am I opposed to games and activities in theory; it's just that in practice they often don't work well or even if they do, aren't worth all the time and trouble.

And don't assume that your students even want to play games and engage in activities. If you're teaching adult students (or even young adults), they may be unenthusiastic about games and activities which they perceive as childish and undignified. I don't blame them. I'm the same way. Your students may be mature and serious-minded and quite accustomed to working hard in class and quite willing to do so in yours. Possibly they or their parents have paid a lot of money for them to attend the school they're in. They want to get their money's worth. The students want to learn quickly and efficiently and may not be interested in what they see as time-wasting silliness. So don't feel that you absolutely must alleviate the excruciating, mind-numbing, soul-crushing boredom of grammar instruction with games and activities. Don't be timid about making your students work hard. Be aware that what you might consider a long day at school and a ton of homework might be considered laughably easy to students who come from countries where much greater demands are routinely made of them.

1.20 Keep 'em talking.
But whatever you do, don't just drone on and on. Even when you're presenting something new, try to interact with the students—ask questions, ask students to read from the book, ask them to go to the board. A good deal of every class should involve students *producing* in one way or another, not just listening to you blabber. Not only does this make sense, it will prevent you from being branded as not being (jargon alert!) *student-centered*. That's a buzzword you definitely need to remember because being considered a *teacher-centered* teacher can be the kiss of death careerwise in some parts. Even though no one really knows what student-centered means, other than making sure you don't do all the talking in class and that your students

do a lot of talking in class, let no one ever doubt that you are a student-centered teacher and that you despise teacher-centered teachers. Be careful, though. Since every teacher has to talk in class once in a while, vindictive supervisors can use the fact that you were overheard talking in class to accuse you of not being student-centered. I'm not kidding!

1.21 Error correction

What about error correction? It's important to understand that errors are broadly categorized as those which interfere with the student's being understood and those which don't. Sometimes these are referred to as (jargon alert!) *global errors,* which interfere with their being understood, and *local errors,* which do not interfere with their being understood. How and when (if at all) to correct errors is tricky. If you correct every error made by every student, you'll never get past page 1 in your textbook. You'll drive your students nuts too.

Correcting errors can be done in a number of ways, sometimes subtly. Often, when I'm repeating an answer made by a student who has made an error, I'll do so with the correct language and stress the correct language so it's obvious what I'm doing—for that student's benefit and the whole class. Sometimes I'll repeat the error with a questioning tone of voice, alerting the student that he or she has made and error and inviting that student to supply the correction.

If it's an error of a more serious nature (which may indicate that I didn't cover something sufficiently in the first place), it might be time for a minireview. Sometimes, especially when it's something I feel the students should know because it's very basic or because I've already told them a million times, I'll feign a heart attack, clutching my chest and staggering around the room. Sometimes I'll pretend to have absolutely no idea what the student is talking about (even though I do), forcing the student to keep trying to get it right. I'll ham it up by acting utterly mystified by what I've just heard. It can be especially fun to pretend incomprehension when students want something—permission to go to the bathroom, for example. With every failed attempt to get it right, I keep pretending not to understand until the student finally does get it right. Then I'll let out a giant, *Ohhhhhhh, NOW I understand* and repeat the correct language for that student's and the entire class's benefit.

Certain errors are more like ingrained bad habits. They don't represent a student's struggling to get it right but, in a way, the opposite—no effort to get it right. My Russian students not using articles, for example, or a certain Spanish speaker I know using *own* for *owe* for the last 25 years (which, coincidentally, is how long I've been married), advanced ESL students who still never add *-s* to the third person singular. These are called (jargon alert!) *fossilized errors*—errors which have become a natural part of their speech, errors, which if they do not prevent them from being understood, they have no incentive to avoid. These can be difficult habits to break, but try. Because these are unconscious habits, frequently (but judiciously) bring the error to the students' attention and make them aware that you are aware of it. Be a stickler—a little pressure will give them an incentive to try a little harder to get it right.

Just as I said that you're always teaching, your error detection radar is always on too. Even when students are chatting with you during down time, be on the alert for errors. As in the classroom, correct errors outside of the classroom selectively and with finesse. The reason why your error detection radar has no off switch is not to torment your students or convince them you're a total jerk but to force them to realize that straining their brains to speak accurately is something they should do all the time, not just when they've been called upon by their teachers. They need to get out of the habit of lapsing into pidgin English when they think accuracy doesn't matter.

Be very careful about the timing of your error correction. Avoid interrupting students when they're speaking. It can have an intimidating effect. Sometimes the student will immediately realize the error and make the correction without any prompting. Don't feel the need to correct every error. If I corrected a Russian student I once had every time he didn't use an article, that's all I would ever have done. It wasn't as if he didn't know to use articles, so just the occasional reminder was sufficient. Increasing speaking fluency is one of your goals too (yes, even in a grammar class), so you don't want to overdo it with the error correction every time your students open their mouths.

Don't be the kind of teacher who criticizes and corrects but never offers praise. Be liberal with praise. Acknowledge improvement, a good question, a good answer or a good effort. How your students react to praise may vary according to their culture, but so what. Do it.

1.22 Deductive/inductive

One important teaching concept to be aware of is the difference between (jargon alert!) *deductive* teaching and *inductive* teaching. What it boils down to is that deductive teaching means telling your students what the rule or system is first and then illustrating that rule or system with examples after. Inductive teaching is the opposite—you give your students some examples first and then challenge them to figure out what the rule or system is after. It is generally believed that inductive teaching is preferable because students are more likely to remember what they've worked out themselves instead of having been told. I agree. My grammar book, *Rocket English Grammar,* employs the inductive approach, and I've tried to build it into this book as well. Not everything can be done inductively, but keep this concept in mind and employ it when you can.

1.23 i+1

Another concept to be aware of is (jargon alert!) *Krashen's theory of i + 1,* where i (i for *input*) is the students' current level of English and 1 refers to one level beyond that. Your immediate goal is to help your students reach that next level, so if the input they receive from you in class is just beyond their current level, it should be comprehensible—students ought to be able to figure it out and move up to that level. This might seem a bit obvious, and it is, but it's a reminder to you to do what I previously advised: build step by step, don't go too fast, don't jump around, build upon what has been learned previously. "Krashen", the term "comprehensible input" and "i + 1" are something you should remember. They're about all many teachers with M.A.s in linguistics remember from their grad school studies, so if you drop those terms into a conversation with them, they'll be impressed.

1.24 Interference

ESL teachers love to talk about (jargon alert!) *interference.* By interference they don't mean their boss telling them how to teach their class. Interference refers to the tendency of (jargon alert!) *L2* (the second language being learned) learners to be subconsciously influenced by the grammar, vocabulary and pronunciation of their L1, their native language. This occurs to some extent to any L2 learner anywhere—regardless of what the L1 and L2 are. Normally it's not something that has to be discussed at great length with students, but you should be aware of it. As you progress in your glamorous, high-paying ESL career, you'll become familiar with the particular errors that are especially common among speakers of particular languages. (And obviously, if you speak your students' L1, you'll be quite familiar with your students' interference errors.) Examples of interference errors would be a Russian speaker saying, for example, *I borrowed book from library,* or an Arabic speaker saying, for example, *My brother he is doctor* or pronouncing *paper* as *baber* or a Spanish speaker saying, for example, *Is hot today* or *Please give me some advices.* In every case, those speakers' brains are trying to make English conform to how things are in their L1. Understanding and being able to predict common interference errors will make you a better teacher.

1.25 Collocations

ESL teachers often speak of (jargon alert!) *collocations.* Collocations are two or more words that often hang out with each other not because some grammar rule requires it but simply because native speakers get in the habit of saying things a certain way even when another way might be perfectly logical and grammatical. That's why we *take a break,* not *have a break.* That's why we *pay attention,* not *give attention.* That's why we *make the bed,* not *do the bed.* That's why we have *big dreams,* not *large dreams.* That's why we have *slight headaches,* not *little headaches.*

It's important to understand that language isn't always about rules; it's often about patterns, habits and custom—things that native speakers just know. Deviating from the collocation a native speaker would use will not always result in misunderstanding. If a nonnative speaker tells me that she is going to *make her homework* after she *does her bed,* I know what she means, but there are times when the lack of the right collocation can interfere with understanding. If you've ever studied a language, you know what it's like to struggle to say something in a foreign language and, for a split second feel proud of your ability to communicate in that language, only to have your listeners either look at you with puzzlement or fall over laughing. You didn't necessarily make a mistake. Maybe you just didn't say it the way they say it.

An understanding of the notion of collocations will help you to help your students understand why, even though what they are saying might be grammatical and logical, native speakers don't always understand them. Make your students aware of collocations (though you don't necessarily have to teach them the term), and encourage them to think in terms of word groups and not just individual words.

Weak collocations are words that are commonly but not exclusively used together, but there are certain words that are virtually never used without one or more other words. These are called *strong collocations.* When do you ever use *inclement* without *weather?* When do you ever use *auburn* without *hair?* There are *fixed collocations* too which don't allow for any deviation (like *kick the bucket*—can you say *knock over the bucket* or *kick the pail?*) And there are words that are literally never used except in one particular collocation. When do you ever use *fro* without *to and?* When do you ever use *roughshod* without *run?*

This idea of words that are often, usually or always used together relates to idioms (like *by the way* or *all of a sudden*), phrasal verbs, many of which are idiomatic, (like *come up with* or *put out*) and *chunks* aka *lexical phrases* (like *once upon a time* or *I would like*—discussed in Section 12.6).

1.26 Heresy

There's plenty of conventional wisdom in this field that I disagree with. Some of it is just plain silly, like not correcting students' papers with a red pen because the color red might traumatize them. Another is that you should never use the students' native language in class. It's very common for ESL teachers to have some knowledge of their students' native language. With lower level students, providing translations or explaining something in their native language can save you a lot of time and result in much better results than if you try to do it all in English, so don't be afraid to do it. Some of the first things you're likely to learn, whether you make a point of studying the students' language or not, is words that are useful in the classroom, for example, the (jargon alert!) *parts of speech* (*verb, noun, adjective, adverb,* etc.), *word, sentence, question, negative, What does* _____ *mean?* These can be an enormous help when you're teaching beginners. But the higher the level, the less you should use their native language. If you can speak your intermediate-level and advanced-level students' language, <u>don't</u> give in to the temptation to do so when it's not necessary. You and they are there in that classroom not so you can practice their language but so they can learn yours. Overdoing it with the students' native language can get you into trouble with the boss too. I've seen it happen. But the odd word now and then, sometimes just for a laugh, is a great way to connect with your students.

Another thing I disagree with is the notion that students should use only monolingual (i.e. English-only) dictionaries. This is the sort of harebrained idea that bosses are good at dreaming up. Remember what I said about metalanguage: If students can understand a teacher's lofty metalanguage, they don't need to be studying English. The same is true of English-only dictionaries. The language in the definitions will often be way beyond your students' comprehension, making the dictionary completely useless. Have you ever studied a language? Very likely you have. Did you use a monolingual or bilingual dictionary? I know the answer. If your teacher had told you not to use a bilingual dictionary, you would have used one anyway, right? Well, good luck telling your students not to use bilingual dictionaries. They will no matter what anyone says, and they should.

1.27 Alphabet soup

You may be wondering *Is this book about how to teach ESL or EFL grammar?* If you are wondering that, stop it right now! Another silly thing about this field is the alphabet soup of names it has: ESL, EFL, ELT, EAL, EIL, ESP, EOP, EAP, ELL, ELF, ESD, ESOL, TESL, TEFL, TESOL (and there are more!). All this alphabet soup does is confuse people. Personally, I prefer ELT, English Language Teaching (or Training—even that isn't agreed upon by all), but since ESL is the most common term, that's what I'll use in this book. Now what about the supposed difference between ESL and EFL? These terms refer to what is imagined by some to be a massive difference between the English that people living in English-speaking countries need to study (ESL) and the English that people living in non-English-speaking countries need to study (EFL). Yes, obviously people who are living in English-speaking countries like the US or Canada or the UK or Australia or New Zealand (and let's not forget Nauru, Tokelau and Pitcairn Island) need to learn the English necessary to avail themselves of government services, to use financial institutions, to shop, to navigate public transportation, etc., as opposed to people in non-English-speaking who don't, but the reality is this is a minor difference that does not justify the fiction that there are two entirely different branches of this field which need to have two different names. The English that these two types of students need is 98.47% the same, according to my calculation. Insisting that every textbook be identified as either an ESL book or EFL book or that teachers in the field identify themselves as either ESL teachers or EFL teachers is nuts. Except for a few books specifically designed for newcomers to English-speaking countries, there is NO difference. I advise you to have little patience with people who make a big deal about whether a book is ESL or EFL or whether you taught ESL or EFL at some previous job.

1.28 AE or BE?

You may be wondering *Is this book about American English or British English?* If you are wondering that, stop it right now! Why? Because it doesn't matter! My mother completely disregarded my wish to be born in Canada and insisted on giving birth to me in the USA. As a result, I speak American English. But what does that mean? It means that the grammar I use is virtually identical to that of my British colleagues. (The Brits say *the team suck,* and I say *the team sucks*—big deal.) It means that my (jargon alert!) *lexicon* is virtually the same as that of my British colleagues. (The Brits say *lift,* and I say *elevator*—big deal.) The idea that there is a massive difference between AE and BE is one of the many myths that exist in the ESL field—as if they were two mutually unintelligible dialects. Book publishers perpetuate this myth, I believe, to sell more books, but the reality is that it is ridiculous to worry students with this. It does them a disservice.

I say "disservice" because your students may very well speak a native language that does indeed have widely divergent and mutually unintelligible dialects (such as Chinese and Arabic), and they may assume—and worry—that the same must be true of English. Exactly the opposite is true. The varieties of English spoken around the world are remarkable for their similarity, not their difference. I have never in my life had any serious difficulty understanding a native speaker from another English-speaking country because of differences in grammar. Have you? I don't mean that you didn't need to listen a bit more closely because of that person's accent or that the occasional vocabulary item was unfamiliar; I mean that you truly did not understand because of major differences <u>in grammar</u>.

I tell my students this and assure them that as far as grammar and vocabulary are concerned, the minor differences between AE and BE are nothing to worry about. (I'm talking about standard vocabulary—not slang, which might be amusing to discuss for a bit but is not their primary vocabulary concern.) What I do tell them is that it's different <u>accents</u> that may give them trouble, not grammar or vocabulary. I strongly encourage them to familiarize themselves with a wide range of accents and point out that there are various accents even within the same country.

Now having said all that, being from the USA, I have naturally written this book in AE. The grammar I teach, the spelling I use (and yes, I hear all you Brits saying *You mean misspelling!*) and the punctuation I use are as we do it in AE. (With the exception of our ghastly American custom of putting periods and commas inside quotation marks when they are not part of the quoted material. It's so illogical that I'm leading a quixotic one-man crusade against the absurd practice.) My British colleagues might feel that I should have given more attention to *shall*, which is virtually extinct in AE, but otherwise, nothing in this book should cause them to freak out.

1.29 Jargon alert!

Keep the jargon to a minimum. Use grammar terminology only insofar as it helps students or is unavoidable. Remember that your goal is to teach your students to speak English, not to train them to be ESL teachers. You want students to learn as effortlessly and as intuitively as possible. You want them to be able to do it, not explain it.

But *you* should know some jargon for two reasons. One, it'll save you from being embarrassed when your colleagues use terms that you're not familiar with and two, it represents important ideas and concepts that you *should* be familiar with. To help you, just as in this introduction, throughout *Secrets of Teaching ESL Grammar,* I've placed "jargon alert!" warnings before terminology that you should remember—terminology commonly used by experienced, trained ESL teachers. It's worth making an effort to learn these terms if you want to be taken seriously as an ESL teacher. Some of you English majors will find that some terms that are quite familiar to you are absent from this book. Studying, analyzing, discussing and teaching English to native English speakers is not the same as it is to nonnative speakers. Nowhere in this book will you find, for example, the terms *predicate, complement, aspect* or *mood* (OK, I do mention complements a couple of times). Never in 26 years of teaching ESL have I had any need to use them in the classroom, and neither will you.

1.30 Leave 'em with a tease.

And finally, I'll pass along something I like to do to at the end of class. In addition to the usual housekeeping things, I like to leave students with a little tease, a little preview of what's to come in the next class. It might be a sentence on the board that I ask the students to think about and try to explain. In a monolingual class it might be how to say something from their native language in English which relates to a grammar topic to be covered in the next class. It might be the answer to a question about that student's country which must be answered using a specified grammar point—maybe about a holiday, tradition or historical event. You get the idea. I tell the students I'm going to ask them about this at the beginning of the next class, and I do. Try this. It's fun and makes you look like a pro who has a master plan, who sees the big picture and in one class is already thinking about the next.

Chapter 2
Be

Could you...

- explain six ways that *be* is used (with adjectives, for example, and five other ways)?
- explain whether *you are* and *you were* are singular or plural?
- explain what is meant by saying that *be* is infinitive? What does *infinitive* mean?

2.1 Focus on form and function will follow.

Be is where every student starts and where every student should start. We can discuss *be* in terms of *form* and *function*. Form means what a word (or grammatical structure) looks like—in this case *be, am, is, are, was* or *were*. Function means what we use these forms for. With *be*, focus on form first—function will follow. Your goal is to help students learn the present forms and the past forms of *be* (don't confuse them with *been* at this point—you can do that later), to learn when to use them, how to make questions and negative sentences with them and how to make contractions with them.

2.2 Tense/aspect/mood?

If you're coming from an English (vs. ESL) major background, you may be familiar with the concepts of (jargon alert!) *tense*, *aspect* and *mood* and how they differ. In the field of teaching ESL, aspect does not exist. The concept is of no help to ESL students and is *not* used. In ESL, everything is a tense: past, present, future (yes, I know that theoretically English has no future tense), continuous and perfect. As for mood, this term is not used either. *Conditional* is used a great deal, *imperative* only rarely (*command* is often used instead), *indicative* and *subjunctive* never (though I'll discuss subjunctive later). *Declarative* and *interrogative* aren't used either. We just have *sentences* which, when necessary, are identified as *negative* or as *questions*. Didn't Einstein say it's better to oversimplify than to overcomplicate? (No, he didn't. I did.)

2.3 *be = am, is, are, was, were*

Be is the (jargon alert!) *infinitive* form. Just what is meant by *infinitive* is always difficult for students, but it's especially difficult with *be*. Why? Because with other verbs which they may already know (or will soon know), verbs like *come, go, eat, sleep, walk, work*, etc., the infinitive form and the present form look <u>exactly the same</u> (with the exception of that crazy *s* which, for some reason that few students ever really understand, we sometimes put on verbs in the present tense—more on that later). Because the infinitive form and the present form of verbs other than *be* look the same (at least when an *s* isn't stuck onto it) and because there is often no great need to understand why they are not the same, most students don't really understand why they are not the same. For example, even at an advanced level, most students would not be able to explain how *eat* in

    2.1   I want to eat.

is different from *eat* in

    2.2   I eat lunch at 12:00.

(but you should be able to, so see Appendix F).

That is not true of *be*, however. The infinitive form of *be* and the present forms are entirely different. But don't confuse your students with talk of the infinitive at this point! Just make sure they understand that *be* is really a group of forms—some present and some past: *be = am, are, is, was* and *were*.

2.4 Uses of *be*

- **six basic ways that *be* is used**

with nouns:	She is a doctor.
with adjectives:	I was sick.
with prepositional phrases:	The students are in the library.
with adverbs:	She was there.
with continuous sentences:	They were working.
with passive sentences:	My car was stolen.

2.5 Start with _be_ + nouns, _be_ + adjectives and _be_ + prepositional phrases.

Look at the six ways to use _be_ above. But before doing so, be aware that this breakdown is somewhat oversimplified. The idea is to get the job done. OK? Now, are you going to teach all of this to your students on day one? No! Focus on nouns, adjectives and prepositional phrases. And don't overdo it with prepositions. Beware that prepositions are potentially confusing. Why? Because no rule or system determines why one preposition is used rather than another or even why a preposition is used at all. Do you know why we say _in the morning_, _at night_ and _on Friday_ or why we say _hear_ but _listen to_ or _watch_ but _look at_? I don't either. When students ask you why, this is one time you can resort to the favorite answer of untrained teachers: _That's just the way it is._ Usually that really means _I don't know_, but in this case it means _Nobody knows_.

Anyway, prepositions won't be a big problem now because all you're going to do is use simple examples like _under the sofa, on the table_, etc. Keep it simple, and students will pick up on their meaning easily. Using people and objects in the classroom in your initial examples will help. (_John is behind Noura, The books are on the desk._) Just between you and me, prepositional phrases _are_ (sort of) adjectives:

> 2.3   He was under the weather.

> 2.4   A man with a gun robbed the bank.

and (sort of) adverbs:

> 2.5   He was under the table.

> 2.6   She lives with her parents.

That's kind of a cool idea to keep in mind for later and definitely not something to confuse your students with now.

2.6 _be_ + continuous (and naughty grammar bits)

The occasional continuous (aka _progressive_) example, as a preview of a lesson to come soon, wouldn't hurt, but don't dwell on it—your focus is on form. Also, it's unavoidable to use subject pronouns and possessive pronouns here before they're actually officially taught. That sort of thing—bits of grammar sneaking into a lesson earlier than the one that they're actually taught in—will happen all the time. Don't worry about it, but be aware of it and limit it so it doesn't confuse your students. In small doses, it's actually a good thing. When you get to some new grammar, it won't always be completely new because the students will already have had a preview of it.

2.7 _you_—singular/plural

Speaking of pronouns, you'll soon be bombarding your students with sentences like these:

> 2.7   You are a student.

and like these:

> 2.8   You are students.

Do you see anything in these two sentences that might confuse them? I do, and here it is: I do not speak every language in the world, but I think it's a fair bet that most of them have some way of distinguishing between singular _you_ and plural _you_. The nouns are the giveaway in 2.7 and 2.8, but what about _You are crazy_? Is there anything in _You are crazy_ to indicate whether the speaker is talking to one person or more than one person? The fact that English uses the same pronoun, _you_, for (jargon alert!) _2nd person singular_ and _2nd person plural_ will strike some of your students as a bit odd and occasionally cause confusion. They'll get used to it pretty quickly, but you should remind them of it once in a while. They'll tend to default to _you_ being 2nd person singular and then be confused by questions with _you_ which are answered with _we_.

2.8 Don't be active with the passive.

The passive (aka the _passive voice_) will come much later—don't even mention it now.

2.9 _be_ + adverbs—not as simple as you think

As for adverbs, what we're really talking about here are adverbs of place—words like _above, away, back, behind, below, downstairs, elsewhere, here, in, indoors, inside, near, nearby, out, outside, somewhere, there, upstairs_. These don't seem like adverbs to you? You thought adverbs were just words like _quickly, slowly_ and _carefully_? Well, think again! As you'll discover later, all sorts of oddball words are adverbs that you've never even thought about. That's something you'll need to use a bit of brainpower later to learn more about.

There are (jargon alert!) _adverbial nouns_ too—_home_ and _downtown_ for example. I don't suggest teaching your students that concept at this early stage. It won't mean a thing to them. When students want to know what's wrong with _He went to home_ or *I went to downtown,* say that *home* and *downtown* are "special" or that they're exceptions. (More on adverbial nouns later.) Like all other languages, I'd guess, English is full of exceptions, and it's something that students need to understand and get used to. Again and again, as you continue to teach grammar, you'll encounter exceptions, and you'll need to explain to your students that they are exceptions. (*Exception* is a handy word to learn how to say in your students' native language.)

2.10 Suggested sequence and sample exercises

▶ Present

It would be easy to make the mistake of assuming that this is very basic and easy and to zoom through it full speed ahead, especially if some of your students are false beginners who have already studied some English, but don't assume anything! For some of your students, this may be completely new, so you need to make sure that they, and all your students, get off to a good start with a solid understanding of which forms go with which persons. By "persons", I mean this basic grammar terminology that you should know.

1st person singular:	I
2nd person singular:	you
3rd person singular:	he, she, it
1st person plural:	we
2nd person plural:	you
3rd person plural:	they

No need to teach your students this "person" business itself—it's the subject pronouns that go along with it that you'll teach them. There are two things to make sure your students understand about subject pronouns:

One is that in English we have three different subject pronouns for the third person singular, *he, she* and *it,* but only one for the third person plural, *they.*

The other is that, as mentioned previously, *you* is singular and plural, which will strike some of your students as odd and take a little getting used to.

Once you feel your students have this down, start replacing pronouns with nouns and proper nouns. Replace *he, she* and *it* with, for example, *Mr. Bean, Maria, the doctor, my father, the book,* etc. Replace *they* with, for example, *Larry and Michael, the boys, my friends, three students,* etc.

Once you feel your students are ready, try some that are a bit trickier: Replace *you* with, for example, *you and Larry, Carlos and you, you and she,* etc. This will puzzle them at first, but the idea is to get them used to the idea that *you* is singular and plural. What I often do is look at one student and say, *You are a student,* (emphasizing *a student*) then point to another while looking at the class and say *She is a student* and then point to both of them and say *You are students* (emphasizing *students*).

Next, try replacing *we* with *Mary and I, my sister and I* or *Carlos, Alan and I,* etc. Let them know that *anybody + I* is the same as *we.*

As you're running around your classroom like a nut doing all of this, I'd recommend little by little creating something like this on the board:

I		am
You		are
He, She, It	(Mr. Bean, Maria, The doctor, My father, The book)	is
We	(Mary and I, My sister and I, Carlos, Alan and I)	are
You	(You and Larry, Carlos and you, You and she, You and I)	are
They	(Larry and Michael, The boys, My friends, Three students)	are

sample exercises 1: Complete the sentences with the correct present form of *be.*

We ___*are*___ tired.

The doctor ___*is*___ in the lab.

1. I _____ the boss.
2. They _____ watching TV.
3. The book _____ there.
4. Mary and Sarah _____ at the beach.
5. My cat _____ fat.

▷ Present contractions

Contractions! Try to force your students to use them. They will resist. With some, it'll be like pulling teeth. We native speakers find it easier to use contractions. We think of them as shortcuts. Actually, children learning English as their first language learn contractions *before* the separate forms, but with second language learners, it's the opposite. They learn the separate forms first, get used to them and want to stick with them.

Why force your students to use contractions? Not because it is *ever* necessary to use them, but because it is absolutely necessary to <u>understand</u> them when they see them and (more difficultly) when they hear them. Forcing your students to use contractions will force them to focus on them and become more familiar with them. You can't emphasize the listening comprehension angle enough. Tell your students that native speakers use contractions 90% of the time in speech and 60% in writing. (I just made up those numbers, but they're probably close to the truth.) Often, more than one contraction will be possible, so in your classroom discussions and in the exercises you assign, you may want to insist, as I did in *Rocket English Grammar,* that both possible contractions be given. However, at other times you'll need to explain that possible contractions are seldom used (like *oughtn't*) or that one of two possible contractions is much more common than the other (like *I won't* vs. *I'll not*).

Put this on the board: (From now on I never put *you* on the board twice. It saves time and students get the idea.)

I am	=	I'm
you are	=	you're
he is	=	he's
she is	=	she's
it is	=	it's
we are	=	we're
they are	=	they're

sample exercises 2: Write sentences with contractions.

We are working.
We're working.

The soup is cold.
The soup's cold.

1. She is angry.
2. I am on the phone.
3. They are watching TV.
4. The door is open.
5. We are here.

sample exercises 3: Write sentences with the correct present form of *be*. Use contractions if it is possible.

a bird/in the tree
A bird's in the tree.

the men/eating
The men are eating.

1. the children/playing in the park
2. Francesca/doing her homework
3. dinner/served at 7:00
4. I/listening to the radio
5. the students/studying

▷ Present negative contractions

The main thing you want your students to understand is that with all subject pronouns except *I,* there are two possible contractions, and they are both equally common. (Pay attention to that idea *common.* How common or uncommon something is will be something that you'll occasionally need to discuss with your students and is something that will determine how you budget your time, which, after all, is not unlimited. Put this on the board:

I am not	=	I'm not		
you are not	=	you're not	=	you aren't
he is not	=	he's not	=	he isn't

she is not	=	she's not	=	she isn't
it is not	=	it's not	=	it isn't
we are not	=	we're not	=	we aren't
they are not	=	they're not	=	they aren't

sample exercises 4: Write sentences with contractions. Write all possible contractions.

She is not watching TV.

She's not watching TV.

She isn't watching TV.

1. They are not outside.
2. The doctor is not at the clinic.
3. You are not listening.
4. He is not an engineer.
5. I am not hungry.

sample exercises 5: Change the sentences to negative. Write all possible contractions.

Mary is inside.

Mary's not inside.

Mary isn't inside.

1. John is a student.
2. We are in front of the supermarket.
3. I am finished.
4. He is in bed.
5. They are here.

sample exercises 6: Write negative sentences with the correct present form of *be*. Write all possible contractions.

she/a student

She's not a student.

She isn't a student.

1. I/eating breakfast
2. Mark/reading a book
3. the projects/finished
4. he and I/mechanics
5. you/washing the car

▷ **Present *yes/no* questions**

Yes/no questions are called that because—brace yourself—they can be answered with *yes* or *no.* It's very important that students understand that when we make questions with *be,* what's happening is that we are (jargon alert!) *inverting* (I say *switching* in class) the subject and *be*:

2.9a   <u>She</u> <u>is</u> from France.

  b   → <u>Is</u> <u>she</u> from France?

Of course, the subject is not always a single word, so you might want to give your students some examples with more complex noun phrases as subjects (but don't overdo it):

2.10a   <u>The tall woman in the blue dress</u> <u>is</u> from France.

   b   → <u>Is</u> <u>the tall woman in the blue dress</u> from France?

We'll be talking about forming questions a lot more later, so the more your students get this idea of *inversion,* the easier it will be.

sample exercises 7: Write answers to the questions with the correct present form of *be.* Use contractions.

   A: Is Mark playing soccer?

   B: Yes, _____*Mark's playing soccer*_____.

1. A: Is the pilot sleeping?

   B: Yes, _____

2. A: Is Ali in the library?

B: No, _____.
3. A: Are the soldiers fighting?
    B: Yes, _____.
4. A: Are Toyotas made in Japan?
    B: Yes, _____.
5. A: Is her sister here?
    B: No, _____.

sample exercises 8: Change the sentences to questions.
       The car is in the garage.
       Is the car in the garage?

1. The cats are under the sofa.
2. Carlos is tired.
3. Tom and his wife are in the gym.
4. You and John are working hard.
5. The house is dirty.

▶ Past

Was and *were* are a little easier to teach since there are only two forms and only one contraction in every case. All you need to do essentially is repeat what you did with present forms of *be*. You could just modify what you've already got on the board:

I		was
You		were
He, She, It	(Mr. Bean, Maria, The doctor, My father, The book)	was
We	(Mary and I, My sister and I, Carlos, Alan and I)	were
You	(You and Larry, Carlos and you, You and she, You and I)	were
They	(Larry and Michael, The boys, My friends, Three students)	were

sample exercise 9: Complete the sentences with the correct past form of *be*.
       Mary ___*was*___ here yesterday.

1. The car _____ very expensive.
2. Sofia and her sister _____ doing their homework.
3. That _____ a good movie.
4. The book _____ written by me.
5. My children _____ there yesterday.

sample exercises 10: Write sentences with the correct past form of *be*.
       Tom and Jerry/at the mall
       Tom and Jerry were at the mall.

1. Noura/dancing
2. the coffee/hot
3. the men/truck drivers
4. the house/sold
5. my parents/there

▷ Past negative and contractions

This will go faster than with present forms. I think you can combine negative with contractions since contractions are used only with *was* and *not* and *were* and *not*. Put this on the board:

I was not	=	I wasn't
you were not	=	you weren't
he was not	=	he wasn't
she was not	=	she wasn't
it was not	=	it wasn't
we were not	=	we weren't
they were not	=	they weren't

sample exercises 11: Write sentences with contractions.

They were not swimming.

They weren't swimming.

1. I was not upstairs.
2. The women were not at the party.
3. She and I were not angry.
4. My house was not clean.
5. Maria was not a secretary.

sample exercises 12: Change the sentences to negative. Use contractions.

Tom was sick.

Tom wasn't sick.

1. John and Mark were in the bank.
2. The keys were in my pocket.
3. I was talking on the telephone.
4. Her cell phone was stolen.
5. Our father was cutting the grass.

sample exercises 13: Write negative sentences with the correct past form of *be*. Use contractions.

the car/in the garage

The car wasn't in the garage.

1. my friends/at the game
2. John/taking a test
3. the door/locked
4. the show/over
5. we/done

▷ **Past *yes/no* questions**

Repeat what you did with present *yes/no* questions. You might want to review the idea of subject/verb inversion.

sample exercises 14: Write answers to the questions with the correct past form of *be*. Use contractions.

A: Were the boys in the library working?
B: No, _____ *the boys in the library weren't working* _____.

1. A: Was the party fun?
   B: Yes, _____.
2. A: Were John and Michael at the meeting?
   B: No, _____.
3. A: Were the students listening to the teacher?
   B: Yes, _____.
4. A: Was the doctor in the clinic?
   B: No, _____.
5. A: Was the movie good?
   B: No, _____.

sample exercises 15: Change the sentences to questions.

The pencils were on the table.

Were the pencils on the table?

1. The calculator was on the table.
2. His father was a police officer.
3. The men were late.
4. The cookies were eaten by the children.
5. The mechanic was fixing the car.

sample exercises 16: Change the sentences from present to past.

Are you busy?

Were you busy?

1. Michael is washing the dishes.
2. Are the girls in the classroom?
3. They're not there.
4. I'm not doing my homework.
5. Is Noura talking to her friend?

sample exercises 17: Change the sentences from past to present.

Mary wasn't playing tennis.
Mary isn't playing tennis.

1. Linda wasn't in the hospital.
2. Three boys were outside.
3. Was the bird flying?
4. Were Tom and Lucy married?
5. She wasn't reading in the library.

▶ **Present and past short answers with *be***

Now teach your students short answers. What do I mean by that? Short answers are answers like this: *Yes, I am, No, he wasn't, Yes, they can.* They're generally pretty easy. It's only with *do, does* and *did* that they can be a bit tricky. One thing to mention is that contractions are used only with negative short answers. We don't say, for example, *Yes, I'm, Yes, he'll, Yes, she'd,* etc.

sample exercises 18: Answer the questions with short answers in the correct tense. Use contractions only in negative short answers. Use only *I, you, he, she, it, we* or *they* in your answers.

    A: Is the girl a good student?
    B: Yes, _____*she is*_____ .

1. A: Are Mary and Gary married?
   B: No, ____*they're not*____ .
2. A: Are you hungry?
   B: Yes, _____ .
3. A: Were Tom and you playing football?
   B: No, _____ .
4. A: Was the test easy?
   B: Yes, _____ .
5. A: Is your sister at the supermarket?
   B: No, _____ .
6. A: Was David eaten by a tiger?
   B: Yes, _____ .

2.11 Ellipsis

Short answers provide the perfect segue to (jargon alert!) *ellipsis.* Ellipsis means not repeating words because it isn't necessary. Why isn't it necessary? Because the intended audience, the reader or listener, understands the words. They've already been heard or read, are remembered and can be mentally filled in. If my friend asks me *Are you hungry?* and I answer *Yes, I am,* she knows that what I mean is *Yes, I am <u>hungry</u>.* Here are some examples with the ellipted words supplied:

2.11a David: Is the girl a good student?
    b Paul: Yes, she is [a good student].

2.12a Sam: Are Mary and Gary married?
    b Sofia: No, they're not [married].

This might seem pretty easy and obvious, and it is here, but later, just like everything else, it'll get more complicated. I would not teach the term *ellipsis* but rather just get your students used to the idea. You might want to use the answers to sample exercises 18 for more practice.

Ellipsis is very common, yet it is barely ever mentioned in grammar books or for that matter in any other area of ESL instruction, including speaking and conversation practice. I think it should be discussed with students, and I included several massive blobs of ellipsis in my grammar book, *Rocket English Grammar* (shameless plug). Discuss it with your students. They'll think you're smart for doing so, and your boss will too.

2.12 Listening practice

What's listening got to do with grammar? As I will remind you again and again, it's very important for students to train their ears to understand the fast, casual speech of native speakers. I have frequently had students tell me that they understand me and their other teachers but not the English speakers they encounter outside the classroom or hear in movies and on TV. To help them with their listening comprehension, I often, toward the end of a grammar lesson, will simply read aloud from whatever examples are at hand—examples and exercise in the textbook and/or on the board—in a way that makes no concession to the students' listening comprehension difficulties but is just as fast and reduced as if I were talking to another native speaker. Do this and repeat, repeat, repeat while your students read along and train their ears. Make sure they understand that this is for their listening comprehension benefit, and that you are definitely <u>not</u> suggesting that they copy your reduced speech. (That would be a mistake—they will have accents which means they need to speak as clearly as possible in order to be understood by native speakers.) Students really appreciate this listening practice, and they'll be impressed that you're smart enough to realize that this should be part of a grammar lesson.

2.13 Three-way speaking practice with *be*

Depending on time (and this is a great way to fill time if you have too much of it), a great exercise that I often do, which I call *three-way speaking practice,* involves the teacher asking one student a question <u>about another student</u>, the first student then asking the second student the question, the second student answering the first and finally the first student answering the teacher with the answer he/she has received from the second. For example,

2.13a	Teacher:	John, is Maria from Peru?
b	John:	Maria, are you from Peru?
c	Maria:	Yes, I am.
d	John:	Yes, she is.

Then keep going so that the second student is now the first. (So now, for example, you're asking Maria a question about Sofia, then Sofia about Ali and so on.) Start (as you always should without being too obvious about it) with the stronger students so that the weaker students have more time to get it. After a bit of confusion at first, they'll catch on quickly.

Chapter 3
Present Continuous and Past Continuous

Could you...

- explain what the continuous tenses are used for?
- explain why *a* and *b* are incorrect?

    a.   He is study.

    b.   He studying.

- explain why *c* is OK but *d* is incorrect?

    c.   I am having fun.

    d.   I am having a computer.

3.1 Relatively easy
It's logical to continue with continuous tenses, but before we do that, a note on terminology: Some books and some teachers prefer the term *progressive* to *continuous*. In my experience *continuous* is more common, and that's what I prefer. OK? Now, why continue with the continuous? Because, in addition to being a very important aspect of grammar that students need to learn early on, it's also relatively easy—a small step for students who have just studied *be*. The main thing is getting them to understand what continuous tenses are used for and to start them on their way to learning new verbs.

And speaking of terminology, remember that since we're teaching our students to speak English, not teach it, we ESL teachers refer to the continuous *tense* and never, ever, confuse students with discussions of *aspect*.

3.2 Continuous used only for now?
So, let me ask, dear reader, is the continuous used <u>only</u> for now, now, now? No! In addition to the past continuous and future continuous, be aware that we often use the present continuous for future. And I don't mean future continuous. I mean sentences like *I'm moving to Florida next month* and *We're eating dinner at 6:00*. But don't tell your students that now! That will come later.

3.3 The *-ing* form
The hardest part of learning how to use continuous tenses has already been done in Chapter 2. Once your students have figured *be* out, it's just a matter of using *be* with the *-ing* form. The what? The *-ing* form. That's easier for students to remember than its more formal name, the (jargon alert!) *present participle*. (When you say it, say the letters: the *i-n-g form*. It doesn't rhyme with *sing*.) I never use the term *present participle* in class. If you do, the students will start confusing it with the *past participle*, so don't.

And don't ever tell your students that the *-ing* form is used <u>only</u> for continuous verbs. As you'll find out, there is a lot more to the *-ing* form than you think.

3.4 Some verbs are never continuous (except when they are).
It's second nature to us native speakers, but students need to learn that some verbs are never continuous, or at least never continuous in a certain sense. These include emotional or mental states like *believe, know, like* and *want*; senses like *hear, see* and *taste* and verbs that relate to how you think or feel about something like *agree, mean, need* and *promise*. But it depends on the meaning. Some verbs are never continuous in one meaning but can be in another. That's why we can say *I'm having a heart attack* but not *I'm having a bicycle*. Actually, most of this is dictated by logic, and students will generally get it without your making a big deal out of it, but it's something you should be aware of.

OK, enough blather. What should you do?

3.5 Simple independent clauses at first
At first, focus on simple (jargon alert!) *independent clauses*, sentences which make sense alone, always with at least one subject and at least one verb. Unless there is also a dependent clause, independent clauses are also called *simple sentences*. See Appendix E for more about this.

When you get to the past continuous, you'll be tempted to start giving your students examples like these, which are <u>not</u> simple sentences:

>   3.1   Larry was studying, but now he's watching TV.

>   3.2   I was sleeping when the phone rang.

Avoid the temptation to go too fast. If you have really good students who catch on quickly, you might want to take it up a notch grammarwise toward the end of the lesson, but at this point, you really don't want to get into the additional grammar these sentences contain—in the case of 3.1, two independent clauses connected by a coordinating conjunction and in the case of 3.2, an adverb clause (a dependent clause attached to an independent clause with a subordinating conjunction). Is that clear? (Before I'm through with you, you'll understand all this stuff.)

3.6 Suggested sequence and sample exercises

Grammarwise, it's all about *be*. It's essentially the same as in Chapter 1—present, past, contractions, negatives, questions, short answers. The only difference is that your students, having already been through it all, will have an easier time of it. At first, all the exercises you'll do will be more or less a repeat of what you did in Chapter 1 except that now they'll all use continuous verbs. So rather than focus on *be*, you're going to focus on teaching your students new and important verbs. You can easily think of several off the top of your head. How about these: *come, go, eat, walk, talk, work, take, study, listen to, watch, read, drive, get, sleep, use, help* and *write*.

You'll need to discuss spelling, but that's not a big deal. It's just a matter of teaching the students to drop the final *e* in verbs like *come* and *take*.

None of the exercises below is different from what you did in Chapter 1, but that doesn't matter; it's still good practice. Remember too that this is an opportunity to teach some new verbs.

sample exercises 1: Write present continuous sentences with the correct form of *be*. Use contractions.
>   she/work
>   *She's working.*

>   1.   the birds/fly
>   2.   I/read a book
>   3.   the pilot/sleep
>   4.   Mark/use his computer
>   5.   the teachers/talk

sample exercises 2: Write negative present continuous sentences with the correct form of *be*. Write all possible contractions.
>   we/study
>   *We're not studying.*
>   *We aren't studying.*

>   1.   the printer/work
>   2.   the children/be bad
>   3.   he/do his homework
>   4.   Alan/help his mother
>   5.   John and his brother/talk to their friends

Look at numbers 2 and 3 in sample exercises 2 above. Don't forget that *be* can be continuous, and don't forget (or learn now) that *do* is both an auxiliary verb and a main verb—that can be confusing for students. (More on that later—wait until then to discuss this with your students.)

sample exercises 3: Write present continuous questions with the correct form of *be*.
>   Michael/read
>   *Is Michael reading?*

>   1.   the cat/look out the window
>   2.   I/do this the right way
>   3.   the mechanic/fix the truck
>   4.   your father/cook dinner
>   5.   the children/be noisy

sample exercises 4: Correct the mistakes in the sentences. Make all of them present continuous.

1. John not working now.
2. The baby's sleep.
3. Is Mark study?
4. I'm no listening to you.
5. Michael is eat breakfast.

sample exercises 5: Write past continuous sentences with the correct form of *be*.

they/eat
They were eating.

1. I/drive my car
2. Alan and I/talk
3. they/try to answer the question
4. the students/do their homework
5. my mother/write a letter

sample exercises 6: Write negative past continuous sentences with the correct form of *be*. Use contractions.

Sarah/watch TV
Sarah wasn't watching TV.

1. Maria and her son/wash the dishes
2. the pilot/talk on the radio
3. I/fly to Poland
4. Tom and I/make dinner
5. her husband/look for a job

sample exercises 7: Write past continuous questions with the correct form of *be*.

John/make a sandwich
Was John making a sandwich?

1. the managers/have a meeting
2. Rosa/plant flowers
3. Alan and his friends/go to the mall
4. you/lie on the sofa
5. the airplane/land

sample exercises 8: Correct the mistakes in the sentences. Make all of them past continuous.

1. Were you do your homework?
2. She was no listening.
3. The bird not singing.
4. John wasn't sleep.
5. Was you studying?

3.7 Mixed review exercises

Next, to strain your students' brains a little more, how about some more difficult exercises where the students need to choose from a range of possibilities and test their knowledge of new verbs?

sample exercises 9: Complete the sentences with the correct form of *be* and the verb in parentheses. Some are present, and some are past. Use contractions if it is possible.

Larry (watch) _____*was watching*_____ TV two hours ago.

1. Look! Those guys (fight) _____.
2. We (not, be) _____ noisy in the library last night.
3. I (work) _____ in the garden all day. Now I am very dirty.
4. _____ you (listen) _____ to the teacher in class yesterday?
5. John and I (not, play) _____ soccer. We're playing baseball.

sample exercises 10: Choose the correct verb. Then complete the sentences with the correct form of *be*.

be ~~cook~~ do play read sleep

1. Michael is in the kitchen. He _____ *is cooking* _____ dinner.
2. Mary was at the library yesterday. She _____ a book.
3. Alan and Carlos are in bed now. They _____.
4. _____ the children _____ football after school yesterday?
5. Call the police! That car _____ stolen.
6. I _____ TV before, but now I _____ my homework.

3.8 Speaking practice—*yes/no* questions

Once you've covered the basics, it's time for some speaking practice. You'll want to go around the classroom having students ask and answer continuous questions. Stick to present continuous. At first, ask and answer the questions <u>yourself</u>. For example,

| 3.3a | Teacher: | Is Ali writing? |
| b | Teacher: | No, he isn't. |

| 3.4a | Teacher: | Are Maria and Sarah listening? |
| b | Teacher: | Yes, they are. |

Then let students answer. At first, pose questions which require the same noun or subject pronoun in the answer. (Whether they answer with long or short answers isn't important.) For example,

| 3.5a | Teacher: | Carlos, is Mary reading? |
| b | Carlos: | Yes, she is. |

Then ask *I/you* questions. You'll be surprised by how much more difficult this will be, so do it a lot. For example,

| 3.6a | Teacher: | Larry, am I teaching? |
| b | Larry: | Yes, you are. |

| 3.7a | Teacher: | Rosa, are you eating a cheeseburger? |
| b | Rosa: | No, I'm not. |

Now you can use the three-way exercise I described in Chapter 1 where you ask S1 (i.e. student 1) a question about S2, S1 then asks S2 the question, S2 answers S1 and finally S1 answers you. For example,

3.8a	Teacher:	Alan, is Carlos drinking coffee?
b	Alan:	Carlos, are you drinking coffee?
c	Carlos:	No, I'm not.
d	Alan:	No, he isn't.

This might all seem pretty basic and obvious, but students need lots of speaking practice. You really can't do too much of this sort of thing. And students like it! It's a great way to liven up a dreary, tedious, mind-numbingly dull grammar class.

3.9 Speaking practice—information questions

Is that all? No! Now it's time to move on to information questions. One thing I like to do is write this on the board:

What is _____ doing?

Maybe you're thinking *doing* is a bit advanced at this point? Maybe, but so what. There are times when you give students previews of grammar soon to come—no harm in that and no need to explain the grammar at great length. Let them figure it out intuitively. If you say no more than this: "question *doING*?, answer <u>ING</u>, for example, *eatING, walkING, workING*" and give them a few examples, they'll catch on. Now go around the classroom posing questions. Answer them yourself, at first, and then ask the students to answer. For example,

| 3.9a | Teacher: | What am I doing? |
| b | Teacher: | I am teaching. |

| 3.10a | Teacher: | What is Maria doing? |
| b | Teacher: | She is listening. |

Follow the same sequence as above—ask and answer questions yourself first; then let students answer. Remember to use a lot of *I/you* questions. Finally, use the three-way speaking practice exercise I discussed in Chapter 1.

3.10 Future continuous?

If you think I've forgotten the future continuous, I haven't. Because the future continuous involves modals—primarily *will*—I think it's better to wait until later and slip it into discussions of the future and discussions of modals.

Chapter 4
Do, Does and *Did*

Could you...

- explain how the verb *study* in *a* is different from the verb *study* in *b*?

    a.   They study English.
    b.   Do they study English?

- explain why the verb *drink* has an *s* in *c*?

    c.   He drinks coffee in the morning.

- explain why the verb *drink* does not have an *s* in *d*?

    d.   Does he drink coffee in the morning?

- explain how *do* is different in *e* and *f*?

    e.   I do the laundry on Saturday.
    f.   I do believe you.

- explain why *g* is OK but *h* isn't?

    g.   Have you a computer?
    h.   Want you a sandwich?

- explain *i* to a student?

    i.   I do do my homework in the bathroom.

4.1 *do, does* and *did*—vitally important and hard as hell

Fasten your seatbelts—you're in for a bumpy chapter. Now you're going to teach your students one of the most difficult aspects of English grammar. But it has to be done and done early. There's no way it can be left until later. Much of what follows builds on this. It is absolutely essential. It's also quite difficult. Many ESL students never really master *do, does* and *did* (Nor do many native speakers—what percentage of native speakers, do you suppose, don't know better than to say *He don't, She don't,* etc.?)

So if it seems as if I'm plodding along at a snail's pace (do snails plod?), it's because, for your students, a solid understanding of how to use *do, does* and *did* is vitally important. You need to spend a lot of time on it. There's no way around it.

But if it's taught right, it doesn't have to be horribly painful. Teaching it right means teaching students <u>patterns</u>—what to do—and not teaching them <u>theory</u>. (And this applies to <u>everything</u> in this book.) Remember, you're teaching your students how to use English, not how to teach it.

4.2 Present simple

Do and *does* are required for what we call the (jargon alert!) *present simple* (aka the *simple present*). What is the present simple? Here's how I explain it to students: the present continuous (which they have just studied) is about something that is happening <u>now</u> (ignoring the past and future continuous for the moment and emphasizing *now*, which they will understand rather than language like *happening, in progress,* etc., which they will not), but the present simple is about *always, sometimes, never, usually*—routine (it's helpful to use a bilingual dictionary to teach them the meaning of *routine*). I'll then give them examples (avoiding the 3rd person singular—the *-s* form of the verb—for now) like *I drink coffee every day. Am I drinking coffee now?* and *You* (to a student) *speak Chinese, right? Are you speaking Chinese now?* You want them to get the idea that the present simple is about things that are generally, always, sometimes, etc. true but not necessarily true about <u>right now</u>. Of course we saw in the last chapter that there are exceptions, like *have* and *live,* but don't mention that.

To help your students understand how the present continuous is different from the present simple, try some exercises like these: (This would be a good time for a quick lesson on the meanings of *always, usually, sometimes* and *never*.)

sample exercises 1: Underline the correct form of the verb.

   Michael (<u>has</u>/is having) three dogs.

Please be quiet. I (study/<u>am studying</u>).

1. We (go/are going) to school at 8:15 every day.
2. Listen to me! I (talk/am talking) to you.
3. My father and my brother are in the garage now. They (fix/are fixing) our car.
4. Sarah and John are doctors. They sometimes (work/are working) in a hospital.
5. I am a teacher. I am in my classroom. I (am teaching/teach) now.

4.3 Start with *do*

Now, let's get to *do*. Write two or three examples on the board. Arrange them horizontally if you have room. Use only *they*, a plural noun or two or more names as subjects:

They live in Canada.   The kids play football.   Sam and Dave have cars.

4.4 Questions with *do*

Simple enough so far, but now we're going to talk about questions and negatives. Start with questions. Under each example, write a *yes/no* question version of the sentences: (Resist the temptation to get into short answer like *Yes, they do* for now.)

They live in Canada.   The kids play football.   Sam and Dave have cars.
Do they live in Canada?   Do the kids play football?   Do Sam and Dave have cars?

It's going to look to your students as if all you need to do to ask a present simple question is stick *do* in front of a sentence, and in this case, that would be right (sort of), but there's more to it than that. You need to understand, even if your students don't, that the verbs in the statements and the verbs in the questions are <u>not</u> the same. Something has changed. Do you know what? The verbs in the statements are in the present tense. The verbs in the questions are infinitives. And they look the same, don't they? The fact that infinitive verbs in English look exactly like verbs in the present simple tense (excluding *be* and the 3rd person singular form—*goes, works,* etc.) will confuse your students to no end if you try to explain it, so my advice is don't try to explain it. Why is this important? Because when you get to *does* and *did,* the verbs will <u>not</u> look the same, and that will confuse your students.

sample exercises 2: Change the sentences to questions with *do*.

    You work in a factory.
    Do you work in a factory?

1. They speak English.
2. Mary and Larry live in Mexico.
3. The teachers eat lunch at 12:30.
4. They have a new car.
5. Your friends know the answer.

4.5 Negatives with *do*

Now write negative versions of the sentences (not negative answers to the questions) under the questions: (Don't discuss contractions yet.)

They live in Canada.   The kids play football.   Sam and Dave have cars.
Do they live in Canada?   Do the kids play football?   Do Sam and Dave have cars?
They do not live in Canada.   The kids do not play football.   Sam and Dave do not have cars.

Clearly, to change a present simple sentence to negative, all you need to do is stick *do not* in the sentence before the verb, and in this case, that would be right (sort of). But once again, the verb has changed to an infinitive, and once again, the infinitive and the present simple verb look the same and once again, they're not actually the same, and once again, they will not look the same with *does* and *did.*

sample exercises 3: Change the sentences to negative with *do not*.

    I drink coffee.
    I do not drink coffee.

1. They have a cat.
2. We speak French.
3. You study in the library.
4. Tom and Alan work in an office.
5. My parents live in Florida.

4.6 Contractions with *do*

Now teach the contraction *don't*. As always, you want to encourage students to use contractions with the understanding that it's never necessary to use them, but it is absolutely necessary to understand them.

sample exercises 4: Change the sentences to negative with *don't*.

> We go to school on Saturday.
> *We don't go to school on Saturday.*

1. You have a big house.
2. The boys listen to the radio.
3. They like pizza.
4. My children play soccer.
5. I live in Spain.

4.7 Short answers with *do*

Now teach your students short answers with *do*. They have already learned short answers with *be*, and the false beginners may be familiar with *Yes, I can* and *No, I can't* and the like, but short answers with *do, does* and *did* will be a bit more difficult because it's the only time that short answers don't always repeat an auxiliary verb from the question. For that reason, spend more time on them than you would with other short answers.

sample exercises 5: Answer the questions with long answers and short answers. Use contractions.

> Do you like football? (yes)
> *Yes, I like football.*
> *Yes, I do.*

> Do Mary and Tom work in a bank? (no)
> *No, they don't work in a bank.*
> *No, they don't.*

1. Do they sit in the back of the classroom? (yes)
2. Do your children play tennis? (no)
3. Do you have a red car? (yes)
4. Do Carlos and Alan speak English? (no)
5. Do you want to eat dinner? (no)

4.8 Speaking practice with *do*

Before going on to *does* and *did,* give your students some speaking practice by asking them questions—similar to the exercises above—all requiring *they,* a plural noun or two or more names as subjects (remember, *does* is going to be a lot harder, so leave it for later). At first, ask all the questions yourself. Then, to get them to practice asking questions, try the three-way speaking exercise I've talked about before. Then transition to *you/I* questions. Encourage but don't insist on contractions in negative answers, and at first don't worry about short answers, but as you continue, try to get your students to use them.

4.9 The accursed *-s* form

Now you're going to do it all over again with *does*. The first thing you have to do is introduce them to the *-s* form of present simple verbs, and that's a big deal, so make a BIG GIANT DEAL out of it! The *-s* form befuddles ESL students the world over. <u>You</u> should know that it's called the third person singular, but there's no need to teach that term to your students. I usually don't. You should also know that the term (jargon alert!) *subject-verb agreement* is often used when discussing the *-s* form. It means that the verb is in the form required for a 3rd person singular subject. It *agrees* with the subject. (And it's the lack of subject-verb agreement that you'll usually be discussing.) Write something like this on the board: (Avoid *has* and *goes* for now.)

> I, You, We, They, The girls, My friends   eat, work, want, speak, like
> He, She, Carlos, Noura, It, The man, Your mother   eat<u>s</u>, work<u>s</u>, want<u>s</u>, speak<u>s</u>, like<u>s</u>

Underline the letter *s* in each verb, just as I have, or better yet, make them huge and fluorescent orange in color. Use fireworks if possible. You really want your students to remember this, and it's not easy.

What you need to make your students understand is that this crazy *-s* form is used for <u>singular</u> subjects—<u>one</u> man, <u>one</u> girl, <u>one</u> teacher, <u>one</u> book, <u>one</u> house (that's actually what I do in class—say "one man, one girl, one teacher, one book, one house" (or something like that) and really emphasize *one*. That's important because students by now will know that we add *s* to <u>nouns</u> to make them plural, and because they've come to associate *s* with plural, sometimes they have a hard time understanding that with verbs, it's just the opposite. That's something for you to be aware of. Also, don't assume that students always understand that by *he, she* and *it,* we also mean the name of any one man, one woman or one thing. Remind them that what applies to *she* also applies, for example, to *Mary* or *my sister.*

▶ Irregular -*s* forms

And now is the time to teach the irregular -*s* forms of *have, go, fly, try* and *cry* (*has, goes, flies, tries* and *cries,* but I think you knew that) and also to point out that *goes* does not rhyme with *does.* Also, that verbs which end with *s, x, sh* and *ch* add -*es.* (But don't turn this into a spelling lesson. You need to mention it, but don't focus on it. Spelling is the least of your students' worries right now.)

Before discussing *does* and questions and negatives, it's a good idea to work hard to reinforce the whole -*s* form thing. Don't rush.

sample exercises 6: Underline the correct form of the verb.
We (<u>work</u>/works) in a factory.

1. I (speak/speaks) English.
2. She (live/lives) in Holland.
3. The teacher (eat/eats) lunch at 12:30.
4. The teachers (eat/eats) lunch at 12:30.
5. Linda and Lucy (work/works) in an office.

So now, you think, they have it all figured out, right? Think again. This won't be easy.

4.10 *does*

OK, let's give them examples. You're essentially going to do what you did before: write two or three sentences on the board but this time with sentences containing 3rd person singular verbs, then change them to questions and then change them then to negatives all the while making a BIG GIANT DEAL out of the verbs in the questions and negatives not having an *s*:

He lives in Canada.	She plays football.	The food tastes good.
Does he live in Canada?	Does she play football?	Does the food taste good?
He does not live in Canada.	She does not play football.	The food does not taste good.

Do your students absolutely need to understand that the tensed verb in the (jargon alert!) *affirmative statements* (statements that are not negative) is changing to the infinitive verb in the questions and negatives. No! All they need to know is that when a sentence is about *He, She, It* or the name of <u>one</u> person or <u>one</u> thing, the verb must be in the -*s* form, and that when it's a question or negative, *does* is used, and the *s* on the verb disappears. That's it.

sample exercises 7: Change the sentences to questions with *does.*
She studies in the library.
Does she study in the library?

1. Maria swims in the lake.
2. Larry sleeps all day.
3. He goes to work at 8:00.
4. John watches TV.
5. The doctor plays tennis.

sample exercises 8: Change the sentences to negative with *does not.*
The doctor works on Saturday.
The doctor does not work on Saturday.

1. Sarah has a computer.
2. His father goes to work at 7:30.
3. My husband washes the dishes.
4. The dog eats potato chips.
5. Mary leaves at 7:00.

Next, teach the contraction *doesn't.*

sample exercises 9: Change the sentences to negative with *doesn't.*
Maria looks sick.
Maria doesn't look sick.

1. Rosa sleeps in class.
2. He leaves at 7:30 every day.
3. My brother lives in a big house.
4. The teacher has a big nose.
5. John watches TV.

Next, short answers.

sample exercises 10: Answer the questions with long answers and short answers. Use contractions.

> Does Tom smoke? (yes)
> *Yes, he smokes.*
> *Yes, he does.*
>
> Does Maria like to dance? (no)
> *No, she doesn't like to dance.*
> *No, she doesn't.*

1. Does Noura listen to the teacher? (no)
2. Does he live in Montana? (yes)
3. Does David know Mark? (no)
4. Does your father have a truck? (yes)
5. Does your mother work at the library? (no)

4.11 Speaking practice with *does*

Do what you did with *do,* but now do it with *does.* Is that clear? The three-way speaking exercise with individual students in the class is excellent *does* practice. It would be almost impossible to overdo this.

4.12 *did*

Did will be both easier and harder than *do* and *does.* Easier because there's only one form to make sense out of—none of this *-s* form nonsense—and harder because your students will have to learn about irregular verbs. I suggest teaching this lesson in two parts—first with regular verbs and then with irregular verbs.

▸ *did* with regular verbs

Once again, you're going to write two or three sentences on the board and change them to questions and negatives, but now they're all going to be in the past tense. At first, use only regular verbs (-*ed* verbs) like *work, talk, watch* and *play.* Go through the same procedure as before only this time show your students how *did* is required for past questions and past negatives (and only *did,* they'll be relieved to hear) and that the verb changes to the…STOP! What are going to tell them? That it changes to the present? That's how they'll see it, but that would be wrong. You know it's actually the infinitive. Are you going to tell them that? It's kind of iffy. My advice is to kind of gloss over this. If you have students who can get it, great—go crazy with your discussion of infinitives. Otherwise, it really doesn't matter if they truly understand what's going on as long as they can do it. Many students—especially the false beginners—may simply refer to it as *verb 1* (and also the past form as *verb 2* and past participles as *verb 3*.) This terminology is common in some countries, and if that's what they're comfortable with, OK. (And you might also hear *1st form, 2nd* form and *3rd form.*) This verb 1, verb 2 and verb 3 terminology is convenient but, strictly speaking, not entirely accurate. Verb 1 (or V1) actually refers to the base form of the present simple—the verb without the *s* that is stuck onto it for the 3rd person singular. (See Appendix F for more about this.)

Put this on the board:

He lived in Canada.	She played football.	The food tasted good.
Did he live in Canada?	Did she play football?	Did the food taste good?
He did not live in Canada.	She did not play football.	The food did not taste good.

▸ *did* with irregular verbs

You've used only regular verbs so far, but now you need to introduce your students to the wonderful world of irregular verbs. You should provide your students with a list of common irregular verbs, and most grammar books will have one. (See Appendix A for a list of irregular verbs.) Focus on the most common verbs for now, and emphasize the need, little by little, to learn them. You might want to offer your students some encouragement to do so by ~~threatening~~ motivating them with an irregular verb quiz in the near future. That's what I often do.

Now go through the same rigmarole as before but with irregular verbs only. Spend a lot of time on this because it's so important to get your students going with learning irregular verbs. Put this on the board, and focus your students on the verb forms. Remind them again about the verbs in negative sentences and questions being in the infinitive form (or verb 1, if you prefer). This will strike them as odd, so be ready to discuss it at length:

He <u>went</u> to Rome.	You <u>had</u> a dog.	The glass <u>broke</u>.
Did he <u>go</u> to Rome?	Did you <u>have</u> a dog?	Did the glass <u>break</u>?
He did not <u>go</u> to Rome.	You did not <u>have</u> a dog.	The glass did not <u>break</u>.

Now you're going to give your students the same sorts of exercises as before except that by now the basic concept will be a lot easier. Now is the time to focus on learning irregular verbs.

sample exercises 11: Change the sentences to questions with *did*.

> They went to the library.
> *Did they go to the library?*

1. Ali finished his homework.
2. Linda saw Larry.
3. He wrote a letter.
4. Carlos slept late.
5. The students read their books. (Talk to your students about this oddball verb and how the past and present are spelled the same but pronounced differently.)

Now teach *didn't*. By now your students should be a lot more comfortable with contractions, so no need to focus on *did not* and *didn't* separately.

sample exercises 12: Change the sentences to negative with *didn't*. Use contractions.

> I went to the supermarket.
> *I didn't go to the supermarket.*

1. Alan thought about the answer.
2. Michael talked to his sister.
3. Mary put the baby on the bed.
4. Your dog ate my dinner.
5. Bill flew to Ecuador.

Short answers with *did* should go fairly easily too.

sample exercises 13: Answer the questions with long answers and short answers. Use contractions.

> Did the boy fall? (yes)
> *Yes, he fell.*
> *Yes, he did.*
>
> Did you go to the mall? (no)
> *No, I didn't go to the mall.*
> *No, I didn't.*

1. Did he take the bus? (yes)
2. Did Sarah eat the apple? (no)
3. Did they see the accident? (yes)
4. Did you drink the milk? (yes)
5. Did your brother work yesterday? (no)

4.13 Speaking practice with *do, does* and *did*

After that, it's time for some speaking practice. Start out with exercises requiring regular verbs and *did* only, then mix it up with irregular verbs, *do* and *does* and more and more *I/you* questions. Encourage but don't insist on contractions and short answers. This sort of speaking practice is tremendously beneficial to students. You could do it for hours, and it wouldn't be too much.

4.14 Strain their brains.

Now, just when your students think they've sort of got this figured out, how about giving them some more difficult exercises? As you can see in number 5 below, I often like to make the last one or two questions a bit more challenging. I'll relax my guard about avoiding grammar that hasn't been taught yet. In this case, *because* and the object pronoun *me* have slipped in. At this point, the students very likely have learned these already, and if not, teach them!

sample exercises 14: Complete the sentences with *do, does, did, don't, doesn't* or *didn't*.

    A: _____*Do*_____ you want to eat lunch now?

    B: Yes, I _____*do*_____. I'm very hungry. I _____*didn't*_____ eat breakfast.

1. A: _____ Mary live in Australia?
   B: No, she _____. She lives in New Zealand.
2. A: I _____ go to work yesterday. I was sick.
   B: _____ you go to a doctor?
   A: Yes, I _____.
3. A: _____ Alan speak Spanish?
   B: Yes, he _____. He speaks it very well.
4. A: _____ Carlos have a car?
   B: No, Carlos _____ have a car. He walks to his job every day.
5. A: I am going to the beach now. _____ you want to come with me?
   B: No, thank you. I _____ like the beach.
   A: Why? Because you _____ like the water?
   B: No, because I _____ like sharks.

sample exercises 15: Write the correct questions for the answers.

    A: *Do you have a car?*

    B: Yes, I have a car.

1. A:
   B: No, he doesn't know the answer.
2. A:
   B: Yes, she went to the bank.
3. A:
   B: Yes, Tom has a cat.
4. A:
   B: No, we don't want to go to the mall.
5. A:
   B: Yes, Mary and Larry took the bus downtown.

There's always a danger that exercises that are all the same will not be challenging enough. They're sort of mechanical—doing the same thing again and again, so I often like to build up to exercises that are tougher, where each question isn't necessarily just like the one before it. Sometimes it's better for your students (and more fun for you) not to warn them—let them strain their brains trying to figure out how each question is different. For example, in the following exercise, I have mixed *be* with *do, does* and *did.* That's no accident.

sample exercises 16: Write the correct questions for the answers.

    A: *Do you have a car?*

    B: Yes, I have a car.

1. A:
   B: Yes, he speaks Korean.
2. A:
   B: Yes, I am hungry.
3. A:
   B: Yes, she read the book.
4. A:
   B: Yes, we are studying. (The correct answer is *Are you studying?* Don't accept *Are we studying?*)
5. A:
   B: Yes, she had breakfast. (This is a good time to explain that in English we *eat* or *have* meals, but we don't *take* meals, as in many languages. This is a common error.)

4.15 Ellipsis with *do, does* and *did*

Ellipsis is very commonly used with *do, does* and *did.* It involves (jargon alert!) *compound sentences*—two independent clauses connected with *and* or *but.* Even though you will not have covered this yet at this point, it's possible your students are already familiar with sentences like these. Still, you need to consider whether they're ready for this or if it would be better to come back to it later. If you decide to wait until later, when you get to conjunctions in Chapter 16 might be a good time.

The tricky bit here is that when the second clause is affirmative, the (jargon alert!) *main verb* (verbs like *come, go, eat, sleep, walk,* etc.) disappears and is replaced by *do, does* or *did*:

4.1a John speaks French, and Mary does too.
 b = John speaks French, and Mary [speaks French] too.

4.2a You have a cat, but they don't.
 b = You have a cat, but they don't [have a cat].

4.3a Larry doesn't know the answer, but John does.
 b = Larry doesn't know the answer, but John [knows the answer].

4.4a Sofia went to college, and Alan did too.
 b = Sofia went to college, and Alan [went to college] too.

4.5a Sam didn't go to college, but Sofia did.
 b = Sam didn't go to college, but Sofia [went to college].

4.6a I don't have a car. Do you?
 b = I don't have a car. Do you [have a car]?

4.7a Linda didn't do her homework. Did you?
 b = Linda didn't do her homework. Did you [do your homework]?

sample exercises 17: Draw a line through the words which can be ellipted.
 My mother drinks coffee, but my father doesn't ~~drink coffee~~.

 The boys played soccer. Did the girls ~~play soccer~~ too?

1. Mary followed the plan, but Michael didn't follow the plan.
2. I feel sick. Does he feel sick too?
3. My mother likes to eat fish, but my father doesn't like to eat fish.
4. We agree with you, but they don't agree with you.
5. Sarah went to the party. Did her brother go to the party?

sample exercises 18: Write the ellipted words.
 Maria has a dog, but I don't [_____ *have a dog* _____].

1. Tom went to the library, but I didn't [_____].
2. I didn't do it. Did you [_____]?
3. Sarah wants to eat, but I don't [_____].
4. Noura drinks coffee, Does Ali [_____]?
5. She did it, but I didn't [_____].

sample exercises 19: Combine the sentences as in the examples. Use ellipsis.
 Larry sleeps a lot. Alan sleeps a lot too.
 Larry sleeps a lot, and Alan does too.

 I went to the baseball game. John went to the baseball game too.
 I went to the baseball game, and John did too.

1. The library closes at 8:30. The supermarket closes at 8:30 too.
2. Susan bought a TV last week. I bought a TV last week too.
3. Mary read that book. Michael read that book too.
4. I know how to swim. My brother knows how to swim too.
5. John thinks it's a good idea. Sam thinks it's a good idea too.

4.16 Alas

As I said, many students will never really get *do, does* and *did* right. They could study English for 20 years, and you'll still hear them say *He no have...* or *I not know...*, etc. It's something you'll want to review again and again. That's what good ESL teachers do—not just go, go, go forward; they frequently go back for minireviews—either planned or when they see a need for it.

4.17 Three more things

We've covered the main things, but I'll finish with three more points—the first of which I'd suggest making part of the lesson above and the other two saving for some time in the future when you feel the time is right. I'm including them here because they relate to *do, does* and *did*.

▶ **One for now:** *Have you a...?*

It's likely that at some point in your *do, does* and *did* lesson that you'll encounter a students who, with the verb *have,* asks and answer questions like this, for example,

4.8a Have you car?
  b Yes, I have.
  c No, I haven't.

rather than this:

4.9a Do you have a car?
  b Yes, I do.
  c No, I don't.

A lot of ESL students who have studied English outside the USA learn this, and <u>there's nothing wrong with it</u>. I explain to the students that this is perfectly good English, but that it's a bit old-fashioned and not often used in modern English. Again, it's absolutely correct, so you don't want to embarrass your students, but you do want to encourage them to use modern grammar.

▶ **And two for later**

Two more things that relate to *do, does* and *did* are a bit advanced and not vitally important at this point—something for later when the time is right, not now when they're having enough trouble with the basics. But they are important. Save these in your bag of tricks for later, *but do do them.*

▷ **Two, the emphatic** *do*

"...*but do do them*"? What kind of crazy sentence was that? Every one of us native speaks, almost every day, probably, says things like this:

4.10 You're wrong! I do love you.

4.11 I'm not kidding. My sister does speak 17 languages.

4.12 Teacher, I'm not lying. My dog did eat my homework.

Now, after all we just discussed about *do, does* and *did,* where does this fit in? Are these questions? No. Are these negative? No. Haven't you just taught your students that *do, does* and *did* are used for questions and negatives? You sure have. But, as you can see, that's not always true. This is called (jargon alert!) *the emphatic do*—emphatic as in *emphasize* as in *make stronger*. We do this when we want to make what we say extra strong so that people know we are serious, not lying, not exaggerating, not kidding. What we're doing is, in effect, taking the tense out of the present simple verb and putting it into *do*—*do* is containing the tense. You can't see that with *do,* but you can with *does* and *did*. Let's look at 4.11 and 4.12 again and see how they look with and without the emphatic *do*. For example,

4.11a I'm not kidding. My sister <u>speaks</u> 17 languages.
  b I'm not kidding. My sister does <u>speak</u> 17 languages.

4.12a Teacher, I'm not lying. My dog <u>ate</u> my homework.
  b Teacher, I'm not lying. My dog did <u>eat</u> my homework.

The emphatic *do* is an essential part of English, so don't neglect it—just wait until your students are a little further along and ready for it.

sample exercises 20: Change the sentences to the emphatic *do*. If numbers 4 and 5 puzzle your students (or you), stay tuned—all will be explained in the next section.

    I drove from New York to Los Angeles in only two days.
    I did drive from New York to Los Angeles in only two days.

1. I went to Mars in a UFO.
2. She has 14 children.
3. I believe you.

4. I did my homework yesterday.
5. I do my homework every day.

One last point on the emphatic *do*. It's <u>very</u> important to explain to students that when speaking, we always stress *do, does* or *did* in the emphatic *do*:

4.13a I DO love you.
    b My sister DOES speak 17 languages.
    c My dog DID eat my homework.

It sounds strange if you don't stress *do, does* or *did* (try it), so be sure you explain this.

▷ **Three, *do* is an auxiliary verb and a main verb**
So how about these questions? Could you explain how *do* is different in these sentences?

4.14 I do my homework in the bathroom.

4.15 Do you know the answer?

OK, I'll tell you. You know that *do* is an auxiliary verb, but *do* is also a main verb. Main verbs are verbs like *eat, sleep, talk, work, go,* etc. So the *do* in *I do my homework in the bathroom* is a main verb, not an auxiliary verb. Now let's imagine that someone doubts that you really do your homework in the bathroom. You want to make that person understand that you are serious, not lying, not exaggerating. So what would you say? This:

4.16 I do do my homework in the bathroom.

In 4.16, the emphatic *do* is being used with the main verb *do*. Like the emphatic *do*, the fact that *do* is also a main verb is not something you want to confuse your students with now. They're confused enough already. Confuse them with this later. Besides, students generally learn that *do* is a main verb intuitively, but there might be a time when it comes up, so now you'll be ready when a student asks you about sentences like these:

4.17 Do your homework.

4.18 He did the laundry.

4.19 She does the dishes.

4.20 I did it wrong.

4.21 Do it now.

sample exercises 21: Change the sentence to negative with *don't* or *doesn't*. Use contractions.
    We do our homework after dinner.
    We don't do our homework after dinner.

1. Lucy does everything well.
2. We do all our shopping on Saturday.
3. I do my homework in the library.
4. She does it carefully.
5. Mark does the dishes after dinner.

sample exercises 22: Change the sentences to questions with *do* or *does*.
    Her brother does his job quickly.
    Does her brother do his job quickly?

1. He does his work slowly.
2. They always do it the wrong way.
3. Sarah does her homework at school.
4. They do their exercises before dinner.
5. He does his work in his office.

sample exercises 23: Change the sentences to negative with *did*. Use contractions.
    He did his work well.
    He didn't do his work well.

1. I did it.
2. He did the laundry.
3. You did the right thing.
4. Tom did everything wrong.
5. Larry did a lot of work.

sample exercises 24: Change the sentences to questions with *did*.

John did a bad job.
Did John do a bad job?

1. She did the best she could.
2. Carlos did a good job.
3. They did the wrong thing.
4. He did it yesterday.
5. She did it right.

Chapter 5
Future

Could you...
- answer this question: Are *will* and *be going to* the only ways we talk about the future?
- answer this question: Are sentences *a, b, c* and *d* future?

    a. We're eating in an hour.
    b. My plane takes off in ten minutes.
    c. We're about to leave.
    d. The President is to address the nation at 7:00 p.m.

5.1 Two stages

My advice is to approach this topic in two stages. The first stage should focus entirely on *will* and *be going to*. Only later, when your students are further along, should you teach them the grammar which answers the questions above.

5.2 *will* and *be going to*

All grammar books, including mine, *Rocket English Grammar,* discuss the differences between *will* and *be going to*. They are different (though not as different as some contend), and you may want to discuss the differences with your students, but many students will never entirely get it. Try, but not too hard, because the good news is that it doesn't matter very much. A nonnative speaker's using *will* when a native speaker would likely use *be going to* or vice versa almost never results in any misunderstanding. I have never found a need to make a big deal of this.

In general, we can discuss *will* and *be going to* in terms of three functions: *expressing willingness, making predictions* and *discussing plans*. As we wade through this, don't worry too much if there seems to be some overlap among these functions. Sometimes more than one will seem to apply. Sometimes your students won't be sure (if you force them to think about it at all, that is) and sometimes you won't be sure either. An English professor could spend an entire semester picking the sample exercises below apart to determine which of the three functions they're performing, but guess what. I don't care, your students won't care, and neither should you. In every case the meaning is obvious—dictated by logic.

Much more important for your students than totally mastering this whole function idea is simply getting the forms right—how to make correct sentences, questions and negatives with *will* and *be going to*. That is what they'll struggle with, not functions.

So nowhere in this chapter will you see an exercise requiring that a student choose between *will* or *be going to* based on whether the sentence is expressing willingness, making a prediction or discussing a plan. That would be totally nuts. It's counterproductive to confuse students with all this function baloney. My advice is to definitely talk about these three functions briefly, but once you finish with that, shut up about it.

5.3 *will* for willingness

Will can be used to say that we are *willing* to do something. It's not a plan—it's an attitude, a feeling about something that is happening now or that may happen in the future. Are you going to write *willingness* on the board and expect your students to have any idea what it means? I hope not. If they knew that, they would certainly also understand *will*. This is where dictionaries come in handy. If you have a class of students who all speak the same language, use your bilingual dictionary. You do have a bilingual dictionary, don't you? You don't believe the nonsense that students should only use monolingual (English only) dictionaries, do you? (As if you could ever enforce a prohibition on bilingual dictionaries outside of the classroom anyway.) If you have a class of mixed language speakers, encourage them to use their own dictionaries (which, I guarantee you, will be bilingual).

In discussing *will* with your students and pulling examples out of your head, you want to be careful not to accidentally stray into conditional sentence territory (e.g. *If you need help, I will help you*). It would be easy to do, but conditional grammar is way over your students' heads right now and will not be taught until much later. The examples below deliberately avoid the conditional:

5.1 Do you need money for lunch? I will give you $10.

5.2 I don't understand my homework. Will you help me?

5.3 My father will not let me drive his car.

Now teach the contraction *'ll*. Later be sure to give your students some listening practice with *'ll*. That's important because sometimes nonnative speakers have trouble hearing *'ll*. For example, someone might say *I'll*, but they'll hear only *I*:

5.4a   He helps me.
    b   → He will help me.
    c   → He'll help me.

5.5a   I do it.
    b   → I will do it.
    c   → I'll do it.

5.6a   They are angry.
    b   → They will be angry.
    c   → They'll be angry.

▶ **With *will* no *do*, no *does*, no *did*, no *s*, no *ed*, no *ing***

After your long hard struggle to teach your students *do*, *does* and *did*, they'll likely be a bit confused about when these words are used and when they are not. It takes time for students to straighten it all out, so remind them that *do*, *does* and *did* are <u>never</u> used with *will* and that verbs after *will* are <u>always</u> verb 1. (The infinitive, of course, but I believe I may already have mentioned the importance of not confusing your students with this. I encourage you to have a look at Appendix F for more discussion of all this infinitive vs. present/verb 1 business.

Give them examples which contrast the tensed forms with the infinitive forms: *he goes/he will go, she is/he will be, he has/he will have*—get the idea? Start with simple examples:

5.7a   He <u>cleans</u> his room.
    b   → He <u>will clean</u> his room.

Make sure they understand that what you said about the infinitive after *will* includes *be*:

5.8a   I <u>am</u> here.
    b   → I <u>will be</u> here.

This will come up again and again as you teach various modals. You need to keep reminding your students that the cloud of main verb forms that they're struggling to make sense out of doesn't matter when the verb follows *will* (or any other modal). Tell them "with *will* no *do*, no *does*, no *did*, no *s*, no *ed*, no *ing*".

This is true of verbs which follow *to* as well. Because you'll soon be discussing *be going to, have to* and *have got to*; and because your students likely have already picked up *want to, like to* and perhaps *hate to, love to, need to* and maybe *have to* already as well, this is the perfect time to discuss this. Often I'll put something like this on the board, using an irregular verb as an example, and making sure the examples I use are 3rd person singular:

after <u>will</u>/after <u>to</u> ONLY <u>verb 1</u>!

↓   ↓

~~do does did~~   She will <u>eat</u>.

work<u>s</u> work~~ing~~ work~~ed~~   He wants to <u>eat</u>.

eat<u>s</u> ~~eating~~ ate ~~eaten~~

sample exercises 1: Change each sentence to future with *will*. Use contractions.
    He works.
    He'll work.

1. I make you a sandwich.
2. They are working.
3. He writes a book.
4. Larry and Carlos go to the mall.
5. He is angry.

5.4 Questions with *will*

Now move on to questions. Teach your students that the subject and *will* are inverted (or *switched*). For practice, have them change some sentences to questions. (Avoid examples with *I* as a subject. It doesn't make sense to ask about your own willingness.) This shouldn't be too difficult:

5.9a   He will wash the dishes.

    b   → Will he wash the dishes?

5.10a   Ali will be there.

    b   → Will Ali be there?

sample exercises 2: Change the sentences to questions.

    You'll meet us for lunch.

    Will you meet us for lunch?

1.   They'll come after dinner.
2.   He will give Mark $1,000.
3.   You'll help me.
4.   Noura will be at the party.
5.   The girls will watch a movie.

A little more of a challenge would be to have your students change some present simple questions to future questions. A bit of new vocabulary sneaks in here and there but nothing that should be a problem:

5.11a   Does Larry cook dinner every day? (tomorrow)

    b   → Will Larry cook dinner tomorrow?

sample exercises 3: Change the sentences to questions with the words in parentheses.

    Do you clean the house every Saturday? (next Saturday)

    Will you clean the house next Saturday?

    Are the students absent today? (tomorrow)

    Will the students be absent tomorrow?

1.   Do you go to work every day? (tomorrow)
2.   Does Sofia take a shower every evening? (this evening)
3.   Are you here every Friday night? (next Friday night)
4.   Do the students have homework every day? (today)
5.   Is Alan studying now? (later)

5.5 Negative contractions of *will*

Now negatives, but first let's look at two tricky things: One is to be sure your students understand that the contraction of *will not* is *won't*. (If English were logical, it would be *willn't*, but what's logic got to do with anything?) The other is to make sure they understand that, even though there are two ways to make negative contractions of *will*, one is <u>much</u> more common than the other, and that is the one they should always use:

    common: I won't, You won't, etc.

    not common: I'll not, You'll not, etc.

Once your students (sort of) understand this, have them change some sentences to negative. Encourage but don't insist on contractions. Only allow *won't* as a contraction. The other way, *'ll not*, is so uncommon that I really discourage it:

5.12a   Alan will wash the car.

    b   → Alan will not wash the car.

    c   → Alan won't wash the car.

sample exercises 4: Change the sentences to negative. Use contractions.

    Mike will win the game.

    Mike won't win the game.

1.   They will help her.
2.   I will go.
3.   He'll change his mind.
4.   Alan will be there.
5.   She'll do it.

Once again, for a little more of a challenge, have your students change some present simple negative sentences to future negative sentences. Encourage but don't insist on contractions:

5.13a I don't help my sister every day. (tomorrow)
   b → I will not help my sister tomorrow.
   c → I won't help my sister tomorrow.

sample exercises 5: Change the sentences to future with the words in parentheses. Use contractions.

Mary doesn't go to school on the weekend. (next weekend)
Mary won't go to school next weekend.

David isn't at work now. (tomorrow)
David won't be at work tomorrow.

1. I don't wake up early on Saturdays. (next Saturday)
2. The teacher doesn't have a class this afternoon. (tomorrow afternoon)
3. Maria doesn't do her homework in the evening. (tomorrow evening)
4. I'm not working now. (later)
5. They don't eat meat on Fridays. (next Friday)
6. They aren't here this week. (next week)

5.6 *be going to*

You've just taught your students how to make contractions, questions and negatives with *will*, so now you'll focus on the same thing with *be going to.* First, however, you need to make it very clear to your students that grammarwise, *be going to* is present continuous, but we native speakers understand that it refers to the future (and don't say *refer* when you explain this— say *is about*). Since *be going to* is present continuous, your students already know how to make contractions, questions and negatives, but didn't someone once say that you should never assume anything about what your students already know? It might seem that the grammar of *be going to* is a no-brainer since it's just present continuous in form, and your students have already studied the present continuous, right? Yes, but it's still a good idea to go over the grammar of *be going to* not just for grammar's sake but to reinforce the whole concept of this seemingly present continuous structure having a future meaning.

sample exercises 6: Change each sentence to future with *be going to.* Use contractions.

She does her homework.
She's going to do her homework.

1. My mother makes dinner.
2. The doctor calls me.
3. We are at the mall.
4. They buy a new car.
5. Larry is late.

sample exercises 7: Change the sentences to questions.

He's going to play football.
Is he going to play football?

1. Sofia's going to have chicken for dinner.
2. You're going to wash your car.
3. Your friends are going to go to Taiwan.
4. He's going to work in the garden.
5. You and she are going to be here next Sunday.

sample exercises 8: Change the sentences to negative. Use contractions.

She's going to help me.
She's not going to help me.

1. He's going to be here later.
2. I'm going to do it.
3. We're going to eat in that restaurant again.
4. He's going to read this book.
5. They're going to have dinner after the movie.

5.7 *be going to* and *will* used for predictions and plans

If you unwisely decide to get further into the functions of *will* and *be going to* with your students, here's what it's all about:

▶ Predictions

Be going to and *will* are used to make *predictions*. That will be a lot easier for students to get than the whole concept of willingness, but be careful to use simple examples. You might want to have them look up *predict* and *prediction* in their bilingual dictionaries. Avoid adverb clauses (like *Mary will be angry when she learns the truth* or *If we don't get to the airport soon, we're going to miss our flight*) and any other unnecessary complexities or needlessly difficult vocabulary. It's easy to make examples overly complicated because you want students to understand the situation, and understanding the situation helps them understand the function that the grammar is serving, or so you might think, but overloading students with new grammar and vocabulary can have the opposite effect. A way to avoid this is to actually make examples consisting of two sentences, as I've done in 5.15 and 5.17:

> 5.14   Alan will get an A on the test.

> 5.15   Don't watch that movie. You won't like it. (Rather than *If you watch that movie, you won't like it.*)

> 5.16   The Cubs are never going to win the World Series.

> 5.17   Larry ate three cheeseburgers, two tacos and a hot dog. He's going to be sick tomorrow. (Rather than *Because Larry...* Also, *be sick* rather than *get sick*—this use of *get,* while very important, is best left for later.)

▶ Plans

Now for a bit of heresy: *Be going to* and *will* are both used for plans. Did you detect the heresy? Some grammar fussbudgets maintain that only *be going to* is used for plans, not *will.* I disagree, and I think you will too if you look at these examples and ask yourself this question: How are these sentences with *will* <u>not</u> plans? For example,

> 5.18   I'll fly to New York tomorrow.

> 5.19   He'll cut the grass on Saturday.

> 5.20   I forgot to get gas today. I'll do it tomorrow. (No way is that willingness or a prediction.)

> 5.21   I'll help you with your homework after dinner. I promise. (ditto)

Convinced? I knew you would be.

Look at 5.21. Some grammar teachers make a distinction between *plans* and *promises* and claim that only *will* is used for promises. I disagree. What is a promise, after all, but an expression of a plan? Aren't they one and the same? I think so, but if this troubles you, go take a sociolinguistics course and see what little use that is in the real world of teaching ESL.

▷ Leave past plans for later.

Also, it might occur to you at this point to teach your students sentences like these:

> 5.22   I was going to call you last night, but I forgot.

> 5.23   Carlos and Alan were going to help me move my sofa, but they didn't.

We often use *was going to* and *were going to* to discuss past plans, especially when what was planned didn't happen (or we don't know if it happened), but this is a bit over your students heads at this point—better to leave it for Chapter 12.

5.8 *go* overload

One word (actually several words) of caution: Expect students to be confused when you discuss the verb *go* in the future with *be going to.* What I mean is this:

> 5.24   I'm going to go to the mall after dinner.

> 5.25   They're going to go to the beach next weekend.

That's a real *go* overload. Expect students to stumble over sentences containing both *be going to* and *go.* This is even more confusing than you realize now because we haven't gotten to present continuous for future yet.

5.9 *shall*?

Some readers may be dismayed that I have so far completely ignored *shall. Shall* has gone the way of the dodo bird and wooly mammoth in American English. It is extinct (or at least pretty close to it). Of course we understand our British cousins when they say *I shall write a strongly worded letter to the Times,* but we never, ever use *shall.* Having said that, I do sometimes mention it in class because *shall* isn't entirely extinct in other parts of the world. I simply explain that *shall* is the same as *will* (yes, with a slight degree of oversimplification—that's what we do sometimes in ESL), give a few examples and move on.

WARNING! READING THIS PARAGRAPH MAY CAUSE BRAIN DAMAGE. If you are aware of the unbelievably archaic notion that *shall* is properly used for the first person and *will* for the second and third persons when used for prediction but exactly the opposite when used for demands, promises or threats, FORGET THIS! Discussions of this still survive in some antiquated books used in remote corners of the globe, but remember, your students have enough work cut out for them learning <u>modern</u> English. This is the LAST thing you should ever consider teaching them. Just thinking about it is making me hallucinate.

5.10 *gonna*

And what about *gonna?*, you might be asking. Yes, *gonna* is very important—important for listening comprehension and even reading since it's common to write *gonna*, so yes, you absolutely should talk about it, and now is the time. But don't tell your students that gonna is "bad English". It's a (jargon alert!) *reduction,* and we all use them—even the most persnickety grammar fussbudgets. I certainly do. *Gonna* is not about good or bad English, it's about casual, fast pronunciation. So rather than speak in terms of good and bad, speak in terms of what is appropriate for a particular (grammar alert!) *register* (the way you adjust your speech, especially the level of formality, to suit a particular situation). Tell your students that *gonna* is OK in informal speech and informal writing but is best avoided when speaking formally and is absolutely not acceptable in formal writing—academic papers, business communications, etc.

5.11 Listening practice

This is the perfect time for some listening practice. It's VERY important to give your students practice understanding the casual, reduced speech of native speakers—I mean normal native speakers, not you—the native speakers they hear outside the classroom, on TV and in movies. I will often, toward the end of a grammar lesson, simply read aloud from whatever examples are at hand—examples and exercise in the textbook and/or on the board in a way that makes no concession to the students' listening comprehension difficulties but are just as fast and reduced as if I were talking to another native speaker. Do this and repeat, repeat, repeat while they read along and train their ears. Students love this. Do it a lot!

Here you'll be doing it with *will* and *be going to.* By all means give your students plenty of practice listening to *gonna,* but also be aware that many students have a hard time hearing the contraction *'ll.* They might, for example, hear

    5.26a   I'll go.

as

      b   I go.

so give them a lot of listening practice with *'ll.*

5.12 Speaking practice

Now for some speaking practice. As always, you want to keep it really simple at first—using only *will* and then only *be going to*—before mixing them up and then at the end doing some of the three-way speaking exercises I've described.

Do not say one word about willingness, predictions and plans. Focus entirely on form and sentence structure. Remember, don't just move from the simple to the more complex in terms of grammar; do the same with your pronunciation. Use *going to* at first then transition to *gonna.* But remember, your goal is for them to understand *gonna,* not say it (though some will try).

Before you get started, give your students examples of short answers. That should be pretty easy. By now you've already thoroughly covered the mechanics of making contractions, questions and negatives with *will* and *be going to,* so there's no need to do it all over again:

    5.27a   Maria: Will you help me?
       b   Carlos: Yes, I will./No, I won't.

    5.28a   Tom: Will he take you to the mall?
       b   Linda: Yes, he will./No, he won't. (NOT *No, he'll not*—strongly discourage this contraction, even though it's
                           100% correct, because it's so rare in modern English.)

    5.29a   Michael: Is John going to be here tomorrow? (Remember to use examples with *be.*)
       b   Alan: Yes, he is./No, he's not./No, he isn't.

Is that all? No, that's not all, but it's all you should try to cover now. There are, however, other important matters relating to the future that you definitely will want to come back to later when you feel the time is right.

5.13 Present continuous for future plans

It is very common in English to use the present continuous for future plans. I'll bet you've never once thought about this, right? Here are some examples: (Using simple sentences without adverb clauses like *We're eating dinner after your father comes home* and avoiding *going* for reasons I'll explain below.)

> 5.30   We're eating dinner at 8:00.
>
> 5.31   I'm flying to Munich next Tuesday.
>
> 5.32   She's leaving soon.

Your students might wonder how on earth we can use the present continuous to talk about the future without being totally confused. It's easy. Point out that *We're eating, I'm flying* and *She's leaving* are indeed present continuous, but when we hear words like *at 8:00, next Tuesday, soon, in ten minutes, after lunch, tomorrow,* etc., we easily understand that the future is being referred to. Also, explain that sometimes, even though future time references aren't used, future is understood from the situation. Don't use that difficult vocabulary, though. Just give examples:

> 5.33a   Michael: What are you doing tonight?
>
>   b   Joe: I'm going to a movie. (This is understood to refer to *tonight*.)

This is a good time to give your students a lesson in *in*. What I mean is that a lot of students will want to say things like this:

> 5.34a   We're having a test <u>after</u> three days.
>
> 5.35a   Wash your hands. We're eating <u>after</u> a few minutes.

Explain to your students that native speakers don't say *after*; they say *in*:

> 5.34b   We're having a test <u>in</u> three days.
>
> 5.35b   Wash your hands. We're eating <u>in</u> a few minutes.

▶ More *go* overload

Remember, I warned that examples with both *be going to* and *go* would confuse your students? Well, it gets even worse with present continuous for future. Imagine your poor students trying to make sense of these three sentences:

present continuous *going*

> 5.36a   I'm going to the library now.

be going to for future

> 5.37a   I'm going to go to the library tonight.

and present continuous for future plans

> 5.38a   I'm going to the library tonight.

Who can blame your students for being confused?

If you want to address this issue, one way is to identify the main verb *go*, in order to distinguish it from the phrasal modal *be going to,* by underlining it or using a different colored whiteboard marker:

present continuous *going*

> 5.36b   I'm <u>going</u> to the library now.

be going to for future

> 5.37b   I'm going to <u>go</u> to the library tonight.

present continuous for future plans

> 5.38b   I'm <u>going</u> to the library tonight.

The best thing to do is wait until the idea of present continuous for future plans has sunk in and your students are fairly comfortable with it. Only then slip in a few examples with *going* and the present continuous for future plans. If you detect the slightest confusion regarding this (and you will), explain it with examples like the ones above.

► **Practice present continuous for future plans.**

The best way to practice this is by having students change future sentences with either *will* or *be going to* to the present continuous. As always, move from easy to more difficult. First, start with *will* only:

5.39a She will visit her mother next week.
   b → She's visiting her mother next week.

5.40a He'll go to the doctor tomorrow.
   b → He's going to the doctor tomorrow.

Then try some with *be going to*: (Leave *be going to go* for last and expect confusion.)

5.41a I'm going to make hamburgers tonight.
   b → I'm making hamburgers tonight.

5.42a Larry's going to go to the beach on Saturday.
   b → Larry's going to the beach on Saturday.

sample exercises 9: Change the sentences so that they use present continuous for future.
     We're going to leave at 2:30.
     We're leaving at 2:30.

     I'm going to go to Germany in a couple of weeks.
     I'm going to Germany in a couple of weeks.

1. Mary's going to call me at 8:00.
2. We're going to eat dinner soon. We're going to have spaghetti.
3. When are you going to do your homework?
4. How many people are going to come to the party?
5. Why are you going to go there?

5.14 Present simple for scheduled future events

It is very common to use the present simple for future events which are on a schedule, timetable, calendar, etc. No new grammar here—just a new idea:

5.43 The game starts at 1:00.

5.44 Flight 420 to Amsterdam leaves in 15 minutes.

We know this is about the future from words like *at 1:00, in 15 minutes, soon, after lunch, tonight, next month,* etc. Make sure to explain that using the present simple for future events is generally done in reference to schedules, timetables, calendars, etc., and is normally used only with a small group of verbs: *be, start, end, begin, finish, open, close, arrive, depart, leave* and a few others that I can't think of right now.

Now have them change some sentences with *be going to* to present simple:

5.45a The store is going to open at 10:00.
   b → The store opens at 10:00.

5.46a My class is going to begin in a few minutes.
   b → My class begins in a few minutes.

Easy enough, right? Well, you'll need to play a cruel trick on your students by giving them some examples with *be*. That will be more difficult:

5.47a The test is going to be next Tuesday.
   b → The test is next Tuesday.

5.48a When is your wedding going to be?
   b → When is your wedding?

Do you see what's going on? *Be going to* is canceled, and the infinitive *be* changes to present simple. Expect your students to be very confused by this. Underline the forms of *be* to help them understand.

sample exercises 10: Change the sentences so that they use present simple for future.
     My flight is going to leave at 11:14.

My flight leaves at 11:14.

When is the graduation going to be?
When is the graduation?

Where is this bus going to go?
Where does this bus go?

1. The show is going to start at 8:00.
2. When is the game going to begin?
3. The store is going to open at 10:00.
4. When is the test going to be?
5. The test is going to be next Tuesday.

5.15 *be about to*

I'm about to discuss another way to talk about the future—in this case about the near future. Grammarwise it's not too difficult. The main thing is to explain that we're talking about the <u>near</u> future. But near is relative, so avoid saying anything like it always means "in a minute", etc. What is near future depends on the situation. If you're going to graduate from college in a couple of days, you might say *I'm about to graduate.* A couple of days is near future in this case. But if you're sky diving, and you're talking about when you're going to open your parachute, a couple of days from now would seem like a long time (more like an eternity).

So anyway, give your students some examples:

5.49   Wash your hands. We are about to eat.

5.50   The bus leaves at 12:15. It's 12:13 now. The bus is about to leave.

It's possible to ask questions with this construction, but not common enough to be worth going into. Don't try any negative examples. *Not about to* has another meaning. It means *no way!*

5.51   I'm not about to let my 16-year-old son drive my new Ferrari.

5.16 *be to*

Huh? Yep, *be to* is a phrasal modal that's used to discuss future official plans and arrangements. Because it's used for other things too, I'll discuss it further in Chapter 12. It's important primarily for advanced students who need English for academic or business purposes, but it can wait until later. But since you're dying to know, here are two examples of *be to* used for future:

5.52   Each student is to be here for the final exam Tuesday at 8:00.

5.53   The two sides are to meet tomorrow to begin peace negotiations.

5.17 Ellipsis with the future

There's no need to keep explaining the concept of ellipsis. The best thing to do is simply present students with several examples and let them see the patterns and refer to them as they do the exercises:

5.54a   I'm not going to be here at 8:00, but I am going to be at 9:00.
   b   = I'm not going to be here at 8:00, but I am going to be [here] at 9:00.

5.55a   I'm not going to be here at 8:00, but I am at 9:00.
   b   = I'm not going to be here at 8:00, but I am [going to be here] at 9:00.

5.56a   We're going to study in the library. Are you going to?
   b   = We're going to study in the library. Are you going to [study in the library]?

5.57a   We're going to study in the library. Are you?
   b   = We're going to study in the library. Are you [going to study in the library]?

5.58a   Noura won't help me, but Carlos will.
   b   = Noura won't help me, but Carlos will [help me].

5.59a   Mary will be at the meeting, but I won't be.
   b   = Mary will be at the meeting, but I won't be [at the meeting].

5.60a   Mary will be at the meeting, but I won't.
   b   = Mary will be at the meeting, but I won't [be at the meeting].

5.61a   I haven't done my homework yet, but I'm about to.
  b   = I haven't done my homework yet, but I'm about to [do my homework].

sample exercises 11:   Draw a line through the words which can be ellipted.

John's going to be late, but Alan isn't going to be ~~late~~.
John's going to be late, but Alan isn't ~~going to be late~~.

I'm going to work in the garden, but she isn't going to ~~work in the garden~~.
I'm going to work in the garden, but she isn't ~~going to work in the garden~~.

1. a   Rosa isn't going to be here today, but she is going to be here tomorrow.
    b   Rosa isn't going to be here today, but she is going to be here tomorrow.
2. a   I'm not going to ride my bike before dinner, but I am going to ride my bike after dinner.
    b   I'm not going to ride my bike before dinner, but I am going to ride my bike after dinner.
3. a   Paul is going to speak at the conference. Is Sam going to speak at the conference?
    b   Paul is going to speak at the conference. Is Sam going to speak at the conference?
4. a   They're going to go, and I am going to go too.
    b   They're going to go, and I am going to go too.
5. a   I'm going to leave early today. Are you going to leave early today too?
    b   I'm going to leave early today. Are you going to leave early today too?

sample exercises 12:   Draw a line through the words which can be ellipted.

Sam won't be here today, but Alan will be ~~here today~~.
Sam won't be here today, but Alan will ~~be here today~~.

Rosa isn't going to go shopping, but Sofia is going to ~~go shopping~~.
Rosa isn't going to go shopping, but Sofia is ~~going to go shopping~~.

Mark won't help you, but Lucy will ~~help you~~.

I told my son to start his homework, and he was about to ~~start his homework~~, but then his friend called.

1. I didn't say anything, but I was about to say something.
2. We'll get to the meeting around 9:00, but Carlos won't get to the meeting until later.
3. I'm not going to be on time for the meeting, but Noura is going to be on time for the meeting.
4. I'm not going to be on time for the meeting, but Noura is going to be on time for the meeting.
5. Linda won't be working when we get there, but Mark will be working when we get there.
6. Linda won't be working when we get there, but Mark will be working when we get there.
7. I won't be at work tomorrow. Will you be at work tomorrow?
8. I won't be at work tomorrow. Will you be at work tomorrow?

sample exercises 13:   Complete the sentences using ellipsis. Use contractions.

A: Is Sarah going to fly to India?
B1: I think she _____*'s going to*_____, but I'm not sure when.
B2: I think she _____*is*_____, but I'm not sure when.

A: Are you and Larry going to go to the mall?
B1: I _____*'m not going to*_____, but Larry is.
B2: I _____*'m not*_____, but Larry is.

A: Are you leaving now?
B: I _____*'m about to*_____, but I have a little more work to do.

1. A: Are you going to sell your car?
    B1: No, I _____ I'm going to keep it.
    B2: No, I _____. I'm going to keep it.
2. A: Will you help me move my piano to the attic?
    B: Yes, I _____, but I don't want to.
3. A: Are you and your brother going to play football?
    B1: My brother _____, but I am.
    B2: My brother _____, but I am.

4. A: Are you going to paint the house this summer?
   B1: Yes, I _____. Please stop asking me.
   B2: Yes, I _____. Please stop asking me.
5. A: You were really angry with your boss today. Did you quit your job?
   B: Almost. I _____, but I changed my mind.

Chapter 6
Nouns and Pronouns

Could you...

- explain why *the* is required in *a* but not in *b*?

  a.   The sugar is in the kitchen.
  b.   Sugar is sweet.

- explain why *c* is wrong?

  c.   Everyone are hungry.

- explain how these sentences are different?

  d.   Do you want anything to eat?
  e.   Do you want something to eat?

- say whether *f* is correct, and if it's not correct, why not?

  f.   One of the cooks cut themself with a sharp knife.

6.1 Subject pronouns and object pronouns

Of course there's no way you've gotten this far without already having used nouns, subject pronouns and articles, but now is the time to actually focus on these and on nouns and pronouns in general. You've already been using subject pronouns, and it's likely your students are fairly familiar with them by now, but a good teacher never assumes anything. So start from square one, as if you had never discussed either. Actually, however, it's object pronouns that will be relatively new and object pronouns that will give your students the most trouble. I always write something like this on the board:

subject pronouns	object pronouns
I	me
you	you
he	him
she	her
it	it
we	us
they	them

Before going on, you should remind your students that *you* is singular <u>and</u> plural. They kind of know that already, but make sure they do, and from now on just write *you* on the board once, as I do (once in each column, that is). Writing it twice might actually confuse them. Also, make sure they know that the subject pronoun *you* is identical to the object pronoun *you*.

Grammarians can't agree on a definition of *subject*, so is it any wonder that they can't agree on the definition of *object* either? It's popular to explain objects as *receiving the action of the verb*. Some don't like this explanation because the word *action* implies, not surprisingly, some sort of action, like *I killed the monster*, but it seems illogical with sentences like *I ignored the monster*. I never use this explanation or any other because I've found that it isn't necessary. Your students will figure out what subjects and objects are just from seeing examples. What you should do is explain that in a basic subject-verb-object (SVO) English sentence, objects and object pronouns follow the verb: (No, not always, but this isn't the time to split hairs, is it?)

6.1   <u>Sarah</u>   ate   <u>dinner</u>.
      subject   verb   object

6.2   <u>She</u>   ate   <u>it</u>.
  subject pronoun   verb   object pronoun

You should also explain that objects and object pronouns follow prepositions:

6.3   <u>The police</u>   looked   for   <u>David</u>.
     subject   verb   preposition   object

6.4   <u>They</u>   looked   for   <u>him</u>.
       subject pronoun   verb   preposition   object pronoun

I've never found it necessary to do more than this to explain what objects are. That doesn't mean all students will instantly get it. You'll still encounter errors and confusion, but they'll figure it out before long without your having to resort to any deep linguistic babble.

Now write some sentences on the board with nouns and proper nouns (names that you would capitalize—people, cities, companies, etc.), and then demonstrate changing the nouns and proper nouns to pronouns, as in 6.2 and 6.4:

> ~~Alan~~ talked to ~~Carlos~~.
> He   him
>
> ~~Mary~~ washed the ~~car~~.
> She   it
>
> I talked to ~~my mother~~.
>   her
>
> ~~The girls~~ looked for ~~the cats~~.
> They   them

Simple enough so far, but what students have the most trouble with is *we* and *us*, so try a few examples like these:

> ~~John and I~~ talked to ~~Mary and Sarah~~.
> We   them
>
> ~~Mary and Sarah~~ talked to ~~John and me~~.
> They   us

and after you do that, give them some more examples. This will be surprisingly difficult, so definitely come back to it for a quick review once in a while.

Try some written exercises like these before going on to speaking practice.

sample exercises 1: Underline the correct pronouns.
      (<u>We</u>/Us) saw (she/<u>her</u>).

1. (Me/I) helped (they/them).
2. (Him/He) will call (us/we).
3. (Them/They) had lunch with (her/she).
4. (We/Us) don't know (he/him).
5. (Her/She) is going to visit (we/us).
6. (I/Me) don't like (her/she).

▸ **Speaking practice**

This is a perfect time for some three-way speaking practice progressing, as always, from easy to more difficult. This will be harder for your students than you think. Even switching from *I* to *you* or *you* to *I* in a question/answer exchange will take some practice. For example,

> 6.5a   Teacher: Rosa, do you see me?
>   b   Rosa: Yes, I see you.

Many a student would stumble over this and answer *Yes, you see me*.

You'll be surprised at how difficult this is for your students. You'll see the need to really practice it, so do it!

6.2 Possessive adjectives

Adjectives in the noun and pronoun chapter? Not in the adjective chapter? Yep. It makes sense to study possessive adjectives and possessive pronouns at the same time. Gotta problem with that? The jump from possessive adjectives to possessive pronouns will be difficult, so better to tackle them one at a time. What are they? (It wouldn't hurt to look up *possession* in a bilingual dictionary.) First, write this on the board: (Remember that how to use possessive adjectives and possessive pronouns is what you're trying to teach them, not terminology. If they can use possessive adjectives and possessive pronouns properly, who cares if they remember what they're called?)

<u>possessive adjectives</u>

> my
>
> your
>
> his
>
> her
>
> its
>
> our
>
> their

Some teachers would write *your* twice, since it's singular and plural, but I see no reason for this (and writing the same word twice might actually confuse your students), but do remind your students that *your*, just like *you*, is both singular and plural. Avoid possessive nouns like *Mary's, The doctor's,* etc. They'll come later.

The first thing to do is to put some examples on the board. Make a big deal out of the fact that a possessive adjective is <u>always</u> followed by a noun. That may seem like a no-brainer to you, but you'll soon see why you should stress this:

> This is <u>my</u> <u>cell phone</u>.
>
> That is <u>our</u> <u>classroom</u>.

A classroom is the perfect place to demonstrate possessive adjectives. Point to objects in and around the classroom, down the hallway or outside that you can see through the window. You may need to work on *this, that, these* and *those* too:

pointing to your desk:	These are my books. This is my pen.
pointing to a student's desk:	That is his dictionary. That's her book.
pointing to your classroom:	This is our classroom.
pointing to a classroom across the hall:	That's their classroom. (Explain *that's = that is*)

▶ **More speaking practice**

Next, go around the classroom asking your students questions. Ask information questions with *what* first. Progressing from easy to more difficult, first point to one student's desk while clearly looking at another student. Ask the student that you're looking at questions about objects on the other student's desk. That's the easiest because they just need *his* or *her*; they don't need to choose between *my/your* or *our/their*. Some will want to answer *It's a book.* That's good English, of course, but you want them to practice with possessive adjectives, so if they do that, pretend (if necessary) to be really dumb: *Yes, it's a book, but is it <u>my</u> book, is it <u>your</u> book* (pointing to another student), *or is it her book?* Do a lot of this, and little by little work in more *my/your* exchanges. That will be more difficult.

Now some three-way exercises. While talking to one student, ask her a question about objects on another student's desk as before, but now make the first student ask the second, obtain an answer and then report back to you with the answer. For example,

6.6a	Teacher:	Maria, is that (pointing to the book on John's desk) my book (pointing to yourself)?
b	Maria:	John, is that his book?
c	John:	No, it's my book.
d	Maria:	No, it's his book.

This is just a model. You could vary this any number of ways, and I guarantee, none of them will go smoothly, but so what—it's a lot of fun, it's good practice and it gets the students talking. It's vitally important that you don't just yak, yak, yak. Get them talking. They need it, and they'll like it. It also looks good when the boss pops in for a visit. And it's a great way to eat up the clock if you find yourself with a few extra minutes before the bell. (This is how real teachers think.)

6.3 Possessive pronouns

Now it's time for possessive pronouns. As a native speaker, your first instinct will be to think that this is just a small step from possessive adjectives and will be easy. It won't. Students have a lot of trouble with this. Put this on the board:

<u>possessive pronouns</u>

> mine
>
> yours
>
> his
>
> hers
>
> ours
>
> theirs

What happened to *its*? Well, when was the last time you said anything like *This is its*? Never, I'll bet. We don't use *its* as a possessive pronoun, so don't even mention it (unless you're asked).

Now your students will see why you made a big deal of nouns always following possessive <u>adjectives</u>: because nouns <u>do not</u> follow possessive <u>pronouns</u>, and that will confuse your students.

Write some sentences on the board similar to those above (or if you haven't erased them, recycle them for this lesson), and cross out nouns and change the possessive adjectives to possessive pronouns:

> This is ~~my cell phone~~.
> This is <u>mine</u>.
> That is ~~our classroom~~.
> That is <u>ours</u>.

Your students may wonder how we know what is being talked about, so make sure they understand that often the noun is understood. That means there's no reason to say it or to repeat it in a conversation. As I keep saying, this will be harder than you think. Before engaging in classroom speaking activities like those above, I suggest some written exercises like these:

sample exercises 2: Underline the correct possessive adjectives and possessive pronouns.
> (<u>Your</u>/Yours) project is very good.

1. This isn't (our/ours). It's (theirs/their).
2. (Mine/My) car is older than (her/hers).
3. (Your/Yours) swimming pool is bigger than (ours/our).
4. I finished (my/mine) homework. Did you finish (your/yours)?
5. Mary took the wrong keys. She didn't take (hers/her). She took (my/mine).

6.4 Possessive nouns

More possessives? Yep, this time it's possessive nouns. Possessive nouns are nouns (including proper nouns) with either *'s* (for a singular noun) or *s'* (for a plural noun) on the end of it. They can be used with or without objects. The best way to explain this to your students is that sometimes a noun can be used the same as a possessive adjective <u>and</u> the same as a possessive pronoun. Write something like this on the board. Use only the possessive adjectives *his, her* and *their*:

> His car is red.
> He talked to her brother.
> Their teacher is nice.
> She likes their house.

Now make a big deal about wondering who *his, her* and *their* refer to. Act as if you're not sure in order to demonstrate why, to be clearer, we sometimes use possessive nouns rather than possessive adjectives.

Now cross out the possessive adjectives and use names instead:

> ~~His~~ car is red.
> John's car is red.
>
> He talked to ~~her~~ brother.
> He talked to Mary's brother.
>
> ~~Their~~ teacher is nice.
> Carlos and Michael's teacher is nice.
>
> She likes ~~their~~ teacher.
> She likes the boys' teacher.

Make sure your students understand the difference between the singular *'s* and the plural *s'*.

Is that all? No! Now you have to discuss possessive nouns used in place of possessive pronouns. Write something like this on the board. Use only the possessive pronouns *his, hers* and *theirs*:

> My car is red and hers is blue.
> This isn't my book. It's his.
> The boy's books are on this table, and theirs are on that table.

Again, act confused about exactly who is being referred to: *Hers?, Who is she?, His?, Who is he?, Theirs?, Who are they?* (Avoid using *whose*, which they probably don't know yet.) Now cross out the possessive pronouns and use common nouns or proper nouns instead:

> My car is red and ~~hers~~ is blue.
> My car is red and Sofia's is blue.
>
> This isn't my pencil. It's ~~his~~.
> This isn't my pencil. It's Mark's.
>
> The boys' books are on this table, and ~~theirs~~ are on that table.
> The boys' books are on this table, and the girls' are on that table.

This is definitely going to cause trouble. One major reason is that many of your students are going to look at Sofia's, for example, and see *Sofia is*. The other reason is that the lack of a noun is going to seem strange to them.

Also, you'll need to tell them about some irregular possessive nouns:

children	men	women	people
→ children's	→ men's	→ women's	→ people's

What to do with words that end with *s*, like *boss*, and names that end with *s*, like, *Carlos*, is a can of worms best left unopened for now.

▶ Even more speaking practice

Now that your students are totally confused, go around the classroom asking questions much as you did with possessive adjectives and possessive pronouns. You want your students to be comfortable with using possessive nouns without objects, but don't go crazy about it. Be happy if they can get them right at all. One way, though, to encourage the use of possessive nouns without objects is to ask them questions which require the correction of a mistaken belief:

6.7a Teacher: Alan, is this your book? (pointing to a book on Mary's desk but clearly addressing Alan, sitting next to Mary)

b Alan: No, it's Mary's.

If Alan answers *No, it's Mary's book,* great, but you could reply *Oh, it's not your book, Alan. It's Mary's* to model the use of a possessive noun without an object.

sample exercises 3: Complete the conversations using the noun or nouns in parentheses.

A: Who were you talking to on the telephone?
B: (wife) I was talking to my _____*wife's*_____ brother.

1. A: Do these toys belong to the boys?
   B: (boys/girls) No, they're not the _____ toys. They're the _____.
2. A: Who is that?
   B: (Larry) That's _____ sister.
3. A: What is the name of the company?
   B: (company) The _____ name is ABC Incorporated.
4. A: Who were you talking to at the meeting?
   B: (children) I was talking to the principal of my _____ school.
5. A: What are the names of the parents of your friend?
   B: (friend/parents) My _____ _____ names are John and Mary.

6.5 Indirect objects

Some verbs can take more than one object. They're called (jargon alert!) *ditransitive*, but no way are you going to confuse your students with that term. By two objects, I'm not talking about saying, for example, *Larry ate a hamburger and a hotdog,* I'm talking about (jargon alert!) *direct objects* and *indirect objects.* That much isn't terribly difficult. The main problem is that these sentences can be written in two ways, so a big part of this lesson is teaching students how to convert from one pattern to the other.

Start by putting some examples like these on the board and underlining both objects:

> Carlos gave <u>a book</u> to <u>Alan</u>.
> My husband is making <u>dinner</u> for <u>me</u>.

In each sentence, there are two objects. The direct objects receive the action of the verb directly. They answer the questions *gave what, is making what?* And you guessed it, the indirect objects are *Alan* and *me*. Explain that and write *d.o.* and *i.o.* under the sentences:

> Carlos gave <u>a book</u> to <u>Alan</u>.
>   d.o.   i.o.

> My husband is making <u>dinner</u> <u>for me</u>.
>   d.o.   i.o.

Tell your students that only the prepositions *to* and *for* are used with indirect objects. Next, show them how these sentences can also be written a different way, without *to* or *for*. Put this on the board:

> Carlos gave <u>Alan</u> <u>a book</u>.
>   i.o.   d.o.

> My husband is making <u>me</u> <u>dinner</u>.
>   i.o   d.o.

Both of these patterns are so effortless for us native speakers that you'll be surprised when your students have difficulty with them—especially the i.o./d.o. pattern. For that reason, give your students some practice with exercises where they have to convert from one pattern to another:

sample exercises 4: Change the sentences as in the example.
> Larry wrote a letter to his father.
> *Larry wrote his father a letter.*

1. I won't give money to him.
2. My mother will bake a birthday cake for me.
3. John bought a car for his son.
4. Noura didn't send an email to Rosa.
5. Do you teach English to them?

sample exercises 5: Change the sentences as in the example. (The choice between *for* and *to* is dictated by logic. Was something done *for* someone's benefit, or was some object or information transmitted, transferred, etc., *to* someone?)
> She read me a story.
> *She read a story to me.*

1. Are you sending Michael a letter?
2. Your teacher left you a message.
3. I'm going to get my daughter a new computer.
4. Maria gave her friends some cookies.
5. Did they show you the picture?

▶ **Slight AE/BE difference**

There is a slight difference between American English and British English here that I don't recommend discussing with your students, but you should be ready if it comes up.

If you're not familiar with BE, and you hear a student say, for example,

  6.8 I gave him it.

it might strike you as an odd mistake whereas, being familiar with BE, it strikes me only as odd.

In AE, <u>when the direct object is a pronoun</u>, only the verb + d.o. + *to/for* + i.o. pattern is followed. The verb i.o. + d.o. pattern is never used. In BE, the verb i.o. + d.o. pattern is also used. For example,

  6.9a I sent <u>a letter</u> to <u>Michael</u>.
  b → I sent <u>it</u> to <u>Michael</u>. (verb + d.o. + *to/for* + i.o., used in BE and the only pattern used in AE)
  c → I sent <u>Michael</u> <u>it</u>. (verb i.o. + d.o., used in BE but not AE)
  6.10a She will give <u>the book</u> to <u>her</u>.
  b → She will give <u>it</u> to <u>her</u>. (verb + d.o. + *to/for* + i.o., used in BE and the only pattern used in AE)
  c → She will give <u>her</u> <u>it</u>. (verb i.o. + d.o., used in BE but not AE)

This leads me to wondering whether a BE speaker would convert, for example, *I gave the books to the students* to *I gave them them.*

6.6 It's easy to get ahead of yourself.

One last thing: It's easy to get ahead of the students grammarwise when you're running around the classroom like a nut pulling questions and examples out of your head. Be careful not to get too far ahead, but don't worry if you occasionally slip something in that they may not have actually gotten to yet—just teach it (or not) and move on. In the case of all this possessive business, it would be very easy to switch, without even realizing it, from *yes/no* questions to information questions using *whose*. If you do, no problem—teach them *whose*, but don't dwell on it. Assure them that you'll talk more about it soon. Other things you will certainly have already used by now, which have not yet been taught, are the conjunctions *and, but* and *or* and question words like *who, what, when, where* and *why*. That sort of thing is going to happen. It happens in textbooks too. It's unavoidable and generally a good thing to give students a preview of what's to come. They're learning even when they don't know they're learning. I am especially happy for students to unconsciously learn prepositions this way because I hate teaching prepositions. Got the idea?

6.7 Articles

No, not magazine articles. *Article* is a fancy word for three very boring words: *a, an* and *the*. Even fancier is that *a* and *an* are called *indefinite articles* and *the* is called *the definite article*. Why even bother to teach something so easy? Because it's not so easy. Many students will have trouble knowing whether to use *a, an* or *the* or whether to use an article at all.

There are three concepts you need to explain to your students. The first is pretty easy—what the difference is between *a* and *an*? Easy—use *an* before a word that starts with a vowel and *a* before a word that starts with a consonant, right? Wrong. Use *an* before a word that starts with a vowel <u>sound</u> and *a* before a word that starts with a consonant <u>sound</u>. Here are some examples to put on the board:

> an hour
> a holiday
> an ugly house
> a university

The second is harder. Tell your students that we use *a/an* when we are discussing a member of a group when the identities of each member in the group are unimportant or unknown. Once we have identified a single member of that group, we switch to *the*. That won't make any sense to them, so better to put some examples on the board:

> <u>A</u> student came to my office. I helped <u>the</u> student with his homework.
> I bought <u>a</u> new car. <u>The</u> car is red.
> I brought <u>an</u> apple to school. I gave <u>the</u> apple to my teacher.

sample exercises 6: Complete the paragraph with a, an or the.

I went to _____*a*_____ restaurant and asked _____*a*_____ waiter for _____*a*_____ cup of coffee. _____*The*_____ coffee wasn't hot, so I asked _____*the*_____ waiter to bring me _____*a*_____ different cup of coffee.

I took _____(1) book out of _____(2) library next to my home, but _____(3) book was very boring, so I returned _____(4) book, and I took out _____(5) different book. I liked _____(6) new book very much, and I told _____(7) friend that she should read it.

The last thing you're going to talk about is *the* used for generalization. In English, we do not use *the* to talk about things in general. Write this on the board:

> Sugar is sweet.
> <u>The</u> sugar is in the kitchen.
>
> Students should work hard.
> <u>The</u> students have a test tomorrow.
>
> Ice cream is delicious.
> <u>The</u> ice cream in this store is expensive.

Make sure your students understand that in the first sentence in each pair, we are talking about <u>all</u> sugar, <u>all</u> students, <u>all</u> ice cream, but that in the second sentence, we are talking about a subset: sugar, students and ice cream in a specific place. It's very handy, when teaching this, to have your students look up *in general* and *specific* in their bilingual dictionaries, not just to facilitate this particular lesson but also because these are very useful words that they should know.

---

sample exercises 7: If *the* is necessary, write it in the blank. If *the* is not necessary, write Ø in the blank (Ø = *nothing*).

Many children don't like to eat _____Ø_____ vegetables.

_____The_____ vegetables we had for dinner last night were good.

1. _____ diamonds are expensive.
2. _____ diamonds in my ring are very small.
3. My father taught me that _____ hard work is important.
4. I never drink _____ coffee in this restaurant. It's very bad.
5. I never drink _____ coffee. I like tea.

6.8 *any* and *some*

You're going to teach your students how *any* and *some* are used in affirmative, negative and interrogative sentences. Interrogative? Yep, that's a fancy word for *question* that I have never once used in a classroom. Don't you use it either. And don't use *affirmative*. Rather, do what I do—use these symbols: +, – and ?. It's a lot easier for students to understand. Put something like this on the board:

+ <u>some</u>
I have <u>some</u> money.
She drank <u>some</u> coffee.

– <u>any</u>
I don't have <u>any</u> money.
Alan doesn't speak <u>any</u> French.

? <u>any or some</u>
Do you have <u>any</u> questions?
Did you buy <u>some</u> milk?

So in questions, *any* and *some* are identical in meaning, right? Not exactly. We use *any* when we really don't know the answer; we use *some* when we think the answer is yes. For example, in 6.11 below, I use *some* because I'm pretty sure the answer is yes:

6.11 Your plane crashed in the desert six days ago, and you've just staggered into town half dead from thirst. Do you want some water?

Whether you explain this to your students is iffy. It really depends. I generally don't unless the students are fairly advanced. Otherwise, keep is simple.

It's a good idea to explain that *some* doesn't automatically mean, as many students think, a small number or small amount. It can mean a little or a lot. To illustrate this, I'll put my hand in my pocket and say something like this:

I have some money in my pocket. Is it one dollar? Maybe. One dollar is <u>some</u> money. Is it one million dollars? Maybe. One million dollars is <u>some</u> money.

You want this *any* and *some* business to sink in because before long, you're going to get to *anyone, something,* etc.

Give your students some written exercises like these. If you have already unwisely confused them by explaining the difference between *some* and *any* for questions, shut up about it now because without knowing the situation, there is no way to say whether the speaker thinks the answer to the questions is yes or not. Just let them answer *any or some* for questions.

sample exercises 8: Complete the sentences with *some* or *any.* Write all possible answers.

There isn't _____*any*_____ money in our bank account.

Does Alan need ___*any or some*___ help?

1. Do you want _____ coffee?
2. I don't have _____ time.
3. There isn't _____ paper in the printer.
4. We don't have _____ apples, but we have _____ bananas.
5. Do you have _____ time to help me?

6.9 Indefinite pronouns and indefinite adverbs

Adverbs in the chapter on nouns and pronouns? Yeah, you gotta problem with that? It makes perfect sense to include them here, and the difference between indefinite pronouns and indefinite adverbs will be entirely lost on your students, which is why you're going to keep your mouth shut about it. OK?

► Indefinite pronouns

First, write the actual indefinite pronouns on the board:

<u>indefinite pronouns</u>
anyone/anybody
anything
everyone/everybody
everything
no one/nobody
nothing
someone/somebody
something

Before continuing, make sure your students understand that *one* and *body* are exactly the same with the slight complication that *no one* is written as two words. Also, make sure they know how to pronounce *nothing* (not like *no thing*).

The main thing is to just get the students to learn the meaning of indefinite pronouns. That won't be too hard, but one trouble spot that you definitely want to discuss is that students often want to say, for example,

> 6.12   Everybody are here.

or

> 6.13   Nobody know the answer.

Why? Because it's perfectly logical—and wrong. Even though it seems as if we are talking about more than one person, indefinite pronouns are singular. Put some examples like these on the board and discuss this:

Everyone <u>is</u> hungry.
Everybody know<u>s</u> the answer.
Nobody was listening.
No one want<u>s</u> to go.

Indefinite pronouns can be subjects or objects. This is pretty straightforward except for *anyone* and *anybody*.

If your students understood the previous section on *any* and *some,* they won't have any trouble with sentence like these:

> 6.14   I didn't know anyone at the party.

> 6.15   She didn't talk to anybody.

but when *anyone* and *anybody* are subjects, they have a different meaning—*any person* and not just *some people*: (Keep it simple—stay away from *Anybody who…,* etc., and yes, *can* has not been taught yet—so teach it!)

> 6.16   Anyone can do it. It's easy.

> 6.17   Anybody can go there. It's a public place.

Now discuss examples with *no one* and *nobody.* The meanings are obvious:

> 6.18   No one can do it. It's difficult.

> 6.19   Nobody likes to pay taxes.

► Indefinite adverbs

So how about indefinite adverbs? I'm talking about *somewhere, everywhere, anywhere* and *nowhere.* Figuring these out should be pretty easy for students who've gotten this far without any problem. That these are adverbs and not pronouns is of no matter. It'll never even occur to your students, so don't make a big deal of it. Don't even make a small deal of it. Just focus on meaning, which shouldn't be difficult. They already know that *nothing, anything, something* and *everything* refer to things and that *someone, everybody, anyone* and *nobody,* etc., refer to people. Now just tell them *somewhere, everywhere, anywhere* and *nowhere* are for places.

sample exercises 9:   Correct the mistakes in the sentences.

1.   No body went to the meeting.

2. I don't have nothing.
3. Are everyone here?
4. Everyone in the office hate the new manager.
5. I didn't go nowhere.

▶ **Indefinite pronouns and indefinite adverbs: two negative patterns**

Now, you'll need to decide whether your students are ready for what follows or whether it's better to leave this for later. It's a bit more advanced than what they've studied up to now. You're going to teach your students two ways to say the same thing. (How much simpler can I put it?) Since we native speakers use both constructions at times, it's a good idea to go over this at some point. Write this on the board:

> I went nowhere.
> Larry wants nothing to eat.
> Talk to no one.

Now write the alternate versions under the three sentences you just wrote:

> I went nowhere.
> = I didn't go anywhere.
>
> Larry wants nothing to eat.
> = Larry doesn't want anything to eat.
>
> Talk to no one.
> = Don't talk to anyone.

How to explain this? What's going on is that in English (unknown to many native speakers) only one negative word is allowed in a sentence (not two!). That's why "double negatives" make English teachers cringe. Look at the first sentence in the three examples above. When there is no *don't, doesn't* or *didn't* in the sentences, the negative idea is conveyed by negative indefinite pronouns or the indefinite adverb *nowhere*. Now look at the second sentence in the three examples above. When *don't, doesn't* or *didn't* are in a sentence, neutral indefinite pronouns or the neutral indefinite adverb *anywhere* are necessary. Got that?

Try giving your students sentences of both varieties and have them change each to the other. This will be lots of fun (and very useful too):

sample exercises 10: Change the sentences as in the examples. Use contractions.

> He did nothing.
> *He didn't do anything.*
>
> Mark doesn't know anything.
> *Mark knows nothing.*
>
> Give it to nobody.
> *Don't give it to anybody.*

1. Michael didn't speak to anybody.
2. She said nothing.
3. He doesn't have any money.
4. I have no idea.
5. She didn't go anywhere.

For even more fun, try some imperatives (aka *commands*):

6. Say nothing to nobody.
7. Don't tell anyone what happened.
8. Let no one in this room.

6.10 Count nouns, noncount nouns and quantifiers

The concept of count nouns and noncount nouns is in itself pretty simple, but when we get into the ways we talk about those count nouns and noncount nouns, it gets more difficult. The basic idea is that in English, some nouns are countable, some are not countable and some are both depending on how they're used.

Start with clear examples of count and noncount nouns before discussing the idea that some nouns are both: (One wretched book that I'm very familiar with actually uses *clothes* as an example of a count noun. How dumb is that?)

count nouns	noncount nouns
car	rice
book	salt
man	money

Show your students that we can talk about *one car* or *two, three, four* or *a thousand cars.* Same with *book* and *man* (a quick review of irregular plurals would be a good idea here). Now explain that we would never talk about *rices* or *salts* or *moneys.* (Don't start looking for obscure exceptions here—yes, in a certain sense almost every noncount noun can be countable, but keep it simple!)

There are, however, some nouns that are both countable and uncountable that you might want to mention—*time* and *room* are good examples.

Students do not need to memorize whether every noun in the English language is countable or uncountable—they generally don't have too much trouble with this anyway, but there are a handful of uncountable nouns which will account for many of the mistakes ESL students make in this area, so it's a good idea to go over them:

advice
equipment
furniture
history
homework
information
research
traffic

sample exercises 11: Find the mistakes in these sentences and correct them.
The teacher taught us many new vocabularies today.
The teacher taught us a lot of new vocabulary today.

1. My friend gave me some bad advices.
2. This book has a lot of interesting informations in it.
3. I was late for work because there was a lot of traffics.
4. We need lots of new furnitures for our new house.
5. The histories of my country are very interesting.

So is that all? Nope. Explain that there are ways of counting uncountable nouns. We don't talk about *rices,* but we do talk about *bags of rice* or *pounds of rice.* We don't talk about *waters,* but we do talk about *liters of water* or *bottles of water.* That's easy enough. I'll often use words like these in my examples:

bag
bottle
box
can
carton
gallon
kilogram
liter
pound

Practice a few, and discuss the need for the preposition *of*: a *can of soda,* a *pound of meat,* etc. You may want to discuss *carton.* In some languages, *carton* means *cardboard.* Explain that in English, cartons are made out of cardboard.

All of the above words describe definite quantities, but the real challenge for students is learning the various expressions of indefinite quantity that we use with count nouns and noncount nouns. Before you get into that, make sure they know what you're talking about. A list of these (jargon alert!) *quantifiers,* (aka *expressions of quantity*) is too much to include here. Here are a few more or less random examples:

count nouns quantifiers	noncount nouns quantifiers
a couple of	a great deal of
a few of	a little of
each of	all of
a lot of	half of
none of	little of
several of	most of
some of	some of

There are many, many more. You'll find one in any good grammar book including a very extensive one in my own grammar book, *Rocket English Grammar* (shameless plug). But here's one thing I'll mention: For perfectly good reasons, students sometimes assume that there's a difference between *a lot of* and *lots of*. Who can blame them? It sure looks like one is plural and one is singular. But there is no difference; tell your students that.

Since this is more of a vocabulary exercise than a grammar exercise, I suggest giving your students a list of quantifiers and then discussing them in class. As I said, there are quite a few. The one in *Rocket English Grammar* is three pages long, which is why you're not seeing it here.

6.11 Reflexive pronouns

- **reflexive pronouns**
  - ○ singular   ○ plural
    - myself   ourselves
    - yourself   yourselves
    - himself   themselves
    - herself
    - itself

▶ **Mistakes that native speakers make with reflexive pronouns (and that might include yourself)**
Now this is an area where most native speakers, including many who care about speaking English correctly (and think they do) make mistakes. So before you start teaching reflexive pronouns to your students, it might be a good idea to make sure you know how to use them properly yourself. So let me begin by asking *you* some questions:

1. Do you see *ourself* and *themself* in the list above? No, you don't. Why?

2. Which of these sentences is incorrect?

   a. Please contact Ms. Smith or myself if you have any questions.
   b. Tom and myself had lunch.
   c. Myself and some friends went to a museum.

Here are the answers:

1. *Ourself* and *themself* are wrong (as in not correct) because *our* and *your* are plural, so it makes no sense to attach the singular *-self* to them. Only *ourselves* and *themselves* are correct.

2. All the sentences are incorrect. Do you know why? Think for a minute while I get a cup of coffee…OK, I'm back. Here's why they're wrong: Anytime you can use *I* or *me* instead of *myself* in a sentence, then *I* or *me* and only *I* or *me* (as in not *myself*)is exactly what you should use. No matter how much the plague of incorrect reflexive pronouns usage has been spread across the land by pompous windbags, if *I* or *me* is possible, then only *I* or *me* is correct and *myself* is wrong (as in not correct). Yes, it's common, but so what. So is *He don't*.

OK, so *I* or *me*, but which one? Well, I sure hope you already know enough about basic English to know the answer, but just in case, here are the corrected sentences:
   a. Please contact Ms. Smith or me if you have any questions.
   b. Tom and I had lunch.

A and *b* were kind of obvious, but what about *c, Myself and some friends went to a museum*? This sentence is an abomination—a crime against English grammar—because it's doubly wrong. Even if you replace *myself* with *I*, it's still wrong. Would you say *I and some friends went to a museum*? Of course not. The correct sentence is

   c. Some friends and I went to a museum.

Now aren't you happy I saved you from teaching your students all that wrong stuff? By the way, that was for your benefit. Those are mistakes that native speakers often make, not ESL students. No need to go into it with them.

OK, now that we've gotten that out of the way, what are you going to teach your students?

▶ **Three uses of reflexive pronouns**
Reflexive pronouns are correctly used for three things:

One, when the subject of the sentence is also the object of the verb:

6.20　She saw herself in the mirror.

Two, when we want to make it clear that we did something without any help:

6.21　I built this house myself.

Three, with *by* when the meaning is *alone*:

6.22　He sat by himself and didn't talk to anyone.

Point out to your students that *yourself* is singular and *yourselves* is plural, and make sure they know that reflexive pronouns are always *one* word (as in <u>never</u> two—a common mistake).

As for exercises, I'd suggest some error correction first with sentences like these. Make sure you explain that reflexive pronouns may not be needed in some of these sentences.

sample exercises 12: Correct the mistakes in the sentences. Reflexive pronouns may not be needed in some sentences.

1. The hunter shot hisself in the foot.
2. Sam and Dave did the work themself.
3. We did all the work ourself. Nobody helped us.
4. Larry and myself will meet with you tomorrow at 10:00.
5. The boss asked Sarah and myself to come to her office.

Now for some fill-in-the-blank exercises, which are also called (jargon alert!) *cloze exercises.* (No, that's not a misspelling.) Use the term *cloze exercise* when you want to impress your colleagues.

sample exercises 13: Complete the sentences with the correct reflexive pronoun.
　　　　I need help. I can't do all this work _____*myself*_____.

1. John didn't do all the work _____. I helped him.
2. You and Mark have to do the work _____. Nobody can help you.
3. I know a lot about cars, so when I have a problem with my car, I can usually fix it _____.
4. I never leave my young children at home by _____.
5. She burned _____ badly when she was cooking.

6.12　Listening practice
Here's another chance to give your students some valuable listening practice. We native speaker have the annoying habit of often not pronouncing the *h* in *he, him, himself, his, her* and *herself.* We also often don't pronounce the *th* in *them.* It's easy enough for us to understand, but pity the poor ESL student trying to tell the difference between these:

6.23　I talked to 'im. (I talked to him.)

6.24　I talked to 'em. (I talked to them.)

Talk about these reductions at some point early in your discussion of pronouns. As I keep saying, tell your students that they never need to do this (and it's better if they don't), but they must understand it. Run down a list of examples, and then occasionally model this in future classes. (These examples are pretty simple and focus only on pronouns. I'll talk about other reductions later.) What's fun is to read these in all their fully reduced glory aloud to your students and then ask them to repeat what you just said. Don't write them on the board—you want them to be listening and trying to understand, not reading. Do it! You'll be surprised at how much trouble they'll have:

6.25　I told 'er I love 'er. (I told her I love her.)

6.26　I'll talk to 'im. (I'll talk to him.)

6.27   I'll talk to 'em. (I'll talk to them.)

6.28   I'll call 'er later. (I'll call her later.)

6.29   I think 'e's a good teacher. (I think he's a good teacher.)

6.30   I asked 'im 'is name. (I asked him his name.)

And that's it!

Chapter 7

Asking Questions

Could you…

- explain why *a* and *b* are not correct?

    a.   Where he went?

    b.   Where he did go?

- explain what tag questions are?
- explain why it's important to talk about intonation with tag questions?
- explain why we ask negative questions?

7.1 Why an entire chapter about asking questions?

Why an entire chapter about asking questions? Because much of language is conversation, and much of conversation is asking questions. Although the grammar of forming questions is covered in other chapters, it's a good idea to focus your students on it because it's an area where they often have trouble and also because they need to learn more than just the usual question words—*who, what, when, where* and *how.*

This is potentially a complicated subject, but it doesn't have to be. I'll teach you how I teach it. It's an approach that has worked well for me and will for you too. It really boils question formation down to its essence in a way that's easy to teach and easy to understand. There is a fair degree of oversimplification here, but I make no apologies—your goal is to learn the basics of how to teach English grammar fast so that you can teach your students the basics of English grammar fast. Remember, it's always better to oversimplify than overcomplicate.

Much of question formation boils down to (jargon alert!) *inversion,* which we've talked about before. You don't have to use that unfamiliar term with your students. I don't. I prefer to speak of *switching.* It doesn't matter really because you're going to be showing your students what you mean on the board. They'll see what you're talking about.

7.2 Two kinds of verbs

First, we need to talk about verbs. I warn you though that in our discussions of (jargon alert!) *auxiliary verbs* (which your students may already know as *helping verbs*), we're jumping ahead somewhat, so be aware of that. Still, by now your students have already learned *will,* and very likely by now they've learned *can* and *should* too. Even though we're going to discuss all modal auxiliary verbs, I suggest limiting your examples and discussion to *will, can* and maybe *should. Have* as an auxiliary verb won't be discussed until later, so you might want to avoid it for now unless you think your students are ready. We'll leave *phrasal modals* until later. Conditional sentences are definitely something you should leave until later. Still, every teacher, every class and every student is different, so how and when to teach these topics is something you need to decide.

All verbs can be classified into two groups—one, main verbs and two, stuff that goes in front of main verbs and, in the case of *be,* other stuff too. (I hope that's not too technical for you.) Remember, main verbs are what immediately comes to mind when you (and your students) think of verbs: *eat, talk, work, say, go, give,* for example. The stuff that goes in front of main verbs basically consists of various auxiliary verbs: *be* (in the form of *am, is, are, was* and *were*), have (in the form of *have, has* and *had*) and do (in the form of *do, does* and *did*) and a subset of auxiliary verbs called *modal auxiliary verbs.*

Sometimes, when I discuss this with students, I'll separate *be* and discuss it as if it were a third group—a group of one. I tell students that *be* is special and different from all other verbs, which is true and is how they will see it. Sometimes I'll have them look up *unique* in their bilingual dictionaries. One thing that always confuses students, that you should be aware of, is that *have* and *do* are both auxiliary verbs <u>and</u> main verbs. But don't make a big deal of that unless it comes up:

- **auxilliary verbs**
    - *be*

      am

      is

      are

      was
- **main verbs (examples)**
    - be*

      come

      do*

      go

      have*

were   see
        talk

  o ***have***
   has
   had

  o ***do***
   do
   does
   did

  o **modal auxiliary verbs**
   can
   could
   may
   might
   must
   shall
   should
   will
   would

  *Be, do and *have* are both main verbs and auxiliary verbs. Are you going to get into that now? I don't recommend it. That *do* is also a main verb was discussed in Section 4.17. That *have* is both a main verb and auxiliary verb is discussed in Section 10.1. That *be* is both a main verb and an auxiliary verb is not something I recommend you *ever* confuse your students with. See Appendix F for a discussion of this.

Are you going to teach all of this to your students now? Only in very general terms. It's better to focus on sentence structure patterns than to go into the deep grammar here. The meanings, or rather the functions, of modals will be covered in Chapter 12. It's the meanings of question words that we'll be focusing on in this chapter.

7.3 Inversion

OK, so what about inversion? All right, pay attention. Questions in English are <u>usually</u> formed by inverting the subject and the stuff that goes in front of the verb. Is it really as easy as that? Well, is anything in life as easy as that? No, sometimes, when the answer to the question is the subject of the answer, we don't invert, but let's leave that for later. As for this inversion business, there's really only one complication. Can you guess what it is? In the each example below, notice how the subject and stuff that goes in front of main verbs switch in order to form a question:

▶ *be*

 7.1a He is sick.
  b → Is he sick?

 7.2a They were studying.
  b → Were they studying?

▶ *have*

 7.3a She has gone to bed.
  b → Has she gone to bed?

 7.4a You have eaten.
  b → Have you eaten?

▶ **Modal auxiliary verbs**

 7.5a He can speak Japanese.
  b → Can he speak Japanese?

 7.6a They will go to the mall after dinner.
  b → Will they go to the mall after dinner?

▶ *do*

7.7 Huh?

Yes, the complication is our old friend *do*. But it's not that complicated if you realize that the job of *do* is to act as a *tense holder*. A what? A container to put the tense it. It has no meaning. It appears out of nowhere when needed to function as a tense holder and disappears into another dimension when it's not needed. Pretty bizarre, huh?

7.4 *do,* a word about nothing

Do is a word about nothing. It has no meaning itself. It conveys meaning only by magically appearing in order to indicate that a sentence is negative, is a question or is emphatic (remember the emphatic *do*?). When it's not needed for one of those functions, it goes back into hiding. (But where does it go?) When it is needed for one of those purposes, it contains the tense. That's why the infinitive *do* becomes the present simple tense *do* or *does* or the past simple tense *did* when it is used (when the tense is put inside it), and that's why the main verb that would otherwise contain the tense if no *do, does* or *did* were present, changes from the present simple or past simple to the infinitive when the tense it contained is transferred to *do, does* or *did*. (Remember that the infinitive has no tense, and remember that to make things extra difficult for you and your students, the infinitive and most forms of the present simple look exactly the same.) Is that clear?

So now you see that sentences without any apparent auxiliary verb actually have one hidden inside the main verb. That auxiliary verb is *do,* but since *do* means nothing, it has no reason to come out of hiding until it's needed to serve as a tense holder in order to make a negative sentence, a question or the emphatic *do*. And when it comes out and makes itself visible, it takes the tense that was in the main verb with it. Isn't grammar weird?

You can see this idea of *do* being a tense holder most easily with the emphatic *do*:

7.8a Larry <u>went</u> to the South Pole.
  b → Larry <u>did go</u> to the South Pole.

You can see that the past simple tense has magically left *went* in *a* and entered *do* in *b* resulting in *went* reverting to the infinitive *go* and the infinitive *do* becoming the past simple tense *did*. Clear as mud, right?

Are you going to tell your students that? No, not unless you're lucky enough to have some really bright students, as I have a few times in my career. But give them a simplified version if you think it would be helpful. Say that *do, does* and *did* also follow the inversion requirement to make questions, but that they're invisible until they're put in front of the subject. Always keep in mind that all that matters is that your students can use English correctly. If they have no idea why they're doing what they're doing but can still do it, great!

Now let's get to what you're really going to focus on: the meanings of various question words and common errors that students make with sentence structure.

First of all, getting many of your students to use inversion when forming questions will be like pulling teeth. They will really prefer to say, for example,

7.9 Where he is?

7.10 Where he has gone?

7.11 When you will go to work?

They'll avoid using *do, does* or *did* entirely:

7.12 Where he went?

and if they do try to use them, they'll put them before the subject:

7.13 Where he did go?

You'll hear a lot of errors like these not just when you're focusing on question formation but long after, even from otherwise fairly advanced students. This inversion business is always a problem. When I hear these (and other) mistakes in the classroom, rather than just correct them, I'll have a lot of fun feigning confusion, befuddlement, perplexity, etc. "What strange grammar is this?" I'll ask. "I just don't understand."

As you practice with question words, you'll have ample opportunity to work on getting your students to get inversion right.

7.5 *yes/no* question inversion practice

But before going on to information questions and question words, give your students some *yes/no* question exercises designed to reinforce inversion and the grammar they have learned so far in general. None of the grammar will be new (except for some naughty bits I've slipped in), but it will still be a very useful and productive review. Just do what you've already done when you taught question formation with *be,* with *do, does* and *did* and with *will.* And don't let your students get lazy about contractions. Remind them that they don't have to use contractions, but they definitely need to understand them—not just when they see them but especially when they hear them. (See my discussion of listening practice at the end of this chapter.)

You'll notice that a few of the examples are passive and that others contain *can, would* and *should.* That's no accident. I've said before that I like to occasionally slip in little bits of grammar that students will get to later as a preview. (And as I've also said before, sometimes it's unavoidable.) No need to go into a huge passive or modal lesson. No need to discuss these at all unless you want to mention them briefly or if a student asks. If they benefit from being exposed to some advanced grammar they'll study later, great, otherwise blame the crazy guy who wrote this book.

sample exercises 1: Change these sentences to *yes/no* questions.

> He was tired.
> *Was he tired?*

1. His mother was sleeping.
2. It's finished.
3. You're sure.
4. It's written in pencil.
5. Linda's being helped by the police officer.

sample exercises 2: Change these sentences to *yes/no* questions.

> He will be here tomorrow.
> *Will he be here tomorrow?*

1. Noura should take her medicine.
2. Carlos can ride a bicycle.
3. You'll help me later.
4. Maria would like to help.
5. We'll be there soon.

sample exercises 3: Change these sentences to *yes/no* questions.

> They work in a factory.
> *Do they work in a factory?*
>
> He lives in Iceland.
> *Does he live in Iceland?*

1. The children make a lot of noise.
2. Her sister lives in San Francisco.
3. Her brothers live in Los Angeles.
4. You play basketball.
5. You and he play tennis.

Next, a mixed review of the previous three exercise sets.

sample exercises 4: Change these sentences to *yes/no* questions.

1. Lucy was driving.
2. Mary will go to Japan.
3. Sam has three children.
4. Tom went to Ireland.
5. Ali had fun at the party.
6. Maria goes to work very early.
7. He'll do it tomorrow.

7.6 Question words and information questions

Now it's time to focus on questions words. (And remember that I prefer the term *question word* to *wh-word* for the simple reason that they don't all start with *wh*.) Did you think question words meant only *who, what, when, where* and *why*? No, there's more to it than that, but that's a good place to start.

Focus on question formation. Be careful when you start making hypothetical answers to all the questions you're going to be discussing. You don't want to open a lot of cans of grammatical cans of worms that are best left unopened for now. Nevertheless, it's hard to avoid some new grammar and vocabulary. You'll have to decide when and how to introduce this material. Maybe start with the basics and come back later for the rest when your students are ready.

So start with *who, what, when, where* and *why*. Discuss their meaning and then for practice with question words and question formation, have your students make questions for given answers. As much as possible, mix questions with *be, do, does* or *did* and the modals *will* and *can*. Unless you're sure your students can handle it, don't get carried away with other modals, and don't get into the present perfect yet.

7.7 *who*

One thing to be careful about is not to accidently pose questions with *who* that ask for the <u>subject</u> of a sentence until you're ready to talk about that. What I mean is questions for which the answer would be, for example, <u>*Mary*</u> *talked to Alan*. Most of your students, if asked to form a question designed to obtain the information that it was Mary who talked to Alan, would say *Who did talk to Alan?*

Since you're focusing on inversion now, you don't want to accidentally stray into this area where inversion is not needed. It's easy to do. You're teaching your students inversion, and suddenly you've given them an example that doesn't seem to work, and you feel foolish. I suggest leaving *who* for the subject questions for later, as I have done in this chapter.

sample exercises 5: Write the correct questions to get the underlined information in the answers.

      A: *Who did you see?*
      B: I saw <u>Carlos</u>.

1. A:
      B: She will talk to <u>Mark</u>.
2. A:
      B: Tom hates <u>Jerry</u>.
3. A:
      B: I'm going to stay with <u>my brother</u>.

7.8 *what*

As with *who, what* can be used to ask for the subject of a question, and as with *who,* I suggest leaving that until later, as I have done.

sample exercises 6: Write the correct questions to get the underlined information in the answers.

      A: *What did she make?*
      B: She made a <u>cake</u>.

1. A:
      B: I bought a <u>pair of shoes</u>.
2. A:
      B: Jim can play <u>the piano</u>.
3. A:
      B: John is making <u>a cake</u>.

7.9 *when*

You could easily use this as an opportunity to teach a lot of time-related language: clock time terminology (*a quarter to, 10 after, 20 past,* etc.), how we use the letter *o* in place of zero (as in 8:07, for example), *last week, next year, the day before yesterday, the day after tomorrow, a year ago, a month from now, in the morning, at night, on Friday, this evening, every week, every other month*—I could go on and on, but you get the idea.)

sample exercises 7: Write the correct questions to get the underlined information in the answers.

      A: *When did she go to her office?*
      B: She went to her office <u>very early</u>.

1. A:
      B: Alan called Sarah <u>yesterday</u>.

2. A:
    B: The class starts <u>at 8.20</u>.
3. A:
    B: I can do it at <u>after dinner</u>.

7.10 *what time*

Explain that *what time* has the same meaning as *when* <u>only</u> when speaking of clock time.

sample exercises 8: Write the correct questions to get the underlined information in the answers.
   A: *What time did you do it?*
   B: I did it <u>at 2:00</u>.

1. A:
    B: She will come <u>at 1:00</u>.
2. A:
    B: Francesca gets home <u>at 3:45</u>.
3. A:
    B: The test is <u>at 9:00</u>.

7.11 *where*

Mention that we sometimes include *to* in the questions with *go*.

   7.14a   Where did you go?
      b   = Where did you go to?

sample exercises 9: Write the correct questions to get the underlined information in the answers.
   A: *Where did they eat?*
   B: They ate <u>in the lunchroom</u>.

1. A:
    B: John was <u>in the lab</u>.
2. A:
    B: Alan will go <u>to the mall</u>.
3. A:
    B: I live <u>in Toronto</u>.

7.12 *why*

Teaching the seemingly easy question word *why* will put you on a slippery slope to teaching the possible grammar used in answers. And there's a lot of it. You'll have to judge for yourself how far to go with it. I would be careful not to suggest that it's necessary to understand it all simply to use the question word *why*.

One of those possibilities is *because*. It's likely that some of your students will not have learned *because* yet. No harm in teaching it now, but keep it simple. Don't get into reversing the dependent clause and independent clause (*Because I have a test, I'm studying/I'm studying because I have a test*).

More useful grammar that you could teach now is the use of *to* and *for* to talk about obtaining something (*I went to the store <u>for</u> a new pen/<u>to get</u> a new pen*) or *to* to talk about accomplishing something (*I called her <u>to ask a question</u>*).

sample exercises 10: Write the correct questions to get the underlined information in the answers.
   A: *Why are you studying?*
   B: I'm studying <u>because I have a test</u>.

   A: *Why did he go to the supermarket?*
   B1: He went to the supermarket <u>to buy some milk</u>.
   B2: He went to the supermarket <u>for some milk</u>.

1. A:
    B: Mary walks to work <u>because she doesn't have a car</u>.
2. A:
    B: The student is absent <u>because he is sick</u>.
3. A:
    B1: I'm going to the library tomorrow <u>for a book</u>.

B2: I'm going to the library tomorrow to get a book.
4. A:
    B: Sofia called her friend to ask her a question.

7.13 *what kind of*

You may also want to teach *what type of* and *what sort of,* but *what kind of* is the most common of these three. You might want to give examples where the name of the group that the answer is a member of is ellipted—not spoken because it's understood. For example, if I'm talking to my friend about cars that we see in the parking lot, I might ask, *What kind is it?* and he would know that I meant *What kind of car is it?*

sample exercises 11: Write the correct questions to get the underlined information in the answers.
    A: *What kind of food does she like?*
    B: She likes <u>Mexican</u> food.

1. A:
    B: It's a <u>shoe</u> store.
2. A:
    B: He reads <u>history</u> books.
3. A:
    B: I'll take <u>business</u> courses.

7.14 *which*

With *which* we sometimes say the name of the group that the answer is a member of, *Which shirt did you buy?*, we sometimes substitute the name of the group with *one* (something you should teach now along with *ones*), *Which one did you buy?*, or we sometimes ellipt it entirely, *Which did you buy?* Also, in informal English, *what* is sometimes used in place of *which*.

sample exercises 12: Write the correct questions to get the underlined information in the answers.
    A: *Which house is yours?*
    B: The <u>big</u> house is mine.

    A: *Which ones did you buy?*
    B: I bought the <u>purple</u> ones.

1. A:
    B: I bought the <u>green</u> shirt.
2. A:
    B: She wants <u>that</u> one.
3. A:
    B: The one <u>with the blue cover</u> is yours.

7.15 *whose*

You might already have touched on *whose* when you taught possessives. Make sure you point out that *whose* sounds exactly like *who's,* and make sure your students know the difference. When the name of the noun in question is understood, it's often not stated: *Whose is it?* or *Whose are they?*

sample exercises 13: Write the correct questions to get the underlined information in the answers.
    A: *Whose car did you drive?*
    B: I drove <u>David's</u> car.

1. A:
    B: It's not my pen. Maybe it's <u>Tom's</u>.
2. A:
    B: I don't know. It's not <u>mine</u>.
3. A:
    B: She went to <u>Mary's</u> house.

7.16 *how much*

Even if you've already taught count nouns and noncount nouns and expressions of quantity, you'll want to review it. If you haven't, then this is the obvious time to do it. Once again, the noun in question is often ellipted if it is understood (*How much ~~money~~ do you have?*).

sample exercises 14: Write the correct questions to get the underlined information in the answers.

     A: *How much of the homework did you finish?*
     B: I finished <u>half of</u> the homework.

  1. A:
      B: I have <u>very little</u> money.
  2. A:
      B: There's <u>a lot of</u> orange juice in the refrigerator.
  3. A:
      B: I didn't buy <u>any</u> coffee.
  4. A:
      B: <u>A million dollars</u> was stolen. (Notice that no inversion is required here.)

7.17 *how many*

Even if you've already taught count nouns and expressions of quantity, you'll want to review it. If you haven't taught these yet, then this is the obvious time to do it. Once again, the noun in question is often ellipted if it is understood (*How many ~~children~~ do you have?*). Be sure to teach your students *How many are…* Sometimes, as in number one below, when students can see that the answer is *one,* they want to ask *How many is…* Point out that until we hear the answer, we don't know if the answer is one or more than one, so the question is always plural.

sample exercises 15: Write the correct questions to get the underlined information in the answers.

     A: *How many children does she have?*
     B: She has <u>four</u> children.

  1. A:
      B: There's only *one book* on the table.
  2. A:
      B: They didn't eat *any* cookies.
  3. A:
      B: *More than 200* people will come to the wedding. (Notice that no inversion is required here.)

7.18 *how often* (and adverbs of frequency)

If you haven't already, you'll need to teach expressions like *once a week, every month, once in a while* etc., and adverbs of frequency (*always, almost always, often, usually, sometimes, occasionally, once in a while, rarely, seldom, hardly ever, almost never, never*). Nothing wrong with teaching *rarely* and *seldom,* but because native speakers rarely say *rarely* and seldom say *seldom,* I think it's important to teach the students what we say more often: *hardly ever.* Also, you'll find that students will answer questions like, for example, *How often do you eat fish?* with *I always fish,* so be prepared to deal with this so that it doesn't sound like they do something 24 hours a day. (See Section 16.5 for more on these.)

You may be tempted to do what many grammar books do: assign percentages to adverbs of frequency. I have a problem with that because which of these adverbs we choose when we speak depends so much on the situation. And then you'll end up, as many books do, teaching your students that *sometimes* means 50%, which makes no sense at all. *Sometimes* is anything between *never* and *always.* It makes as much sense to say *It sometimes snows in Saudi Arabia* (it really does) as it does to say *It sometimes snows in Canada.* Once, I was teaching from a book which said that *usually* means 90%, and a student raised his hand and asked, in all seriousness, *What about 91%?*

sample exercises 16: Write the correct questions to get the underlined information in the answers.

     A: *How often do you drink coffee?*
     B: I <u>never</u> drink coffee.

  1. A:
      B: He goes shopping <u>twice a week</u>.
  2. A:
      B: He <u>hardly ever</u> works on Saturday.
  3. A:
      B: Alan was <u>almost always</u> late.

7.19 *how far is/was it* (*from* + location) *to* + location

Occasionally some pesky student might ask just what *it* is in sentences like, for example, *It was cold yesterday* or *It is Monday.*

The answer is that *it* isn't really anything (another word about nothing). Its only function is to satisfy the requirement that all English sentences must have a subject. You can't just say, *Is hot today*, for example. *It* used in this way is called an (jargon alert!) *expletive* or *dummy subject*, but no need to teach your students that.

sample exercises 17: Write the correct questions to get the underlined information in the answers.

    A: *How far is it from New York to Los Angeles?*
    B: It's <u>around 2,450 miles</u> from New York to Los Angeles.

1. A:
    B: It's <u>very far</u> to the park—maybe <u>250 miles</u>.
2. A:
    B: It was about <u>15 miles</u> from my house to Larry's house.
3. A:
    B: It's around <u>three miles</u> from here to the beach.

7.20 *how*

How alone has many functions, but the ones to focus on at this point are asking about how something is done and how a goal is achieved. Are you going to confuse your students with that explanation? I hope not—just show them a bunch of examples. Be aware that many questions like these would likely be answered by a native speaker with a gerund in the answer, and gerunds are (you guessed it) a can of grammatical worms you should leave unopened until later.

sample exercises 18: Write the correct questions to get the underlined information in the answers.

    A: *How will she cook it?*
    B: She'll cook it <u>in the oven</u>.

1. A:
    B: I get to work <u>by bus</u>. (This important use of *get* is something you might want to teach now along with *get here* and *get there*.)
2. A:
    B: She fixed it <u>with a screwdriver</u>.
3. A:
    B: You can lose weight <u>by eating less and exercising more</u>.

7.21 *how* with adverbs

Good examples to use are *well, fast, hard, quickly, long, early* and *late*. Make sure you're up to speed regarding the differences between adverbs and adjectives. Don't forget that *well, fast, hard, long, early* and *late* are adjectives as well as adverbs, and make sure you understand the difference between *bad* and *badly*. See Section 16.3 for more about this.

Often we default to the better or greater of two opposite adverbs in a question. Only if the opposite adverb has been established do we ask as to the degree of that adverb. For example,

  7.15a Rosa: How well does Larry sing?
     b Ali: He doesn't sing well. He sings badly.
     c Rosa: Really? How badly does he sing?
     d Ali: How badly? Very badly.

Sometimes, when the answer might be a range of adverbs, we don't specify the adverb in the question:

  7.16a Tom: How does John drive?
     b Bill: He drives recklessly.

sample exercises 19: Write the correct questions to get the underlined information in the answers.

    A: *How does Tom drive?*
    B: He drives <u>fast</u>.
    A: *How fast does Tom drive?*
    B: He drives <u>very</u> fast.

1. A:
    B: She plays tennis <u>well</u>.
2. A:
    B: She plays tennis <u>very</u> well.

3. A:
    B: They came home <u>very</u> late—around 2:00 a.m.

7.22 *how* with adjectives
As with adverbs, we often default to the better or greater of opposite adjectives when asking a question. Only if the opposite adjective has been established do we ask as to the degree of that adjective:

7.17a	Gary:	How tall is your brother?
b	Sarah:	He's not tall at all. He's short. (Be ready to explain *at all* if you use this example.)
c	Gary:	Really? How short.
d	Sarah:	Less than 150 centimeters. (To my metrically challenged fellow Americans, that's about 4' 11".)

Sometimes this will seem illogical to students, for example, asking *How old...* to ask the age of a baby or *How big...* to ask the size of something known to be very small.

Note that it is the adjective *long* which is used in *How long* to ask questions (answered with *be*) about the length of objects like rivers, books, movies, etc., and the adverb *long* which is used to ask questions (answered with verbs) about lengths of time spent doing things, which is discussed separately below.

An interesting aside here might be a discussion of adjectives with different opposites depending on the situation. For example, *short/tall* for vertical stuff like people, trees and buildings but *short/long* for horizontal stuff and *young/old* for people but *young/new* for other things. (And you might as well talk about *right/wrong* and *right/left* while you're at it.)

sample exercises 20: Write the correct questions to get the underlined information in the answers.
A: *How deep is the pool?*
B: The pool is <u>10 feet deep</u>.

1. A:
    B: The book is <u>434 pages long</u>.
2. A:
    B: It's <u>not hard</u>. It's <u>easy</u>.
3. A:
    B: I'm <u>29 years old</u>.
4. A:
    B: I was very sick, but I'm <u>much better</u> now.

7.23 *how long* for lengths of time
How long used for lengths of time isn't terribly difficult, but this is the obvious time to teach expressions for lengths of time that we might use to answer questions with *How long...* For example, *for ten minutes, for three days, forever, since last week, all day, all year, all my life, from/to, from/till, from/until.* (When you get to the perfect tenses, *for* and *since* will come up again. An important part of teaching the perfect tenses is the difference between *for* and *since*. But leave that for later.)

sample exercises 21: Write the correct questions to get the underlined information in the answers.
A: *How long did you study?*
B: I studied <u>for three hours</u>.

1. A:
    B: I'll be in Australia <u>for a month</u>.
2. A:
    B: My students were sleeping <u>all day</u>.
3. A:
    B: She worked <u>from 8:00 until 12:30</u>.

7.24 *how long* + modal/a form of *do* + *it take* (someone) *to*
Wow, what a mess. It's not as bad as it looks. What it really means is how much time was required or needed to do something:

| 7.18a | Paul: | How long did it take you to write your book? |
| b | David: | It took me <u>two years</u> to write my book. |

| 7.19a | Maria: | How long will it take you to get here? |
| b | Tom: | It'll take me <u>only a few minutes</u> to get there. |

sample exercises 22: Write the correct questions to get the underlined information in the answers.

    A: *How long does it usually take you to get over jet lag?*
    B: It usually takes me a week to get over jet lag.

1. A:
    B: It takes her <u>around 25 minutes</u> to drive to work.
2. A:
    B: It took me <u>three hours</u> to do my homework.
3. A:
    B: It will take <u>about 30 minutes</u> to install this program.
4. A:
    B: It took me <u>an hour</u> to get there.

7.25 *what* + a form of *do* used when the answer to a question is a verb

One thing that students sometimes don't get about *do* is that it's used in questions when the answer to the question is a verb. Put this on the board:

    A   What is Michael doing?
    B   He is making something.
    A   What is Michael making?
    B   He is making a dog house.

Now ask them how they are different. Why *doing* in *What is Michael doing?* Why *making* in *What is Michael making?* Tell them that in the first conversation, we don't know that *making something* is the answer. We don't know if he is *making, reading, cleaning, cooking,* etc. In the second conversation, we know *making,* but *making what?* Underline as shown:

    A   What is Michael <u>doing</u>?
    B   He is <u>making something</u>.
    A   What is Michael <u>making</u>?
    B   He is making <u>a dog house</u>.

Do can be used in this way in any tense, but don't overdo it in your examples (so no future perfect passive continuous examples like *What will have been being done by him?*). As we've discussed, it's very common to ask questions about future plans with the present continuous: *What are you doing tomorrow?* (see Section 5.13.)

sample exercises 23: Write the correct questions to get the underlined information in the answers.

    A: *What did you do yesterday?*
    B: I <u>stayed home and studied for my exam</u>. (What will you say if a student asks "Why not to home"?)

    A: *What's your sister doing on the weekend?*
    B: She's <u>visiting her friend in the hospital</u>.

1. A:
    B: I <u>watched TV</u> last night.
2. A:
    B: We're <u>studying</u>.
3. A:
    B: He'll <u>wash his car</u> on Saturday.
4. A:
    B: She's going to <u>clean her house</u> tonight.
5. A:
    B: I'm <u>going shopping</u> tomorrow.

7.26 *who* and *what* used when the answer to a question is the subject

One thing that never fails to confuse students, after you've been pounding them over the head with inversion and *do, does* and *did* is that, strangely, there are times when it is not correct to use inversion or *do, does* and *did*. I don't mean when another auxiliary or modal auxiliary verb is called for. I mean examples like these (again with the information the question is designed to obtain underlined). Put these on the board and ask your students what the correct question is for these answers:

A

B   Sarah danced with Michael.

A

B   A tree fell on the house.

I guarantee many, maybe most, will answer *Who did dance with Michael?* and *What did fall on the house?* If these were emphatic *do* questions, these would be correct, but these are not emphatic *do* and are not correct. (And don't even mention that.) So why are the students confused? Because when the answer to the question is the <u>subject</u>, no inversion or *do, does* or *did* is required. In the answers above, *Sarah* and *a tree* are the <u>subjects</u> of the answers. No need to get into a deep discussion of subjects and objects (or, God forbid, *complements*). I explain this to students in terms of "<u>before</u> the verb" and "<u>after</u> the verb". Just tell them: When the answer to the question is <u>before</u> the verb, "no switching and no *do, does* or *did*".

Exercises meant to practice this are such no brainers that it's more effective to mix them—have them come up with questions that call for either subjects or objects.

sample exercises 24: Write the correct questions to get the underlined information in the answers.

A: *Who saw Mary?*
B: <u>Sofia</u> saw Mary.

A: *Who did Sofia see?*
B: Sofia saw <u>Mary</u>.

1. A:
   B: John is helping <u>Carlos</u>.
2. A:
   B: <u>John</u> is helping Carlos.
3. A:
   B: <u>The fire</u> damaged the museum.
4. A:
   B: The fire damaged <u>the museum</u>.

7.27 *whom*

Teaching your students to use *whom* correctly should not be high on your list of priorities. It's not something you probably want to spend a lot of time on, and if you do cover it, it might be something you come back to later. But if you're asked, and you might be; if you have more advanced students who are ready for it or if you just want to know something that most native English speakers don't, you should know how to use *whom*. And actually, asking questions with *whom* isn't really that difficult. The basic idea is that *who* is for subjects and *whom* is for objects, but in modern English, most people use *who* for both. Why? Simple—they have no clue as to when or how to use *whom*. But very shortly, you will have a clue, and you'll be able to casually slip *whom* into a conversation with your loser friends from high school. That'll impress them. Don't overdo it though. The reality is that even people who do have a clue usually use *who* instead of *whom*. This is so common that *who* is considered acceptable, with *whom* as an option when you want to show off.

Here's what it boils down to: If the answer to the question is the object and a person, then *whom* can be used (even though it usually isn't):

7.20a John: Who(m) did Larry see?
   b   Carlos: Larry saw <u>Sam</u>.

7.21a Lucy: Who(m) is the teacher helping?
   b   Gary: The teacher is helping <u>Rosa</u>.

7.22a Joe: Who(m) will Carlos meet?
   b   Sam: Carlos will meet <u>the manager</u>.

Is it that easy? Of course not. Sometimes *whom* must be used: If the object in the sentence is the object of a preposition, then there is the option of (jargon alert!) *fronting* the preposition. When this is done, *whom* is not optional. It must be used:

7.23a Michael: Who(m) did you listen <u>to</u>?
   b   = <u>To</u> whom did you listen?
   c   John: I listened <u>to Mary</u>.

7.24a	Mark:	Who(m) are the police looking <u>for</u>?
b		= <u>For</u> whom are the police looking?
c	Sarah:	The police are looking <u>for Alan</u>.

This can be done with any preposition:

7.25a	Rosa:	Who(m) does John sit <u>in back of</u>?
b		= <u>In back of</u> whom does John sit?
c	Gary:	John sits <u>in back of Larry</u>.

If this comes up at all, and for most students it never will, it's another one of those things that is never necessary to use but is a good idea to understand, especially for students learning English for academic or business purposes.

sample exercises 25: Write the correct questions to get the underlined information in the answers.

A1:	*Who(m) will Rosa eat lunch with?*
A2:	*With whom will Rosa eat lunch?*
B:	Rosa will eat lunch with <u>Linda</u>.

1. A1:
   A2:
   B: John sits next to <u>Maria</u>.
2. A1:
   A2:
   B: Ali is dancing with <u>Noura</u>.
3. A1:
   A2:
   B: He looked at <u>Alan</u>.
4. A1:
   A2:
   B: Sam will make dinner for <u>his wife</u>.

7.28 Negative questions—three functions

This is a useful lesson, but it might be another thing you come back to when you feel your students are ready for it. In this chapter, we've spent a lot of time talking about how to form questions, and in previous chapters, we've spent a lot of time talking about how to make negative sentences. But in reality, we often combine the two and make negative questions. The grammar isn't really anything new, but the functions of negative questions are what will be new and what you should teach your students. There are three reasons we ask negative questions.

▶ **To start a conversation**

When you ask a question, people usually feel that they must answer you, and that's a good way to get a conversation going:

7.26 Isn't it a nice day? (to a stranger outside)

7.27 Aren't the bridesmaids' dresses hideous? (at a wedding)

▶ **To confirm information that we already think is correct**

7.28 Isn't your name Larry?

7.29 Weren't you in my English class last year?

▶ **To make a point**

In this case, you're asking a question but not in order to obtain information. You want to stick it to somebody—to express annoyance or displeasure or to point out that you were right in the first place:

7.30 Didn't I tell you to clean your room? (a parent to a child who did not clean her room as instructed)

7.31 Aren't you going to help me? (to a lazy husband who is watching football on TV while his wife cleans the house)

7.32 Didn't I tell you it would be closed? (to your friend upon arriving at a store that you said would be closed)

7.33 Didn't I tell you he was no good? (from a mother to a daughter whose husband has just been arrested)

sample exercises 26: Write negative questions that you think are correct for the situation. (Even though these might be hard for your students at first, if you're a good entertainer—and a good teacher is a good entertainer—you can have a lot of fun hamming it up with these scenarios and others that you think up.)

> Your son should be doing his homework, but he isn't.
> *Shouldn't you be doing your homework?*

1. You are talking to your friend, but he is not listening to you.
2. You are a teacher, and you are upset because a student did not do her homework.
3. You want to start a conversation with somebody standing next to you in an art museum. You think that the painting you are both looking at is beautiful.
4. You think your friend is asking a lot of dumb questions. He acts like he doesn't know anything.
5. You think my name is Carl, but you're not 100% sure.

7.29 Tag questions

You use tag questions, don't you? You saw that that was a tag question, didn't you? That was pretty clever of me, wasn't it? We use tag questions to change a sentence that is not a question into a sentence that is a question. These are very common in conversation and therefore something you should definitely teach to your students.

The grammar can get a bit tricky, but the basic idea is that if the sentence is affirmative, the tag question will be negative and vice versa. To illustrate this when I teach tag questions, I use positive symbols (+) and negative symbols (−) so that the students can see that the statement and the tag question are opposite:

         +   −

You understand this, don't you?

      −   +

It's not hard, is it?

▶ Making tag question

▷ *be*
The form in the base sentence is the same in the tag question:

7.34   He <u>wasn't</u> at the meeting, <u>was</u> he?

7.35   Mary <u>is</u> very intelligent, <u>isn't</u> she?

▷ Modals/*do, does, did*
The modal or negative form form of *do, does* or *did* is repeated,

7.36   You <u>won't</u> forget, <u>will</u> you?

7.37   He <u>can</u> speak Spanish, <u>can't</u> he?

7.38   She <u>doesn't</u> have a car, <u>does</u> she?

but when there is no modal or negative form of *do*, use *don't, doesn't* or *didn't*:

7.39   You live in Atlanta, <u>don't</u> you?

7.40   He works in a library, <u>doesn't</u> he?

7.41   Lucy went to Scotland, <u>didn't</u> she?

▷ Perfect tenses
Have, has and *had* are repeated:

7.42   You've eaten, <u>haven't</u> you?

7.43   He <u>hadn't</u> done it yet, <u>had</u> he?

▷ *this, that, these, those*
Use *it* or *they*:

7.44   That <u>is</u> your pen, <u>isn't</u> it?

7.45   These <u>aren't</u> John's books, <u>are</u> they?

7.46 There isn't a computer in the classroom, is there?

7.47 There are five players on a basketball team, aren't there?

▷ *everybody, something*, etc.
Use *it* or *they*:

7.48 Everybody came to the conference, didn't they?

7.49 Nothing is broken, is it? (This doesn't violate what I said about positive and negative because nothing is negative.)

▶ **Two functions of tag questions**
We use tag questions for two reasons, and we use (jargon alert!) *intonation,* (variations in the *pitch* of our voice used to convey meaning) to indicate which of those two reasons we have in mind:

▶ **To confirm information that the speaker thinks is probably true** (and sometimes to also make a point)
If this is the reason, when we get to the tag question, the voice goes <u>down</u>. Model these for your students:

7.50 You weren't listening to a word I said, were you? ↘

7.51 You should be studying for your test and not watching TV, shouldn't you? ↘

7.52 This garlic ice cream isn't very good, is it? ↘

▷ **To learn the answer to something we're really not sure about**
If this is the reason, when we get to the tag question, the voice goes <u>up</u>. Model these for your students:

7.53 The teacher said to read Chapter 7 for tomorrow, didn't she? ↗

7.54 I go north to get to the beach, don't I? ↗

7.55 That guy's name is David, isn't it? ↗

7.30 *aren't I?* NO!!!
One last thing. Please don't teach your students *aren't I.* This is wrong and just plain awful. Teach them *am I not.*
I'm right about *aren't I* being an abomination, am I not?

sample exercises 27: Write tag questions. (Model the rising and falling intonation when you say the completed sentences in class, but don't expect the students to be able to tell you whether the intonation should rise or fall because there's no way to know—it all depends on the situation.)

You went to Poland last year, _____ *didn't you* _____?

1. She hadn't been there before, _____?
2. There are 30 days in April, _____?
3. He wouldn't do it, _____?
4. I'm right, _____?
5. She's not angry, _____?

7.31 Listening practice
One web site advises ESL students that "You need to use reductions in order to sound more natural." This is bad advice. Regardless of what your students want, what they really need and what they should want is to be understood by native speakers when they speak. It's the rare ESL student who does not have an accent—in fact, it's not rare—it's unknown. Your students will all have accents, sometimes very strong accents, which means that native speakers will have to work hard, sometimes very hard, to understand them when they speak. For that reason, your students need to speak clearly. Attempting to imitate the reduced speech of native speakers won't make them "sound more natural". It will make them sound comical and perhaps even incomprehensible. Forget that. What is very important is that they *understand* reductions. This is tremendously important. That's the way native speakers talk everyday—even English teachers.

OK, so what's this got to do with questions? A lot. In *yes/no* questions, forms of *do* and *be* are often reduced—sometimes reduced into nonexistence, and in information questions, question words are often mangled horribly. My advice is that as you teach your students question formation and question words, you continually model reductions. Don't go crazy with it. Think of it as a continuum—you start out any lesson speaking clearly and a little more slowly than you normally would and then gradually speak in a more natural fashion. Finally, toward the end of the lesson, focus on reductions. The focus here is on questions, but discuss the way native speakers like to pronounce *t* as *d* when it comes after a vowel (all native speakers do this, though Americans seem to do it the most); how *h* is reduced or entirely silent in *he, him, himself, her, herself* and *his*; how the *th* in *them* is often silent; how *o* changes to *a* in *you* and *to*; how *of* often changes to *a* (the *f* being completely silent) and how we all sometimes do what our mothers told us not to do: drop our *g*s (*goin', doin'*).

To amuse yourself, read these aloud in class, just as you would after a couple of beers, and ask your students to repeat what you just said in standard, <u>unreduced</u>, pronunciation (unreduced because the idea is to see if they understood what you said, not to imitate it). It won't be easy for them, but it's fantastic listening practice, and students love this kind of stuff. They often have a better idea of the importance of learning to understand the reduced speech of native speakers than their teachers do. (I'll get to *gotta* and *hafta* later, so no need for that now. Also, *wouldja, couldja*, etc., will come later.)

▸ Reduced *yes/no* questions

7.57   Da ya wanna eat? (Do you want to eat?)

7.58   Ya wanna eat? (Do you want to eat?)

7.59   Wanna eat? (Do you want to eat?)

7.60   Ja go da the store? (Did you go to the store?)

7.61   Ze doin' it? (Is he doing it?)

7.62   I'she angry? (Is she angry?)

▸ Reduced information questions

7.63   Whoz 'e think 'e is? (Who does he think is?)

7.64   Who ja go da the party with? (Who did you go to the party with?)

7.65   Whoz 'ere? (Who's there?)

7.66   Whacha want for dinner? (What do you want for dinner?)

7.67   Whad 'e do last night? (What did he do last night?)

7.68   Whaja do yesterday? (What did you do yesterday?)

7.69   Whenz 'e comin'? (When is he coming?)

7.70   Where ya goin'? (Where are you going?)

7.71   Wherez 'e going? (Where is he going?)

7.72   Where da ya go after class? (Where do you go after class?)

7.73   Wherez 'e go on the weekend? (Where does he go on the weekend?)

7.74   Where ja go last night? (Where did you go last night?)

7.75   Whyd 'e go there? (Why did he go there?)

7.76   Whyz 'e wanna go da the library? (Why does he want to go to the library?)

7.77   Howja get there? (How did you get there?)

7.78   How ya doin'? (How are you doing?)

7.79   Howz 'e dance? (How does he dance?)

7.80   Howbowchoo? (How about you?)

7.81   Whadabouchoo? (What about you?)

Chapter 8
Phrasal Verbs

Could you...

- explain why *take on* isn't the opposite of *take off*?
- explain why *come up with* isn't the opposite of *come down with*?
- explain why *a* is correct but *b* is not correct?

  a. I turned it on.
  b. I turned on it.

- answer this question: Can phrasal verbs be used as adjectives?
- answer this question: Can phrasal verbs be used as nouns?

8.1 Phrasal verbs are verbs!

Phrasal verbs might seem like something that should be in a vocabulary book rather than a grammar book, but there are aspects of phrasal verbs that it makes sense to discuss here. First of all, use the term *phrasal verb* rather than *two-word verb* for the simple reason that they don't always have two words. Some have three. Also, never tell your students that phrasal verbs are informal or substandard or that they are idioms (though they are idiomatic). Phrasal verbs are verbs—it's as simple as that. The more your students think of them that way, the more they'll realize how important it is to learn them. As with all main verbs, some are informal, of course, but most are not. There's nothing substandard about phrasal verbs, and by giving your students the idea that phrasal verbs are oddities that should be classified with other expressions, like *raining cats and dogs,* you're doing your students a disservice. Phrasal verbs are an absolutely essential part of the English (jargon alert!) *lexicon,* the vocabulary or (jargon alert!) *word stock* of a language, and something every student needs to give attention to.

Essentially, there are four things you need to teach your students. One is about vocabulary (which is not our focus here), and the other three are about grammar.

8.2 Phrasal verbs are everywhere.

Make your students understand just how important phrasal verbs are. Tell them that there are (I'm not kidding) thousands of them. Narrowing it down to 400 for my book, *The Ultimate Phrasal Verb Book,* wasn't easy. In case they have any doubt that phrasal verbs are common and important, give them some examples that they very likely already know: *turn on the light, turn off the TV, put on your shoes, take off your coat* and one I use frequently in my classroom, *WAKE UP!* Also, make sure to tell them that the most important thing about phrasal verbs is <u>not</u> the grammar that we're going to focus on here; it's learning the meanings of common, essential phrasal verbs that they'll see and hear every day.

8.3 Separable or inseparable?

The majority of phrasal verbs have two parts—the verb and the (jargon alert!) *particle*. Particles are sometimes prepositions and sometimes adverbs. Don't go there! It's another can of grammatical worms best left unopened. Just call them particles. Some phrasal verbs can be separated and some cannot. That means the object can sometimes be placed between the verb and the particle and sometimes not. Why are some phrasal verbs separable and some not? Trust me, you don't want to know. It's just something we, as native speakers, know instinctively, but students need to learn (*how,* not *why*). I've never found this to be a serious difficulty, however. Students seem to pick this up fairly easily. Here are some examples:

8.1a <u>turn on</u> the TV
  b   = <u>turn</u> the TV <u>on</u>

8.2a <u>put on</u> your shoes
  b   = <u>put</u> your shoes <u>on</u>

Is it as simple as that? What do you think? When a noun is replaced by a pronoun, it <u>must</u> be between the verb and the particle. Why? Good question, but that's the way it is:

8.3a <u>turn on</u> it
  b   = <u>turn</u> it <u>on</u>

8.4a <u>put</u> <u>on</u> them
   b = <u>put</u> them <u>on</u>

sample exercises 1: All of the phrasal verbs in this exercise are separable. Use the objects in parentheses to write each sentence three ways.

> Sam cut up. (the meat, it)
> *Sam cut up the meat.*
> *Sam cut the meat up.*
> *Sam cut it up.*

1. I made up. (a story, it)
2. The teacher will call off. (the test, it)
3. He called back. (his friend, him)
4. Please clean up. (this mess, it)
5. They're tearing down. (the building, it)

sample exercises 2: All of the phrasal verbs in this exercise are inseparable. Use the objects in parentheses to write each sentence two ways.

> Mark ran into. (a tree, it)
> *Mark ran into a tree.*
> *Mark ran into it.*

1. Jack cheats on. (the tests, them)
2. She looked for. (her son, him)
3. I'll get on. (the horse, it)
4. I'm counting on. (John, him)
5. Don't fall for. (his lie, it)
6. I dealt with. (the problem, it)

8.4 Nouns made from phrasal verbs

Many phrasal verbs can be *turned into* nouns. What does a teacher *hand out*? *Handouts.* When a car *breaks down* and traffic *backs up,* what's your excuse for being late to work? A *breakdown* on the highway caused a big *backup.* When you *screw up* at work, why is your boss is *pissed off*? Because of your big *screwup.*

Don't tell your students that when a phrasal verb is used as a noun, it's always written as one word. That's often the case, but there's no general agreement about this. Sometimes they're written as one word, sometimes with a hyphen. The idea that phrasal verbs can be used as nouns is what's important here, not hyphens.

sample exercises 3: Decide which word is correct—the phrasal verb or the noun—and underline it. (Here all the nouns are written as one word or with hyphens.)

> I'm going to (<u>stop over</u>/stopover) in Frankfurt.

> I have a (stop over/<u>stopover</u>) in Frankfurt.

1. The salesperson made a (follow up/follow-up) call.
2. You should (back up/backup) your important computer files.
3. The company is going to (lay off/layoff) 5,000 workers.
4. I had a (get together/get-together) at my house.

8.5 Adjectives made from phrasal verbs

It is very common to use some phrasal verbs as adjectives. When you *space out* and drive right past your exit on the interstate and *end up* in the middle of nowhere, what was the problem? You were *spaced-out.* When you *lock* yourself *out* your house, what's the problem? You're *locked out.* When you have a big decision to make and have no idea what to do, what's your problem? You're *mixed up.*

Once again, not everyone agrees about whether these should be written as two words, one word or whether they should be hyphenated, and once again, that's not what's important.

What we're seeing here is actually about main verbs in general not just phrasal verbs. All of these adjectives made from phrasal verbs are the past participles of the phrasal verbs. Many past participles, of phrasal verbs and otherwise, are also adjectives. That's something you'll want to talk about with your students when you focus on adjectives and maybe come back to when you get to the passive voice. Sometimes it's easy to confuse participle adjectives with present participles and past participles—but I'm getting way ahead of myself—much more about this later (maybe too much).

sample exercises 4: Write *adj* in the blank if the words in italics are an adjective. Write *v* in the blank if the words in italics are a phrasal verb.

The application isn't *filled out*. ___adj___

I *used up* all the paper in the copier. ___v___

1. Why is Sofia all *dressed up*? Is she going to a party? _____
2. We *fixed up* our old house before we sold it. _____
3. You can't print because your printer's not *turned on*. _____
4. Alan bought a new monitor, but it isn't *hooked up* yet. _____
5. I was really *worn out* after the game. _____
6. The baker really *screwed up*. He used salt instead of sugar in the wedding cake. _____

Chapter 9
Have Got and *Have Got To*

Could you…

- explain what *got* means in *a*?

   a. I have got a dog.

- answer this question: Are *b* and *c* the same?

   b. I have got to go.
   c. I gotta go.

- explain why *d* is not correct but *e* is correct?

   d. She doesn't have got a job.
   e. She doesn't have a job.

9.1 Why an entire chapter on *have got* and *have got to*?

Have got is an idiom and *have got to* is an idiomatic phrasal modal auxiliary verb. Why do I feel like I gotta devote an entire chapter to them? After all, there's another chapter all about modal auxiliary verbs. The reason is that *have got* and *have got to* are both <u>very</u> idiomatic, which makes them extra difficult for students, and they are also <u>very</u> common and therefore <u>very</u> important. I can't exaggerate how important they are (actually I can: They're the most important things in the universe) for students to understand these—for all the four skills but especially for listening comprehension. I have given this lesson many times, and invariably students are interested and grateful for the big boost it gives them in their listening comprehension. Before continuing, make sure your students understand that they never need to use *have got* and *have got to* (which will be a great relief to them), but they absolutely must understand them.

I'm going to tell you a secret. Let's keep it between you and me for now. You can tell your students later but not until we've made them jump through a few hoops. OK, here's the secret: *have got* means <u>exactly</u> the same thing as *have*, and *have got to* means <u>exactly</u> the same thing as *have to*. *Have got* and *have got to* are not informal; they are not slang; they are not "American". *Have got* and *have got to* are perfectly acceptable English used by native English speakers around the world. And they're not just occasionally used in place of *have* and *have to*; they are very often and I believe for many people <u>usually</u> used in place of *have* and *have to*—especially when speaking.

9.2 So what does *got* mean?

So, you may be wondering, just what does *got* mean? Why is it there? Where did it come from? Where did we all come from? What does it all mean? The answer to all of those questions is a mystery, and this isn't the time or place to try to answer them. All I need to say to you for now—all you need to say to your students later—is that *have got* is a very good examples of an idiom—and by that we grammar weenies mean a word or combination of words that cannot be figured out simply by knowing what the words mean—the words have a *figurative* meaning that is separate from their *literal* meaning. Native speakers know the figurative meaning—for them it's not a problem. They know, for example, that *as well* means *also*, that *so long* means *good bye* and that *how come* means *why*. They're not confused because the literal meanings of these words have nothing to do with what we use them for. There are many of these in English. We saw that many phrasal verbs are idiomatic: *Fall down* isn't too hard for students to figure out, but why should *put up with* mean *tolerate*? How could any student understand the meaning of *put up with* without learning the figurative meaning? The literal meaning doesn't make any sense at all.

So *have got* and *have got to* are idioms. Got it? (And by that, of course, I really mean *Have you got it?*)

OK, now remember what I just said—all of this is top secret for the moment. Don't explain anything to your students yet. You're going to have some fun with them first.

9.3 Bewilder your students (for a good cause).

Write these two sentences on the board:

   I have a car.   I have got a car.

Now ask your students to explain how these sentences are different. Obviously, the one on the right has *got* in it, but how are they different in meaning? Let your students ponder and puzzle. Let them be baffled and bewildered. Let them talk among themselves. Let them offer suggestions that will all be wrong. The most likely one won't be at all unreasonable—that the sentence on the right is present perfect. It's not unreasonable because in British English, the past participle of *get* is *got*, not *gotten*, as in American English. But it's not present perfect.

This is what we call (jargon alert!) *inductive teaching*. It boils down to giving students examples first and then letting them figure out what it's all about rather than telling them what it's all about first and then giving them examples after. That's what's called *deductive teaching*. The *Could you...* questions that I start every chapter with are an example of inductive teaching. Inductive teaching is student-centered, which is something very important that all supervisors want teachers to be even though nobody has any idea what it means other than putting students in groups so they can yak in their native language. Nevertheless, if anyone asks if you're a student-centered teacher, explode with indignation at the very suggestion that you might not be.

OK. My digression is over and your students are still befuddled. Now it's time to tell them our big secret: these sentences have <u>exactly the same meaning</u>. Let this shocking revelation sink in for a minute and then give them a simplified version of what I said above: *got* means nothing...it's an idiom...what's an idiom...very common...especially in speaking...very important... not slang...don't have to use...must understand...blah, blah, blah. (DO NOT discuss *have got <u>to</u>* yet. One thing at a time.)

At this point your students may be wondering if you are slightly nuts. Maybe you are, but you know what you're talking about here, and you're going to prove it to them by giving them what is a very important part of this lesson—listening practice. But first, remind them that contraction of *have* is *'ve*.

Write several more sentences under the two that you just wrote on the board and underline as shown. Use only the pronouns *I, you, they* and *we*:

<table>
<tr><td>I <u>have</u> a car.</td><td>I <u>have got</u> a car.</td></tr>
<tr><td>I <u>have</u> three children.</td><td>I <u>have got</u> three children.</td></tr>
<tr><td>You <u>have</u> a dictionary.</td><td>You <u>have got</u> a dictionary.</td></tr>
<tr><td>They <u>have</u> a big house.</td><td>They <u>have got</u> a big house.</td></tr>
<tr><td>We <u>have</u> a fat cat.</td><td>We <u>have got</u> a fat cat.</td></tr>
</table>

9.4 Listening practice

Now give your students a good sample of what we native speakers sound like when we actually use *have* and *have got*. Say each sentence as a native speaker would. In the <u>left</u> column, reduce the *h* in *have* to almost nothing, as we native speakers do. (Do not use the contraction *'ve*, since this is very uncommon). Now do the same with the sentences in the right column. Do it several times. Start by pronouncing each word clearly, without contractions, and then get more and more casual, more and more real in your pronunciation—using contractions— so that finally, the *'ve* contraction disappears—in other words, you've gone, for example, from *I have got* to *I've got* to *I got*. That's when you'll see the light go on in your students' faces—the *ah ha!* moment when they get it—when they realize that's what all those native speakers have been saying that they never understood before. Now they'll know why you're making such a BIG GIANT DEAL of this.

Now change the sentences on the board so that all the pronouns are *he* and *she* and every instance of *have* is now *has* and do it all over again only this time the *'s* contraction is <u>not</u> reduced to nothing.

9.5 Grammar stuff

Is that all? Of course not. You need to teach your students some grammar stuff now. Before getting to questions and negatives, you should give them some practice changing sentences from *have* to *have got*. That will seem incredibly simple—just stick *got* in the sentence after *have*—but it won't be as simple as that, and also, you want to keep reminding their ears how we use or don't use contractions and how we make reductions when we speak, so keep modeling these.

sample exercises 1: Change the sentences so that they use *have got*. Use contractions.

> We have a lot of work.
> *We've got a lot of work.*
>
> Larry has a good job.
> *Larry's got a good job.*

1. I have brown hair.
2. He has brown hair too.
3. We have a small house.

4. Paul has a broken arm.
5. You have a big mouth.

9.6 Negative with *have got*

Next, teach your students how to make negative sentences with *have got*. Write sentences with *have* in a column on the left and with *have got* on the right, and then show how they are changed to negative differently:

I <u>have</u> a car.	I <u>have got</u> a car.
→ I <u>don't have</u> a car.	→ I <u>haven't got</u> a car.
We <u>have</u> a fat cat.	We <u>have got</u> a fat cat.
→ We <u>don't have</u> a fat cat.	→ We <u>haven't got</u> a fat cat.
She <u>has</u> a pencil.	She <u>has got</u> a pencil.
→ She <u>doesn't have</u> a pencil.	→ She <u>hasn't got</u> a pencil.
He <u>has</u> a bicycle.	He <u>has got</u> a bicycle.
→ He <u>doesn't have</u> a pencil.	→ He <u>hasn't got</u> a bicycle.

If anyone wants to say *We haven't a…* or *He hasn't a…*, for the sentences on the right, discourage this and see my comments in Section 4.18. Do not let any student say *I've not got…* or *We've not got…* for the sentences on the right. Although these would be correct grammar, this pattern is so uncommon that it is really best avoided.

But strongly encourage your students to use the *'ve* contraction with *have got* and the *'s* contraction with *has got*. <u>Not</u> using these contractions is so rare that it would sound strange not to.

Emphasize that *do, does* and *did* are <u>never</u> used with *have got* (or *have got to*).

sample exercises 2: Change the sentences so that they use *have got*. Use contractions.
My sister doesn't have a computer.
My sister hasn't got a computer.

1. Our house doesn't have a garage.
2. We don't have enough time.
3. Carlos doesn't have a calculator.
4. Tom and Linda don't have any children.
5. The children don't have their homework.

9.7 Questions with *have got*

Next, you're going to teach your students how to make questions with *have got*. Write sentences with *have* in a column on the left and with *have got* on the right, and then show how they are changed to questions differently:

You <u>have</u> a car.	You <u>have got</u> a car.
→ <u>Do</u> you <u>have</u> a car?	→ <u>Have</u> you <u>got</u> a car?
They <u>have</u> a fat dog.	They <u>have got</u> a fat dog.
→ <u>Do</u> they <u>have</u> a fat dog?	→ <u>Have</u> they <u>got</u> a fat dog?
She <u>has</u> a pencil.	She <u>has got</u> a pencil.
→ <u>Does</u> she <u>have</u> a pencil?	→ <u>Has</u> she <u>got</u> a pencil?
He <u>has</u> a bicycle.	He <u>has got</u> a bicycle.
→ <u>Does</u> he <u>have</u> a pencil?	→ <u>Has</u> he <u>got</u> a bicycle?

(If anyone wants to say *Have they a…* or *Has she a…*, discourage this and see my comments in Section 4.18.)

sample exercises 3: Change the questions so that they use *have got*.
Do you have a computer?
Have you got a computer?

1. Do you have enough money?
2. Does Lucy have a problem?
3. Does her house have a basement?
4. Do I have food in my teeth?
5. Does Mark have brown hair?

9.8 *have to = have got to*

Now you're going to do it all over again but with *have got to*. It'll go a lot faster this time though. All the grammar is the same but with the addition of *to*.

But first, what do *have to* and *have got to* mean? Don't forget to explain that. You need to teach them that *have to* and *have got to* are about obligation—something that you have no choice about. It might help if they look up *obligation* in their bilingual dictionaries. It's very likely that some of your students will already know *must*. That'll help them understand the meaning of *have to* and *have got to*. If they already know *should,* and that's very likely, they may mistakenly think that *have to* and *have got to* are the same as *should*. This is a very common misunderstanding. Just tell that that's not true and then focus on making them understand that *have to* and *have got to* have the same meaning as *must*. This is something of an oversimplification, however. It would be counterproductive at this point to tell them that what I just said isn't exactly true. We often use *must, have to* and *have got to* as a strong form of *should*. For example,

9.1 You've really got to see *Zombies Ate My Brain*—it's a fantastic movie!

9.2 Mary keeps telling me how good that restaurant is. I have to go there someday.

9.3 Oh you simply must see Mary's new house—it's fabulous.

Leave that alone for now. It's discussed in Chapter 12. Instead, write this on the board:

> I <u>have</u> <u>to</u> go.   I <u>have</u> <u>got</u> <u>to</u> go.

You've already had your fun asking your students how *I have a car* and *I have got a car* are different, so you can't do that again with these two. They'll know what you're up to. What you're going to do now is dazzle your students with another demonstration of reduction which will once again amaze them when they realize what all those native speakers have been saying that they never understood before.

First, look at your watch and repeat the sentence on the left with urgency and without the *h,* which as you know, is often reduced right out of existence. Now look at your watch again and repeat the second sentence again and again starting with all the words (not contractions) slowly and clearly, then with the contraction but again slowly and clearly, then keep repeating so that eventually the *'ve* contraction disappears entirely and *got to* becomes *gotta,* and then, when you get to *I gotta go,* run out the door! After you come back in, give them some more examples with *gotta*:

9.4 I gotta finish my homework.

9.5 They gotta work tomorrow.

9.6 You gotta pass the test.

Got it?

Now give them examples with *has got to*:

9.7 She's gotta talk to her boss.

9.8 He's gotta make dinner.

9.9 My wife's gotta go to the doctor.

Remind them the *'s* contraction is never silent. We always say it.

Now, be <u>very</u> sure to tell your students two things:

One, that they <u>never</u> have to use *have got to. Have to* is always perfectly OK (and at this time I tell them that *must* is actually much less common for this purpose than *have to*), but they absolutely have got to understand *have got to* (and *gotta*) when they see it and hear it because all native speakers, including all English teachers, use it frequently. If you think I'm exaggerating how common it is, try listening for it in your speech and that of other people. You'll see what I mean.

And two, you have got to tell your students is that *gotta,* while common and OK in informal writing, is <u>not</u> acceptable for any sort of formal, serious writing such as academic papers and business communications.

sample exercises 4: Change the sentences so that they use *have got to.* Use contractions.

> I have to work tomorrow.
>
> *I've got to work tomorrow.*

> Rosa has to do her homework.
> *Rosa's got to do her homework.*

1. I have to take my son to soccer practice.
2. The pilot has to fly to Norway.
3. They have to take a test.
4. Michael has to clean his house.
5. I have to get to work early tomorrow.

9.9 Negative with *have got to*

Next, you're going to teach your students how to make negative sentences with *have got to*. This will be a lot easier than with *have got*. Write sentences with *have to* and *has to* in a column on the left and with *have got to* and *has got to* on the right, and then show them how they are changed to negative differently:

You <u>have</u> <u>to</u> be here at 8:00.	You <u>have</u> <u>got</u> <u>to</u> be here at 8:00.
→ You <u>don't</u> <u>have</u> <u>to</u> be here at 8:00.	→ You <u>haven't</u> <u>got</u> <u>to</u> be here at 8:00.
She <u>has</u> <u>to</u> leave now.	She <u>has</u> <u>got</u> <u>to</u> leave now.
→ She <u>doesn't</u> <u>have</u> <u>to</u> leave now.	→ She <u>hasn't</u> <u>got</u> <u>to</u> leave now.

If anyone wants to say *You haven't to…* or *She hasn't to…*, for the sentences on the left, don't let them—it's so rare that it would sound very strange to a native speaker. And don't let any student say *You've not got to…* or *She's not got to…* for the sentences on the right. Although these would be correct grammar, this pattern is so uncommon that it really should be discouraged.

But strongly encourage your students to use the *'ve* contraction with *have got to* and the *'s* contraction with *has got to*. <u>Not</u> using these contractions is so rare that it would sound strange not to.

sample exercises 5: Change the sentences so that they use *have got to*. Use contractions.
> I don't have to help my father.
> *I haven't got to help my father.*

1. I don't have to go to the meeting.
2. Carlos doesn't have to go to school on Thursday.
3. You don't have to do it.
4. The store doesn't have to return your money.
5. They don't have to get there until 11:00.

9.10 Questions with *have got*

Next, you're going to teach your students how to make questions with *have got to*. Write sentences with *have to* in a column on the left and with *have got to* on the right, and then show them how they are changed to questions differently:

They <u>have</u> <u>to</u> wash the car.	They <u>have</u> <u>got</u> <u>to</u> wash the car.
→ <u>Do</u> they <u>have</u> <u>to</u> wash the car?	→ <u>Have</u> they <u>got</u> <u>to</u> wash the car?
He <u>has</u> <u>to</u> help his sister.	He <u>has</u> <u>got</u> <u>to</u> help his sister.
→ <u>Does</u> he <u>have</u> <u>to</u> help his sister?	→ <u>Has</u> he <u>got</u> <u>to</u> help his sister?

sample exercises 6: Change the questions so that they use *have got to*.
> Do you have to leave now?
> *Have you got to leave now?*

1. Do they have to fly to Beijing?
2. Does she have to be here early tomorrow?
3. Do I have to wear a suit?
4. Does Mary have to pick up her friend at the airport?
5. Does Alan have to wash the car?

What about past? Tell your students that *have got* and *have got to* (along with *must*) are never used in the past. It's a present thing only. Only *have* and *have to* are used in the past. That'll be a relief to them.

9.11 Bad but sadly common grammar

Sadly, many native speakers mangle these two forms into these mutants:

9.10a I don't got...

   b He doesn't got... (or worse yet, *He don't got...*)

9.11a I don't gotta...

   b He doesn't gotta... (or, egad, *He don't gotta...*)

Probably your students will not say any of these or ask about them, so no need to even mention them, but occasionally you have students who've lived among native speakers for a long time and picked up bad habits. Also, you might get some young hotshot who has grown up on American movies, has learned a lot of slang and bad grammar from them, and wants to use it either because he doesn't know any better or because he wants to sound cool.

9.12 Listening practice

Every native speaker says *gotta*, even English teachers, even me, so you gotta let students know how important it is to understand it even if they never use it. And given the extra complicated grammar of *have got* and *have got to,* most never will use it, and that's OK!

9.13 Ellipsis with *have got*

Ellipsis with *have got* and *have got to* is nothing more than the type of short answers we've seen already. That's what short answers (like *Yes, I am, No, he doesn't. Yes, she can,* etc.) are, after all, but examples of ellipsis. So this won't be terribly difficult, but it's good practice for your students:

9.12a Rosa: Have you got a DVD player?

   b Ali: No, I haven't.

   c   = No, I haven't [got a DVD player].

9.13a Tom: Have your children got computers?

   b Sofia: Our son has, but our daughter hasn't.

   c   = Our son has [got a computer], but our daughter hasn't [got a computer].

sample exercises 7: Rewrite the B sentences with ellipsis.

     A: Have Sam and Lucy got a dog?

     B1: No, they haven't got a dog.

     B2: *No, they haven't.*

1. A: Has Linda got a pen?

     B1: No, she hasn't got a pen.

     B2:

2. A: Has your house got a basement?

     B1: Yes, it's got a basement.

     B2:

3. A: Have you and your wife got passports?

     B1: I haven't got a passport, but my wife's got a passport.

     B2:

4. A: Have you got jobs?

     B1: I've got a job, but he hasn't got a job.

     B2:

9.14 Ellipsis with *have got to*

9.14a Tom: Have you got to go to the meeting?

   b Jerry: Yes, I've got to.

   c   = Yes, I've got to [go to the meeting].

9.15a John: Have you and Mary got to work tomorrow?

   b Joe: I've got to, but Mary hasn't got to.

   c   = I've got to [work tomorrow], but Mary hasn't got to [work tomorrow].

sample exercises 8: Rewrite the B sentences with ellipsis.

     A: Have you got to pick up Tom at the airport?

     B1: Yes, I've got to pick up Tom at the airport.

     B2: *Yes, I've got to.*

1. A: Have you got to pay the bill?
   B1: Yes, I've got to pay the bill.
   B2:
2. A: Has your brother got to wear a tie at his new job?
   B1: No, he hasn't got to wear a tie at his new job.
   B2:
3. A: Have Carlos, Alan and John got to be here early tomorrow?
   B1: Carlos and Alan have got to be here early tomorrow, but John hasn't got to be here early tomorrow.
   B2:
4. A: Has Michael got to do it today?
   B1: Yes, he's got to do it today.
   B2:

In reality, native speakers would often answer questions like these with *do* or *does*. There's no rule that a question with *have got* or *have got to* must be answered with *have got* or *have got to* rather than *have* or *have to* (or *do* or *does* in a short answer):

9.16a	Tom:	Have your children got computers?
b	Sofia:	Our son <u>does</u>, but our daughter <u>doesn't</u>.
c		= Our son [has a computer], but our daughter doesn't [have a computer].

9.17a	Larry:	Have you and Mary got to work tomorrow?
b	Carlos:	I <u>do</u>, but Mary <u>doesn't</u>.
c		= I [have to work tomorrow], but Mary doesn't [have to work tomorrow].

Chapter 10
Perfect Tenses

Could you…

- answer this question: Is *a* about the past or the present?

  a.   I have eaten.

- explain how *b* and *c* are different?

  b.   They've been to Rome.
  c.   They've gone to Rome.

- explain the purpose of *ever* in *d*?

  d.   Have you ever flown in a hot air balloon?

- explain how *for* and *since* are used in perfect sentences?
- explain the future perfect?

10.1 *have*: auxiliary verb and main verb

Although by now your students have already seen examples of auxiliary verbs, the use of *have* as an auxiliary verb is still likely to confuse them. Perfect sentences using *have* as both an auxiliary verb and main verb will confuse them even further. And who can blame them for being confused by *I had had lunch,* for example? Be aware of this. Avoid examples with *have* as both an auxiliary verb and main verb until you're far enough into your discussion of the perfect tenses that it won't totally bewilder your students.

10.2 Three types of perfect sentences

I don't mean past, present or future—we'll get to that later. I mean three types of time relationships that are described by the perfect tenses. Perfect sentences show a relationship between

one, an earlier time and a later time:

Figure 10.2a

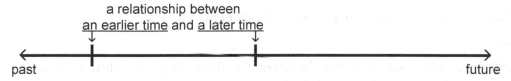

two, two or more earlier times and a later time:

Figure 10.2b

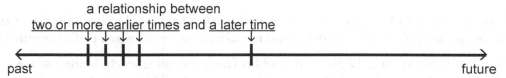

or three, a continuous time and the end of that continuous time:

Figure 10.2c

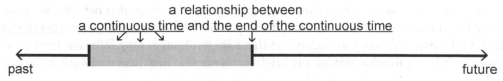

This applies equally to the past perfect, the present perfect and the future perfect. It will help both you and your students to keep this in mind.

10.3 Past participles

But before getting into perfect tenses at all, plan to spend a fair amount of time introducing your students to past participles. This will likely be the first time your students have had to use past participles. Although some of them may be vaguely aware of their existence, assume nothing.

Because the students' grasp of past participles will be a bit shaky at first, avoid overloading them with irregular forms. Keep stressing the need to work hard to memorize irregular past participles. It's especially important that you familiarize your students with *been,* the past participle of *be.* Provide them with a list of irregular verbs, such as the one in Appendix A, and tell them that it's very important to learn them not only for the perfect tenses but for other things that they'll study later. If necessary, motivate them with the magic word: *quiz.*

10.4 Focus on the present perfect (especially) and the past perfect.

Start with and focus on the present perfect (especially) and the past perfect. The future perfect is much less common than the present perfect and past perfect. Many native speakers live their entire lives without using it. I'd recommend budgeting your perfect lesson time like this: 60% for the present perfect, 30% for the past perfect and 10% for the future perfect (if even that much). Don't completely ignore the future perfect, however. Depending on the level of your students, you may want to discuss it after you have finished with the present perfect and past perfect, and you certainly want to be ready if a student asks you about it.

10.5 Three uses of the present perfect

The present perfect (*have* or *has* + past participle) shows a relationship between one or more events or a continuous period of time in the past and the present:

> 10.1   I haven't finished my project yet.
>
> 10.2   We have eaten in that restaurant twice.
>
> 10.3   He has been in the hospital for three days.

▶ **One, to connect a past time and the present**

Figure 10.5a

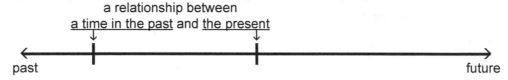

Write this sentence on the board: (Don't use contractions at first—talk about those later.)

> **I have eaten lunch.**

Ask your students whether the sentence is about the past or the present. Let them struggle. Let them ponder. Let them agonize. Let them puzzle. Try not to look too amused. Do not help them!

After a few minutes, some will answer *past,* some *present* and maybe one or two bright students will hesitantly say *both.* Don't tell them!

Now choose a student (let's say her name is Maria), and explain a hypothetical situation to the class: (Use the present tense because this is hypothetically happening right now—you don't want to make this seem like a past perfect situation.)

> I eat lunch at 12:00. Then I visit Maria at 12:30. Maria and her family are eating lunch. Maria asks me to eat lunch with her family. But I ate lunch at 12:00. I am not hungry now. I tell Maria that I am not hungry because I have eaten lunch." (Stress *have eaten,* and repeat the scenario a couple of times.)

Now once again, ask your students whether *I have eaten lunch* is about the past or the present. After a little more pondering, it's time for the major revelation: *I have eaten lunch* is about the past <u>and</u> the present. How can that be? (Ponder, ponder, ponder.) *I have eaten lunch* gives you information about <u>two</u> times and it tells you that there is <u>a connection between them</u>. One, you understand that I ate lunch in the past and two, you understand that I am not hungry <u>now</u>. Why am I not hungry now? Because I ate lunch <u>in the past</u>. Don't forget to acknowledge any bright students who may have said *both* in the first place.

▶ **Two, to connect two or more past times and the present**

Figure 10.5b

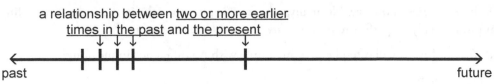

Now write this sentence on the board:

> I have seen that movie four times.

Ask your students to explain the sentence. Some will get that this seems to be about not one time in the past but four times in the past—but what's the connection to the present? In present perfect sentences, the connection to the present can sometimes be a bit vague. Students will often not see why the past simple, *I saw that movie four times,* doesn't have the same meaning. The connection to the present is often simply that *It is true now that…* So in this case, what you are saying is *It is true now that I have seen that movie four times.* Why say this and not *I saw that movie four times*? Perhaps to emphasize your love of that movie, perhaps to emphasize your thorough familiarity with that movie, perhaps to explain why you don't want to go with your friends who have invited you to the cinema to see it with them. In one way or another, the fact that you saw it four times in the past has some connection to the present.

At this point, it's very important to make sure your students understand that when there is not a connection between the past and the present—when we're talking about that past <u>only</u>—we use the past simple. That's often how a conversation flows: from the present perfect to the past simple. For example,

10.4a	Larry:	Do you want have lunch?
b	Mary:	No thanks, I <u>have eaten</u> lunch.
c	Larry:	When did you eat lunch?
d	Mary:	I <u>ate</u> lunch at 12:00.

Another thing to mention is that when there is a specific time reference, the past simple is used. The way to explain this to your students is to tell them that when we say, for example, *last week, ten minutes ago, in 2008, yesterday,* etc., we use the past simple. Don't get into *for* and *since* yet. We'll get to that later.

sample exercises 1: Choose past simple or present perfect. Underline the correct answer.
> Alan (<u>saw</u>/has seen) that movie last week.
> Alan (saw/<u>has seen</u>) that movie many times.

1. I (ate/have eaten) in that restaurant twice since I moved to this city.
2. I (ate/have eaten) in that restaurant twice last week.
3. I (am/have been) here since 1:30.
4. Tom is married now. He (was/has been) married for 17 years.
5. Mary is single now. She (was/has been) married for 12 years.

▶ **Three, to connect a continuous time which started in the past and the present**

Figure 10.5c

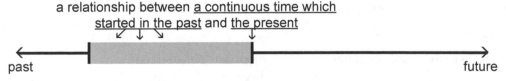

Emphasize that in this case, we are not talking about one or more separate events but a non-stop situation or activity that began in the past and continues to the present. Write these on the board and ask your students to explain the past/present connection: (We'll focus on *for* later, but it's impossible to avoid in these examples, so you may want to jump ahead to Section 10.15 and come back to this afterward.)

> Michael has known David for a long time.
> John has been in the hospital for three days.
> Mark has been studying for two hours.

The answer, of course, is that in each case, the situation or activity described started in the past and continues to the present. It was true or was happening before, and it's true or happening now.

Two verbs you should discuss here are *live* and *work*. Normally, whatever applies to verbs in the present regarding whether they are continuous or not applies equally to perfect tenses, but *live* and *work* are exceptions.

Present perfect sentences with *live* and *work* will often be present simple with no difference in meaning:

10.5a   Mary has been living in Spain for seven years.
    b   = Mary has lived in Spain for seven years.

10.6a   I have been working for the ABC Company for 16 years.
    b   = I have worked for the ABC Company for 16 years.

sample exercises 2: Make one present perfect sentence from the two sentences.
      Larry became a pilot three years ago. He is a pilot now.
      Larry has been a pilot for three years.
      They started waiting for Alan 15 minutes ago. They are waiting for Alan now.
      They have been waiting for Alan for 15 minutes.

1.   Rosa came here 30 minutes ago. She is here now.
2.   I got sick a week ago. I am sick now.
3.   Maria started to clean three hours ago. She is cleaning now.
4.   We bought this car five years ago. We have this car now.
5.   The baby fell asleep two hours ago. The baby is sleeping now.

sample exercises 3: Complete the sentences with present continuous or present perfect continuous. Use contractions.
      I (paint) _____*'m painting*_____ my house now. I _____*'ve been painting*_____ it for two hours.

1.   My mother (read) _____ now. She _____ since 11.00.
2.   The girls (study) _____ in the library now. They _____ for two hours.
3.   I (drive) _____ now. I _____ for five hours, and I'm really tired.
4.   Paul (watch) _____ TV at the moment. He _____ TV all day.
5.   We (look) _____ for John's house. We _____ for it for 20 minutes.

10.6   Mechanics and memorization

You'll want to keep working on getting your students to memorize irregular past participles. Since they're somewhat random in nature, there's not much you can tell them (other than "The irregular past participle quiz is next week") that will help, but one thing I always point out is that all irregular verbs with *-ought* and *-aught* in the past tense are exactly the same in the past participle.

Also, we haven't said anything about questions, negatives and short answers. That's because these should be fairly simple at this point, except for one involving contractions. Your students have seen the inversion question pattern before: *He has…/ Has he…?* That will be easy. But what about contractions and short answers?

10.7   Contractions and short answers

Once again, stress that it is never necessary to use contractions, but it is absolutely necessary to understand them. Explain the two ways to make contraction with *have* and *has,* but emphasize that one of the two ways is <u>much</u> more common than the other.

Emphasize that *do, does* and *did* are <u>never</u> used for questions or negatives sentences with the perfect tenses.

10.8   Present perfect contractions

● **affirmative**	● **negative** (more common)	● **negative** (less common)
I've	I haven't	I've not
You've	You haven't	You've not
It's	It hasn't	It's not
She's	She hasn't	She's not
We've	We haven't	We've not
They've	They haven't	They've not

As for short answers, remind them that contractions are used only in negative short answers: (In other words, we would never answer, *Yes, I've* or *Yes, she's.*)

- **negative** (more common)
  No, I haven't.
  No, you haven't.
  No, it hasn't.
  No, she hasn't.
  No, we haven't.
  No, they haven't.

- **negative** (less common)
  No, I've not.
  No, you've not.
  No, it's not.
  No, she's not.
  No, we've not.
  No, they've not.

Write these on the board, and ask the students to explain *he's* in both sentences:

> He's sick.
>
> He's eaten.

Of course, one is *He is* and the other is *He has*. You need to remind students that *'s* is the contraction of both *is* and *has*. Until now, the students have seen *'s* only as the contraction of *is*. That *'s* is also the contraction of *has* will be something new to them. They'll understand easily enough when you explain it, but you need to emphasize the need to remember this when they are reading or listening.

The fact that many past participles are also participle adjectives, so that *He's finished* could be both *He is finished* or *He has finished,* is a can of grammatical worms you don't want to open now. Better to wait until you're teaching adjectives. (And to review it when you get to the passive.)

sample exercises 4: Change the sentences to questions.
> You've finished.
> *Have you finished?*

1. You've ridden a donkey.
2. They have gone home.
3. She's fallen asleep.
4. Sarah and her sister have seen that movie.
5. Francesca has painted her room pink.

sample exercises 5: Change the sentences to negative. Use contractions.
> The children have cleaned their room.
> *The children haven't cleaned their room.*

1. They've been there before.
2. She's met him.
3. Jim's worn his new shoes.
4. We've had dinner.
5. I've taught this class.

sample exercises 6: Change the sentences from past simple to present perfect. Use contractions.
> Mark drove to New York.
> *Mark's driven to New York.*
>
> They had a party.
> *They've had a party.*

1. She threw the ball.
2. Sofia wrote a letter.
3. We did our work.
4. The show began.
5. They took a taxi.

sample exercises 7: Complete the sentences with *have* or *has* and the correct form of the verbs. Some are negative.

be	do	fall	~~give~~	go	read

1. I don't know what my grade is. The teacher ____*hasn't given*____ it to me.
2. This is a great book. _____ you _____ read it?
3. Look! A tree _____ _____ on that house.

4. You are so lazy! You _____ _____ anything all day!
5. How long _____ your sister _____ married?
6. Where _____ she _____? I can't find her anywhere.

10.9 Three ways to use the past perfect

The past perfect (*had* + past participle) shows a relationship between one or more events or a continuous period of time in the past with a later time in the past. Be aware that when we use the past perfect, we often use it with dependent clauses, independent clauses and subordinating conjunctions. You probably haven't done any of that with your students yet. All of it is covered in great detail in Chapter 16, but I wouldn't jump ahead to that with your students, though you may want to yourself. For now, I'd give your students a short lesson on *before*, *after* and *because* (without using the terms *dependent clause*, *independent clause* or *subordinating conjunction*!) as they are used in past perfect sentences. Put examples like these on the board demonstrating the two patterns:

Because I had studied,   **I knew the answer.**
Before/After/Because + past perfect clause,   past simple clause. (Point out the comma.)

I knew the answer   **because I had studied.**
past simple clause   *before/after/because* + past perfect clause. (no comma)

Once you've done that, discuss these examples:

10.7   Larry told me that he had finished his homework.

10.8   He had been sick for six months before he died.

10.9   I was very angry when they finally arrived because I had been waiting for a long time.

▸ **One, to connect an earlier past time with a more recent time in the past**

Figure 10.9a

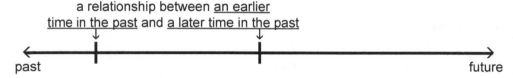

To teach the past perfect, take the scenario you created to teach the present perfect and transfer it to the past. Quickly review the Maria/lunch scenario, and then (making sure that *I have eaten lunch* is still on the board) ask the students to imagine that you are talking about the same events, but it all happened yesterday (or in other words, it's now tomorrow, and today's events are now in the past). Retell the story, but in the past:

> Yesterday I ate lunch at 12:00. Then yesterday I visited the home of Maria at 12:30. Maria and her family were eating lunch. Maria asked me to eat lunch with her family. But I ate lunch at 12:00. I was not hungry at 12:30. I told her I was not hungry because I had eaten lunch." (Stress *had eaten*, and repeat the scenario a couple of times.)

▸ **Two, to connect two or more past times and a more recent time in the past**

Figure 10.9b

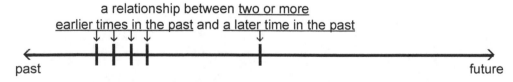

10.10   John had failed the exam four times before he passed it.

10.11   After Sofia had looked at five houses for sale, she bought a house on Main Street.

Often, however, because *before* or *after* make the order of events clear, native speakers use the past simple instead of the past perfect:

10.12   John failed the exam four times before he passed it.

10.13   After Sofia looked at five houses for sale, she bought a house on Main Street.

▶ **Three, to connect a continuous time and a more recent time in the past**

Figure 10.9c

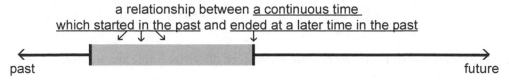

a relationship between <u>a continuous time</u>
<u>which started in the past</u> and <u>ended at a later time in the past</u>

past   future

10.14   When the ABC Company went out of business, I had been working there for 10 years.

10.15   Larry had been sleeping for 12 hours before he finally woke up.

10.16   After being married for five years, Sarah and Tom got divorced.

10.10 Past perfect contractions

Nothing new here except for *had* replacing *have* and *has*:

• **affirmative**	• **negative** (more common)	• **negative** (less common)
I'd	I hadn't	I'd not
You'd	You hadn't	You'd not
It'd	It hadn't	It'd not
She'd	She hadn't	She'd not
We'd	We hadn't	We'd not
They'd	They hadn't	They'd not

As for short answers, remind your students that contractions are used only in negative short answers: (In other words, we would never answer, *Yes, I'd* or *Yes, she'd.*)

• **negative** (more common)	• **negative** (less common)
No, I hadn't.	No, I'd not.
No, you hadn't.	No, you'd not.
No, it hadn't.	No, it'd not.
No, she hadn't.	No, she'd not.
No, we hadn't.	No, we'd not.
No, they hadn't.	No, they'd not.

sample exercises 8: Change the sentences from present perfect to past perfect. Use contractions.
> I've been to France.
> *I'd been to France.*

1. She hasn't left yet.
2. He's lived in Chicago since 1985.
3. They've already had dinner.
4. I've never been to Timbuktu before.
5. We've never driven on that road.

sample exercises 9: Change the sentences to questions.
> She'd just left.
> *Had she just left?*

1. They'd had breakfast.
2. He had given her some money.
3. You'd been reading.
4. Tom had already arrived.
5. Sofia had just gone to bed.

sample exercises 10: Change the sentences to negative. Use contractions.
> Mike had done it before.
> *Mike hadn't done it before.*

1. Maria had spoken with her sister.

2. I'd told her the answer.
3. They'd been watching TV.
4. We had taken the bus.
5. They'd done it already.
6. Paul had gone home.

sample exercises 11: Complete the sentences with *had* and the correct form of the verbs. Some are negative.

~~build~~   do   fall   ride   see   tell

1. I was surprised when Carlos told me that he ____*had*____ ____*built*____ his house by himself.
2. Mary didn't know where John was. She _____ _____ him.
3. I _____ _____ a camel only one time in my life.
4. My teacher was angry because I _____ _____ my homework.
5. _____ you _____ in love before?
6. My wife didn't know that I lost my job. I _____ _____ her yet.

10.11 Past perfect used to show causality

(jargon alert!) *Causality?* That's a fancy way to talk about a *cause and effect relationship* (which is a fancy way to talk about using *because* to explain why something happened). You've already discussed *because,* and your students should already understand it, but it wouldn't hurt to focus on it and do the really useful exercise below. You should stress the importance of using nouns in the first clause and pronouns in the second:

10.17a   Because <u>Tom</u> had been there many times before, <u>he</u> didn't get lost.
   b   = <u>Tom</u> didn't get lost because <u>he</u> had been there many times before.

10.18a   <u>The children</u> were very tired because <u>they</u>'d been playing soccer for three hours.
   b   = Because <u>the children</u> had been playing soccer for three hours, <u>they</u> were very tired.

sample exercises 12: Write past perfect sentences as in the example. Be careful to put nouns and pronouns in the correct positions.

> Mary forgot to bring cash. Because of this, she couldn't pay for her lunch.
> *Mary couldn't pay for her lunch because she had forgotten to bring cash.*

1. Larry's car broke down. Because of this, he was late for work.
2. Sofia went to bed. Because of this, I didn't talk to her when I called.
3. Bill didn't study for the test. Because of this, he failed it.
4. I forgot to bring my lunch to work. Because of this, I was hungry all day.
5. I didn't pay attention to the teacher. Because of this, I didn't know what to do.
6. She hadn't brought her ID. They wouldn't let her in the bar.

10.12 Three uses of the future perfect (in case your students aren't totally confused already)

The future perfect (*will have* + past participle) is <u>much</u> less common than the past perfect and present perfect. Many, maybe most, native speakers of English go through their entire lives without using it, but it's not totally extinct, and it does come in handy sometimes, so it's something you should at least spend a little time on, and it's certainly something you should be prepared to explain if you're asked about it.

Explain that the future perfect is used to describe a relationship with one time in the future and another time that is also in the future but will be in the past at a future time. Confusing enough? It'll confuse your students too. Let's imagine, for example, two future events: taking the final exam and graduating. Right now, they're both in the future, but on the day I graduate, that final exam will be in the past: *When I graduate, I will (already) have taken the final exam.*

My advice is to cover the future perfect only briefly. Spend 90% or more of your time on the past perfect and present perfect and make your students understand that these are what they should focus on. As with the past perfect, we're getting a little ahead of ourselves grammarwise—using grammar not discussed until Chapter 16. Keep it simple for now. The future perfect isn't worth confusing your students with now by jumping ahead to what will be a pretty difficult topic. Just explain that we use time references like *when, by the time, in July, at that time, next year, before, after, as of,* etc., to indicate the future with the future perfect. If necessary, point out that when those future time references are used in a dependent clause, the dependent clause is in the present tense. You should point out that it's very common to use *already* with the future perfect.

▶ **One, to connect an earlier time in the future with a later past time in the future**

Figure 10.12a

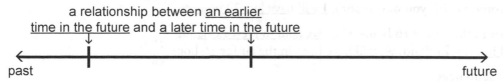

10.19   The movie will have started by the time we get to the theater. (If you use *by the time* in your example, be ready to explain it.)

10.20   It's too late to go to the bank. When you get there, it will already have closed.

▶ **Two, to connect two or more times in the future and a later past time in the future**

Figure 10.12b

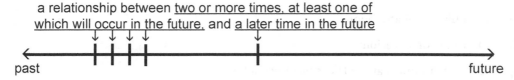

10.21   When we go to Las Vegas next month, we will have been there six times.

10.22   Next semester, I will have taught this class four times.

▶ **Three, to connect a continuous time in the future and a later time in the future**

Figure 10.12c

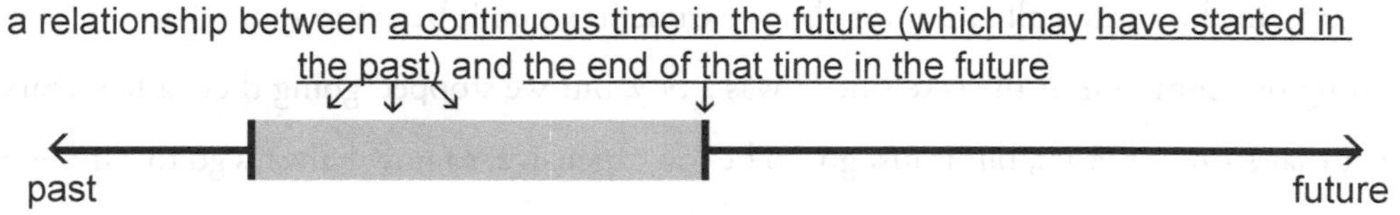

a relationship between <u>a continuous time in the future (which may have started in the past)</u> and <u>the end of that time in the future</u>

past   future

10.23   My wife and I will have been married for 25 years on August 19.

10.24   I will have been working here for five years as of next Tuesday.

10.13 Future perfect contractions

It is <u>not</u> common to use contractions with the future perfect. People say *I will have* rather than *I'll have, I will not have* rather than *I'll not have/I won't have,* etc. I suppose the reason for this is that the speaker doesn't want to confuse the listener any more than necessary with this rare grammatical structure or maybe it's to be sure to get full credit for using it. This is not something to spend more than a few minutes of class time on.

sample exercises 13: Complete the sentences with the future perfect. Some are negative.

      We've lived in this city for 14 years, so next year we _____*will have lived*_____ here for 15 years.

1.   I'm sick. I got sick six days ago, so tomorrow I _____ sick for one week.
2.   It's 2:00. I want to go home at 4:00, but it will take me three hours to finish my work. I can't leave at 4:00 because I _____ my work yet.
3.   I've been waiting for 55 minutes. In five minutes, I _____ for one hour.
4.   I always get to my office at 8:30, so if you call me at 8:15. I _____ there yet.
5.   My parents were married 39 years ago, so next year they _____ married for 40 years.

10.14 Past perfect and future perfect tenses and reversible clauses

To give your students a little more practice, you might want to review how sentences with dependent clauses can be reversed by rewriting a few of the examples. (If you're not sure what a dependent clause is, see Section 16.13 and Appendix E.) Point out that a comma is used only when the dependent clause comes first (or as we grammar weenies say, is *fronted*):

10.25a   The children had been playing baseball all afternoon <u>when it began to rain</u>.
    b   = <u>When it began to rain</u>, the children had been playing baseball all afternoon.

10.26a   I ran into a tree because <u>I had been talking on my cell phone</u>.

    b   = Because <u>I had been talking on my cell phone</u>, I ran into a tree.

10.27a   <u>I will have lost 20 pounds</u> by the time I come to visit you next month.

    b   = By the time I come to visit you next month, <u>I will have lost 20 pounds</u>.

10.28a   We will have been in the air for 16 hours <u>when we land in New Zealand</u>.

    b   = <u>When we land in New Zealand</u>, we will have been in the air for 16 hours.

10.15 Continuous perfect sentences

By now your students should understand continuous sentences fairly well, though as always, you should never assume anything, so it wouldn't hurt to do a quick review. What will be new to the students is the use of *been* with the *-ing* form of the verb (aka *the present participle,* but don't confuse them with that) in continuous perfect sentences.

▶ Present perfect continuous

Sometimes present perfect sentences are used to talk about an activity that has been continuous up to the present time:

10.29   He's been studying for two hours.

10.30   Larry's been working on his car all afternoon.

or a repeated past action that still occurs on occasion:

10.31   We have been spending our summers at the lake since I was a boy.

10.32   I've been shopping at that store for years.

▶ Past perfect continuous

A past perfect form of these sentences would often be used with an adverb clause or in a compound sentence:

10.33   He'd been studying for two hours when the library closed.

10.34   Larry had been working in the garden all afternoon, but he came in when it began to rain.

10.35   We had been spending our summers at the lake since I was a boy, but we stopped going there a few years ago.

10.36   I'd been shopping at that store for years, but it just got to be too expensive, so now I always go to a different store.

▶ Future perfect continuous

You might want to discuss continuous future perfect sentences if you have extra time and some really motivated and capable students, but it could be easily skipped:

10.37   I will have been working in this factory for 35 years by the time I retire next year.

10.16 *for* and *since*

A lesson on *for* and *since* should always be a major part of any discussion of perfect tenses. This will be surprisingly difficult for some students, so the best thing to do is write this on the board and review it again and again:

       for <u>how much time</u>   since <u>the start of the time</u>

and then give them several examples (*since* will be a little more difficult for them):

       for <u>how much time</u>   since <u>the start of the time</u>
            ↓   ↓

       for three years   since 1959

       for two minutes   since March

       for a long time   since yesterday

       for years   since last week

       forever   since this morning

       since she was 18 years old   since I got married

It's the *since* business that will be the most difficult, so really work on it. What will confuse students is that some of this language doesn't leap out at them as *the start of a time*. Obviously, language, for example, like *2009, October 19, last year,* etc. clearly refers to a time in the past, but for many students, language like this:

10.38a   since <u>we were young</u>

    b   since <u>she moved here</u>

    c   since <u>they were in high school</u>
    d   since <u>Christmas</u>
    e   since <u>breakfast</u>

will be more difficult. These aren't so obvious, so work on it!

sample exercises 14: Choose *for* or *since*.

    The baby has been asleep _____*since*_____ 3:00.

    The baby has been asleep _____*for*_____ two hours.

1. I've lived here _____ a year.
2. She has worked there _____ February.
3. The children haven't eaten _____ breakfast.
4. I haven't changed my car's oil _____ six months.
5. Noura hasn't called me _____ last week.
6. I haven't seen her _____ a long time.
7. They have been in the waiting room _____ only a few minutes.

10.17 *just, yet* and *already*

Always include *just, yet* and *already* in your perfect tense lesson:

▶ *just*

Explain that *just* is used to say that something happened <u>only a short time ago</u>:

    10.39   I've just seen a ghost.

    10.40   I called her, but she'd just left.

Say that *just* is placed between *have, has* or *had* and the verb. Be sure not to tell your students that a short time ago is, for example, *five minutes ago*, etc. What would be considered a short time ago depends on the situation—it could be minutes, hours, days, weeks…you get the idea.

▶ *yet*

Yet is used to say that something hasn't happened, but that it is (or was) expected to happen. (You may have to explain the meaning of *expect*.) The idea that it's something that, even though it has not happened, is something you are sure will happen, is always difficult. For example, you wouldn't say *I haven't been to the Moon yet* because you will never go to the Moon. *Yet* is placed after *not* or more commonly at the end of a sentence or clause containing a perfect tense:

▷ **Simple sentence**

    10.41a   I have not <u>yet</u> eaten lunch.
        b   I have not eaten lunch <u>yet</u>.

▷ **Compound sentence (two independent clauses joined by a conjunction)**

    10.42   I haven't seen that movie <u>yet</u>, but I will see it soon.

    10.43   She has finished her classes, but she hasn't taken her final exams <u>yet</u>.

▷ **Complex sentence (an independent clause and a dependent clause joined by a subordinating conjunction)**

    10.44   We hadn't started eating <u>yet</u> because the rice wasn't ready.

    10.45   Because Mary hadn't passed calculus <u>yet</u>, she couldn't graduate with the rest of her class.

▶ *already*

Already is used to say that something happened before, but that this fact was not known. This can also be hard for students to understand. Use your bilingual dictionary, encourage students to use theirs, and don't believe the nonsense that students should never use bilingual dictionaries:

    10.46a Mother: Turn off the TV and do your homework.
        b Son: I've already done my homework.

Say that *already* is placed between *have, has* or *had* and the main verb. Like *yet*, it can be used in any perfect sentence or clause.

As for discussing *just, already* and *yet* with the future perfect, the future perfect is so rarely used that's it not worth the time it would take, but if you have unlimited time, go for it!

sample exercises 15: Complete the conversations with *just, already* or *yet*. There may be more than one good answer.

1. A: When are you going to do your homework?
   B: I've _____ done it. I did it three hours ago.
2. A: Have you begun working on your project _____?
   B: Yes, I have. I started it last night.
3. A: Hello, may I speak with Maria please?
   B: Sorry, she was here five minutes ago, but she's _____ left.

10.18 *ever*

Ever must also be part of your perfect tense lesson. On the board write a few present perfect questions, for example,

> Have you eaten Ethiopian food?
> Has she flown in a hot air balloon?
> Have you been to the zoo?

and then change them like this:

> Have you <u>ever</u> eaten Ethiopian food?
> Has she <u>ever</u> flown in a hot air balloon?
> Have you <u>ever</u> been to the zoo?

Now ask your students how the two groups of sentences are different (in meaning—obviously there is an additional word in the second group). Let them puzzle and ponder for a minute or so, and then tell them that there is <u>no</u> difference between the two groups. So what is the purpose of *ever*? *Ever* simply makes it clear that we are asking about all time and not just today or recently. In some cases, this is obvious, but in others it isn't, so *ever* is often used.

For past perfect sentences with ever, simply change some of the examples so that they are past perfect:

> Had you <u>ever</u> eaten Ethiopian food?
> Had she <u>ever</u> flown in a hot air balloon?
> Had you <u>ever</u> been to the zoo?

You might mention that it would be very common to use *before* in sentences like these.

Ever is about meaning, not grammar. Often, when the meaning is clear, there is no need for *ever* and many native speakers wouldn't use it. *Ever* is used when there is a need for clarity of meaning, not to satisfy some grammatical requirement. Also, in informal English, many native speakers would use the past simple:

10.47   Did she ever fly in a hot air balloon?

10.48   Did you ever eat sushi before you went to Japan?

10.49   Did you ever go to the zoo?

So what about this? It's not the best grammar, but that's reality. Normally, I'm all in favor of teaching what real native speakers say—correct or not, but in this case I wouldn't confuse students with this. They're confused enough already, and besides, if they heard a native speaker say something like this, it wouldn't be hard to understand. But what about teaching students grammar that is totally wrong, like *He don't*? What is your goal? Is it to teach students to speak only perfect English so they can communicate only with other speakers of perfect English in a perfect world? I think you know the answer to that question. Ideally, your students will learn and use only perfect English, but they need to be prepared for the real world where native speakers routinely use informal, casual and sometimes just plain wrong grammar.

sample exercises 16: Use *ever* and the words in parentheses to make present perfect questions.
> (you, see, that movie)
> *Have you ever seen that movie?*

1. (John, write, a book)
2. (your father, drive, a truck)
3. (you, be to, Japan)

4. (Carlos, read, this book)
5. (you, have, a broken heart)

10.19 *been to*

Been to is highly idiomatic (and you do know what that means, don't you?) and absolutely must be part of your present perfect lesson. When discussing going to a place and having returned from that place, it is very common to use *been to* in past perfect and present perfect sentences:

10.50   I've never been to Poland.

10.51a   John: Have you ever been to Peru?
    b   Mary: No, I haven't, but I've been to Bolivia.

10.52   We'd never been to that restaurant, but last night we went there, and the food was terrible!

If a student asks, be ready to explain that this is an idiom which is used <u>only</u> with past perfect and present perfect sentences.

Sometimes (and many grammar books make a big deal of this), there is a difference between *been to* and *gone to*. The difference is that *been to* implies that a person has returned from a place, but *gone to* implies that he or she is still there.

sample exercises 17: Complete the sentences with words from this list.

am	~~are~~	been	been	been
did	~~doing~~	go	have	have
have	have	reading	went	

Jim: Hi Bob, What _____*are*_____(1) you _____*doing*_____(2)?
Bob: Hi Jim, I _____(3) _____(4) a book about India. _____(5) you
    ever _____(6) to India?
Jim: Yes, I _____(7). India is a very interesting country.
Bob: When _____(8) you _____(9) there?
Jim: I _____(10) to India three years ago.
Bob: What about Nepal? _____(11) you ever _____(12) there?
Jim: No, I _____(13) never _____(14) to Nepal.

10.20 *not* vs. *never*

Explain that in short negative answers, *not* is used,

10.53a   David: Have you ever eaten to Ethiopian food?
    b   Carlos: No, I haven't.

but in long negative answers, it's common to use *never* (or *ever*):

10.54a   Ali: Had she ever flown in a hot air balloon?
    b   Noura: No, she hadn't flown in a hot air balloon.
    c   = No, she had never flown in a hot air balloon. (more common)
    d   = No, she hadn't ever flown in a hot air balloon. (less common)

Don't even think about discussing *ever* with the future perfect.

10.21 Listening

It's very important to give your students practice hearing how native speakers use the past perfect and present perfect outside of the classroom. Emphasize that native speakers almost always use contractions when they speak and that the contractions *'s*, *'ve* and *'d* are very hard to hear when people speak quickly and casually. I will often, toward the end of a grammar lesson, simply read aloud from whatever examples are at hand—examples and exercise in the textbook and/or on the board in a way that makes no concession to the students but are just as fast and reduced as if I were talking to another native speaker. Do this and repeat, repeat, repeat while they read along and train their ears. Students love this. Do it a lot!

10.22 Ellipsis with perfect tenses

10.55a   We've been to Tibet. Have you?
    b   = We've been to Tibet. Have you [been to Tibet]?

10.56a   We've been to Tibet. Have you been?

   b   = We've been to Tibet. Have you been [to Tibet]?

10.57a   Sofia's eaten pineapple pizza, but we haven't.

   b   = Sofia's eaten pineapple pizza, but we haven't [eaten pineapple pizza].

10.58a   I'd heard that joke before, and Mary had too.

   b   = I'd heard that joke before, and Mary had [heard that joke before] too.

sample exercises 18:   Write the ellipted words.

    The boys have cleaned their room, but the girls haven't [*cleaned their rooms*   ].

1.   I haven't been there. Have you been [_____]?
2.   I haven't been there. Have you [_____]?
3.   John's finished dinner, but Mary hasn't [_____].
4.   Linda's been studying all day, but Sofia hasn't been [_____].
5.   Linda's been studying all day, but Sofia hasn't [_____].
6.   I'd heard about the change, but I didn't know if he had [_____].

Chapter 11
Adjectives

Could you...

- explain the difference between *embarrassed* and *embarrassing* in *a* and *b*?

    a. I was embarrassed.
    b. It was embarrassing.

- explain *c* to a student? Why *got*?

    c. I got used to it.

- explain whether *closed* in *d* is an adjective or a verb?

    d. The door was closed.

- explain how *e* and *f* are different?

    e. I saw a man-eating alligator.
    f. I saw a man eating alligator.

- explain whether *g* is correct or incorrect, and if it is incorrect, why?

    g. I feel badly.

- explain whether *h* is correct or incorrect, and if it is incorrect, why?

    h. I feel good.

- explain how a noun can be used as an adjective?

11.1 Two basic patterns of adjective use

How hard can it be to teach words like *good, bad, hot, cold, happy, angry, big, small, tall* and *short*? Harder than you think. After making sure your students know what adjectives are, which they very likely do by the time you actually get around to focusing on them (but assume nothing!), the first thing to do is to teach your students the two basic patterns of adjective use:

- **before nouns**
    This is <u>hot coffee</u>.
    My son's got a <u>new job</u>.
    He is a <u>good dancer</u>.
    They have a <u>big house</u>.
    I saw a <u>pink elephant</u>.
    Mary <u>seems angry</u>.
    Your hair <u>looks beautiful</u>.
    She <u>became sick</u>.
    Larry <u>got ready</u>.

- **after linking verbs (aka copular verbs)**
    The water <u>is cold</u>.
    The flowers <u>smell good</u>.
    I <u>feel hot</u>.
    The cake <u>tastes delicious</u>.
    The music <u>sounds wonderful</u>.

11.2 Before a noun

An adjective before a noun is pretty basic. One thing to mention is that the noun is (jargon alert!) *stressed*. That means the intonation (the pitch, or level, of the voice) is higher when we say the noun than it is when we say the adjective. Also, depending on the native language of your students, you might need to explain that adjectives in English don't need to agree with person or gender or number, but this is very seldom a problem.

11.3 After a linking verb (aka copular verb)

So what are linking verbs, and why are they also called *copulas* (aka *copulative verbs* or *copular verbs*)? Is *copula* related to *copulate*? Yes, it is (and why are you thinking about that?) because the idea is *connecting* or *joining*, and isn't that what copulating is all about? Think of them as all being some kind of weird equals sign. You're saying that what is on the left of the linking verb is equal to what is on the right. It's kind of obvious with *be*. If you say *He is happy*, you're essentially saying *he = happy*, and if *he = happy*, then logically, *happy = he*. Do the math—*he* and *happy* are one and the same. You can switch sentences with linking verbs around, and they still make sense and have the added benefit of making you sound like Yoda:

11.1   Cold is the water.

11.2   Delicious tastes the cake.

11.3   Sick became she.

11.4   Powerful is the Force.

Nobody talks this way normally, and certainly don't explain any of this to your students, but I want you to see how these are sort of like algebra: If X = 3 then 3 = X. As you can see, linking verbs can relate to the senses, and most are pretty straightforward—*taste, smell, sound, look*—but some will take a bit more effort to teach.

Feel has several meanings, but the one that concerns us here is *to have an emotion, quality or internal sensation*: *I feel angry, Your skin feels soft.* We use adjectives to describe these emotions, qualities or internal sensations, not adverbs, so no matter how many times you hear people say *I feel badly*, it's wrong and now you know it's wrong. (Unless they mean that the nerves in their fingertips are malfunctioning.) *I feel bad* is what's correct. Also correct is the opposite of *I feel bad, I feel good.*

Well is confusing to native speakers too. It's an adverb, of course: *She sings well,* but it's also an adjective meaning *not sick,* which is why *I don't feel well* means *I feel sick.*

Seem seems as if it should be easy to teach, but how do you explain the difference between these?

11.5a   She looks angry.
    b   She seems angry.

Do your best to convey the idea of nonvisual cues, but if that fails, get out the bilingual dictionary.

It might surprise you that *get* is a linking verb. This use of *get* is extremely important, and I'll talk more about it later in this chapter along with *become*.

Other verbs that are sometimes linking verbs are, in case you're dying to know, *act, remain, continue, stay, grow, appear, turn,* and *prove*. (And let's not forget *wax*. If you're like me, hardly a day goes by when you don't make a comment about someone *waxing philosophical*.)

How much of this grammar are you going to teach to your students? Not much because it really isn't necessary. The grammar here is pretty easy. More useful would be to make sure your students know the meaning of these linking verbs.

sample exercises 1: Complete the sentences.
    Jim's shirt is orange.
    He has an _____*orange shirt*_____.

1. The perfume smells nice.
    It's _____.
2. Your idea sounds good.
    I think it's a _____.
3. This answer seems wrong.
    I think this a _____.
4. Your house looks fantastic.
    You have a _____.
5. The man became very angry.
    He was a very _____.

sample exercises 2: Answer the questions.
    That's terrible music. How does the music sound?
    It sounds terrible.

1. I think Alan might be upset. How does Alan seem?
2. The baby has soft skin. How does the baby's skin feel?
3. Sofia has beautiful hair. How does her hair look?
4. Carlos has stinky feet. How do his feet smell?
5. Larry was not tired before, but now he is tired. How did Larry get?

11.4 Comparative and superlative forms

The biggest part of your adjective lesson is going to be (jargon alert!) *comparative* and *superlative* adjective forms. The basic concept isn't terribly difficult, but as usual, there are plenty of complications. Every adjective can be used as a comparative or superlative:

- **base form**
- **comparative form**
- **superlative form**

tall   taller   tallest

OK, simple enough, but we don't say *expensiver* or *expensivest*, do we? Of course not. We say this:

expensive   more expensive   most expensive

11.5 Opposites of comparative and superlative forms

We'll be talking about opposites too, and there are different ways to do that. Sometimes with an opposite word:

tall	taller	tallest
short	shorter	shortest

sometimes with a negative prefix:

happy	happier	happiest
unhappy	unhappier	unhappiest

sometimes with *less* and *least*:

important	more important	most important
less important	least important	

and yes, we can also say:

unimportant	more unimportant	most unimportant

11.6 Comparative forms

So what's it all about? Comparing, of course. Unfortunately, talking about comparatives and superlatives always ends up being more of a boring spelling lesson than a thrill-packed grammar lesson, but it's unavoidable, so let's get it over with (how's that for an idiom?):

▶ **Comparative adjective forms**

- **one-syllable: add -*er***

cold	colder
nice	nicer (don't double the *e*)
big	bigger (double final consonant when the adjective is consonant-vowel-consonant)

- **two- or more syllables: use *more* or *less***

modern	more/less modern
difficult	more/less difficult
beautiful	more/less beautiful

- **two syllables ending in -*y*: cancel -*y* and add -*ier***

happy	happier
easy	easier
lazy	lazier

- **irregular comparative forms**

good	better
well	better
bad	worse
far	farther/further

With comparative forms, the main thing is to teach your students to use *than*:

11.6   China is bigger <u>than</u> India.

11.7   A BMW is more expensive <u>than</u> a Toyota.

But once that has soaked in and your students think there is no way that you can ever use a comparative without *than,* you have to tell them that this isn't true. Often, the *than*-phrase is ellipted when it is understood. This will confuse students, so be sure to explain it:

11.8a   A: Is the USA bigger than Canada?
   b   B: No, Canada is bigger [than the USA]. (We understand *than the USA,* so there's no need to repeat it.)

Be sure to thoroughly cover irregular comparatives. There aren't many, but they're important. Generally, as adjectives, *farther* and *further* are both used for distance:

11.9   It took five hours to drive there. It was farther/further than I thought.

but there are some other less common ways for which only *further* is used as an adjective. Rather than provide *further* explanation, I refer you to a dictionary. And don't forget, we're talking about adjectives here. *Far* is also an adverb. The differences between *farther* and *further* that you think I'm forgetting relate to the adverb *far.*

Also, what about *well*? *Well* is an adverb, but it's also an adjective meaning *not sick, proper, in good condition.* The comparative form is *better* and the superlative form is *best* (exactly the same as *good,* which would confuse your students if you made a big deal out of it, so don't.) It has a few common uses:

11.10   I am well.

11.11   Get well soon.

11.12   I hope you feel better.

For extra credit, explain this (to yourself, not your students!): *All's well that ends well.*

sample exercises 3: Complete the sentences with the correct comparative form of the adjective in parentheses.
   (bad) My grade was _____*worse*_____ than yours.

1.   (tall) I am _____ than my brother.
2.   (dangerous) Motorcycles are _____ than cars.
3.   (easy) My math class is _____ than my English class.
4.   (well) I didn't feel well yesterday, but I feel _____ today.
5.   (far) My house is close to the lake. Mark's house is much _____.

sample exercises 4: Correct the mistakes in the sentences.

1.   Your house is small. My house bigger.
2.   Is Beijing more small than Shanghai?
3.   Emeralds are more expensives than diamonds.
4.   French food tastes gooder than English food.
5.   I got a bad grade on the Spanish test, but Mary's grade was worser.

11.7 Superlative forms
Superlative adjectives are all about <u>the</u> maximum, <u>the</u> minimum: <u>the most</u>, <u>the least</u>, <u>the biggest</u>, <u>the smallest</u>, etc. Did you notice: *the, the, the, -st, -st, -st*? That's what the following dull lesson is all about:

▶ **Superlative adjective forms**

- **one-syllable: add *-est***
  cold   coldest
  nice   nicest (don't double the *e*)
  big   biggest (double final consonant when the adjective is consonant-vowel-consonant)

- **two- or more syllables: use *most* or *least***
  modern   most/least modern
  difficult   most/least difficult
  beautiful   most/least beautiful

- **two syllables ending in *-y*: cancel *-y* and add *-iest***
  happy   happiest
  easy   easiest

lazy   laziest

- **irregular superlative forms**
  good   best
  bad   worst
  far   farthest/furthest

Grammarwise, it boils down to using *the* with the superlative form:

11.13   Russia is <u>the</u> biggest country.

11.14   Chinese is <u>the</u> most difficult language. (That's what some people say, though this has also been said about Japanese and Arabic. There's no way to determine this scientifically, but it makes for an interesting classroom discussion.)

As for irregular superlatives, *furthest* and *farthest* are both used for distance, though *furthest* sounds snootier and is therefore better (not really). These are really much more common as adverbs, so as far as adjectives, it's time to move on.

sample exercises 5: Complete the sentences with the correct superlative form of the adjective in parentheses.

(tall) Gary is the _____*tallest*_____ player on the basketball team.

1.   (modern) We use only the _____ technology in our company.
2.   (simple) That was the _____ quiz that I've ever taken.
3.   (expensive) What is the _____ car in the world?
4.   (bad) This student's essay is the _____ that I have ever read.
5.   (good) Which student had the _____ score?

sample exercises 6: Correct the mistakes in the sentences.

1.   Is the Amazon River longest river in the world?
2.   Sam is the most crazy guy I know.
3.   I got a 99 on my quiz. That was the goodest score in my class.
4.   My most young child is eight years old.
5.   Yesterday was the worse day of my life.

11.8 Modifying comparative forms of adjectives

Quite a few expressions are used to modify comparative forms. We can say that *Larry is taller than Gary*, but how much taller—*a lot taller?*, *a little taller?*, *a great deal taller?*, *considerably taller?*, *way taller?* We can say that *Chicago is less expensive than New York*, but how much less expensive—*slightly less expensive?*, *not quite as expensive?*, *far less expensive?*, *nowhere near as expensive?*

There are too many expressions such as these for a complete list here, but there is one in my *Rocket English Grammar* (shameless plug).

Exercises for these, as with other expressions we'll talk about, depend more on logic than grammar.

sample exercises 7: Circle the letter of the best answer.

1.   Sarah is 43 years old, and Mary is 11 years old. Sarah is _____ Mary.
     a.   not nearly as old as
     b.   a lot older than
     c.   as old as
     d.   a little older than

2.   Michael's watch cost $150. My watch cost $145. My watch was _____ Michael's.
     a.   not quite as cheap as
     b.   just as cheap as
     c.   a great deal cheaper than
     d.   a bit cheaper than

3.   A mouse is _____ an elephant.
     a.   somewhat smaller than
     b.   as big as
     c.   almost as big as
     d.   nowhere near as big as

4. Linda is 1.7 meters tall, and her brother is 1.7 meters tall. Linda is _____ her brother.
   a. nearly as tall
   b. just as tall as
   c. a great deal cheaper than
   d. not as tall as

11.9 Using superlatives

Is Cairo the biggest city *in Africa*? Is it the biggest city *in the world*, or is it *one of* the biggest cities *in the world*? If not Cairo, what is the biggest city *of all*?

Are Florence and Venice *two of* the most beautiful cities *in Italy*? Absolutely. Are they *the two* most beautiful cities *in Italy*? I think so, but are they *the two* most beautiful cities *in the world*? I don't know. What do you think is the most beautiful city *of all*?

As you can see, we can use superlatives to discuss whether some member of a group is at or near the maximum or minimum quality of that group. And often we make it clear just what that group is—*all the cities in Africa* or *all the cities in the world*.

We talk of *the biggest* or *the smallest* or *the most* or *the least*, but sometimes we talk about *three of the biggest* (three in a larger group, but not necessarily numbers one, two and three) or *the three biggest* (numbers one, two and three). To be clear, we often specify just what the group is that we're talking about with prepositional phrases:

11.15   This is the worst seat <u>on the airplane</u>.

11.16   He is the dumbest guy <u>in my class</u>.

11.17   What is the most expensive car <u>in the world</u>?

or with an adjective clause (aka *relative clause*) starting (optionally) with *that, which, who* or *whom* (more on this in Chapter 13):

11.18   This is one the most boring books <u>(that) I have ever read</u>.

11.19   That's the craziest thing <u>(which) I've ever heard</u>.

11.20   Gary is one of the funniest guys <u>(whom) I know</u>.

11.21   The most interesting person <u>(whom) I have ever met</u> was Larry.

and when we want to be very clear that we mean the entire group and not some subset of that group, we say *of all*.

sample exercises 8: Use the correct maximum superlative form of the adjective in parentheses to complete the sentence.
   (boring) This is one of the _____*most boring*_____ books I have ever read.

1. (hard) One of the _____ classes I ever took was economics.
2. (stupid) That was one of the _____ things that I have ever done.
3. (expensive) Moscow is one of the _____ cities in the world.
4. (large) The _____ ocean of all is the Pacific Ocean.
5. (interesting) I fell asleep during my geometry class. It was one of the _____ classes I have ever been in.

11.10 Participle adjectives

Explain to your students that the past participles (aka *verb 3*, aka *the 3rd form*) of many verbs are also adjectives. Actually, we saw this already when we looked at phrasal verbs. This generally isn't very difficult to teach, though *done* (as in *finished*) and *left* (as in *remaining*) are a bit idiomatic and should be explained:

bored	broken	burned	closed	confused
crowded	divorced	done	dressed	drunk
engaged	finished	forbidden	frightened	gone
hidden	hurt	interested	invited	involved
left	lost	married	mistaken	scared
tired	worried	written		

This is a good time to review past participles too, so to do that and to give your students a little bit of a challenge, how about having them try to tell the difference between past participles and a participle adjectives?

sample exercises 9: Use the past participle of the verb in parentheses to complete the question, and then write *v* if the past participle is being used as a verb or *adj* if the past participle is being used as an adjective.

    (break) I have to wear my old glasses today. I have _____*broken*_____ my new glasses. ___*v*___

    (break) I have to wear my old glasses today. My new glasses are _____*broken*_____. ___*adj*___

1. (worry) Where have you been? We've been very _____ about you. _____
2. (marry) I'm _____, and I have three children. _____
3. (hide) I have _____ a key outside of my house. _____
4. (do) I can't go home yet. I'm not _____ with my work. _____
5. (lose) I've _____ my pen. Have you seen it? _____

11.11 Adjective + preposition combinations

One of the most difficult things for students to learn about adjectives is that many of them are used with prepositions when they are followed by an object. And which preposition? Why do we say *ready <u>for</u>* but *bored <u>with</u>* but *interested <u>in</u>* but *married <u>to</u>* but *good <u>at</u>* but *curious <u>about</u>* but *absent <u>from</u>*? If you know, please tell me, because I don't. Here and elsewhere with prepositions, there's no system to it, so there's nothing you can teach your students other than the need to memorize common adjective + preposition combinations. Here are several examples, and there's a much longer list in Appendix C:

absent from	angry about/with	bad for/at	bored with	confused about
curious about	different from	engaged to	finished with	frightened of
good for/at	happy about	hidden from	interested in	involved in
mad about/at	made of	married to	mistaken about	ready for/to
responsible for	right about	scared of	sure about	tired of
used to	worried about	wrong about		

As you can see, some of the adjectives are shown with two prepositions.

Food is either *good for* you or *bad for* you, but people are either *good at* or *bad at* doing things.

My wife can be *mad at* me but *mad about* what I did. (*Mad* generally means *angry* in American English as opposed to *crazy* in British English.)

Same with *angry*: I can be *angry with* my wife or *angry about* what she did. (Though, of course, it was actually my fault.)

Also, you are *ready for* the test but *ready to* take the test.

In American English we generally say *different from* though many, to the horror or grammarians, say *different than*. The British say *different to*.

Exercises for this are more about reinforcement than right or wrong. You should focus not on teaching new grammar but on teaching your students the meanings of these adjectives and the importance of memorizing the prepositions that are used with them—in other words, memorizing them as a single (jargon alert!) *lexical phrase* (a word or group of words that act as a single unit of meaning).

sample exercises 10: Complete the sentences with the correct adjective + preposition combination from the list above. There may be more than one good adjective + preposition combination for some.

    I am very _____*confused about*_____ my homework. I don't understand it at all.

1. I was _____ class yesterday because I had to go to the doctor.
2. Are you _____ go yet? We need to leave now, or we'll be late.
3. What Mary said to me yesterday was terrible. I am very _____ her.
4. My house is _____ wood.
5. I packed my suitcases yesterday. I'm _____ my vacation.

11.12 *get* used with adjectives

Get is certainly one of the most important verbs in the English language. In addition to its basic meaning, it has enough idiomatic meanings to fill up several pages in a dictionary. Do you *get it*? To your students, these meanings of *get* have a tendency to all sort of blend together into one confusing blob. We've already talked about *have got*, which looks an awful lot like the present perfect, even though it isn't, and if your students were sufficiently motivated by your phrasal verb lesson to study more phrasal verbs, they know that there are dozens that begin with *get*. (I included 22 of them in my *The Ultimate Phrasal Verb Book*.)

So now we come to another vitally important use of *get*: to talk about the <u>change</u> from one adjective to another adjective. *Change* is what it's all about and *change* is what you're going to keep repeating to your students. *Transition* would be a good word to use here, but your students know *change*, and it's not likely they know *transition*, so stick with *change*. (Or have your students look up *transition* in their bilingual dictionaries!)

I'm talking about sentences like these:

11.22   Carlos got sick yesterday.

11.23   My wife gets mad when I forget birthday.

11.24   I'm getting hungry.

11.25   If you say that again, I'll get angry.

11.26   Larry used to be thin, but he's gotten fat.

So why explain this to your students in terms of change? Because you want them to understand that we're not talking about *being sick*, for example, we're talking about the change from *not being sick* to *being sick*.

What I always do when I teach this is write two columns of opposite adjectives on the board. But, you say, not all adjectives have opposites. Right you are. There is no common opposite to *hungry*, for example (Remember, we're keeping it simple here. Nobody ever says *satiated*, and that includes you.) So here is what we do:

<u>before</u>	→	<u>change</u>	→	<u>after</u>
not sick	→	I <u>got</u> sick yesterday.	→	sick
not mad	→	My wife will <u>get</u> mad when [insert joke here].	→	mad
happy				sad
not hungry				hungry
not tired				tired
not ready				ready

Start giving your students before and after examples. Point to the left column and say *I was not sick two days ago*. Next, point to the right column, put your hand on the belly, moan, groan, collapse on the floor, writhe around in agony, pretend you're near death and say *Now, I am sick*. Next, get up off the floor and write *I got sick yesterday* in the center, between the two columns. I draw arrows on the board pointing from left to right to emphasize the idea of changing from one adjective to the opposite adjective.

Again, point to the left column and say *My wife is not mad now*. Next, point to the right column and say *My wife will be mad*. Next, write *My wife will get mad when [insert joke here]* in the center.

Get the idea? Keep doing it with more examples. When coming up with examples, there's a tendency to lapse into making all the examples past simple tense, so try not to do that—vary the tenses, and be sure to include some continuous examples.

sample exercises 11: Complete the sentences with the correct form of *get*.

Mary and Larry _____*got*_____ married last week. Now they're on their honeymoon.

1. I've been working all day. I'm _____ tired. I need to take a break.
2. Did you see Maria? She used to be thin, but she has _____ very fat.
3. My father was driving in Boston, and he _____ totally lost.
4. Don't do that again! If you keep doing that, I'm going to _____ angry.
5. It's 2:30 in the morning, and my daughter still hasn't come home. I'm _____ worried.

11.13 *get used to* and *be used to*

One last thing: If you find yourself with a lot of time to fill, this might be a good time for a side lesson on the very useful but very idiomatic adjective *used to*, as in *I am used to my new job*. If you have students from hot climates now studying somewhere in the USA where it's cold as hell in the winter (or year-round in Canada), you can have fun with examples like *Khalid is from Kuwait. He wasn't used to cold weather, but now he's getting used to it.*

Accustomed to has the same meaning as *used to*, but it's so much less common than *used to* that it's not terribly important to mention it unless your students are Spanish speakers. *Be used to* in Spanish is *estar acostumbrado a*. Obviously, *acostumbrado* is a (jargon alert!) *cognate* (words in different languages with a common origin) of *accustomed*. That'll be easy for them, and they'll want to stick with *accustomed to*. Nothing wrong with that, but make sure they understand that in English *used to* is actually much more common.

11.27a   No estoy acostumbrado al pinche clima frío en este loco país.
   b   = I am not used to the cold weather in this country.

sample exercises 12: Complete the sentences with *used to* or the correct form of *get used to*. Some are negative.

   After we moved to this city, I didn't like it, but now I am _____*used to*_____ it.

   I keep pushing the wrong buttons on my new remote control. I still haven't _____*gotten used to*_____ it.

1.   I've lived in Mexico for many years, so I am _____ spicy food now.
2.   It's been hard to _____ the new system, but little by little, I'm _____ it.
3.   When I moved to England, it was a difficult to drive on the left side of the road. It took me a long time to
     _____ it.
4.   Everyone at my school is confused about the new schedule. We're not _____ it.
5.   It takes a long time to _____ the time change when you fly from the USA to China.

WARNING! *Used to* is a very useful thing to talk about, and this is the logical time to do it, but it could easily lead you into two topics your students might not be ready for:

One is the difference between the adjective *used to* discussed above and the expression *used to* as in *I used to smoke, but now I don't*. This discussion WILL happen, but now is not the time for it. Wait until you get to modals and phrasal modals.

The other is gerunds. It would be very easy to slip in a few examples like this:

11.28   I have a new job. I have to wake up every day at 4:30 in the morning. Before I hated <u>waking up</u> at 4:30, but now
        I am getting used to <u>waking up</u> at 4:30.

But *waking up* is a gerund, and your students haven't gotten to gerunds yet. If you want to give them a little preview, go for it, but otherwise avoid gerunds for now.

11.14   *-ing/-ed* participle adjectives

Is a book *interested* or *interesting*. Are you a *bored* teacher or a *boring* teacher (or maybe both)? Part of every lesson on adjectives should be a discussion of what I call *-ing/-ed* adjective pairs. These pairs of adjectives will be a challenge for your students—more than you think, but if you teach them as I recommend, it will be easier. First of all, <u>all</u> of these adjectives are derived from regular verbs. The *-ing* form is what is called the *present participle* of the verb (a term I don't use with my students), and the *-ed* form is the past participle of the verb.

It's all about *cause* and *effect*. The *-ing* adjective is always the cause, and the *-ed* form is always the effect. But are you going to talk to your students about cause and effect? No. Why confuse them with new terminology? Use *why* and *because*. Put this (or a shortened version) on the board:

<u>why?</u>	<u>because</u>
↓	↓
amazed	amazing
amused	amusing
annoyed	annoying
bored	boring
challenged	challenging
confused	confusing
depressed	depressing
disappointed	disappointing
disgusted	disgusting
embarrassed	embarrassing
excited	exciting
exhausted	exhausting
fascinated	fascinating
frightened	frightening
insulted	insulting
interested	interesting
irritated	irritating
relaxed	relaxing

shocked	shocking
surprised	surprising
threatened	threatening

Ask and answer several questions with these adjectives. Emphasize *why* and *because* and point to adjectives on the left and right as you do it. Of course, this will be as much a vocabulary lesson as a grammar lesson. A lot of these adjectives will be new to your students, so start with adjectives they might already know. You don't need to use the entire list. For example,

> I love this book (holding imaginary book turning page after page), I want to read and read it and read it.
> I am very <u>interested</u> in this book. Why am I <u>interested</u>? Because this book is <u>interesting</u>.

or

> I'm at a movie. This movie is bad, bad, bad (pretend to be dozing off). I am <u>bored</u>. Why am I <u>bored</u>? Because this movie is <u>boring</u>.

Do that a few more times and then encourage them to memorize this: Why *-ed*?, Because *-ing*.

One thing I've found is that speakers of some languages have a hard time distinguishing between *interested/interesting* and *excited/exciting*. If you encounter this, try to explain that *interested/interesting* is intellectual and *excited/exciting* is emotional. Point to your head and say "Interesting is here. This book is very good. I am interested" and then point to my heart and say "Exciting is here. I will go on vacation tomorrow. I am excited." Then reach for the bilingual dictionary.

Sometimes students get the idea that *-ing* adjectives are always about things and *-ed* adjectives are always about people. This is not true, so do not let them get this idea.

Once they've got the basic idea down, go down this list or whatever you're working on and, once again, remember to focus on teaching some new and useful vocabulary.

sample exercises 13: Complete the sentences with the correct form of the adjective.

(surprise) David is an excellent student, so I was very _____*surprised*_____ that he failed the exam.

1. (confuse) I don't understand my homework at all. It's very _____.
2. (embarrass) Everybody laughed when I made a mistake. I was very _____.
3. (embarrass) Everybody laughed when I made a mistake. It was very _____.
4. (excite) I think travel is very _____, and I'm _____ about my trip to Paris next week.
5. (irritate) Sarah did not think my joke about her big feet was funny. She was very _____.

11.15 Nouns used as adjectives (aka compound nouns)

Did you know that a noun can be an adjective? If you've ever talked about a *coffee cup*, a *book store*, a *roommate* or a *school bus*, you've used a noun as an adjective. We do it all the time in English, and it's not hard to teach to your students though you'll need to stress an important point about listening comprehension and pronunciation.

What I do is put a couple of sentences like these on the board. Be sure to stress *big* and *green*:

> I have a <u>big</u> garden.
> That is a <u>green</u> bottle.

Now ask and answer questions like these:

> What kind of garden is it? It's a big garden. I know it's a big garden because *big* is an adjective. And what kind of bottle is it? It's a green bottle. How do I know? Because *green* is an adjective.

Now cross out *big* and write *vegetable*. Then cross out *green* and write *water*. Now say (stressing *vegetable* and *garden*):

> What kind of garden is it? It's a vegetable garden. I know it's a vegetable garden, but is *vegetable* an adjective? No, *vegetable* is a noun. And what kind of bottle is it? It's a water bottle. I know it's a water bottle, but is *water* an adjective? No *water* is a noun.

Now you'll explain that nouns used in this way do the job of adjectives. That won't be hard, and they'll learn more examples from the following exercise, but first, it's important to talk about listening comprehension and pronunciation (or more accurately, *intonation*).

Repeat these to your class, and ask them to tell you which word is stressed: (When does the voice go up?)

vegetable garden
water bottle
cat food
coffee table
pencil sharpener

This is important for their listening comprehension <u>and speaking</u> (contrary to what I've said previously about reductions). Try saying some of these without stressing the first noun, and you'll see that it sounds so strange that a native speaker might actually not understand.

11.16 Most common mistake with nouns used as adjectives (aka compound nouns)

The most common mistake students make with compound nouns (other than not stressing the first noun) is making the first noun plural when it seems logical to do so. Your students will want to say, for example,

book<u>s</u> store
car<u>s</u> factory

Don't let them!

11.17 Two words?, hyphenate?, one word?

Are compound nouns always written as two words? No, nothing would ever be that simple in English, would it? They are usually written as two words, but not everyone agrees about this (to the extent that they think about it at all). You will see, for example, *paper clip, paper-clip* and *paperclip*. All are correct. Are you going to discuss this at great length with your students? I hope not, but just in case some troublemaker asks you why you wrote a compound noun one way and his or her electronic dictionary shows it another way, you've got your answer: you didn't make a mistake; there's no general agreement about this, but usually they're written as two words.

sample exercises 14: Complete the sentences.
I need a bowl for my soup. I need a _____*soup bowl*_____.

1. They play football in that stadium. It's a _____.
2. Carlos likes juice from apples. He likes _____.
3. I need an opener for this can. Do you know where the _____ is?
4. Lucy teaches at a school. She is a _____.
5. Sam is the driver of the bus. He's the _____.

11.18 Compound adjectives

With a handy little punctuation gizmo known as a hyphen, almost anything can be turned into an adjective. Don't believe me? Compare these pairs of sentences—the first in each pair with an ordinary adjective and the second with a compound adjective:

11.29a   We stayed in a <u>nice</u> hotel room.
    b   We stayed in a <u>$300-a-night</u> hotel room.

11.30a   It was a <u>long</u> flight to Brazil.
    b   It was a <u>14-hour</u> flight to Brazil.

11.31a   It's a <u>sad</u> story.
    b   It's an <u>all-too-familiar</u> story.

11.32a   She has a <u>good</u> job.
    b   She has a <u>full-time</u> job.

11.33a   He's a <u>busy</u> man.
    b   He's a <u>32-year-old</u> man.

Now do you believe me? This is an extremely handy thing to teach your students. The main thing with compound adjectives is for students to be aware of their existence and, ideally, the meanings of many common compound adjectives. As far as producing compound adjectives themselves, they need to know when hyphens are necessary and when they are not (and therefore wrong). Hyphens are used only when the words modify a noun that immediately follows them. Compare these pairs of sentences:

11.34a   We stayed in a <u>$300-a-night</u> hotel room.
    b   Our hotel room cost <u>$300 a night</u>.

11.35a   It was a <u>14-hour</u> flight to Brazil.

     b   The flight to Brazil was <u>14 hours</u> long.

11.36a   It's an <u>all-too-familiar</u> story.

     b   The story is <u>all too familiar</u>.

11.37a   She has a <u>full-time</u> job.

     b   Her job is <u>full time</u>.

11.38a   He's a <u>32-year-old</u> man.

     b   He is <u>32 years old</u>.

All sorts of words can be combined to make compound adjectives (with one exception discussed below). I suggest that you emphasize this more as a vocabulary lesson than a grammar lesson, however. There's no point in spending time on all the various possible combinations and certainly no point in having your students memorize them. The most useful thing your students can take away from this lesson is an awareness of how compound adjectives are made and an understanding of some of the more common compound adjectives. Foremost among these, I'd say, are the various ones with numbers in them. These would be the most useful to learn and the most useful for your students to practice creating themselves.

I have grouped these according to what parts of speech or verb forms they're combinations of, but as I said, that's not the main thing—you want your students to remember what some of these mean, to be able to recognize a compound adjective when they see one and to be able to produce compound adjectives as well, especially number-related compound adjectives:

- **number + period of time**
  a 50-minute class
  a two-week vacation
  a three-hour tour

- **number + noun**
  a $400-a-night hotel room
  a 340-page book
  a 2,000-seat theater
  a three-car garage
  a one-way street
  a 55-mile-per-hour speed limit
  a 20-kilometer drive
  a ten-foot pole

- **phrases**
  a do-it-yourself project
  an off-the-shelf solution
  a black-and-white movie

- **adverb + past participle**
  a brightly-lit room
  a well-known author
  a badly-behaved child
  a densely-populated country

- **noun + past participle**
  a hand-made table
  a self-taught guitar player
  a gas-powered engine

- **noun + present participle**
  a record-breaking speed
  a labor-saving device
  a French-speaking country
  a mouth-watering dinner

- **noun + adjective**
  a world-famous singer
  a sugar-free drink
  a smoke-free hotel
  a brain-dead politician

- **adjective + noun**
  a last-minute change
  a full-length version
  a high-speed train

- **noun + noun**
  a part-time job
  a full-time job

- **adjective + past participle**
  an old-fashioned idea
  a long-awaited sequel
  a warm-blooded animal
  a cold-blooded killer

- **adjective + present participle**
  a good-looking guy
  a long-lasting friendship

- **adjective + adjective**
  bitter-sweet memories
  Anglo-American relations

11.19 Common compound adjective mistakes

A very common mistake is making number-related compound adjectives plural. It will seem logical to say, for example,

a $400-a-night hotel room (pronounced *dollars*)
a two-weeks vacation
a 340-pages book
a three-cars garage
a 20-kilometers drive
a 45-years-old man

and that's why your students will want to do it. But it's wrong, so don't let them!

11.20 Adverbs and compound adjectives

The adverb *very* and adverbs ending with *-ly* are not hyphenated when they precede compound adjectives:

11.39   He's a very good-looking guy.

11.40   That's an extremely old-fashioned idea.

Strictly speaking (and we grammarians always speak strictly), because *best, well* and *fast* are both adverbs and adjectives, to avoid confusion, a hyphen should follow them when they are used as adverbs:

11.41a   I saw a well-trained elephant. (an elephant that has been trained well)
     b   I saw a well trained elephant. (a trained elephant that is not sick)

In reality, hyphens are often not used for two reasons: one, in common expressions like *a well known person* or *a part time job* or *a three bedroom house,* people know exactly what is meant and there is no danger of confusion and two, most native speakers haven't got a clue about any of this stuff.

Stay tuned for a lot more about adverbs used with adjectives.

sample exercises 15: Rewrite the sentences so that they use compound adjectives.
It takes 12 hours to fly to Thailand.
It's a _____*12-hour*_____ flight to Thailand.

1. His salary is $50,000 a year.
   He has a _____ job.
2. Mary lives in a house with four bedrooms.
   Mary lives in a _____ house.
3. The race was 100 meters.
   It was a _____ race.
4. John gave a presentation that lasted 20 minutes.
   John gave a _____ presentation.
5. Rosa works four days a week.
   Rosa has a _____ job.

11.21 Making comparisons with *same, similar, different, like* and *alike*

Grammar books teach these words, but two things about this lesson always bug me: one, who says *alike*? and two, does *like* mean *exactly the same* or does it mean *kind of the same* (in other words, *similar*)? and when things are only *kind of the same* doesn't that mean that they're *kind of different too?*, so how can things be *like* each other (or *alike*) and *different* too??? Is *like* like *same*? Is *like* similar to *same*? Is *like* different from *same*? I think I'm going crazy!!!

Actually, I'm not going crazy because, as a native speaker, I can deal with this ambiguity. With the imperfect tools that English provides, I know what people mean, and I know how to make them understand what I mean. It's easy for us native speakers but not always easy for students of English trying to make sense of it all. You want to keep lessons simple, so do you deliberately avoid discussions of ambiguities which may only confuse your students, or do you oversimplify, you tell yourself, because it's easier for your students but also, you know, because it's easier for you?

What's the answer? There is no good answer that always applies. You have to consider your students—will they be enlightened or befuddled by your efforts to clarify ambiguity? You have to consider whether it's worth the effort. Are you going to use up 20 minutes of valuable class time to discuss a matter that will very likely never come up?

Anyway, teaching these words isn't terribly difficult. It boils down to teaching two patterns. Put this on the board:

> A and B <u>are</u> _____.
> A <u>is</u> _____ B.

▶ *same*

Emphasize *as* and the need to remember *the*:

> A and B are <u>the same</u>.
> A is <u>the same as B</u>.

▶ *similar*

Emphasize *to*:

> A and B are <u>similar</u>.
> A is <u>similar to</u> B.

▶ *different*

Emphasize *from*. Also, you might mention that some people say *different than* and *different to*:

> A and B are <u>different</u>.
> A is <u>different from</u> B.

▶ *like/alike*

Don't emphasize anything, least of all *alike*, since it's not really common, and be ready to explain that *like* can sometimes mean *the same as* and sometimes *almost the same as, similar to, kind of the same as, sort of the same as*. *Kind of* and *sort of*, used to modify adjectives, is something we'll talk about in a page or two. These are useful and quite common, so why not give your students a preview?

> A and B are <u>alike</u>.
> A is <u>like</u> B.

Regarding prepositions, once again, there is no system to it. Why, for example, *the same <u>as</u>* but *similar <u>to</u>* but *different <u>from</u>*? There's no answer. It's just something that students need to memorize.

sample exercises 16: Correct the mistakes in the sentences.

1. My house same as your house.
2. This book is different of that book.
3. My house and your house are not same.
4. Paul's bicycle is similar my bicycle.
5. These shoes are alike those shoes.

sample exercises 17: Use *be* and the words in parentheses to write two present tense sentences as in the example.

(my coat, your coat, similar)
My coat and your coat are similar.
My coat is similar to your coat.

1. (New York City, Los Angeles, different)
2. (my tie, your tie, alike, like)
3. (Larry, his twin brother, same)
4. (my car, your car, similar)
5. (these tires, those tires, same)

11.22 Adjectives modified by adverbs

How do you feel about teaching adjectives? Do you feel *a bit confused?*, *rather confident?*, *pretty good?*, *100% ready?* What I have just cleverly done is show you examples of how adverbs are used in English to modify adjectives. Normally, the adverb precedes the adjective:

11.42   He is totally crazy.

One exception is *enough*:

11.43   This isn't good enough.

That adverbs can modify adjectives (and not just verbs, which you already knew) is a fundamental concept to keep in mind. (It will come up again when we focus on adverbs in Chapter 16.) Of course it's not as simple as that. Adjectives can be (jargon alert!) *gradable* (aka *qualitative*) or *non-gradable,* and that determines the type of adverb that can modify them. So what does it boil down to adverbwise? Grading adverbs modify gradable adjectives, and non-grading adverbs modify non-grading adjectives.

▶ Grading adverbs used to modify gradable adjectives

Gradable adjectives can vary in degree. *Hungry,* for example: You can be *a bit hungry, somewhat hungry, very hungry* or *extremely hungry.* Also, gradable adjectives have comparative and superlative forms.

- **grading adverbs**
  - **weak**
    a bit
    a little
    slightly

  - **moderate**
    fairly
    kind of
    moderately
    rather
    somewhat
    sort of

  - **strong**
    awfully
    extremely
    highly
    pretty
    quite
    really
    terribly
    very

You may recall way back in Chapter 2 that I said that you would see that all sorts of oddball words are adverbs that you never even thought of. And here you see what I mean. Would you ever have guessed that *a bit* or *kind of* or *pretty* would be classified with adverbs? Totally amazing, isn't it? *Pretty* used this way often strikes students as pretty weird, especially when I tell them that we native speakers might say that some unfortunate person is *pretty ugly*. This is also a good time to teach the very common reductions *kinda* and *sorta*.

▶ **Non-grading adverbs used to modify non-gradable adjectives**

Non-gradable adjectives can't vary in degree because one, they represent extremes: you can't be *very freezing* or *very excellent* because the idea *very* is implicit in the meaning of the adjective, because two, they represent (jargon alert!) *absolutes*: you can't be *very perfect* or *very dead* or because three, the adjective serves to classify: something cannot be *very nuclear* or *very monthly*—it either is or it isn't. Non-gradable adjectives do not have comparative and superlative forms. (At least not in the literal sense of the adjective—yes, we can say *This is the deadest party I've ever been too* or *Some Americans are more equal than others*.) The non-grading adverbs' function is not to convey any notion of degree but to amplify, to dramatize the adjective.

- **non-grading adverbs**
  100%
  absolutely
  completely
  entirely
  totally

▶ **Staying out of trouble with the grammar police (not your students, you!)**

One thing to be aware of to stay out of trouble with the grammar police is to understand that in English you can't (as we grammar weenies say) *qualify an absolute*. What does that mean? As we saw, some adjectives can vary in degree. You can be *extremely hungry*, but you can't be *extremely dead*. You're either *dead* or *not dead*—there's no in between (though I have had students who made me wonder). *Dead* is an absolute adjective. The two absolutes that you want to be especially careful about are *unique* and *perfect*. These are the two that the grammar police are always on the alert for. When I'm with a fellow grammarian club member, and we hear a potential member say, for example, that something is *extremely unique* or *the most perfect*, my fellow grammarian club member and I will grimace and look knowingly at each other with raised eyebrows. After hurriedly ridding ourselves of this wretched person's presence, my fellow grammarian club member and I will snicker cruelly and say, "Egad! Did you hear what he said? It was ghastly. It was just ghastly. Good lord, he's obviously not one of us. He has no hope whatever of being admitted to our prestigious and exclusive grammarian club. Let us shun him henceforward." Yes, it's brutal, but that's life. Don't let this happen to you.

Are you going to explain all of this to your students? Other than the two main things to avoid—qualifying *unique* or *perfect*—no, that's the least of their worries.

To show you how pathetic the life of a grammar teacher is, I've had long discussions with a colleague about *somewhat* and *quite*. One book we are both familiar with claims that *somewhat* is stronger than *quite*. I say this is quite wrong. But it's all in the ear of the beholder. There isn't any absolute answer. And speaking of *quite*, I guarantee you students will confuse it with *quiet* and *quit*, so make sure to go over this—spelling, meaning and pronunciation.

Also, there are certain patterns to how these words are used which have more to do with custom than right or wrong. We can say *I'm highly suspicious*, but why can't we say *I'm highly hungry* or *I'm highly tired*? (Actually, we can, and I just did, but why wouldn't we *normally* say these?) Why teacher, why, why, why??? What are you going to say? It can be frustrating. You want to explain everything to your students, but there are times when there really is no explanation that will help them. Time spent exploring the topic would be counterproductive and a useless.

Exercises such as the one below are very useful for getting students to think and talk. They're not about correct and incorrect grammar. All the answers are grammatically correct, but they're not all logical (and now is a good time to teach them the meaning of *logical*.) It's about getting students to understand the meanings of these words and how we use them.

sample exercises 18: Underline the best adverb to finish the sentences. There may be more than one good answer. Be ready to explain your answer.

Mary will not speak to me. She's (a bit/moderately/<u>pretty</u>) angry with me.

1. Francesca got a 94 on her test. That was a (slightly/somewhat/pretty) good score.
2. I was (a bit/terribly/completely) late to work—only five minutes.
3. John's mother died yesterday. He is (a bit/sort of/terribly) upset.

4. I couldn't do it. It was (slightly/totally/kind of) impossible.
5. I want to buy my wife a big diamond ring, but they're (a little/kind of/extremely) expensive.
6. My essay is (a little/rather/quite) short. The teacher said it should be 20 pages long, and mine is 19 pages long.
7. The boss said my idea was (somewhat/very/absolutely) perfect.

Chapter 12
Modals and Phrasal Modals

Could you…

- give a simple answer this question: What does *would* mean?
- explain how *must* is very commonly used in a way that has nothing to do with *obligation* or *having to do something*?
- explain how *should* is very commonly used in a way that has nothing to do with *advice* or *something being a good idea*?
- answer this question: Are *should, ought to* and *had better* the same or different? If they are different, how are they different?
- answer these questions: Is *had better* about the past? If not, why not?

12.1 Go beyond the basics

Modals and phrasal modals are an essential part of English, but they're something that few ESL students learn beyond the basics. One of the best things you can do for your students is give them a solid foundation in modals and phrasal modals.

12.2 Terminology

First of all, let's get our terminology straight. *Modals* are also known as *modal auxiliaries* and *modal auxiliary verbs*. I prefer just *modals*. A modal is one word. A *phrasal modal* is two or more words. Phrasal modals are also called *semi-modals*:

- **modals**
  can
  could
  may
  might
  must
  shall
  should
  will
  would

- **phrasal modals**
  be able to
  be going to
  be supposed to
  be to
  had better
  have got to
  have to
  ought to
  used to

12.3 Easy and not easy

Modals and phrasal modals are both easy and one of the most difficult things you will teach.

They're easy because the mechanics of making questions, negatives and short answers is the same as what students have already seen. I'm not—and you're not—going to focus on that. There aren't going to be any basic grammar exercises in this chapter—change to questions, change to negatives, etc. Your students should already know that by now. There's the odd complication we'll talk about here and there, but no big deal.

They're not easy because every modal and semi-modal does double, triple and quadruple duty, so what you need to do is get your students to focus on (jargon alert!) *functions* rather than meaning.

12.4 Meaning and functions

Functions? Not meaning? Meaning is a difficult concept when it comes to modals and phrasal modals. Whenever your students think they've got the meaning of one of them nailed down, along comes another that blows their understanding out of the water. I like to use the analogy of pumpkin seeds. Anyone who as ever carved a pumpkin knows what it's like to pick a pumpkin seed up off the floor. Just when you think you've got it, the slimy little thing flies out of your hand to parts of the kitchen unknown. So I'll tell you right now: regarding the meaning of modals and phrasal modals, they mean a lot more than you think they mean. That's what makes modals so useful but also what makes them so difficult to teach and learn. Two or more modals will have the same function, and as soon as your students have that figured out, they'll discover that those same modals now have different functions. It'll drive your students nuts!

So is our strategy going to be to focus on those many meanings? No! We're going to focus on functions. What are functions? Functions are the reasons we use language—the work we want to do with this tool we call language. Do we want to predict the future? Do we want to express willingness? Do we want to express ability? Do we want to express doubt? Do we want express opinion? Do we want to obtain somebody's opinion? Do we want to give permission? Do we want to ask for someone's permission? These are functions.

Often, functions involve expressing how we feel about a situation or a bit of information, and different people don't always feel the same way about a situation or a bit of information, do they? Imagine that two of my colleagues and I are discussing a student and his chances of passing the test tomorrow. We might say something like this:

12.1   Teacher 1:   He <u>will</u> pass the test.

12.2   Teacher 2:   He <u>might</u> pass the test.

12.3   Teacher 3:   He <u>had better</u> pass the test.

You can see that we have used different modals to express our different feelings about the same thing.

Don't believe me? Here's another example. Imagine I notice that one of my students is absent. I have no idea why, but two other students and I speculate as to the answer:

12.4a   Teacher: She <u>must</u> be in the library.
  b   Student 1:   She <u>might</u> be in the library, or she <u>might</u> be in the bathroom.
  c   Student 2:   The library is closed. She <u>can't</u> be in the library. She <u>may</u> be in the bathroom, or she <u>could</u> be in the principal's office.
  d   Teacher: Whatever, she <u>should</u> be here in the classroom.
  e   Student 1:   Relax teacher, she <u>should</u> be here soon. (Student 1 is a smartass.)

Isn't it cool what modals can do? See how they're used to express how different people can perceive the same situation differently? Did you notice how *must* was used? Did it have anything to do with *obligation*? No, it didn't. Did you notice the two ways that *should* was used? Do you understand how the second is different from the first? Remember what I said about modals having more functions than you realize?

For almost every function we'll discuss, more than one modal or phrasal modal can be used, so for example, instead of focusing on learning the meanings of *would,* we will focus on learning the different ways *would* and other modals and phrasal modals are used for various functions.

This is what I stress again and again with my students. Yes, by all means encourage your students to look in their bilingual dictionaries and see what it says for *would,* for example, but make sure they understand that there is NO WAY that any language will have one equivalent word only for *would* that will always work for every function.

So functions! Got it? But are you going to use that word? No! (But you should use it with your fellow teachers—it's a good little bit of jargon.) You're going to use your (or your students') bilingual dictionary to teach your students the word *situation*. That's what I do, and it's a good vocabulary word for them. So from now on, we're talking about <u>situations</u>, OK?

Also, the list of words at the beginning of this chapter is the last time you're going to see modals and phrasal modals treated separately. From now on they'll be treated as one group. We'll discuss them without regard to whether they are modals or phrasal modals. The differences in how questions and negatives are formed with them is not something that you should need to explain at this point, though of course review it if you see the need.

And a word on contractions: Some modals and phrasal modals have contractions which are very commonly used, and others have contractions which are possible but which are seldom if ever used. (When was the last time you said *hadn't better, mayn't, mightn't, mustn't, oughtn't to* or *shan't*?) Why aren't these contractions used? It's custom, not right or wrong. All these oddball contractions are perfectly good English and might be found in an old book and in your students' dictionaries. Do not even mention uncommon contractions. Your students will subconsciously get a feeling for which ones are common and those are the one they'll learn and use. If they never see or hear *mightn't*, they'll never want to use it. If they see and hear *wouldn't* all the time, they will want to use it. Oddball contractions are the least of your students' (and your) worries. Instead, familiarize your students with common contractions and only get into this if it comes up.

12.5 Asking for permission with *may, could* and *can*

May, could and *can* are all used to ask for permission:

    12.5a   May I use your telephone?
       b   = Could I use your telephone?
       c   = Can I use your telephone?

You can see right off that your students will see this as kind of bizarre. How can three words all have the same meaning? Of course, you and I know that it's not that they have the same meaning but that they are all used for the same function. It's something your students need to get used to. In this particular case, you may find that some students have gotten the idea from other books or teachers that *may* is vastly more formal and polite than *can* and *could,* as if only dukes and duchesses say *may* and the rest of us schlubs say *can* and *could*—words that are almost obscene in their crude informality. This is nonsense. I tell my students that *may* is a bit more formal perhaps, but there is nothing at all wrong with using *can* or *could* and that this is nothing to give any thought to.

You can talk about typical answers to these requests. Obviously, short answers like *Yes, you can, No, you can't, Yes, you may* or *No, you may not* are possible, but *Yes, you could* or *No, you couldn't* are not (because it would sound like a conditional sentence, which it isn't.) Also *Sure, OK, Of course, No problem,* etc. No grammar here but useful conversation help.

sample exercises 1: What would you say in these situations? Write answers with *may, could* or *can.* Do not use the same modal for each answer. Practice using all of them.

> You are at my house, and you want to use my computer. What do you say to me?
>
> *May I use your computer?*
> *Could I use your computer?*
> *Can I use your computer?*

1. You want to open the window in my house. What do you say to me?
2. You and your friend are at work, and you both want to go home early. What do you say to your boss?
3. You are at a friend's house, and you want a glass of water. What do you say to your friend?
4. Your sister wants to use my car. What do you say to me?
5. You are talking to your teacher, and you want more time to finish your project. What do you say to your teacher?

12.6 Asking for permission with *would you mind* and *do you mind*

The questions in Section 12.5 above:

    12.6a   May I use your telephone?
       b   = Could I use your telephone?
       c   = Can I use your telephone?

could be rephrased as this:

    12.7   Would mind if I used your telephone?

or as this:

    12.8   Do you mind if I use your telephone?

These are useful and handy and something you should teach your students, but they'll need to understand the meaning of *mind.* Try explaining it in terms of *bother, be a problem.* Then get out the bilingual dictionary. You'll also need to explain that no means yes: *No, I wouldn't mind* or *No, I don't mind* mean *Yes, OK, Sure, No problem,* etc. And finally, *would you mind if…* is a conditional sentence, and that's not something your students have gotten to yet. BUT, you need to teach your students to use the past form of the verb with *would you mind.* That will strike them as odd, but assure them that it's correct and that all will be revealed later. Teach it as a (jargon alert!) *chunk* (aka *lexical phrase*). What's that? A group of words that are memorized without regard to the grammar involved. Students even at a low level can memorize lots of useful phrases and what they mean without necessarily knowing all the grammar involved. A good example of this is *I would like* and *I would like to* which students generally learn mean *I want* and *I want to* long before they get to conditional sentences and learn the grammar involved.

sample exercises 2: Change these requests so that they use *would you mind* and *do you mind.*

   May I sit down?
   Would you mind if I sat down?
   Do you mind if sit down.

   1. May I close the door?
   2. Can my son swim in your pool?
   3. May I turn up the heat?
   4. Can I speak with your manager?
   5. Can I not go shopping with you tonight?

How about number 5? Sometimes questions like these can be negative. These are the answers:

   12.9   Would you mind if I didn't go shopping with you tonight?

   12.10 Do you mind if I don't go shopping with you tonight?

12.7 Asking people to do something with *would*, *could*, *will* and *can*

How about four modals all with the same function? *Would, could, will* and *can* are all used to ask people to do something:

   12.11a   Would you help me?
      b   = Could you help me?
      c   = Will you help me?
      d   = Can you help me?

Once again, short answers are possible, though more common would be *I'd be happy to, Sure, OK, Of course, No problem,* etc.

So why do I say short answers would be less likely? The goofy nature of modals is that because they have so many functions, they have the potential for being misunderstood. It'll be a while before we get to conditional sentences, but in reality the sentences above are examples of conditional sentences. What's really being asked is this:

   12.12a   Would you help me if I asked you?
         = Could you help me if I asked you?
         = Will you help me if I ask you?
         = Can you help me if I ask you?

And that's not all. There's ellipsis afoot here. What's really, really being asked is this:

   12.13a   Would you help me if I asked you to help me?
      b   = Could you help me if I asked you to help me?
      c   = Will you help me if I ask you to help me?
      d   = Can you help me if I ask you to help me?

Are you going to explain any of this to your students now? No, you are not! Not until you get to conditionals. These are conditional questions, and because of that, answers like *Yes, I would, Yes, I could, Yes, I will* and *Yes, I can* don't come across as a solid yes. They have a conditional sound that might sound odd—as if there is some reluctance on the part of the speaker to give a firm yes or that saying yes depends on something. This is true of other requests with modals as we have seen and will see again.

And if you're not sure why the examples above with *would* and *could* contain the past form of *ask* (*asked*), but the examples with *will* and *can* contain the present form (*ask*), that will be explained in the conditional chapter. No need to get into any of this with your students now!

sample exercises 3: What would you say in these situations? Write answers with *would, could, will* or *can.* Do not use the same modal for each answer. Practice using all of them.

   You want your friend to give you a ride. What do you say to her?
   Would you give me a ride?
   Could you give me a ride?
   Will you give me a ride?
   Can you give me a ride?

   1. You want me to fix your bicycle. What do you say to me?
   2. You want your friend to help you with your homework. What do you say to him?

3. You want me to open the window. What do you say to me?
4. You want your sister to turn off the TV. What do you say to her?
5. You want me to pick you up at the train station. What do you say to me?

12.8 Asking people to do something with *would you mind*

Here again your students are going to get a preview of grammar to come later. Gaze upon these examples:

12.14 Would you mind giving me a ride to the airport?

12.15 Would you mind not saying that anymore?

12.16 Would you mind shutting up?

What we see here are *gerunds*. *Giving, saying* and *shutting* are gerunds—verbs in the *-ing* form used as nouns. We will have a lot more to say about gerunds later, but as far as your students are concerned (if they ask), there is nothing continuous about these sentences—no form of *be* is anywhere to be found. And speaking of *be*, *be* can be a gerund too:

12.17 Would you mind being quiet?

And here we see also something we'll see again later when we get to gerunds—negative gerunds:

12.18 Would you mind not talking so loudly?

As for answers, it may strike your students as odd that the way to say yes is to say no:

12.19a John: Would you mind washing the dishes?
   b Mary: No, I wouldn't mind [washing the dishes]. (= Yes, I will [wash the dishes].)

so you might want to work on that.

sample exercises 4: Change these requests so that they use *would you mind*.
          Could you get me a sandwich?
          Would you mind getting me a sandwich?

1. Can you move this sofa for me?
2. Will you take us to the library?
3. Would you go shopping with me tomorrow?
4. Can you be here at 7:00?
5. Can you not walk so fast?

12.9 *borrow* and *lend*

These are important words that we native speakers use easily, so you'll be surprised at how much difficulty students have with them. You want to reinforce that *borrow* is similar to *take* and that *lend* is similar to *give*. That won't be terribly difficult, though a bilingual dictionary might help. The real problem your students will have is keeping them straight. They'll confuse them no end.

Asking to borrow something is like asking for permission. In both cases—asking to borrow something or asking for permission—you are asking for something. It's also like asking someone *to do* something because you're asking someone to lend you something. So a good way to teach *borrow* and *lend* is to use the grammar you've already taught your students—first with *give* and *take* and then with *lend* and *borrow*:

12.20a I forgot my calculator. May/Can/Could I <u>take</u> yours?
    b = I forgot my calculator. May/Can/Could I <u>borrow</u> yours?

12.21a I forgot my calculator. Would you mind if I <u>took</u> yours?
    b = I forgot my calculator. Would you mind if I <u>borrowed</u> yours?

12.22a I forgot my calculator. Would/Could/Will/Can you <u>give</u> me yours?
    b = I forgot my calculator. Would/Could/Will/Can you <u>lend</u> me yours?

12.23a I forgot my calculator. Would you mind <u>giving</u> me yours?
    b = I forgot my calculator. Would you mind <u>lending</u> me yours?

That's quite an explosion of grammar, isn't it? Of course, it's a bit of an oversimplification meaningwise to imply that *lend* = *give* and that *borrow* = *take*, but I've never had any problem with that. Even though your students will certainly know *give* and *take* by now, the idea that *borrow* and *lend,* though opposite in meaning, just like *give* and *take,* can be used to say the same thing, just like *give* and *take,* will confuse them. To reinforce this idea, put something like this on the board:

> Can <u>I borrow</u> $10?
>
> = Can <u>you lend me</u> $10?
>
> Would you mind <u>if I borrow</u> $10?
>
> = Would you mind <u>lending me</u> $10?

One thing to work on is that *borrow* never needs an indirect object, but *lend* usually does have one. In this sentence, *his pen* is the object:

12.24   I borrowed his pen.

In this sentence, there are two objects: *me* is the indirect object, and *his pen* is the direct object:

12.25   He lent me his pen.

That's a lot of jargon. It all boils down to not saying *borrow me,* so you might want to keep it simple: emphasize *lend me/ borrow ~~me~~.*

You'll need to teach your students that *lend* is irregular (*lend/lent/lent*) and also that, as much as it pains me to say it, many people nowadays use *loan* as a verb rather than *lend.* (Ghastly!)

In situations like this, when I've dropped a ton of grammar on my students' heads, rather than simply expecting them to master is all in a few minutes, which isn't realistic, I like to give them exercises which call for some sort of error correction. That's essentially what the exercise below is—three (jargon alert!) *distractors* (the wrong answers in a multiple choice exercise, a good bit of jargon you definitely should know) with errors in them and one correct answer.

sample exercises 5: Circle the letter of the best answer.

1.   I don't have any money. _____ $20?
     a.   Could you lend
     b.   Could I lend me
     c.   Could I borrow
     d.   Could you borrow me

2.   I forgot my pen. _____ your pen?
     a.   Would you mind lending me
     b.   Could you mind lending
     c.   Would you borrow me
     d.   Would you mind me borrowing

3.   My father's car is at the mechanic. _____ your car?
     a.   Can you lend
     b.   Can you lend him
     c.   Can he lend you
     d.   Can you borrow him

4.   I forgot my umbrella. _____ your umbrella?
     a.   Would I mind if you borrowed
     b.   Would you mind if lent
     c.   Would you mind borrowing me
     d.   Would you mind if I borrowed

5.   Mary forgot her tennis racket. _____ yours?
     a.   Would you borrow her
     b.   Would she borrow you
     c.   Would you lend her
     d.   Would she lend you

Here's something a little more challenging:

sample exercises 6: What would you say in these situations? Write one answer with *borrow* and one answer with *lend*.

You want your friend to give you some money.
- a. (may, borrow) *May I borrow some money?*
- b. (would, mind, lend) *Would you mind lending me some money?*

1. You want to use your friend's bicycle.
   - a. (can, borrow)
   - b. (would, mind, lend)

2. You want to use your sister's football.
   - a. (would, lend)
   - b. (may, borrow)

3. You want your friend to give you her dictionary.
   - a. (would, mind, borrow)
   - b. (will, lend)

4. You want your friend to give you his snow shovel.
   - a. (could, borrow)
   - b. (will, lend)

5. You want to use your neighbor's grill.
   - a. (would, mind, borrow)
   - b. (would, mind, lend)

12.10 Saying something was necessary in the past with *had to*

Recall that an entire chapter was devoted to *have/have to* and *have got/have got to*. *Have to* and *have got to* are phrasal modals and could have been included in this chapter, but because *have got* and *have got to* are so important as well as so idiomatic, they really need the extra attention. At least that's what I think. As we saw, in the present, *have to*, *have got to* and *must* all have the same function (except when negative). How about the past? What are the past forms and past participles of *have to*, *have got to* and *must*? Well, in the case of *have got to* and *must*, nothing—they don't exist. They can't be used in the past. Only *have to* has a past form and a past participle: *had to* in both cases.

sample exercises 7: Change the sentences to past simple.

Sarah has to go to the library.
Sarah had to go to the library.

I must pay my telephone bill.
I had to pay my telephone bill.

My father's got to go to the dentist.
My father had to go to the dentist.

1. Mark must do his homework.
2. I've got to go to the airport.
3. He's got to help his father.
4. Do you have to wake up early?
5. Have you got to make dinner?

12.11 Saying something is not necessary with *have to* or is not allowed with *must*

Remember when I said that *have to* and *must* are the same? I lied. These negative sentences with *have to* and *must* aren't the same, are they?

12.26   You don't have to do it. (but you can if you want to. It's allowed.)

12.27   You must not do it. (It's not allowed.)

As you can see, *don't have to* means that something is allowed but that it isn't necessary, and *must not* means that something is *forbidden, not allowed*.

In reality (as opposed to grammar fantasyland), who ever uses *must not* to say something is not allowed? (I'm <u>not</u> talking about a very different, common and important way to use *must not* that we'll talk about later.) What most people use is the imperative. Imperative sentences are also known as *commands* or *orders*. Grammarwise, they're interesting, at least to pathetic people like me, because they have no subject. The subject of imperative sentences is always understood to be *you*. We would not say

12.28   You don't say that again!

We would say

12.29   Don't say that again!

Anyway, here are some fairly easy exercises to reinforce this idea:

sample exercises 8: Write *NN* after the sentence if it means that something is not necessary. Write *NA* if it means that something is not allowed.

> You don't have to go to the meeting. ___*NN*___
>
> You must not talk to anyone during the exam. ___*NA*___

1. Sarah doesn't have to take her brother to work. _____
2. You must not smoke in a supermarket. _____
3. I don't have to go with my brother. _____
4. You must not tell anyone. _____
5. You must not let your cat jump on the dinner table. _____

12.12 Saying something is a good idea or a bad idea in the present or future with *should*, *ought to* and *had better*

▶ *should*

Now we're getting into the fun stuff. This is the function of *should* that your students have probably already learned by now—giving advice, saying something is a good or a bad idea—*You should study hard, You should not smoke,* etc. But is that what we native speakers *always* say? No. We also use *ought to* and *had better* for the same purpose, and both of those are problematic.

▶ *ought to*

First of all, you need to teach your students some things about *ought to*:

Number one is that, in modern English, it's always *ought to* and never just *ought*.

Two is that *ought to* is never negative. So no *ought not to* or *oughn't to*. (Remember we're talking about modern English here, which is all your students care about and all you should be teaching them.)

Three is that *ought to* is never used in questions. No *Ought you to...?* (modern English!), and finally, native speakers VERY commonly reduce *ought to* to *otta*. That's something you *otta* teach them, but you *otta* remind them that they *don't hafta* say *otta*, but they *gotta* understand it.

So now that we got all that out of the way, what matters to your students is that *should* and *ought to* are really the same. Put this on the board so there's no mistake:

> should = ought <u>to</u>

and an example:

> I <u>should</u> lose weight.
> = I <u>ought to</u> lose weight.

(Of course, if that happens to actually be true about you, the last thing you need is a bunch of students nodding their heads in agreement, so come up with something else.)

▶ *had better*

If you though *ought to* was problematic, welcome to *had better,* an idiomatic disaster area. Try for a moment to understand the grammar of *had better*. I'll check my email while you think about it...OK, I'm back. What did you come up with? What? Are you serious? That's ridiculous. You're wrong. *Had better* is an idiom that cannot be understood literally. It makes no sense grammarwise so there's nothing to explain to your students other than it's an idiom and it makes no sense grammarwise and that it's like *should* and *ought to* <u>but stronger</u>. And that's a big BUT. That *had better* is stronger than *should* and *ought to* is what gets *had better* out of bed in the morning. We native speakers save it for situations where we want to say that there will be a negative consequence for not doing something or not taking some advice. Sometimes we say what the negative consequence is

12.30a   You'd better go now, or you'll be late for school.

and sometimes we don't say it. It's only implied:

12.31a   You'd better not do that again (or something bad will happen)!

As you saw in the examples above, we native speakers almost always use the contraction of *had, 'd,* and VERY important to your students, we VERY often omit *had* or *'d* entirely. We say, for example,

12.30b   You better go now, or you'll be late for school.

12.31b   You better not do that again!

This really is something you need to give your students a lot of listening practice with. As always, remind them that they don't necessarily need to copy the reduced English that you're modeling (and probably shouldn't), but that they must understand it. And actually, it gets even worse: in imperative sentences we often say only *better,* without any subject at all. I do, and you do to. Better not deny it. I know you do:

12.32   Better go now, or you'll be late for school.

12.33   Better not do that again!

See how *You should...* has turned into *Better...*? Sometimes I wonder how anyone can learn this language.

And we're not done yet! Make sure your students know that the only negative form of *had better* is *had better not.* There is no *had not better* or *hadn't better.* (modern English! I don't care what may have been said decades or centuries ago, neither do your students, and neither should you.)

Also, since *had better* contains the past form of *have,* your students might understandably get the idea that *had better* is about the past. It's not, so make sure they don't.

And finally, in modern English, *had better* isn't used in questions.

Had better is incredibly useful and important, but you really need to emphasize the idea that there is always a stated or implied negative consequence. We don't use it when there is no idea of a negative consequence. To reinforce this, the exercises below ask students to consider whether a situation is dire enough to warrant *had better.* Also, in some cases, either *should* or *ought to* will work, but in other cases no. And you know why, don't you? *Ought to* won't work in questions or a negative sentences. In some cases, however, there may be more than one good answer. There's nothing wrong with that! Talk to your students about it. Get their opinions as to why one answer is better than another or as good as another. It's an excellent opportunity for some conversation practice.

sample exercises 9: What would you say in these situations? Use *should, ought to* or *had better* to complete the sentences. There may be more than one good answer for some. Be ready to explain your answer.

1. Fire! You _____ call the fire department right now!
2. Your hands are dirty. You _____ wash them before you make dinner.
3. You're sick. You _____ wash your hands before you make dinner.
4. Michael, you _____ not eat with your mouth open.
5. I'm getting angry. You _____ not say that again!

12.13 Saying something was a good idea or a bad idea in the past with *should*
The good news for you and your students is that the big mess that we talked about in the previous section gets a lot tidier in the past. *Ought to* (modern English!) and *had better* are not used in the past—only *should.* (OK, on rare occasions you might hear *ought to have.*)

It's all about *should have*:

12.34   I should have studied for the test.

12.35   You shouldn't have eaten three hot dogs, two hamburgers and five pieces of cake.

It's really so much easier than what we saw in the previous section, but listeningwise, there's one thing you need to talk about here that will come up again and again as we continue our merry journey: *should have* is very often reduced to *shoulda.* Your students need to understand this, but—you know what I always say next, so I won't say it. (You think you're so smart.)

You can have a lot of fun with these in class—inventing terrible things that happened to you or massive blunders that you made and asking your students for their advice. Here are some exercises like that. When I say there may be more than one possible answer, I mean that the advice could be phrased any number of ways. For example,

12.36   "My wife asked, 'Am I fat?' and I said yes. Now she won't talk to me." What do you think?

---

possible answers:

12.37a   You shouldn't have said yes.
  b   You should have said no.
  c   You should have kept your mouth shut.
  d   You should think before you talk.
  e   You should grow a brain.
  f   Your wife shouldn't have married you.

sample exercises 10:   What would you say about the people in these situations? Use *should have* or *should not have*. You are giving advice, so there may be more than one possible answer for some. Be ready to explain your answer.

> I didn't go to the party, and now my friends are telling me that it was a great party.
> *You should have gone to the party.*
>
> Maria locked her keys inside her house, so she had to break a window to get in.
> *She shouldn't have locked her keys inside her house.*

1.   I didn't eat breakfast. Now I'm hungry.
2.   I tried to start a fire with gasoline. Now I'm in the hospital.
3.   Noura didn't keep her big mouth shut. Now her sister is very angry with her.
4.   Alan didn't call his father. Now his father is upset.
5.   Carlos forgot to bring his glasses to the movie theater. Now he can't see the movie.

12.14   Talking about ability in the past, present and future with *can, could* and *be able to*

Here we will see that, in a kinda, sorta way, *could* is the past form of *can*. And while we're on the subject of modal past forms, *would* is the past form of *will, might* is the past form of *may* and get this—*should* is the past form of *shall*. This is a very small part of a much bigger modal picture and not worth making a big deal out of. I actually NEVER mention this to students except in the case of *can* for present ability and *could* for past ability. However, you'll find that some students fixate on this—usually because they've gotten it from some old-fashioned book in their native country—as if that's all one needs to know about these modals. In this case, at least, it does help your students to understand *could* is the past of *can*.

▶ *can* and *be able to* for present ability

Both *can* and *be able to* are used in the present. There's no new grammar here. Your students know how to make questions, negatives and short answers with *can* and *be*. One thing you may want to remind your students about is that *can* is used for ability and permission. Native speakers don't confuse the two, but your students might.

▶ *could* and *be able to* for past ability

A question regarding past ability starting with *Could you...?*, out of context, could conceivably be misunderstood to be a request for someone to do something. That's what happens with these modals which are used for many functions: The meaning might not be clear because of *could*'s conditional function. If I say, for example,

12.38   Could you do it?

what do I mean? Do I mean

12.39   Could you do it at some time in the past?

or do I mean

12.40   Could you do it now if I asked you to do it?

Of course in reality, we native speakers are seldom confused in this way—words like these aren't uttered in isolation but as part of a conversation and in a situation understood by all involved in the conversation. But it's a lot harder for your students. It's something for you to be aware of and sensitive to. You can see why I've advised you to focus on functions and the (usually) more than one modal and phrasal modal which can be used to perform these functions.

Not much to say about *be able to* in the past. Obviously, it's a way to avoid the confusion discussed above.

▶ *could* and *will be able to* for future ability

This gets confusing. We use *can* to speak about future ability, but not in the sense of knowledge of how to do something. We would <u>not</u> say

12.41   I'm starting a course in French. I can't speak French now, but after I finish my course, I can speak French.

That doesn't make any sense. However, we do use *can* for future ability when we speak of having the power to do something in the future:

> 12.42   I don't have time now, but I can help you tomorrow.

Will be able to works in both situations:

> 12.43   I'm starting a course in French. I can't speak French now, but after I finish my course, I will be able to speak French.

> 12.44   I don't have time now, but I will be able to help you tomorrow.

In the exercises below, you'll see that both *could* and *can* are good answers for numbers 5 and 6, which take place in the present. That's because they could be understood to be questions as to whether someone is able to do something or requests that someone actually do something. Confusing enough? Sometimes modals will make your head spin.

sample exercises 11: Complete the sentences with *can* or *could* and the verb in parentheses. Use contractions.

> I'm really tired. I (not, sleep) _____*couldn't sleep*_____ last night.

1. Sarah (walk) _____ when she was only six months old.
2. (understand) _____ you _____ what the teacher was talking about yesterday?
3. Mary has to work Friday night. She (not, come) _____ to the party.
4. I forgot my cell phone, so I (not, call) _____ you last night.
5. Oh no! My computer is screwed up again. Michael, (figure out) _____ you _____ what's wrong with my computer?
6. (tell) _____ you _____ me what this says? I forgot my glasses, and I (not, read) _____ it.

sample exercises 12: Rewrite the sentences using the correct form and tense of *be able to.*

> I can't do it.
> *I'm not able to do it.*

> Could you hear what he said?
> *Were you able to hear what he said?*

1. I can't sleep on airplanes.
2. Could the tech guy figure out what was wrong with your computer?
3. Mark can see a lot better with his new glasses.
4. The doctors couldn't save him.
5. I couldn't get my car started.

12.15   Talking about repeated past actions and past situations with *used to* and *would*

Here you need to make an important distinction—past actions and past situations. Put this on the board:

past actions	past situations
used to	used to
	would

Here's what it's all about:

For past actions, both *used to* and *would* are possible:

> 12.45   When I was a boy, we <u>would go</u> to the beach every weekend.

> 12.46   When I was a boy, we <u>used to go</u> to the beach every weekend.

With past situations, only *used to* is possible. Make sure your students understand that this a past situation which no longer exists:

> 12.47   I <u>used to</u> live in Oregon, but now I live in California.

Simple enough? Not really. *Used to* never fails to confuse students mainly because of its similarity to *be used to,* as in *be accustomed to,* which we discussed in Section 11.13. Before discussing the two, which you inevitably will (and it's a great way to eat up class time if you need to), teach your students how to make questions and negatives with *used to*: *I didn't use to...* and *Did you use to...* (Notice that *used* has changed to *use.*)

Also, teach your students that we do not use *used to* to talk about past situations when the time of the past situation is given.

Compare these examples:

12.48   My father <u>used to work</u> for the ABC Company.

12.49   My father <u>worked</u> for the ABC Company <u>from 1998 to 2007</u>.

sample exercises 13: Underline *would* or *used to*. If both are correct, underline both.
I (would/<u>used to</u>) love basketball when I was young. I (<u>would</u>/<u>used to</u>) play every day after school.

1. My sister (would/used to) have five dogs. They (would/used to) bark all night and wake up the neighbors.
2. I (would/used to) to work at the First National Bank on Main Street. When I worked there, I (would/used to) eat lunch at Sam's restaurant across the street almost every day.
3. Michael (would/used to) be thin, but he's gained a lot of weight in the last few years.
4. When I shared an apartment with my brother, he (would never/never used to) help me clean.
5. When I was young, my parents (wouldn't/didn't use to) let me go out on school nights.

12.16 Using modals with the phrasal modals *have to* and *be able to*

Modals (especially *will, would, might, may* and *should*, are often used with the phrasal modals *have to* and *be able to*. *Ought to* is not common and *have got to* is never used:

12.50   I might have to work tomorrow.

12.51   Mary may not be able to come to the party.

sample exercises 14: Complete the sentences with the words in parentheses.
Tom is going to try to fix my old TV, so I (not, have to, buy, may) _____ *may not have to buy* _____ a new one.

1. Carlos told me that he (come, be able to, not, will) _____ to my wedding.
2. If you're over 65, you (not, have to, may, pay) _____ full price. You (get, might, be able to) _____ a discount.
3. I'm sorry, but your essay wasn't very good. You (have to, will, rewrite) _____ it.
4. After you finish your driver's education course, you (pass, be able to, should) _____ the driver's license exam.
5. When you're in Norway, you (be able to, might, see) _____ the Northern Lights.

12.17 *would rather*

I made a BIG GIANT DEAL out of *would rather* in my book *Rocket English Grammar* (shameless plug), and believe me, it gave me a headache, and I know it's going to give me another headache now as I write this, but here goes.

So why did it give me a headache? Because of *ellipsis*—and you know what that is: not saying or repeating words because they are implied or understood. This is a very important part of learning English, especially for listening comprehension.

But first, let's get the basics out of the way. *Would rather,* of course, is used to talk about preferences. Often in writing and almost always in speaking, *would* is contracted to *'d*. This contraction of *would, 'd,* is something you want to train your students to listen for. It's very hard to hear when native speakers are speaking a mile a minute, and for ESL students, that's a problem.

OK, back to ellipsis. Here are some question and answer examples which will illustrate various patterns in which *would rather* is used and also several common ways that ellipsis is used. The words in brackets show the words that could be said but could also be, and probably would be, ellipted.

When one verb is used with two or more objects, often the objects are repeated but not the verb:

12.52   I'd rather play tennis than [play] soccer.

12.53   He'd rather be studying medicine than [be studying] law.

In conversation, often everything after the first object is not repeated:

12.54a   David: What would you rather do—play tennis or play soccer?
    b   John: I'd rather play tennis.
    c   = I'd rather play tennis [than play soccer].

12.55a   John: Would Mark rather be studying medicine or studying law?
    b   Ali: He'd rather be studying medicine.
    c   = He'd rather be studying medicine [than be studying law].

Sometimes the choice is between something and nothing:

12.56a Lucy: Would you like to help me give my cat a bath?
 b Sarah: I'd rather not.
 c = I'd rather not [help you give your cat a bath].

Here are some more examples:

12.57a Sofia: Would you rather eat Chinese food or Mexican?
 b = Would you rather eat Chinese food or [eat] Mexican [food]?
 c Joe: I'd rather eat Mexican food than Chinese.
 d = I'd rather eat Mexican food than [eat] Chinese [food].

12.58a Rosa: What do you want to do—play basketball or watch TV?
 b Paul: I'd rather play basketball.
 c = I'd rather play basketball [than watch TV].

12.59a Carlos: Do want to go shopping with me?
 b Gary: I'd rather not.
 c = I'd rather not [go shopping with you].

Here are some common question patterns:

12.60a What would you rather have—chocolate ice cream or vanilla ice cream?
 b Would you rather have chocolate ice cream or [have] vanilla ice cream?
 c Would you rather have chocolate ice cream than [have] vanilla ice cream?
 d Wouldn't you rather have chocolate ice cream than [have] vanilla ice cream?

So how about your students? If you want to teach them all these patterns, go for it, but you may want to keep it simple and teach them the most common pattern: *I'd rather (verb) than (verb)*. You could practice this by going around the classroom asking questions like these:

12.61 Michael, would you rather go to the dentist or [go to] the beach?

12.62 Sarah, would you rather watch TV or do your homework?

without discussing the many variations and ellipsis possibilities. You have to judge what your students need and are ready for. If you really want to go all out, try this exercise.

sample exercises 15: Ask questions with *would rather*.
 A: What _____ *would you rather have—apple juice or orange juice* _____?
 B: I'd rather have apple juice [than have orange juice].
 A: What _____ *would you rather do—walk to the store or drive there* _____?
 B: I'd rather walk to the store [than drive there].
 A: Would _____ *you rather go to a movie than visit my mother* _____?
 B: I'd rather go to a movie [than visit your mother].
 A: Wouldn't _____ *you rather watch TV than clean the garage* _____?
 B: Yes, I'd rather watch TV [than clean the garage].

 1. A: What _____?
    B: I'd rather stay home [than go to the library].
 2. A: Wouldn't _____?
    B: Yes, I'd rather leave tomorrow [than leave today].
 3. A: Would _____?
    B: He'd rather drive all night [than stop at a motel].
 4. A: Where _____?
    B: He'd rather go to Munich [than go to Berlin].
 5. A: Wouldn't _____?
    B: No, she wouldn't rather be married [than be single].

sample exercises 16: Write two answers to the questions. In the first answer, do not use ellipsis. In the second answer, use ellipsis as much as possible. Often there is ellipsis in the question. Try to replace the ellipted words in the B1 answer as in the example.

      A: Would you rather have coffee or tea?
         (You prefer tea.)
  B1: I'd _____ *rather have tea than coffee* _____ .
  B2: I'd _____ *rather have tea* _____ .

1. A: Would he rather go to London or Paris?
      (He prefers London.)
  B1: He would _____ .
  B2: He would _____ .

2. A: What would you rather do—play tennis or go swimming?
      (You prefer to play tennis.)
  B1: I'd _____ .
  B2: I'd _____ .

3. A: Wouldn't you rather drive to the beach than walk to the beach?
      (You prefer to walk to the beach.)
  B1: Yes, I would _____ .
  B2: Yes, I would _____ .

4. A: Would you rather go shopping with me or stay home?
      (You prefer to stay home.)
  B1: I'd _____ .
  B2: I'd _____ .

5. A: What would she rather do—take a taxi or go in my car?
      (She prefers to take a taxi.)
  B1: She'd _____ .
  B2: She'd _____ .

12.18 Certainty, predictions and expectations

The next few sections will deal with how we use modals and phrasal modals to discuss degrees of certainty, to make predictions and to talk about expectations regarding the past, present and future. Actually though, certainty, predictions and expectations boil down to the same thing—how sure we are about what *has happened, is happening* or *will happen*. The idea of degree is very important, as you will see. As usual, we'll see that sometimes two or more modals and phrasal modals will have the same function, and as usual, we'll come across various complications and exceptions.

12.19 Degrees of certainty about the present with *must, have to, have got to, may, might, can* and *could*

Must, have to, have got to, may, might, can and *could* are all used, in one way or another, to discuss how certain we are about something in the present. Yes, seven different modals and phrasal modals. But in this case they are <u>not</u> all the same, with the exception of *may, might* and (sort of) *could*. The main thing here is the degree of certainty—emphasize that to your students.

The use of *must* that we will discuss here and in the next section, called (jargon alert!) *logical probability*, is very important—important because it's a very common aspect of everyday English—far more common than what is probably the only thing your students have learned so far about *must*: that it's for *obligation*. I think this use of *must* is one of the most important things you can teach your students about modals.

Your students already know *maybe* by now. They know that we say *maybe* when we are not sure. Now we are discussing several modals that we use for the same purpose, and *may* is one of them. The difference between *maybe* and *may be* never fails to confuse students, so you need to work on it.

▸ + 100% sure (no modal or phrasal modal)

When we are 100% certain, we do <u>not</u> use modals or phrasal modals:

  12.63 Mary <u>is</u> sick.

  12.64 Carlos <u>speaks</u> Spanish.

▸ + Very certain (*must, have to* or *have got to*)

When we are very certain, but not 100%, we use *must, have to* or *have got to*. Make sure your students understand that the functions they see here are different from the functions discussed previously. They are <u>not</u> about obligation. They are used to say that we are very certain about something because it is logical to think as we do. *Must* is the most common. *Have to* and *have got to* are used only when we want extra emphasis to make what we say stronger:

12.65   The teacher is wearing a wedding ring. He has never told me that he is married, but if he's wearing a wedding ring, he <u>must be</u> married.

12.66   David is an excellent piano player. He <u>must practice</u> a lot.

12.67   It takes an hour to drive to the mall, and they left three hours ago, so they <u>have to</u> be there now.

12.68   I don't understand this math problem. Alan is really good at math. Let's ask him. He <u>has to know</u> the answer.

12.69   That's the craziest thing I have ever heard! You<u>'ve got to be</u> joking.

▶ **+ Maybe (*might, may* or *could*)**

When we are not very certain, we use *might, may* or *could*. There is no difference in meaning (or at least none that is of any concern to ESL students) when they are used for this function:

12.70   Larry is often absent from class, and he's absent today. He <u>might be</u> sick, but I'm not sure.

12.71   John knows a little about French history, so he <u>may know</u> the answer to your question.

12.72   Where are my keys? I think they <u>could be</u> under the sofa, or they <u>could be</u> in my coat pocket.

▶ **– Maybe not (*might not* or *may not*)**

When we are not very certain, and the emphasis is on the negative, we use *might not* or *may not* (but not *could not*) in negative sentences:

12.73   The mechanic told me that my car would be ready around 2:00, and it's 1:50 now, so it <u>might not be</u> ready yet.

12.74   I asked a man for directions to the bank, but he just smiled and kept walking. I think he <u>may not speak</u> English.

▶ **– Very certain with emphasis on the negative (*must not*)**

When we are very certain, and the emphasis is on the negative, we use *must not*. *Have to* and *have got to* are not used in negative sentences. The contraction *mustn't* is possible, but it is not common, so don't let your students use it:

12.75   John isn't eating any of the food on his plate. He <u>must not be</u> hungry.

12.76   Everyone at the party was dancing except Larry. He <u>must not know</u> how to dance.

▶ **– Almost 100% sure with emphasis on the negative (*cannot* or *could not*)**

When we are almost 100% sure, and the emphasis is on the negative, we use *cannot* or *could not*. Notice how the meaning of *could* is different in negative sentences than it is in affirmative sentences:

12.77   Your husband wants to quit his job at the bank and become a circus clown? You <u>can't be</u> serious.

12.78   Somebody told you he invented a car that runs on sea water? That <u>couldn't be</u> true. I think you made a mistake.

▶ **– 100% sure with emphasis on the negative (no modal or phrasal modal)**

When we are 100% certain, and the emphasis is on the negative, we do <u>not</u> use modals or phrasal modals:

12.79   Sofia <u>is not</u> here.

12.80   John <u>doesn't live</u> in California.

Remember, modals are about how we perceive or feel about a situation, and because different people can perceive a situation differently or feel differently about a situation, it's difficult to make exercises where there is only one right answer. To reinforce students' understanding of modals, I think it's better to ask them to choose from two (and sometimes more) answers so they can consider what is appropriate in different situations. In some cases, it's clear why one answer is the best answer, but in other cases, it might not be so clear or a case could be made for more than one of the answers. That's a good thing. It makes your students think, and it's a great opportunity for some classroom discussion.

sample exercises 17: What would you say in these situations? Study the examples to better understand when each modal is used. Then underline the words that you think are the best in each situation.

I forgot my dictionary, and I need one for the English test. Maria sometimes has a dictionary, so I'll ask her. She (<u>may have</u>/has got to have) one.

---

1. That movie was fabulous! I loved it! It (might be/has to be) the best movie in the universe!
2. Alan never goes in the deep end of the swimming pool. He (doesn't know/must not know) how to swim.
3. It's 9:00 p.m. I just called my sister, but there was no answer. She (may be/must be) sleeping.
4. It's 2:00 a.m. I just called my sister, but there was no answer. She (may be/must be) sleeping.
5. Your 18-year-old daughter is going to marry an 83-year-old man? You (can't be/aren't) serious! You (have got to be/could be) joking!

12.20 Degrees of certainty about the past with *must, have to, have got to, may, might, can* and *could*

Again we see that seven modals and phrasal modals are used discuss about how certain we are about something in the past. Your students might wonder how we can be uncertain about the past—the past has already happened, right? Yes, sometimes we are certain of what has happened, but at other times we don't know for certain what has happened. Then we express our thoughts as to the likelihood of what may or may not have happened with modals and phrasal modals. A review of past participles, especially *been,* might be a good idea at this point.

▶ **+ 100% sure (no modal or phrasal modal)**

When we are 100% certain, we do not <u>use</u> modals or phrasal modals:

12.81   Carlos <u>has eaten</u> dinner.

12.82   Mark <u>was</u> here yesterday.

12.83   My brother <u>went</u> to the library.

▶ **+ Very certain (*must have*)**

When we are very certain, we use *must have.* Remind your students again that the function of *must* that they see here is different from the function discussed previously. It's not about obligation. It's about how certain we are about something. *Have to have* and *have got to have* are possible, but they are not common:

12.84   Sarah isn't answering her telephone. She <u>must have gone</u> to bed.

12.85   I saw Carlos leave for work in the morning but turn around and go back into his house. He <u>must have forgotten</u> something.

12.86   Michael borrowed Mary's car, and he crashed it. Mary <u>must have been</u> very angry.

▶ **+ Maybe (*might have, may have* or *could have*)**

When we are not very certain, we use *might have, may have* or *could have.* There is no difference in meaning when they are used for this function:

12.87   John didn't come to work today. I think he <u>might have gone</u> to the baseball game.

12.88   I hurt my finger badly today. I'm going to go to the hospital because I think I <u>may have broken</u> it.

12.89   Somebody called but didn't leave a message. It <u>could have been</u> my son calling to wish me happy birthday.

▶ **– Maybe not (*might not have* or *may not have*)**

When we are not very certain, and the emphasis is on the negative, we use *might not have* and *may not have* (but not *could not have*) in negative sentences:

12.90   I left a message for Mary to call me tonight, but she hasn't called me yet. I think she <u>might not have gotten</u> the message.

12.91   Our teacher told all of us to come to the library today, but Carlos isn't here. He <u>may not have been listening</u> when the teacher told us to come here.

▶ **– Very certain with emphasis on the negative (*must not have*)**

When we are very certain, and the emphasis is on the negative, we use *must not have.* Notice that *have to* and *have got to* are not used in negative sentences. The contraction *mustn't have* is possible, but it is not common:

12.92   Ali got a bad grade on his English test. He <u>must not have studied</u>.

▶ **– Almost 100% sure with emphasis on the negative (*cannot have* or *could not*)**

When we are almost 100% sure, and the emphasis is on the negative, we use *cannot have* or *could not have.* Notice how the meaning of *could have* is different in negative sentences than it is in affirmative sentences:

12.93   Your teacher told you that the sun rises in the west? You <u>cannot have heard</u> her correctly.

12.94   Carlos says that he read a 500-page book last night, but he <u>couldn't have read</u> such a long book in one night.

▶ – **100% sure with emphasis on the negative (no modal or phrasal modal)**

When we are 100% certain, and the emphasis is on the negative, we do not use modals or phrasal modals:

12.95   John <u>hasn't been</u> here all day.

12.96   Michael and Sarah <u>weren't</u> at the party.

12.97   They <u>didn't go</u> to the park.

Are you going to expect your students to memorize all of that? Of course not. Again, the best thing you can do is get them familiar with these modal and phrasal modals uses and reinforce that familiarity with exercises like these.

sample exercises 18:   What would you say in these situations? Study the examples to better understand when each modal is used. Then underline the words that you think are the best in each situation.

1.   It takes three hours to fly to Paris from here, and Sarah left five hours ago. She (must have arrived/might have arrived) in Paris.
2.   It takes three hours to fly to Paris from here, and Alan left three hours ago. He (must have arrived/might have arrived) in Paris.
3.   It takes three hours to fly to Paris from here, and Michael left two hours ago. He (cannot have arrived/might not have arrived) in Paris.
4.   I left a message for Jim about my party. I was sure he would come, but he didn't. He (may not have gotten/did not get) my message.
5.   I saw Linda across the street. I waved to her, but she didn't wave back. She (didn't see/may not have seen) me.
6.   Maria didn't answer her phone. She (didn't hear/might not have heard) it ringing.

12.21   *may have* and *might have*: slightly different

What would any discussion of modals be without complications? I sort of oversimplified when I said that *may have* and *might have* were 100% the same. Actually, there is a distinction, but it's unknown to most native speakers and is probably not worth adding to your students' burden of making sense of all these slippery devils. In a weird way, *might* is the past of *may*. The idea of modals having a past and present form isn't something I like to dwell on because one, there's rarely a need to, unless you're talking about *can* and *could* and present and past ability, and because it gives students the idea that this is the key to understanding modals, which it hardly is.

But for reasons that will be explained in Chapter 18, this idea—modals having a past form and a present form—is important when we talk about things that *could be real, possible,* etc., and those which are *not real, not possible,* etc., (or at least *almost certainly not real or almost certainly not possible*). What we'll see is that we use the past <u>form</u> of verbs (why I make a point of emphasizing *form* will be explained in Chapter 18), including modal auxiliary verbs, when we talk about things that are not real, not possible, etc.

This idea applies to our discussion here of *may* and *might*. When we speculate about the present/future (remembering that we make no distinction between the present and future—the future starts right now), the whole idea is that we are not sure, so using either *may* or *might* to make a distinction between what is sure and what isn't sure doesn't make sense. Nothing is sure, so no distinction is made between *may* and *might* in this situation, and they have become synonymous.

But what about the past? Well, it is possible to speculate about a future outcome in the past and to be either sure or unsure whether that outcome occurred.

When <u>we know</u> how things turned out, we use *might have*. If I say

12.98   That shark <u>might have</u> eaten me.

we know that the shark didn't eat me because if it had, I wouldn't be writing this. I'm using *might have,* the past <u>form</u> of *may have,* because this possible outcome didn't happen. It is impossible that I was eaten by the shark.

But what if we <u>don't know</u>? If we don't know how things turned out, we use *may have*:

12.99   I was swimming with David. I got away from the shark, but David is missing. I think the shark <u>may have</u> eaten him.

In poor David's case, we are talking about something that is possible—maybe the shark did eat David. That's why we use *may have.*

This is a pretty fine point to be teaching to your students, so are you going to? As I said, many (probably most) native speakers haven't got a clue about any of this and use *may have* and *might have* interchangeably. Normally I wouldn't mention this to students, but if you get some really motivated and capable students who ask you about this, now you know. (And lucky you!) Regardless of whether you teach this to your students, if it's not entirely clear to you, you might want to come back to it after studying Chapter 18 on conditionals.

12.22 Degrees of certainty about the future, part 1, with *will*, *be going to*, *might*, *may* and *could*
Future gets a bit tricky because, in addition to using *will*, *be going to*, *might*, *may* and *could* to express our thoughts as to the likelihood of what may or may not happen in the future, we also use various adverbs to say precisely how certain we are. In order to focus your students on the most essential aspects of this and not smother them in grammar, I think this should be taught in two parts—the basics and the finer points. The finer points could wait until later when you think your students are ready for it.

And while you're talking to your students about *probably*, you should give them a little listening exercise: native speakers almost always say *probly* instead of *probably*. You *probly* do too, and you should model that for your students with the usual reminder to listen and learn, not copy.

▶ **+ 100% sure (*will* or *be going to*)**
When we're 100% certain, we use *will* and *be going to*: (And as we saw in Chapter 5, also the present continuous and the present simple. Mention that too, if you want, but I wouldn't now—keep it simple.)

12.100   Maria <u>will make</u> an apple pie.

12.101   They'<u>re going to</u> win the game.

▶ **+ Somewhat certain (*will probably* or *be probably going to*)**
When we're somewhat certain, but not 100%, it's common to use *probably*:

12.102   Carlos is usually late, so he'<u>ll probably be</u> late today.

12.103   I might go to the party, but I'<u>m probably going to stay</u> home tonight.

▶ **+ Maybe (*might*, *may* or *could*)**
When we are not very certain, we use *might, may* or *could*. There is no difference in meaning when they are used for this function:

12.104   I think it <u>might rain</u> soon.

12.105   The meeting tomorrow <u>may be canceled</u>.

12.106   My grandfather is very sick. He <u>could die</u> at any moment.

▶ **− Maybe not (*might not* or *may not*)**
When we are not very certain, we use *might not* or *may not* (but not *could not*) in negative sentences:

12.107   Larry <u>might not like</u> this shirt that I got him for his birthday.

12.108   Are you sure you want to go to a Japanese restaurant? You <u>may not like</u> the food.

▶ **− Somewhat certain with emphasis on the negative (*probably will not* or *be probably not going to*)**
When we are somewhat certain, but not 100% sure, and the emphasis is on the negative, we use *probably*:

12.109   Alan is so lazy. You can ask him to help you, but he <u>probably won't do</u> it.

12.110   I'm not feeling well today. I'<u>m probably not going to go</u> to work tomorrow.

▶ **− 100% sure with emphasis on negative (*will not* or *be not going to*)**
When we are 100% certain, and the emphasis is on the negative, we use *will not* and *be not going to*:

12.111   The store <u>won't be</u> open when we get there.

12.112   My speech <u>isn't going to last</u> longer than 30 minutes.

sample exercises 19: What would you say in these situations? Study the examples to better understand when each modal is used. Then use *will, be going to, might, may* or *could* to complete the sentences. Use *not* and *probably* when you think they are necessary. Remember that modals are used to say how people feel about or understand a situation, so it is possible for different people to feel about or understand the same situation in different ways. For this reason, there may be more than one good answer for some. Be ready to explain your answer.

1. Today is Sunday, and sometimes stores are closed on Sunday, so if we go shopping, some of the stores _____ be closed.
2. I'm feeling a little sick. I _____ go to work tomorrow.
3. I'm feeling very sick. I _____ go to work tomorrow.
4. My doctor's appointment is at 9:00, and the meeting starts at 10:00, so I _____ be late for the meeting.
5. My doctor's appointment is at 9:00, and the meeting starts at 1:00, so I _____ be late for the meeting.

12.23 Degrees of certainty about the future, part 2, with *will, be going to* and a bunch of adverbs

In addition to *probably,* we use also use several other adverbs. There are 1,001 and variations on all of this. (I counted them.) Here are a few:

+

12.113a   I will almost certainly do it.
    b   I am almost certainly going to do it.
    c   I will most likely do it.
    d   I will very likely do it.
    e   I likely will do it.
    f   I am most likely going to do it.
    g   I am very likely going to do it.
    h   I am likely going to do it.

    i   Whatever.

    j   I am not likely going to do it.
    k   I am very likely not going to do it.
    l   I am most likely not going to do it.
    m   I will not likely do it.
    n   I will not very likely do it.
    o   I will most likely not do it.
    p   I am almost certainly not going to do it.
    q   I will almost certainly not do it.

—

And of course, let's not forget that we also use the present continuous and present simple for future. And let's not forget that we sometimes use *never* instead of *not.* I could fill the next several pages with examples, but you get the idea.

There are even variations within variations. Several of the examples above would be just as acceptable with the words slightly rearranged. I used the word order that seemed the most natural to me. *Almost, certainly, probably, likely, never* and *not* are adverbs, and adverbs have a lot more freedom to move around in sentences than other parts of speech. Are you going to teach all 1,001 variations to your students? No, I don't recommend it, but some? Yes, maybe that's a good idea. But how many should you teach your students? Good question. That often happens: You're faced with deciding what to teach your students and what to skip—where do you quit? How much is too much? Are you a being a good teacher by teaching your students every conceivable variation, or are you being a bad teacher by overwhelming and confusing them? Are you being a good teacher by keeping it simple and not mentioning things that you know are out there so as not to overwhelm and confuse your students, or are you being a bad teacher by not teaching them as must as possible? What's the answer? I DON'T KNOW!!!

I like to imagine my student's ability to use English as a building. I can't build the entire building for them, but I can help them build the framework. Completing the building will have to come later, but I can help them with some of that too. But what help and how much? There is no right or wrong answer—there are so many factors to consider. What are your students' needs? Can they handle tons of grammar, or will it blow them away? What needs explaining, and what can they easily figure out on their own later? How much time do you have? How common is the grammar in question? And just between you and me, I have heard rumors that there are some teachers—terrible, unprofessional, disgrace-to-the-profession teachers—who actually sometimes—brace yourself—consider what is on the test (egad!) to be an important factor. Of course, this isn't *anything* I have *ever* given *any* thought to, and I'm sure you never will either.

12.24 Certainty: talking about expectations based on previous knowledge or experience with *should* and *ought to*

This is often overlooked or covered quite briefly by grammar books, but I feel that it's important and deserves a lot more attention than that. For that reason, I made a BIG GIANT DEAL of it in my book, *Rocket English Grammar* (shameless plug). As with *must* for logical probability, I think this is one of the most useful things you can teach your students about modals.

First of all, in no way, shape or form does this have anything to do with giving advice. As soon as your students hear *should* (and to a lesser extent, *ought to*), they'll think *advice*. So make it clear from the beginning that this is not about giving advice.

And superficially, this might seem like what we've already been talking about—using different modals and phrasal modals to discuss how certain we are about something. For example,

12.114   He will screw it up.

12.115   She might not pass the test.

12.116   Brazil is going to beat the USA in the World Cup 20 to 0.

12.117   They may have gotten lost.

And superficially, that is sorta, kinda true, but *should* and *ought to* are different in a very important way, and that is why I have separated this from our discussion of certainty using other modals and phrasal modals. In the sentences above, if I had said these sentences, I might know what I'm talking about, <u>or I might not</u>. Maybe I'm just a babbling idiot who hasn't got a clue what he's talking about—there's nothing about the sentences above that tells you that what I say is <u>definitely</u> based on any experience or knowledge I have of the situation.

But what about these examples? Read them and ask yourself this question: Is it understood that they are based on my previous experience or knowledge of a situation?

12.118   I don't know the answer to your question, but Maria knows a lot about that subject. Let's ask her. She should know.

12.119   I don't want to see Linda at the gym. She always goes there in the morning. It's 3:00 in the afternoon now, so if I go to the gym now, she shouldn't be there.

12.120   Follow these directions to get to the clinic: First, drive three miles north on Main Street. Then turn left on Oak Street and go about one mile. You should see the clinic on the right.

12.121   The coffee shop opens really early, so let's go now. It's 8:30 already. They ought to be open.

As you can see, we use *should* and *ought to* to discuss our certainty about people or situations which we <u>already know about and understand</u>. We want to say that we are quite certain about something because we <u>already</u> have experience with or knowledge of these people or situations. *Should* is more common than *ought to*. Remember to remind your students that *should = ought to* and that *ought to* is usually pronounced *otta* (with the usual reminder to listen and learn, not copy). Also, remind them that *ought to* is almost never used for questions and negative sentences.

We use *should* and *ought to* when we <u>do not know</u> if what we expected really happened, but we're quite certain that it did:

12.122   It usually takes ten minutes to drive to the bank, and John left an hour ago, so he ought to be there by now. (The speaker doesn't know if what he or she expected has happened but is pretty sure that it did.)

and when what the speaker expected did not happen, contrary to what we were quite certain would happen. Is that clear?

12.123   He told me he was going to come to this party, so where is he? He ought to be here. (The speaker knows that what he or she expected hasn't happened.)

Should and *ought to* are used for the present and future. *Should have* and *ought to have* are used for the past. (And needless to say, *should have* is more common.)

Let's look at some past examples. First, examples where the speaker <u>doesn't know what happened</u>:

12.124   Francesca's father told her to finish her homework before dinner. She had just a little homework, so she shouldn't have needed more than 15 minutes to finish it. (Did she need more than 15 minutes? The speaker doesn't know but is pretty sure that she didn't.)

12.125   John flew to Los Angeles this morning. He left four hours ago, and it usually takes two hours, so he should have arrived by now. (Has John arrived? The speaker doesn't know but is pretty sure that he has.)

12.126 Larry had a test yesterday. I haven't talked to him, so I don't know how the test went, but he's a really good student, so the test ought to have been easy for him. (Was it easy? The speaker doesn't know but is pretty sure that it was.)

and some examples where the speaker <u>knows what happened</u>:

12.127 I'm getting worried about my wife. It's 6:00, and she always comes home from work at 4:00. She should have come home two hours ago. Where is she? (The speaker knows that his wife didn't come home at 4:00, contrary to what he expected.)

12.128 Lucy, this was a small project. You took two weeks to finish it. It shouldn't have taken you more than one week. (The speaker knows that Lucy didn't finish the project in one week as he or she expected.)

sample exercises 20: What would you say in these situations? Use *should, should have* or *ought to* and the correct form of the verb in parentheses to complete the sentences. Write all possibilities. Some are negative. Remember that it is not common to use *not* with *ought to*.

1. The train is supposed to come at 7:14, and it's already 7:24. The train (come) _____ soon.
2. It's really easy to do this. It (not, take) _____ you more than a few minutes last night, so why haven't you finished yet?
3. My wife loves to make Italian food, so she (love) _____ this pasta maker I'm buying for her.
4. Linda and her husband went to Tom's Diner. That isn't a very expensive restaurant, so dinner for two people (not, cost) _____ more than $40.
5. The mail is delivered every morning at 10:00, and it's 11:30 already. It (come) _____ by now.
6. It's really easy to do this. It (not, take) _____ you more than a few minutes tonight, but call me if you have a problem.

12.25 Plans: talking about past plans with *be going to*
We've already talked about how the phrasal modal *be going to* is used to talk about future plans, but what about past plans? We use *be going to* for that too. As we saw with *should* and *ought to* in the previous section, we can distinguish between past plans which we know the outcome of and those which we don't. In other words, whether the plans worked out or did not work out. When what we plan actually happens, we normally use the past simple:

12.129 Alan went to the beach yesterday. (I know he went to the beach.)

but when those plans don't work out, we often use *be going to*:

12.130 Alan was going to go to the beach yesterday, but it was too cold. (I know he didn't go the beach.)

We also use *be going to* discuss past plans that may or may not have worked out. We don't know the outcome:

12.131 Carlos was going to go to the beach too, but I don't know if he did.

Here are some more examples. First, with a known outcome. What was planned didn't happen:

12.132 I was going to make a chocolate cake last night, but I didn't.

12.133 You were going to be here at 8:00, but you came at 9:00. Why were you late?

12.134 Look! Larry got a tattoo! He said he wasn't going to get one, but he did.

12.135 Sarah said she wasn't going to be at the meeting, but I saw her there.

12.136 Gary, why are you smoking? You told me you weren't going to smoke anymore, remember?

12.137 Francesca was going to go shopping today, but she changed her mind and stayed home.

12.138a Tom: Is Noura here?
   b Jerry: Noura was going to be here, but she isn't.

and second, with an unknown outcome. We don't know if the plans happened:

12.139a Sam: Were your friends going to eat at that new French restaurant last night?
   b Dave: Yes, they were going to eat there, but I don't know if they did.

12.140 I need to know what happened at the conference yesterday. Mary was going to attend. I'm going to call her to find out what happened.

12.141   John wanted to make an appointment to see his doctor today, but he couldn't. The doctor was going to be in surgery at the hospital.

12.142   Don't call Carlos. He's not home. He was going to go to the museum today.

12.143a Sam: Is your sister at work now?
     b   Alan: She wasn't going to go to work today, but I just called her, and she isn't home, so maybe she did go to work.

To further confuse your students, explain that we also use past forms of *be going to* to discuss plans made in the past for a future time:

12.144   I talked to Mary last night, and she said she was going to visit us next Saturday.

12.145   They said they were going to deliver my new sofa tomorrow.

It would be useful to your students if you discussed some similar ways we talk about past plans. *Plan to, plan on* and *intend to* have a similar meaning:

12.146a I was going to wash my car yesterday, but I didn't.
     b   = I planned to wash my car yesterday, but I didn't.
     c   = I planned on washing my car yesterday, but I didn't. (*Washing* is a gerund, which you haven't gotten to yet.)
     d   = I intended to wash my car yesterday, but I didn't.

It occurs to me that it might occur to you to ask whether this is grammar or vocabulary? Wouldn't vocabulary be a different class, a different teacher, a different book? Throughout this book, in addition to discussing how to teach your students grammar, I've given you advice about how to help them with speaking (a little), listening (a lot), and I've also provided you with many useful words to teach them (with many more to come). Are these, strictly speaking, grammar? No. Do I care? No. What is *your* goal? For your students to understand the English that they read in their grammar book and hear in your classroom? Yes, that's great, but your real goal is for them to understand and use English beyond their grammar book and outside the walls of their classroom. That's what really matters.

sample exercises 21: Complete the sentences with *be going to*. Some are negative.
      A: I'm surprised to see you here, Linda. You _____*weren't going to*_____ come, but here you are.
      B: You're right. I _____*was going to*_____ stay home tonight, but I changed my mind.

1.   A: Did Mark and Sarah go to Hawaii last year?
      B: They _____ go, but they didn't.
2.   A: Why are you here at work? You _____ take today off, right?
      B: No, I _____ take today off. Sam _____ take today off.
3.   A: You lost your job? When _____ you _____ tell me?
      B: Yes, I lost my job. I _____ tell you tomorrow.
4.   A: My parents visited me last night, so I had to cancel all my plans.
      B: What _____ you _____ do?
      A: I _____ have lunch with Tom, and then we _____ play golf.

12.26 Talking about expectations with *be supposed to*

Be supposed to is the Swiss Army Knife of phrasal modals—it has many uses.

We use *be supposed to* to talk about what we expect because it is a rule or a law:

12.147   You're supposed to stop when the light is red.

12.148   You're not supposed to smoke in a movie theater.

We use *be supposed to* to talk about what we expect because it is the correct way to do something:

12.149   You're supposed to take this medicine twice a day.

12.150   Parents are supposed to teach their children about right and wrong.

We use *be supposed to* to talk about what we expect because it's a plan or a schedule:

12.151   The meeting tomorrow is supposed to start at 10:00.

12.152   I'm waiting for Maria. She's supposed to meet me here at 11:30, and then we're going to eat lunch.

We use *be supposed to* to talk about unfulfilled plans:

12.153   The meeting yesterday was supposed to start at 10:00, but it started late.

and unconfirmed plans:

12.154   John was supposed to meet Mary this morning at 8:00. I hope he remembered.

Be supposed to is used to talk about the past, present and future, but only the past simple and present simple form of *be* are used because, as we'll see later, no distinction is made between the present and future. The future starts right now. Compare these two examples:

12.155   My sister is supposed to call me any second.

12.156   My sister is supposed to call me tomorrow.

Also, *be supposed to* is never continuous.

I wouldn't advise teaching your students the verb *suppose* here because that's not likely to help with *be supposed to*. But some troublemaker might ask what it means, so if you do discuss *suppose*, try to teach them that it's similar to *assume, presume, believe*, and then when that fails, get out the bilingual dictionary. If you're lucky, it might have a definition of *be supposed to*.

And make sure your students understand that in written form, it's always *suppos<u>ed</u>*, never *suppose*, but when we native speakers say it, the *-ed* is usually silent or close to it. To reinforce the mechanics of *be supposed to*, how about a little error correction?

sample exercises 22:   Correct the mistakes in the sentences.

1.   I supposed to finish this work before I go home.
2.   You're not suppose to talk in a library.
3.   John will be supposed to give a presentation next week.
4.   Are we supposed read Chapter 5 or Chapter 6 for our homework?
5.   The show is supposing to start at 9:00.

sample exercises 23:   Complete the sentences with the correct form of *be supposed to*. Some are negative.

A: Why is Mark angry with you?
B: Because I _____*was supposed to*_____ take him to the airport, and I forgot.

1.   A: When does the meeting begin? (Present simple used for future, remember?)
     B: It _____ begin at 11:00.
2.   A: Did Mary meet you at the mall this morning?
     B: She _____, but she didn't.
3.   A: How long should I cook this cake for?
     B: You _____ cook it for 45 minutes.
4.   A: Is it OK to smoke here?
     B: No, you _____.
5.   A: When _____ I _____ be home tonight?
     B: I already told you. You _____ be home at midnight.

12.27   *be to*

Believe it or not, our long strange trip through the modal looking glass (how's that for mixing musical and literary allusions?) is almost over. We finish with *be to*, a little gem of a phrasal modal that, hidden in plain sight, you might not even have known existed even though you've used it and heard it a million times—maybe a billion times.

Be to is a classic example of how, when you study a language, it's the little words that can be the biggest problem. How many of your students, would you say, are aware that there's something about the words *be* and *to* that they still need to learn? Not many, but then they come across sentences like these:

12.157   He was not to have done that.

12.158   You are to do it at once.

or a headline like this:

12.159   President to Address Nation at 8:00 (Where's *be*?)

and they think what anyone who has studied a language has thought many a time—*I know every one of these words, and I have no idea what this means.*

So should you definitely teach *be to*? Not necessarily. It depends on whom you're teaching. For more advanced students who will use English for academic or business purposes, I usually do. Otherwise, I skip it. *Be to* is also useful, as we'll see, for making sense out of signs and article headlines on the internet and in newspapers.

So what's it all about? *Be to* is used in formal English to talk about something that is expected because it is an order or a rule:

12.160   This is secret. You are not to tell anyone. Do you understand?

12.161   You were to finish your homework assignment three days ago. Why haven't you finished yet?

12.162   Students are to complete the first part of the exam before 10:30 and the second part before 11:45.

12.163   You are not to open this door when the red light is on. Do you understand?

or about something that is expected because it is an official plan or arrangement:

12.164   The President is to speak to the nation at 8:00 Tuesday evening.

12.165   The meeting was to have ended at 4:00, but it didn't end until 5:30.

12.166   The president of the company is to speak to the conference at 9:00.

12.167   The king and the prime minister were to meet yesterday in the royal palace.

Present perfect and past simple forms of *be to* can be used with little difference in meaning:

12.168a   The king and the prime minister were to meet yesterday in the royal palace.
       b   = The king and the prime minister were to have met yesterday in the royal palace.

12.169a   He was to be in his lawyer's office at 1:00.
       b   = He was to have been in his lawyer's office at 1:00.

but it is more common to use the past simple of a main verb or *be* (not *be to*) when we are talking about plans and arrangements that we know really happened:

12.170   The king and the prime minister met yesterday in the royal palace.

12.171   He was in his lawyer's office at 1:00.

Present perfect and past simple forms of *be to* are usually used for unrealized expectations:

12.172a   The president of the company was to speak to the conference at 9:00, however her speech was canceled.
       b   = The president of the company was to have spoken to the conference at 9:00, however her speech was canceled.

and unconfirmed expectations:

12.173a   He was to be in his lawyer's office at 1:00, but I don't know if he went.
       b   = He was to have been in his lawyer's office at 1:00, but I don't know if he went.

You can see how similar *be to* is to *be supposed to*. If you've covered *be supposed to*, discussing this similarity would help your students understand *be to*.

sample exercises 24: You are to use the correct form of *be to* to complete the sentences. Some are negative.

You _____*were to*_____ be at the meeting yesterday. Where were you?

You _____*were to have*_____ been at the meeting yesterday. Where were you?

You _____*are to*_____ be at the meeting tomorrow. Is that clear?

1.   You _____ sit here, do your work and be quiet. Do you understand?
2.   This information is secret. You _____ discuss it with anyone. Is that clear?
3.   The flight from Madrid to Mexico City_____ arrived at 2:10, but it didn't. In 30 minutes an airline official _____ announce some important information regarding the missing plane.
4.   You _____ submitted your report by yesterday. Why didn't you?
5.   The judge _____ announced her decision today, but she postponed it until tomorrow.
6.   Several executives from our company are going to speak at the conference next week. The advertising manager

_____ speak about the new advertising campaign, and then Ted MacDonald, Phil Shepardson and Joe Samuelson _____ give a presentation about plans for the next year. Chris Pinkerton, the CEO of the company, _____ spoken at the conference as well, but he had to cancel.

12.28 Headlinese

A semi-invisible form of *be to* is often seen in headlines. By "semi-invisible", I mean partially ellipted. Look at these headlines:

12.174   Teachers to End Strike

12.175   Johnson to Testify

12.176   Microsoft to Lay Off 11,000

As a native speaker, you understand these headlines to be a way of discussing the future, but can you imagine your poor students trying to make sense out of the grammar in these headlines? They all contain ellipted forms of *be to*. Without ellipsis, this is what the headlines are really saying:

12.177   Teachers Are to End Strike

12.178   Johnson Is to Testify

12.179   Microsoft Is to Lay Off 11,000 (In case you haven't checked your style manual lately, I'm following the convention of not capitalizing prepositions and articles unless they beging the title.)

Of course, even without ellipsis, these would be a challenge for most students because of *be to*. You could rephrase these as:

12.180   Teachers Are Going to End the Strike

12.181   Johnson Is Going to Testify

12.182   Microsoft Is Going to Lay Off 11,000

Using *be to* in this way (with *be* ellipted), is one aspect of what is called *headlinese*. It all boils down to saving space—packing a lot of info into a small space.

Here are some other forms of headlinese. They have nothing to do with *be to* or modals or phrasal modals at all, but so what.

It's common to ellipt *be* entirely from passive verbs:

12.183   Three [Were] Shot in Robbery

Articles are often ellipted too:

12.184   [A] New York Man Sells [the] Brooklyn Bridge to [a] Stupid Tourist

One last thing, verbs in headlinese (unless they are passive) are usually present simple instead of past simple or present perfect. So, for example, this:

12.185   New York Man Sells Brooklyn Bridge to Stupid Tourist

instead of this:

12.186   New York Man Has Sold Brooklyn Bridge to Stupid Tourist

A lot of this also applies to signs. For example,

12.187   Tobacco Not Sold to Minors

12.188   Library Closed on Sunday

are ellipted versions of these:

12.189   Tobacco [Is] Not Sold to Minors

12.190   [The] Library [Is] Closed on Sunday

So once again, we return to the question of how much of this you are going to teach your students, and once again, I return to the answer *it depends*. As is so often the case, it depends on variables—how much time you have, who your students are, what their needs are, how motivated they are and even, sometimes, (shhh) what's on the test. Things like this, which to you seem useful and interesting but are hardly absolutely essential, might fascinate one class and put another class into a coma.

One class might look at you like you're the coolest, smartest teacher in the world and another like you're some kind of weirdo (which you may be). Knowing what to skip, what to teach and how to teach it comes from experience, but no class ever works out just as you expect. That's why I'm not a huge fan of detailed lesson plans. Yes, I speak heresy, but when I go to class I know what I want to cover. I may have decided on certain activities, pages and exercises, and I may have written out what I want to put on the board, but students may breeze through something you thought would take forever, they might have a lot of trouble with something you thought would be easy, they might ask you to review something you've covered previously, you might see the need to review something you've covered previously, a student might ask you a question that takes you off in another direction to a useful and interesting topic and you decide to go with it and finish tomorrow what you had planned for today.

Of course you think about every class in advance, but don't go in with some meticulously detailed lesson plan that you refuse to deviate from. You'll bore your students to death and besides, a flexible and spontaneous teacher will be a more entertaining and therefore better teacher. Some of the best classes I've ever taught have been ones that were the least planned. Yes, it's easy to give advice like this when you have a lot of experience. Inexperienced teachers lack confidence and want to make sure they don't screw up. That's only natural, but remember that you cannot predict everything. Be ready to adjust to the class as it actually turns out rather that forcing the class to conform to your expectations. Don't apologize for going in a new, unplanned direction, but explain why you're doing it and why it's a good idea. And don't be afraid to ask your students what they think. They'll appreciate that.

Well, that was quite a digression. Getting back to our topic, headlinese, how do you test your students' understanding? What I've had a lot of fun with is giving students examples of headlines and then asking them to rewrite them as complete sentences, without any of the omissions we've discussed. Try to keep the vocabulary simple. There will often be more than one good answer. Often, more than one tense will make sense.

sample exercises 25: Rewrite the headlines as complete sentences. There may be more than one good answer.

> Man Bites Dog
> *A Man Has Bitten a Dog*
> *A Man Bit a Dog*
>
> Governor to Resign
> *The Governor Is to Resign*
> *The Governor Is Going to Resign*

1. Two Killed in Crash
2. Pope to Visit White House
3. Hurricane Destroys Miami
4. Bank Robber Arrested
5. ESL Teachers Demand Pay Raise
6. Mayor to Declare City Bankrupt

And by the way, there's more to headlinese than I've discussed here. Another aspect is the frequent use of certain words like *probe, slam* and *hit*. And sometimes the results of headlinese can be ambiguous and unintentionally amusing:

> Red Tape Holds Up New Bridge
> Kids Make Nutritious Snacks
> Teacher Strikes Idle Students
> Include Your Children When Baking Cookies
> Juvenile Court to Try Shooting Defendant
> Prostitutes Appeal to Pope
> Two Sisters Reunited After 18 Years at Checkout Counter
> Patient at Death's Door—Doctors Pull Him Through
> Is There a Ring of Debris around Uranus?

Google "crash blossoms" (that's what they're called) for a good laugh.

12.29 Ellipsis with modals and phrasal modals

12.191a	Mary:	Is the supermarket open now?
b	John:	It must be. It's open 24 hours a day.
c		= It must be [open now]. It's open 24 hours a day.

12.192a	Tom:	Susan works at the same company as your brother. Do you think she knows him?
b	Ali:	She must. It's a very small company.
c		= She must [know him]. It's a very small company.

12.193a	Sam:	Misaki is from Japan. Does she speak Japanese?
b	Sofia:	She has got to. How could she be from Japan and not?
c		= She has got to [speak Japanese]. How could she be from Japan and not [speak Japanese]?

12.194a	Bill:	I called Carlos five times last week, but there was no answer. I wonder if he was on vacation.
b	Alan:	He might have been.
c		= He might have been [on vacation].

12.195a	Gary:	Has Mary gone to bed?
b	Tom:	It's almost midnight. She must have.
c		= It's almost midnight. She must have [gone to bed].

12.196a	Sarah:	Are you still going to go to the doctor tomorrow?
b	John:	I might not. I'm feeling a lot better.
c		= I might not [go to the doctor tomorrow]. I'm feeling a lot better.

12.197a	Linda:	Is Francesca here?
b	Rosa:	She ought to be, but she isn't.
c		= She ought to be [here], but she isn't [here].

12.198a	Mark:	Has Sarah called you yet? She said she would call at 4:30, and it's 5:00 now.
b	Ali:	She should have by now, but she hasn't.
c		= She should have [called me] by now, but she hasn't [called me].

12.199a	John:	Did you go shopping last night?
b	Maria:	I was going to, but I didn't.
c		= I was going to [go shopping last night], but I didn't [go shopping last night].

12.200a	Lucy:	Did you return the library book yesterday?
b	Joe:	I was supposed to, but I didn't.
c		= I was supposed to [return the library book yesterday], but I didn't [return the library book yesterday].

12.201a	Ali:	The members of the committee were to have met yesterday. Is that correct?
b	Sam:	Yes, that is correct. They were to have, but I don't know if they did.
c		= They were to have [met yesterday], but I don't know if they [met yesterday].

sample exercises 26: Rewrite the B sentences with ellipsis.

    A: Can I park here?
    B1: No, you're not supposed to park here.
    B2: *No, you're not supposed to.*

1. A: Larry left for Medford two hours ago. I wonder if he has arrived.
    B1: Medford is only 15 miles from here. He must have arrived by now.
    B2:

2. A: Look! Is that Michael's car?
    B1: It's got to be Michael's car. It looks exactly like his car.
    B2:

3. A: Have Lucy and Sam moved? I haven't seen them for a long time.
    B1: I don't know. They might have moved.
    B2:

4. A: Are Rosa and Sofia in the classroom?
    B1: They ought to be in the classroom, but they're not in the classroom.
    B2:

5. A: Has Larry left yet?
    B1: It's after 5:00, so he should have left by now, but I don't know if he has left yet.
    B2:

6.   A: Your father asked you to cut the grass today. Did you?

     B1: I wanted to cut the grass today, I was going to cut the grass today, and I should have cut the grass today, but I didn't cut the grass today.

     B2:

7.   A: Did you take your kids to the movie last night?

     B1: I was going to take my kids to the movie last night, but I was busy, so I didn't take my kids to the movie last night.

     B2:

8.   A: Did you pay the rent yesterday?

     B1: I was supposed to pay the rent yesterday, but I didn't pay the rent yesterday.

     B2:

9.   A: Wasn't the sales manager to have completed her monthly sales report by the end of the month?

     B1: Yes, she was to have completed her monthly sales report by the end of the month, but she didn't complete her monthly sales report by the end of the month.

     B2:

10. A: Do you think Mary's home now?

     B1: She should be home now. She never goes anywhere in the evening.

     B2:

11. A: Is Larry going to go to France next summer?

     B1: He may go to France next summer. He's not sure.

     B2:

12. A: Did the judges announce their decision yesterday? That was the plan, wasn't it?

     B1: Yes, the judges were to have announced their decision yesterday, but they postponed their decision.

     B2:

Chapter 13
Adjective Clauses and Adjective Phrases

Could you...

- help a student understand why these sentences with common errors are incorrect?

    a. The test was very difficult which I took.

    b. I bought a book which it cost $25.

- explain why it's OK to omit *that* in *d* but not in *f*?

    c. The movie that I saw was boring. (OK)

    d. The movie I saw was boring. (OK)

    e. I saw a movie that was boring. (OK)

    f. I saw a movie was boring. (not OK, Why?)

- explain why commas are required in *h* but not *g*?

    g. A woman who works in my office is from Costa Rica.

    h. Cristina Ramos, who works in my office, is from Costa Rica.

- explain why *i* is OK but *j* is not?

    i. Cristina Ramos, who works in my office, is from Costa Rica. (OK)

    j. Cristina Ramos, that works in my office, is from Costa Rica. (not OK, Why?)

13.1 Adjective clauses do the same job as adjectives

Adjective clauses (aka *relative clauses*) are used in sentences like these. The adjective clauses are underlined:

13.1 The car <u>that I bought</u> is a piece of junk.

13.2 John made a cake <u>which was delicious</u>.

13.3 Marie Curie, <u>who died in 1934</u>, was the winner of two Nobel Prizes.

13.4 I know a woman <u>whose husband is a pilot</u>.

When I teach adjective clauses, I begin by telling my students that adjective clauses are a way to combine short sentences with one idea into longer sentences with more than one idea, and that knowing how to use adjective clauses will help them to write and speak in a more natural way. To illustrate this, what I do sometimes is give an example of writing or speaking made up of short single-idea sentences and then show them how much better that writing or speaking can be with adjective clauses. For example, read this to them (or write it on the board), and ask if it sounds like good English:

> We saw a movie. We liked it very much. It was about a man. He went to Mars. On Mars, he married a woman. She was the queen of Mars. After the movie, we went to a restaurant. It has good pizza.

Don't explain anything yet. Let them try to figure out why it sounds so odd and unnatural. Then give your students this version:

> We saw a movie that we liked very much. It was about a man who went to Mars. On Mars, he married a woman who was the queen of Mars. After the movie, we went to a restaurant which has good pizza.

Ask your students if it sounds better the second time. Unless they're completely clueless, they'll say that it does. Point out how shorter sentences have been combined to make longer sentences. They'll be dazzled.

Almost certainly they will already have heard or read adjective clauses many times without really realizing what was going on grammarwise. Even if they're sort of vaguely aware that they exist, they likely won't know how to use them very well (if at all) because they can get a bit tricky.

It would help your students to remind them first what an adjective is—a word that modifies, identifies or describes (or, as I often phrase it, *gives information about*) a noun. Once that has sunk in, tell them that an adjective clause is a group of word (specifically, a group of words containing a subject and a verb) that do the same job as a single adjective: give information about a noun.

13.2 Subject adjective clauses

Start with the easiest type of adjective clause: subject adjective clauses.

Put two simple pairs of sentences on the board like these. Make one about a thing and the other about an unnamed person. Just about anything will work, but keep it simple. Make sure there's only one noun in it:

> I heard a song.
> The man is noisy.

Then write two more sentences after the first two with some information about the thing and unnamed person. Again, almost anything will do, but keep it simple, and make sure the thing and unnamed person are the subject of the second sentences:

> I heard a song. It was beautiful.
> The woman is noisy. She lives next to me.

It doesn't matter if you use nouns or pronouns in the second sentences. You could write them like this:

> I heard a song. The song was beautiful.
> The woman is noisy. The woman lives next to me.

but I usually go with the pronouns.

So now what? Just show the students what to do? That wouldn't be inductive, would it? No, now ask your students to try to combine each pair of sentences to make one sentence. You'll likely get something like this:

13.5   I heard a song it was beautiful.

13.6   The woman is noisy she lives next to me.

Or some wise guy might rewrite these sentences like this:

13.7   I heard a beautiful song.

13.8   The noisy woman lives next to me.

13.7 and 13.8 aren't wrong, but tell the wise guy that that's a different grammar lesson. We don't have the option of rewriting them entirely here, and that's not always possible anyway.

So assuming this is what's on the board:

> I heard a song. It was beautiful.
> The woman is noisy. She lives next to me.

here's what you're going to do. Let's start with the first pair:

> I heard a song. It was beautiful.

First, ask your students which noun in the first sentence is the same as something in the second. Most will figure out that *song* and *it* are the same thing. Now cross out *it*:

> I heard a song. ~~It~~ was beautiful.

and rewrite the sentence like this:

> I heard a song <u>which</u> was beautiful.

Tell your students that *which was beautiful* is an adjective clause and emphasize that it is now directly after the noun it is modifying (but don't say *modifying*—say *describing, giving information about,* or *identifying*).

Now do the same with the second pair of sentences, but this time with *who*:

> The woman is noisy. ~~She~~ lives next to me.
> The woman <u>who</u> lives next to me is noisy.

This is a lot to digest. You might want to give them two or three more examples. Tell your students, if they haven't figured it out already, that *which* is for things and *who* is for people. Once that's clear, tell them that we can use *that* for both. DO NOT repeat the myth that *that* is somehow informal and that *who* and *which* are preferable. This is nonsense. *That* is perfectly acceptable. What I do tell students is that, though all three of these words are perfectly fine, what is most common among native speakers is *who* for people and *that* for things. Don't dwell on *that* vs. *who* and *which*. Be happy if they can get it right with any of these. By the way, *who, which* and *that* are called (jargon alert!) *relative pronouns,* but there's no need to teach that term to your students. I don't.

One thing to watch out for is that students often get the idea that adjective clauses always go at the end of the sentence, as it did in the first example above (and why I made sure this was not true of the second example). If that is the case with too many of the examples you discuss in class, that's what they'll think. Emphasize that the adjective clause goes directly after the noun that it modifies. (Actually, this isn't always true, but better to oversimplify at this point than overcomplicate and confuse your students any more than they are already.)

Another thing to watch out for is this: Students will often not want to *cancel* (as I phrase it—they'll know the word *cancel*— they won't know *omit*) the second noun or pronoun, and they'll end up with, for example,

13.9   I heard a song which <u>it</u> was beautiful.

13.10   The woman who <u>she</u> lives next to me is noisy.

You'll encounter this error again and again. Like many errors, it's very predictable, so you want to anticipate it and address in your initial presentation.

That's a lot for your students to make sense out of, and as usual, it only gets worse, so take it step by step and reinforce their (jargon alert!) *acquisition* of subject adjective clauses with some exercises at this point.

sample exercises 1: Cross out the word in the second sentence that would be canceled in a subject adjective clause.
The student is absent today. ~~She~~ was sick yesterday.

1.   A man is very lazy. He works in my office.
2.   I bought a car. It cost $25,000.
3.   The people make a lot of noise. They live next to me.
4.   What did the man say? He called you.
5.   I know a girl. She is from Milan.

sample exercises 2: Write *who/that* or *which/that* in the blanks. Then put parentheses around the adjective clause.
The student (_____*who/that*_____ was sick yesterday) is absent today.

1.   Some people _____ live near me were hurt in an accident.
2.   Ali read a book _____ was 450 pages long.
3.   I heard a joke _____ was really funny.
4.   The waiter _____ waited on us wasn't friendly.
5.   John told us a crazy story _____ didn't make any sense at all.

sample exercises 3: Combine the sentences using the second sentence as an adjective clause. Use only *who* or *that.*
The boy broke his arm. He fell out of a tree house.
The boy who fell out of a tree house broke his arm.

1.   She told me a story. It was interesting.
2.   My wife bought some shoes. They cost $70.
3.   The people talked a lot. They sat behind us at the movie theater.
4.   How many people speak Spanish? They live in Florida.
5.   The teacher asked me a question. It was very difficult.

13.3 Object adjective clauses

I hope you've made a big deal out of replacing the <u>subject</u> with a relative pronoun in <u>subject</u> adjective clause, because now we're going to be replacing the object with a relative pronoun in object adjective clauses, and that's a lot more difficult. Once again, you're going to write two pairs of sentences on the board—one about a thing and one about a person:

Everyone liked the cake. Rosa made <u>it</u>.
The guy is crazy. I work with <u>him</u>.

First of all, make a big deal out of a word in the first sentence of each pair being the same as the <u>object</u> of the second. So *cake* is the same as *it,* and *The guy* is the same as *him.* The second example is especially handy for reinforcing the concept of adjective clauses having the function of identifying a noun. Say that there are a lot of guys in this world, but which one are you talking about? Ohhhhhhh, the guy you *work* with. *He's* the crazy guy. (Also, *guy* is a word you should teach—students absolutely need to know common informal words like *guy* and *bunch* and *stuff* and *junk,* etc. Just make sure they know they're informal.)

Now for the fun stuff. Always start with the pair that is about things (as opposed to people). Skip the inductive approach, since none of your students will have any idea what to do, cross out the object and write the sentences with adjectives clauses (in this case, object adjective clauses). Make a big deal out of word order—the relative pronouns *which* and *that* not only replace the object in the second sentence but now <u>precede</u> the subject of the second sentence, and once again, the adjective clause follows the noun that it modifies:

> Everyone liked the cake. Rosa made ~~it~~.
> = Everyone liked the cake <u>which Rosa made</u>.
> = Everyone liked the cake <u>that Rosa made</u>.
> = Everyone liked the cake <u>Rosa made</u>.

Yep, three ways to do it! The first two, with *which* and *that,* won't freak your students out too much. They've seen these relative pronouns before, but what about the last? No relative pronoun at all? That's right. You can show it as I have above, which I prefer, or use, as many books do, the symbol 0:

13.11   Everyone liked the cake <u>0 Rosa made</u>.

Now it's time for the second pair, about people. I always cover that second because it's more difficult:

> The guy is crazy. I work with <u>him</u>.
> = The guy <u>whom I work with</u> is crazy.
> = The guy <u>who I work with</u> is crazy.
> = The guy <u>that I work with</u> is crazy.
> = The guy <u>I work with</u> is crazy.

Four ways! That'll blow your students away. What about *whom*? What are you going to tell your students about that? We've talked about *whom* already, so no need to repeat it all. Here's what I tell students about *whom* in regard to object adjective clauses: I say that *whom* is the very best English, and if they are sure it is correct, then by all means use it, but since most native speakers use *who* all the time, then they certainly can too if they're not certain. *Who* is so common that even I, an unapologetic (jargon alert!) *proscriptionist,* (an annoying, friendless know-it-all who goes around pointing out the mistakes people make in their English and telling them what they should say instead) am inclined to accept it. Tell your students that *who* vs. *whom* is the least of their problems. Understanding it is more important than using it.

More important to them is what native speakers really say. While making it clear that *all* of the options above are perfectly acceptable, I tell my students that in everyday English, nothing—no relative pronoun at all—is the most common way, but in writing, in longer and more complicated sentences or when we just want to be extra clear, we usually use *that* for things and *who* for people. Dispel any notions that *that* is somehow informal. That's baloney.

As with subject pronouns, two errors are frequent: tacking the adjective clause onto the end of the previous sentence rather than putting it after the noun that it modifies, for example,

13.12a   The homework was very difficult <u>which I did last night</u>.

rather than

b   The homework <u>which I did last night</u> was very difficult.

and not canceling the object in the second sentence:

c   The homework which I did <u>it</u> last night was very difficult.

sample exercises 4: Cross out the word in the second sentence that would be canceled in an object adjective clause.
   The books are about Spain. I got ~~them~~ at the library.

1.   The potato salad was delicious. We ate it at the picnic.
2.   The man is not friendly. I live next to him.
3.   A woman came to my office. I had never met her before.
4.   What did the people say? You were talking to them.
5.   I'm not used to the shoes. I bought them yesterday.

sample exercises 5: Write *who(m)/that* or *which/that* in the blanks. Then put parentheses around the adjective clause.
   The student (_____*who/that*_____ was sick yesterday) is absent today.

1. The tacos _____ we had last night weren't very good.
2. Did you see the dress _____ she wore to the party?
3. The flight attendant _____ I talked to was from Montreal.
4. The soup _____ he made was too salty.
5. The guy _____ I sat next to on the plane had bad breath.

sample exercises 6: Combine the sentences using the second sentence as an adjective clause. Give all possible answers.

> The girl was pretty. I saw her.
> *The girl whom I saw was pretty.*
> *The girl who I saw was pretty.*
> *The girl that I saw was pretty.*
> *The girl I saw was pretty.*

1. The mechanic said it would cost $1,000 to fix my car. I talked to him.
2. We don't understand the language. She speaks it.
3. Some people never take a bath. I know them.
4. The guy is interesting. We live next to him.
5. The man was very tall. I saw him.

13.4 Object adjective clauses with verb + preposition combinations

Part of your discussion of object adjective clauses has to be about verb + preposition combinations as they are used in object adjective clauses. What is a verb + preposition combination? Many (jargon alert!) *transitive verbs* (verbs that either can or must have an object), require that a certain preposition be after it. Even apart from this discussion of object adjective clauses, this is something your students should be aware of. To illustrate, I write pairs of sentences like these on the board to show how common these verb + preposition combinations are as well as to show how the preposition, though it is required, doesn't have any grammatical function since these verbs can often be virtually interchangeable with main verbs of a similar meaning which don't require prepositions:

> I watch the children.
> I look <u>at</u> the children.
>
> I hear the radio.
> I listen <u>to</u> the radio.

Remind your students to memorize verb + preposition combinations as a single unit. Some are frequently categorized with phrasal verbs and identified as inseparable. This is a convenient way to teach them, but there's more to it than that, though nothing would be accomplished by getting into deep grammar with your students (other than totally befuddling them). (For more examples of verb + preposition combinations, refer your students to Appendix B.)

Getting back to object adjective clauses, when a verb is followed by a preposition, the preposition can be placed before the relative pronouns *whom* and *which*. When the preposition is moved in this way, it's not possible to use *that*—<u>only</u> *whom* and *which* are used and they <u>must</u> be used:

13.13	<u>look for</u> the car	→	The car <u>for</u> which <u>I looked</u> was red.
13.14	<u>listen to</u> music	→	The music <u>to</u> which I <u>listened</u> was beautiful.
13.15	<u>work with</u> Frank Smith	→	Frank Smith, <u>with</u> whom I <u>work</u>, speaks Arabic.
13.16	<u>live next to</u> a man	→	The man <u>next to</u> whom we <u>live</u> has a big dog.

Sometimes there's an indirect object between the verb and preposition:

13.17	<u>receive</u> a letter <u>from</u> the lawyer	→	The lawyer <u>from</u> whom we <u>received</u> a letter is a crook.
13.18	<u>make</u> a cake <u>for</u> the wedding	→	The wedding <u>for</u> which my mother <u>made</u> a cake was canceled.
13.19	<u>write</u> your name <u>on</u> the paper	→	Where is the paper <u>on</u> which you <u>wrote</u> your name?
13.20	<u>fix</u> my car <u>with</u> my father	→	My father, <u>with</u> whom I <u>fixed</u> my car, is a mechanic.

Try to use a variety of prepositions in your examples, and remind them that prepositions aren't always single words. There are also (jargon alert!) *phrasal prepositions* like *instead of, in front of* and *next to*.

The good news for your students is that they never need to do this. I always stress that, but I also stress that they need to understand it—especially if they're learning English for business or academic purposes, where this sort of snooty grammar is more common.

sample exercises 7: Change the adjective clauses so that the preposition is before the relative pronoun. Use only *which* or *whom*.

> The house that I live in is very old.
> *The house in which I live is very old.*

> General Mills, whom Captain Crunch served under, was injured during the war.
> *General Mills, under whom Captain Crunch served, was injured during the war.*

1. The boy whom I sat next to in grammar school is a lawyer now.
2. I didn't get the job that I applied for.
3. The woman I work with is from Lebanon.
4. The subject she gave a presentation about was interesting.
5. The opera I slept during was by Wagner.

sample exercises 8: Combine the sentences using the second sentence as an adjective clause with the preposition before the relative pronoun. Be careful about punctuation.

> The city was very small. I grew up in it.
> *The city in which I grew up was very small.*

1. I don't know the man. You were talking to him.
2. The student is from Germany. I sit in front of him.
3. I saw a movie with some friends. I work with them.
4. The woman plays loud music all night. We live under her.
5. It is an amazing story. Many books have been written about it.

13.5 Amazing additional info on verb + preposition combinations

Many verbs and many adjectives must be used with certain prepositions. (Adjective + preposition combinations are discussed in Section 11.11.) A list of verb + prepositions combinations is found in Appendix B. This might be good time to have a look at them. Keep in mind, though, that in the case of verb + preposition combinations and adjective + prepositions combinations, it's mostly about vocabulary—memorizing the meanings of the verbs and adjectives along with memorizing which prepositions are used with them (which can alter the meaning of the verb or adjective).

Here's something else interesting (at least to pathetic people like me) about verb + preposition combinations: They provide the key to one of the great riddles of our time: what's the deal with inseparable phrasal verbs. Well, (and this is entirely for your elucidation, not something to confuse your students with), it turns out that inseparable phrasal verbs are actually—brace yourself for some deep grammar—verbs which require an (jargon alert!) *adverbial complement* starting with a certain preposition. If you are totally blown away by that major revelation, great; if not, forget it

13.6 *whose* in subject adjective clauses

The meaning of *whose* was discussed in Section 7.15, though it wouldn't hurt to review it and also to review possessive adjectives. (In fact, you definitely should review both.) Now we're going to focus on how to use *whose* in subject adjective clauses. Again, we'll start with a pair of sentences. Put these sentences on the board:

> I talked to a man. His name was Bill.

Now cross out the possessive adjective:

> I talked to a man. ~~His~~ name was Bill.

and rewrite it as one sentence with *whose*:

> I talked to a man <u>whose</u> name was Bill.

As a reminder that the noun being modified can appear anywhere in a sentence, discuss this example:

> The children were happy. ~~Their~~ school burned down.
> The children <u>whose</u> school burned down were happy.

Normally, this is done with the possessive adjectives *his, her* and *their*, but what about *its*? Is it OK to say, for example, this:

13.21   The car whose battery was dead wouldn't start.

or this?

    13.22   We ate in a restaurant whose food was terrible.

The answer is yes. Although using *whose* for inanimate objects is a bit uncommon, and most native speakers usually rephrase examples such as these, there is absolutely nothing wrong with it. Anyone who tells you otherwise is wrong. Are you going to spend a lot of time on this with your students? No, but it might come up, so you should mention it.

sample exercises 9: Combine the sentences. Use the second sentence as an adjective clause. Use only *whose*.
    The woman called the police. Her son was lost.
    The woman whose son was lost called the police.

    1.   I talked to a man. His wife is an artist.
    2.   Did the woman go to the hospital? Her arm was broken.
    3.   The airplane crashed. Its wing fell off.
    4.   Where is the man? His wallet was stolen.
    5.   The actor was working as a waiter. His show was canceled.

13.7 Relative adverbs *where* and *when* used in adjective clauses

Where and *when* can be used to make adjective clauses. When *where* and *when* are used in this way, they're called (jargon alert!) *relative adverbs,* but no need to dazzle your students with that fascinating fact. Your students won't detect any difference between relative pronouns and relative adverbs, so don't even bring it up.

Start with two pairs of sentences. Make sure you have *there* and *then* in them because that's what the relative adverbs are going to replace. Then cross out *there* and *then*:

    The office is on the fifth floor. I work ~~there~~.
    There is no day next week. I can meet you for lunch ~~then~~.

Now rewrite them with adjective clauses:

    The office <u>where</u> I work is on the fifth floor.
    There is no day next week <u>when</u> I can meet you for lunch.

Easy!

My advice is to demonstrate these exactly as I have done and go straight to the exercises. This isn't usually very difficult, but in case it comes up (which is unlikely), be aware that the relative adverbs are replacing relative pronouns used as objects of prepositions:

    13.23   The office <u>in which</u> I work is on the fifth floor.

    13.24   There is no day next week <u>on which</u> I can meet you for lunch.

sample exercises 10: Combine the sentences. Use the second sentence as an adjective clause. Use only *where* or *when*.
    Saturday is the day. Many people do their shopping then.
    Saturday is the day when many people do their shopping.

    That is the building. I work there.
    That is the building where I work.

    1.   That's the park. We play soccer there sometimes.
    2.   I still remember the day. My son was born then.
    3.   Is there a day? I can meet with you then.
    4.   Did he tell you the restaurant? He was going there.
    5.   The day was the worst day of my life. My parachute didn't open then.

13.8 Relative adverb *why* used in adjective clauses

Why is also a relative adverb which can introduce adjective clauses. It's usually used with *reason* in sentences like these:

    13.25a   That is the reason. He was fired from his job for this reason.
       b   That is the reason <u>for which</u> he was fired from his job.
       c   That is the reason <u>why</u> he was fired from his job.

Amazing huh? If you put these on the board, I'd skip the *for which* example:

Adjective Clauses and Adjective Phrases

That is the reason. He was fired from his job for this reason.

That is the reason <u>why</u> he was fired from his job.

sample exercises 11: Combine the sentences. Use the second sentence as an adjective clause. Use only *why*.

What was the reason? She was angry for this reason.

What was the reason why she was angry.

1. Did Larry tell you the reason? Mary went to the hospital for this reason.
2. That was the reason. David was arrested by the police for this reason.
3. Does anyone know the reason? The ESL teacher jumped out the window for this reason.
4. Nobody knows the reason. She was so angry for this reason.
5. I wonder if we will ever know the reason. We are put on this Earth for this reason.

13.9 Punctuation of adjective clauses—restrictive and nonrestrictive

So far we have discussed adjective clauses as being necessary to identify something. If I say this:

13.26a   The man speaks Chinese.

how do you know which man I'm talking about? There are a lot of men in the world. But if I say this:

b   The man who lives above me speaks Chinese.

the adjective clause *who lives above* me distinguishes the man from all the other men in the world. Now you know which guy I'm talking about—the one who lives above me. In this case, the adjective clause is (jargon alert!) *essential* to identify which man I'm talking about.

But what if we already know this guy, and we know that his name is Paul Moss? I want to tell you that he speaks Chinese and also, by the way, that he lives above me, but is the fact that he's the guy who lives above me necessary to identify him? No, we already know who he is. He's Paul Moss. The information that he lives above me is not necessary to identify him. In this case, we would say this:

c   Paul Moss, who lives above me, speaks Chinese.

Why the commas? Because in this case *who lives above me* is <u>not</u> necessary to identify the guy I'm talking about. We already know who he is. He's Paul Moss. That he lives above me is just some extra information that I stuck in the sentence. It's (jargon alert!) *nonessential*.

And wouldn't it be easy if the terms *essential* and *nonessential* were the only terms that grammar nerds ever used to describe these things, but noooooooo, we have to use something more obscure and therefore way cooler. The most common terms are (jargon alert!) *restrictive* and *nonrestrictive*:

restrictive   =   essential

nonrestrictive   =   nonessential

And do I ever teach any of these terms to my students? No, but you should be able to explain the basic concept to your students so that they understand why commas are sometimes necessary and sometimes not.

This restrictive/nonrestrictive business applies to

subject adjective clauses:

13.27a   A woman who works in my office is from Costa Rica.

b   → Cristina Ramos, who works in my office, is from Costa Rica.

object adjective clauses:

13.28a   The book which I took with me to read on the plane was really boring.

b   → *Ulysses,* which I took with me to read on the plane, was really boring.

whose:

13.29a   The man whose daughter graduated at the top of her class was very proud.

b   → Tom Johnson, whose daughter graduated at the top of her class, was very proud.

and *where* and *when*:

13.30a   The town where I grew up is a small town.

b   → Springfield, where I grew up, is a small town.

13.31a   The day when I met her was the best day of my life.
b   → November 17, when I met her, was the best day of my life.

But of course there are complications. In nonrestrictive adjective clauses, it is not possible to use *that,* and it is not possible to use no relative pronoun or no relative adverb at all.

Don't assume that the giveaway that commas are needed is a proper noun. It really depends on the situation. Imagine we're talking about two men in a car accident. One man was OK, but regarding the other man, we might say this:

13.32a   The man who was injured was taken to the hospital.

Because there were two men in the accident, the adjective clause is essential to identify which of the two men was taken to the hospital.

Now imagine that there was only one man in the car accident. Then we would say this:

b   The man, who was injured, was taken to the hospital.

In this case, there was only one man, so we've already identified him as the man who was in an accident, and the adjective clause is nonessential.

So how are you going to teach this? By focusing on the idea of essential and nonessential. Have your students ask themselves if the information in the adjective clause is needed to identify a noun in the main clause or if it's just extra information.

sample exercises 12: Put commas around the adjective clauses that are only for extra information and not for identification.
    A man who called yesterday wants to talk to me about a job.
    no change
    Larry Smith who called yesterday wants to talk to me about a job.
    Larry Smith, who called yesterday, wants to talk to me about a job.

1.   A man who had escaped from prison was captured by the police.
2.   Elephants which are native to Africa and Asia are very intelligent.
3.   The boy who was bitten by a dog was crying.
4.   Coffee which originally came from the Middle East is now grown in many countries.
5.   The city where I live now is very boring.

13.10 Nonrestrictive adjective clauses and quantifiers

You've just taught your students how to make nonrestrictive (with commas) subject and object adjective clauses (remembering that the subject and object I refer to are the subject and object in the second sentence, the one that the adjective phrase is made from):

13.33a   Larry and his three daughters had lunch with us. His daughters are very nice.
b   → Larry and his three daughters, who are very nice, had lunch with us.

13.34a   Questions 6 to 10 on the exam were very difficult. They were about trigonometry.
b   → Questions 6 to 10 on the exam, which were about trigonometry, were very difficult.

13.35a   My wife has many relatives Mexico. I have never met them.
b   → My wife has many relatives in Mexico, whom I have never met.

13.36a   Mark Stewart has written nine books. I have read them.
b   → Mark Stewart has written nine books, which I have read.

Easy enough, but what if we change the sentences as follows? Now what?

13.37a   Larry and his three daughters had lunch with us. <u>Two of his daughters</u> are doctors.

13.38a   Questions 6 to 10 on the exam were very difficult. <u>All of them</u> were about trigonometry.

13.39a   My wife has many relatives Mexico. I have never met <u>many of them</u>.

13.40a   Mark Stewart has written nine books. I have read <u>some of them</u>.

This is what:

13.37b   Larry and his three daughters had lunch with us. <u>Two of his daughters</u> are doctors.

     c   → Larry and his three daughters, <u>two of whom</u> are doctors, had lunch with us.

13.38b   Questions 6 to 10 on the exam were very difficult. <u>All of them</u> were about trigonometry.

     c   → Questions 6 to 10 on the exam, <u>all of which</u> were about trigonometry, were very difficult.

13.39b   My wife has many relatives Mexico. I have never met <u>many of them</u>.

     c   → My wife has many relatives in Mexico, <u>many of whom</u> I have never met.

13.40b   Mark Stewart has written nine books. I have read <u>some of them</u>.

     c   → Mark Stewart has written nine books, <u>some of which</u> I have read.

Expressions like *two of, all of, many of, some of,* etc., are called quantifiers or expressions of quantity (mentioned in Section 6.10). There are a lot of them, and they can be, and in formal English often are, used in adjective clauses. Before looking at more examples, look at example 13.33b. Do you notice something odd about it? How did *who* in 13.33b turn into *whom* in 13.37c? Isn't it a subject adjective clause? Isn't *who* used in subject adjective clauses? *Who* has become *whom* because in 13.37c, *his daughters* is <u>not</u> the subject. *Two* is the subject *His daughters* is now the *object* of the preposition *of,* and *whom* is used for objects. Pretty wild, huh? Here are a few more examples:

13.41   Tom had several suggestions, few of which made any sense.

13.42   The students, a number of whom failed the test, complained to the principal.

13.43   India has 1.2 billion people, 31% of whom are aged 14 or below.

This sort of grammar is quite common in more formal English, especially in business and academia, so if that's where your students are headed, this is worth having a look at. There's more, but first some exercises with quantifiers:

sample exercises 13: Combine the sentences to make one sentence with an adjective clause with *of whom* or *of which.* Remember to use commas.

     Two people were killed in the accident. Neither of them was wearing a seatbelt.
     Two people, neither of whom was wearing a seatbelt, were killed in the accident.

1. The desserts were fantastic. Most of them were made by Sofia.
2. We checked in 11 pieces of luggage. British Airways lost all of them.
3. Almost 40 people applied for the job. Few of them were qualified.
4. At the conference, I spoke to 300 people. Hardly any of them were interested in what I had to say.
5. Every year, Canada produces 27 million liters of maple syrup. Most of it comes from the province of Quebec.

(And if you're thinking that this:

13.44a   Almost 40 people, few of whom were qualified, applied for the job.

would sound better as this:

     b   Almost 40 people applied for the job, <u>few of whom were qualified</u>.

your thinking is good. Moving adjective clauses and adjective phrases to the end of the sentence in this way is discussed shortly. One thing at a time!)

13.11 Nonrestrictive adjective clauses and superlatives

This *of which/of whom* business is also used with superlatives:

13.45a   Maria bought three pairs of shoes. <u>The most expensive of them</u> cost $75.

     b   → Maria bought three pairs of shoes, <u>the most expensive of which</u> cost $75.

13.46a   Ten guys tried out for the basketball team. <u>The tallest of them</u> is 214 centimeters tall.

     b   → Ten guys, the tallest of whom is 214 centimeters tall, tried out for the basketball team.

(For my metrically challenged fellow Americans, that's just over seven feet.)

sample exercises 14: Combine the sentences to make one sentence with an adjective clause with *of whom* or *of which.* Remember to use commas.

     Northern California is home to the world's tallest trees. The tallest of them is 379 feet tall.

Northern California is home to the world's tallest trees, the tallest of which is 379 feet tall.

1. Larry caught five fish. The largest of them weighed five pounds.
2. Twenty girls skated in the competition. The youngest of them was only 15.
3. Alan took five courses last semester. The hardest of them was calculus.
4. We looked at seven houses in San Francisco. The least expensive of them cost more than a million bucks.
5. My mother has three brothers. The oldest of them is 47 years old.

13.12 Adjective clauses reduced to restrictive adjective phrases

We native speaker say things like these examples every day:

13.47 The guy standing over there is a jerk.

13.48 A woman wearing a red coat was following me.

13.49 People living in Alaska are used to cold weather.

13.50 I heard a sad story about an ESL teacher with a family, school loans and a mortgage.

13.51 The police found the car driven by the bank robbers.

Do these seem in any way similar to adjective clauses? Well, in a way they started out as adjective clauses until the speaker reduced them to (jargon alert!) *adjective phrases*. (They're phrases and not clauses because there's no subject or tensed verb.) Let's see the evolution of 13.47-13.51:

13.52a The guy is a jerk. He is standing over there.
   b → The guy who is standing over there is a jerk.
   c → The guy standing over there is a jerk.

13.53a A woman was following me. She was wearing a red coat.
   b → A woman who was wearing a red coat was following me.
   c → A woman wearing a red coat was following me.

13.54a People are used to cold weather. They live in Alaska.
   b → People who live in Alaska are used to cold weather.
   c → People living in Alaska are used to cold weather.

13.55a I heard a sad story. It was about an ESL teacher with a family, school loans and a mortgage.
   b → I heard a sad story which was about an ESL teacher with a family, school loans and a mortgage.
   c → I heard a sad story about an ESL teacher with a family, school loans and a mortgage.

13.56a The police found the car. It was driven by the bank robbers.
   b → The police found the car which was driven by the ban robbers.
   c → The police found the car driven by the bank robbers.

Grammar at this level can get pretty murky—not just for students but teachers as well, so go get a double espresso and hold on tight. Rather than focusing your students on grammar and terminology, which obviously you'll have to do to some extent, put your students to work actually forming sentences like these in the hope that it will become automatic. Like riding a bicycle: you don't think about the physics involved—you just do it.

In the examples above, I've actually mixed three things: adjective clauses derived from (jargon alert!) *active verbs* (i.e. not passive verbs), prepositional phrases and passive verbs. To help you and ultimately your students, I'll focus on each of them separately.

▶ **Restrictive present participle phrases**

Adjective phrases derived from active verbs use the present participle, the *-ing* form of the verb. For that reason, they're called (jargon alert!) *present participle phrases*.

(In case you're thinking these are gerunds, stop thinking that right now! They're not gerunds. It's a very common mistake to mix up present participles, which have an adjectival function (remember *-ing* and *-ed* participle adjectives?) and gerunds, which are nouns. Remember that verbs in the *-ing* form which are <u>not</u> being used as continuous verbs are not automatically gerunds instead. We haven't gotten to gerunds yet, so you shouldn't even be talking about them now.)

Anyway, let's look again at our examples:

13.57a The guy is a jerk. He is standing over there.

b → The guy who is standing over there is a jerk.

c → The guy standing over there is a jerk.

13.58a A woman was following me. She was wearing a red coat.

   b → A woman who was wearing a red coat was following me.

   c → A woman wearing a red coat was following me.

13.59a People are used to cold weather. They live in Alaska.

   b → People who live in Alaska are used to cold weather.

   c → People living in Alaska are used to cold weather.

You don't see any commas anywhere, do you? That's because all of the adjective clauses are restrictive (essential). Keep this in mind; it'll be important later.

As you may recall from Section 11.10, many present participles and past participles are used as adjectives. As far as I'm concerned, they _are_ adjectives. That's how students see them, and that's how I teach them. I've never seen any point in confusing students by explaining that, in a mysterious, magical, mystical, metaphysical way, they're not exactly adjectives but participles functioning as (masquerading as?, pretending to be?, shape shifting as?) adjectives. They're like photons that can't decide whether they're waves or particles, and just when you observe that they're one, they change to the other. Explaining this adjective-participle duality will only confuse your students, so don't even bring it up. However, here's an example of what I'm talking about. First, a present participle phrase:

13.60a I heard a baby <u>crying in the next room</u>.

If, as I contend, the present participle _crying_ is basically an adjective with (jargon alert!) _modifiers_ (fancy talk for _stuff after it_), can we put the adjective and its modifiers in front of the noun where adjectives normally go?

   b I heard a <u>crying in the next room</u> baby.

No, we can't, but what if we get rid of the modifiers. Is this OK?

   c I heard a <u>crying</u> baby.

Yes, it is. See how easily a present participle can turn into adjective? (Or are they two sides of the same coin? Are they some kind of portal to another dimension? What do ancient astronaut theorists have to say about this?)

   d I heard a baby <u>crying</u>.

   e I heard a <u>crying</u> baby.

Adjective or present participle? Wave or particle? If you have to be Albert Einstein to answer these questions, can you really expect your students (or yourself, or me) to answer them? As far as your students are concerned, participle adjectives are adjectives and what we're doing here has nothing to do with participle adjectives, so don't even mention them.

Earth to Carl! What _do_ you say to your students? Show them some examples of how adjective clauses can be reduced to adjective phrases (in this case, present participle phrases). That's really all you need to do without going into quantum physics or deep grammar. Stick to surface grammar—what your students can see. That's all that matters to them.

First, start out with exercises in which the sentence being turned into an adjective phrase is continuous and therefore already in the _-ing_ form. That's less confusing, but there is actually a difference between the continuous verb and the present participle. Your students won't get that at all. I mention it because, as you will see shortly, the adjective phrase verb isn't always continuous.

sample exercises 15: Cross out the words which can be canceled.

   A girl ~~who was~~ selling cookies knocked on the door.

   Did you see the eagle ~~which was~~ flying over our house?

1. I don't like the girl who is dancing with my brother.
2. What's the name of the cat which is sleeping on the sofa?
3. The loud music which was playing outside kept me awake all night.
4. Some of the people who are coming to our party are really weird.
5. The lions ate a man which was bothering them at the zoo.

sample exercises 16: Make subject adjective clauses. Then reduce them to adjective phrases.

   Larry helped a man. He was having car problems.

Larry helped a man who was having car problems.
Larry helped a man having car problems.

The woman works in the finance department. She is talking to the sales manager.
The woman who is talking to the sales manager works in the finance department.
The woman talking to the sales manager works in the finance department.

1. The teacher noticed a boy. He was cheating on the test.
2. I saw an elephant at the circus. It was riding a bicycle.
3. A bus plunged into the valley below. It was carrying 39 passengers.
4. Look! There's a guy. He is trying to break into that house.
5. A woman left a message for you. She was asking about the painting you're selling.

Make sure your students understand that the present participle phrase will always be in the *-ing* form regardless of what form it's in in the adjective clause. In the exercise below, that's just what they'll see:

sample exercises 17: Write sentences with adjective phrases.
People who live in New Zealand are called kiwis.
People living in New Zealand are called kiwis.

Millions of people who hoped to become rich bought lottery tickets.
Millions of people hoping to become rich bought lottery tickets.

1. I can't eat food which contains a lot of salt.
2. Anyone who visits that country must have a visa.
3. The family which lives next to us has a swimming pool.
4. People who live in glass houses shouldn't throw stones.
5. Kids who go to that school have to wear uniforms.

▶ **Restrictive past participle phrases**
Before we go any further, I have to warn you that we haven't gotten to the passive yet, but this chapter on adjective phrases is the logical place to include this aspect of the passive. You may want to jump ahead to Chapter 15 and come back to this later.

Everything I said about the ill-defined border between present participles and adjectives applies to past participles and adjectives as well. Actually, I like to think of present and past participles and adjectives as overlapping rather than having any distinct dividing line.

Anyway, many past participles are also used as participle adjectives. Let's start with a passive sentence:

13.61a   The FBI agent discovered the microphone <u>hidden by the spy</u>.

This is obviously a passive sentence and *hidden* is obviously a past participle. But let's get rid of the *by*-phrase that marks this as a passive sentence. For the sentence to make sense and have the same meaning, it has to be changed to this:

b   The FBI agent discovered the <u>hidden</u> microphone.

If you were to ask your students, they would say that *hidden* is an adjective, and why wouldn't they? As far as they're concerned, it is an adjective, and as far as I'm concerned it is an adjective, so leave it at that.

But what if we hadn't gotten rid of the *by*-phrase? Could we say this?

c   The FBI agent discovered the <u>hidden by the spy</u> microphone.

No we couldn't.

Let's backtrack and see how 13.61a is a reduced subject adjective clause:

d   The FBI agent discovered the microphone. It was <u>hidden by the spy</u>.
e   The FBI agent discovered the microphone ~~which was~~ <u>hidden by the spy</u>.
f   The FBI agent discovered the microphone <u>hidden by the spy</u>.

As with present participle phrases with *be*, the relative pronoun and whatever form of *be* is in the adjective clause are cancelled. The verb will not change. It will be a past participle in the adjective clause and in the adjective phrase too.

Restrictive past participle phrases aren't as common as restrictive present participle phrases, but we'll be talking later at great length about nonrestrictive past (and present) participle phrases. Bet you can't wait.

sample exercises 18: Make subject adjective clauses. Then reduce them to adjective phrases.

The man was identified as Frank Smith. He was arrested by the police.
The man who was arrested by the police was identified as Frank Smith.
The man arrested by the police was identified as Frank Smith.

1. Some buildings were never rebuilt. They were destroyed by the tornado.
2. The desk was sold for $1,000,000. It was used by Homer when he wrote *The Odyssey*.
3. The money was returned to the bank. It was stolen by the bank manager.
4. Did you hear about the explorer? He was eaten by cannibals.
5. The jewels were valued at $65,000. They were taken by the thieves.

▶ **Restrictive adjective phrases with actual adjectives**

All participle phrases are adjective phrases, but all adjective phrases are not participle phrases. Believe it or not, you can turn an adjective clause with actual adjectives in it into an adjective phrase with actual adjectives in it? Who would have guessed?

The main thing is to make sure your students understand that the adjectives all have (jargon alert!) *modification*—stuff after them. Because of that stuff, they can't go in front of the nouns they are modifying as they normally would. For example, these sentences:

13.62a   A boy sat next to me on the flight. He was sick with the flu.

could be combined as this:

   b   A boy who was sick with the flu sat next to me on the flight.

or this:

   c   A boy sick with the flu sat next to me on the flight.

but not this:

   d   A sick with the flu boy sat next to me on the flight.

sample exercises 19: Make subject adjective clauses. Then reduce them to adjective phrases.

I stayed in a hotel room. It was smaller than a closet.
I stayed in a hotel room that was smaller than a closet.
I stayed in a hotel room smaller than a closet.

A man committed the crime. He was insane with jealously.
A man who was insane with jealousy committed the crime.
A man insane with jealousy committed the crime.

1. People take the train or just stay home. They are afraid of flying.
2. She has a heart. It's as cold as ice.
3. Mark has a dog. It's bigger than a horse.
4. A man sat down beside me. He was bent with age.
5. We saw mountains. They were white with snow.

This sort of adjective phrase isn't as common as participle adjective phrases or adjective phrases with prepositional phrases (discussed next). I think most native AE speakers would use the adjective clause rather than the adjective phrase. Using the adjective phrase has a certain literary quality, and most AE speakers do not have a literary quality. But they're worth having a look at.

▶ **Restrictive adjective phrases made with prepositional phrases**

Would you believe that prepositional phrases can serve as adjective phrases? Amazing, but true. Not very difficult either. Once again, it boils down to canceling the relative pronoun and whatever form of *be* appears in the adjective clause. (And remember, *A bird ~~which is~~ in the hand is worth two [birds] ~~which are~~ in the bush*.)

sample exercises 20: Make subject adjective clauses. Then reduce them to adjective phrases.

I heard a tragic story. It was about an ESL teacher with a family, school loans and a mortgage.
I heard a tragic story that was about an ESL teacher with a family, school loans and a mortgage.
I heard a tragic story about an ESL teacher with a family, school loans and a mortgage.

The woman checked out at 7:00 a.m. She was in room 217.
The woman who was in room 217 checked out at 7:00 a.m.

The woman in room 217 checked out at 7:00 a.m.

1. The teacher said the words might be on the test. They were on the board.
2. A Chinese family moved into the house. It is next to us.
3. The car belongs to my uncle. It's in the garage.
4. I grew up in a town. It is near Chicago.
5. What's the name of that guy? He's by the door.

13.13 Adjective clauses reduced to nonrestrictive adjective phrases

Now that you've finished teaching your students various types of restrictive adjective phrases reduced from restrictive adjective clauses, you're going to teach them about nonrestrictive adjective phrases. To complicate matters, when nonrestictive adjective phrases are stuck in the middle of a sentence, they sometime get restless and decide to just get up and move to the front or back of a sentence. When they move to the front, we say they are (jargon alert!) *fronted*. At the back, we say they are (jargon alert!) *extraposed*.

Although these various adjective phrases can be rewritten as adjective clauses, the resulting adjective clause can be a bit unnatural and awkward, so from now I'm going to go straight from two sentences to one with an adjective phrase without the intermediate adjective clause stage. I think that will be better for your students, and by now that shouldn't be a problem.

▶ **Nonrestrictive present participle phrases (fronted and extraposed)**

Remember that adjective phrases derived from active verbs use the present participle, the *-ing* form of the verb, and for that reason, they're called present participle phrases. In Section 13.12 we looked at restrictive present participle phrases. Now we're going to look at nonrestrictive present participle phrases. You might want to remind your students of the whole essential/nonessential, comma/no comma deal discussed in Section 13.9.

First, show your students a simple example like this:

13.63a Bill sneaked out of the room. He walked softly.
 b Bill, walking softly, sneaked out of the room.

and then show them how the adjective phrase can be fronted:

 c Walking softly, Bill sneaked out of the room.

Pretty cool, huh? This sort of thing is very common, so I suggest emphasizing it. In fact, there will be times when it sounds odd *not* to front the adjective phrase, especially when the subject of the main clause is a pronoun. Despite this, I suggest you have students create these odd sentences to help them understand just where the adjective phrase they're fronting has come from. Remind your students that, unlike before, the information is not essential for identifying anyone or anything—it's extra, additional information added to the sentence—not essential but perhaps helpful in explaining or describing the information in the main clause.

sample exercises 21: Combine the sentences to make two sentences as in the examples.
 Michael knew his wife would get angry. He didn't tell her what happened.
 Michael, knowing his wife would get angry, didn't tell her what happened.
 Knowing that his wife would get angry, Michael didn't tell her what happened.

 I sneaked out the back door. I didn't want my boss to see me leaving early.
 I, not wanting my boss to see me leaving early, sneaked out the back door.
 Not wanting my boss to see me leaving early, I sneaked out the back door.

1. Rosa had to use her credit card. She didn't having any cash.
2. I waited for him to come home. I got angrier and angrier.
3. Alan left for his job interview. He wore his only suit.
4. Maria didn't see the alligator. She was lying on the beach with her sunglasses on.
5. Larry watched the birds for hours. He wished he could fly.

Now let's look at present participle phrases which end sentences. They normally modify the subject of the base sentence and could be placed immediately after the subject, but they're often extraposed—moved to the end of the sentence. When that happens, sometimes other words will get between the noun or noun phrase and the extraposed present participle phrase that's modifying it. That's OK as long as the meaning is clear. For example,

13.64a The police arrested him and took him to jail. They didn't believing a word he said.

b → The police, not believing a word he said, arrested him and took him to jail.
c → The police arrested him and took him to jail, not believing a word he said.

is clear, but if too much intervenes, as in this example,

13.65   The police arrested him and took him to jail despite his claim that his 88-year-old grandmother robbed the bank and hid the money taken in the robbery under his mattress, not believing a word he said.

it not would be clear, but that's an extreme example.

sample exercises 22: Combine the sentences to make two sentences as in the examples.
Carlos woke up early and got ready for work. He forgot that it was Saturday.
Carlos, forgetting that it was Saturday, woke up early and got ready for work.
Carlos woke up early and got ready for work, forgetting that it was Saturday.

Sarah is looking for a new job. She had heard that her company might go out of business.
Sarah, having heard that her company might go out of business, is looking for a new job.
Sarah is looking for a new job, having heard that her company might go out of business.

1.   Maria sat for hours by the phone. She wondered why he didn't call.
2.   I told her the whole story. I knew she would think I was nuts.
3.   Frank ran into the truck. He didn't notice that the light was red.
4.   Alan lied to his father for months. He didn't have the nerve to tell him the truth.
5.   John and Mary didn't want to go to the movie with us. They had heard that it was terrible.

▶ **Nonrestrictive adjective phrases with actual adjectives (fronted and extraposed)**
We have already discussed restrictive adjective phrases with actual adjectives, and we saw that they're relatively uncommon, but much more common are nonrestrictive adjective phrases with actual adjectives. Just like present and past participle phrases, they're frequently fronted and extraposed.

Keep reminding your students about this nonessential/nonrestrictive idea—that it is extra information not essential to the sentence—the sentence would still make sense without it.

No new concepts here, so you might as well have your students dive right in to the exercises. First, fronted nonrestrictive adjective phrases with actual adjectives:

sample exercises 23: Combine the sentences to make two sentences as in the examples.
The ESL teacher ran screaming down the hallway. He was fed up with his rude and lazy students.
The ESL teacher, fed up with his rude and lazy students, ran screaming down the hallway.
Fed up with his rude and lazy students, the ESL teacher ran screaming down the hallway.

Mark got up and left. He was tired of waiting to see the doctor.
Mark, tired of waiting to see the doctor, got up and left.
Tired of waiting to see the doctor, Mark got up and left.

1.   Bill went inside and took a shower. He was hot and dirty from working in the garden all day.
2.   Baffin Island has a population of only 11,000. It is more than twice the size of Great Britain.
3.   Michael sat quietly at his desk. He was angry about his manager's criticism.
4.   The girls left the room. They weren't interested in hearing Bob's dumb jokes.
5.   I felt like punching him in the nose. I was mad as hell.

Now extraposed nonrestrictive adjective phrases with actual adjectives:

sample exercises 24: Combine the sentences to make two sentences as in the examples.
Mark refused to shake my hand. He was angry that I hadn't chosen him for the job.
Mark, angry that I hadn't chosen him for the job, refused to shake my hand.
Mark refused to shake my hand, angry that I hadn't chosen him for the job.

The students entered the school. They were wet from the rain.
The students, wet from the rain, entered the school.
The students entered the school, wet from the rain.

1.   John arrived at the party. He was nervous about running into his ex-wife.
2.   Bill kept his mouth shut. He was afraid to say a word.

3. Larry lay awake all night. He was sick with worry.
4. Linda walked along the beach. She was sad and lonely.
5. The children went to bed. They were terrified of the monster they knew was in the closet.

13.14 Appositives

Appositives are another type of adjective phrase. They are nouns and noun phrases which modify other nouns or noun phrases. Appositives can modify any noun or noun phrase in a sentence—subject, object, object of a preposition, whatever. They can be a bit tricky—all sorts of things are appositives that you'd never have guessed—so it makes sense to treat them separately. And don't get hung up on terminology. Who cares if your students even remember the term *appositive* as long as they can use them?

Appositives can be rewritten as adjective clauses, but the results can sound weird, so I think it's counterproductive to talk about that with students, so don't.

What it boils down to is that with appositives, we're inserting a noun or noun phrase immediately after (usually, but not always) another noun or noun phrase in order to identify, define, explain or clarify that noun or noun phrase. The noun or noun phrase we've inserted (jargon alert!) *renames* the noun or noun phrases it modifies. Here are some examples with the appositives underlined. Can you figure out why 13.66, 13.67 and 13.68 have commas but 13.69, 13.70 and 13.71 don't?

13.66   The new manager of the sales department, <u>Julie Jones</u>, spoke at the meeting.

13.67   Tom Davis, <u>my father's best friend</u>, died last week.

13.68   You dope! That isn't a horse or a donkey. It's mule, <u>a cross between a horse and a donkey</u>.

13.69   My son <u>Alan</u> isn't a college student.

13.70   The fact <u>that Larry lied about me</u> made me angry.

13.71   My friend <u>Keith</u> lives in Abu Dhabi.

In each example, the appositive identifies, defines, explains or clarifies the noun or noun phrase it follows. It does that by renaming it, by saying that the two nouns or noun phrases are one and the same:

The new manager of the sales department	=	Julie Jones
Tom Davis	=	my father's best friend
a mule	=	a cross between a horse and a donkey
my son	=	Alan
the fact	=	that Larry lied about me
my friend	=	Keith

Now how about those commas? Do you remember a few pages ago we talked about essential and nonessential information? We said that some adjective clauses provide essential information, in which case no commas are used, but others provide nonessential extra information—perhaps helpful, interesting and useful—but not necessary for identification. Well, it's the same deal here. The appositives in 13.66, 13.67 and 13.68 provide nonessential information, but the info in 13.69, 13.70 and 13.71 is essential for identification. Remember, just to cause extra confusion, instead of the easily-understood terms *essential* and *nonessential,* we grammarians insist on using *restrictive* and *nonrestrictive.*

▶ Nonrestrictive appositives

Commas are (usually) used with nonrestrictive appositives—two when it is inserted within the sentence or one when it's at the beginning or end of the sentence: (Dashes and colons can be used instead of commas for more oomph—dashes just like commas but only a single colon at the end of a sentence. Should you confuse your students even further with that? Hmmmm. I'll leave that up to you.)

13.72   <u>An expert mechanic</u>, Carlos immediately knew what was wrong with my car.

13.73   Carlos, <u>an expert mechanic</u>, immediately knew what was wrong with my car.

13.74   When I have a car problem, I always take my car to Carlos, <u>an expert mechanic</u>.

This seems pretty simple so far, but appositives can be a lot longer and more complicated than these example:

13.75   Jim Smith, my creepy college roommate from Alabama who used to wash his underwear in the kitchen sink and had such terrible B.O. that I couldn't breathe whenever he was around, called me yesterday.

That's a rather extreme example, but you get the idea. As your students get into more advanced grammar, it might be easy for them to confuse appositives with other modifying phrases. Just remember, an appositive is a noun or noun phrase. It could always be rephrased in a sentence with *be*: He is _____, She was _____, They are _____, It was _____, etc:

13.76a   Jim Smith, <u>my college roommate</u>, called me yesterday.

    b   → Jim Smith called me yesterday. He was <u>my college roommate</u>.

As you go over this with your students, give them practice listening to how we native speakers lower our intonation, when we say the nonrestrictive appositive. That's important! Encourage them to do the same because without the lowered intonation, a sentence with an appositive would sound odd to a native speaker and might not be understood.

sample exercises 25: Combine the sentences to make one sentence with an appositive. There may be two answers from some. If you think two answers are possible, write both answers.

    I asked Bill Nelson about my computer problem. He's a guy I work with.
    I asked Bill Nelson, a guy I work with, about my computer problem.

    John knew that Frank was lying about his war experiences. John is a retired Army captain.
    John, a retired Army captain, knew that Frank was lying about his war experiences.
    A retired Army captain, John knew that Frank was lying about his war experiences.

1.   We saw Michael eating lunch with Bob Jackson. He's the man who wants to buy Michael's business.
2.   I asked Rosa to bake a cake for the party. She is my sister-in-law.
3.   Her husband lost $85,000 in Las Vegas. That was their life's savings.
4.   I ran into Steve Barkley at the supermarket. He was my high school English teacher.
5.   My ex-brother-in-law shocked everyone with his rudeness. He's a complete lunatic.

▸ **Restrictive appositives**

Whether information is essential or nonessential isn't always obvious from an isolated sentence. It often depends on the situation—the prior knowledge that the speaker and listener have. For example, does this sentence need commas?

13.77   My cat Larry is very fat.

Hard to say. How many cats do I have? Maybe just one cat (and you know that), so no commas because *Larry* is nonessential, or maybe I have several cats (and you know that), so commas are needed because *Larry* is essential to specify which of my cats I'm talking about. How could any student know this? Yes, sometimes it's obvious, but not always, so that's why I don't think it's a good idea to get too hung up on punctuation by asking students to insert or not insert commas—better to focus on sentence structure.

Anyway, remind your students that these appositives provide essential information, so that's why there are no commas in any of them.

sample exercises 26: Combine the sentences to make one sentence with an appositive.

    My cousin visited me last night. His name is Tom.
    My cousin Tom visited me last night.

1.   Have you read the novel? The name of the novel is *War and Peace*.
2.   The discovery shocked everyone. The discovery was that Frank was the murderer.
3.   We aren't paid enough. We are ESL teachers.
4.   I went to the party with my friend. Her name is Sarah.
5.   The fact prevented me from going on the trip. The fact was that I had a broken leg.

▸ **Nonrestrictive appositives (fronted and extraposed)**

Just like other nonrestrictive adjective phrases, nonrestrictive appositives are frequently fronted:

13.78a   Niagara Falls is visited by millions of people every year. It is a popular honeymoon destination.
    b   Niagara Falls, a popular honeymoon destination, is visited by millions of people every year.
    c   A popular honeymoon destination, Niagara Falls is visited by millions of people every year.

and extraposed. Sometimes, when the appositive modifies a noun or noun phrase at the end of the sentence, no extraposition is necessary:

13.79a   The next morning, we arrived in Cusco. It was the ancient capital of the Inca Empire.
    b   The next morning, we arrived in Cusco, the ancient capital of the Inca Empire.

but sometimes, when a few words follow the noun or noun phrase being modified, extraposition is possible as long as the meaning is clear:

13.80a   We arrived in Cusco. It was the ancient capital of the Inca Empire.
    b   We arrived in Cusco, the ancient capital of the Inca Empire, the next morning.
    c   We arrived in Cusco the next morning, the ancient capital of the Inca Empire.

sample exercises 27: Combine the sentences to make one sentence with an appositive. Write two versions as in the example.
  My father offered to help the police. He is a retired detective.
  My father, a retired detective, offered to help the police.
  A retired detective, my father offered to help.

1. Carlos always gets good grades. He is an excellent student.
2. Nicholas is hated by many who have worked for him. He is a liar and a bully.
3. Greenland has a population of only 57,000 people. It is the largest island in the world.
4. Sarah can never pass a used book store without going in for a look. She is a book lover.
5. Yosemite is 140 miles east of Los Angeles. It is one of the USA's most popular national parks.

sample exercises 28: Combine the sentences to make one sentence with an appositive. Write two versions if it is possible to move the appositive to the end of the sentence.
  I was robbed of $700 by the thief. That was money I needed to pay bills.
  I was robbed of $700, money I needed to pay bills, by the thief.
  I was robbed of $700 by the thief, money I needed to pay bills.

  Rosa went to Florida with Sofia. Sofia is her sister who lives in Wisconsin.
  Rosa went to Florida with Sofia, her sister who lives in Wisconsin.

1. The police suspected his wife of the crime. She was a woman with a history of poisoning husbands.
2. David lives in Kempton. It's a small town in the middle of nowhere.
3. I had to pay $2,000 to get my car fixed. That was a lot more than I expected.
4. We ate lunch at El Taco Loco. It's a Mexican restaurant near our house.
5. I hired Mary Jones for the job. She's a woman with an excellent resume.

13.15 *which* used to modify an entire sentence
This is the last section in the adjective clause chapter, which will come as a relief to you. Did you see what I just very cleverly did? I used *which* to modify an entire sentence. Here are some more examples:

13.81   Linda and Sam got married, which Linda's parents were not happy about.

13.82   Bill failed the final exam, which really surprised his teacher.

This is pretty simple to figure out and teach, and it's something you *should* teach because it's very common. Be forewarned that some people have a silly notion that this is somehow informal and not suitable in proper English. This is nonsense, and why anyone thinks so is a mystery to me.

So how to teach this? Put pairs of sentences like these on the board:

  Our team won a game. This was a miracle.
  He said yes. This surprised me.

Then simply rewrite them as below. Pretty simple, huh?

  Our team won a game, which was a miracle.
  He said yes, which surprised me.

sample exercises 29: Use the second sentence as an adjective clause. Be sure to cancel *this*.
  I forgot my wife's birthday. This made her angry.
  I forgot my wife's birthday, which made her angry.

1. A man helped me fix my bicycle. This was very nice of him.
2. Sarah is very sick. This makes me worry.
3. Joe crashed his car. This didn't surprise me because he always drives too fast.
4. The doctor said my friend doesn't have cancer anymore. This was great news.
5. Last year we went to Venice. This, in my opinion, is the most beautiful city in the world.

Chapter 14
Noun Clauses

Could you…

- explain why *a* and *b* are wrong?

  a.   I don't know when does the movie start.

  b.   Can you tell me where is the bank?

14.1 Definition of noun clause

Noun clauses give ESL students a lot of trouble. So first of all, what's a noun clause? A noun clause is a dependent clause (meaning it wouldn't make sense on its own) <u>with a subject and a tensed verb in it</u>. (Whenever you hear *clause*, you know there's a subject and a tensed verb in there somewhere.)

Two common kinds of noun clauses are *that-clauses*:

14.1a   When I saw the bear, I knew <u>that I was in trouble</u>.

and *question word-clauses* (aka *wh*-clause, but since not all *wh* words start with *wh,* I prefer the term *question word*):

14.2a   Did you hear <u>what the teacher said</u>?

You can see that noun clauses do the job of single nouns by replacing the noun clause with single nouns:

14.1b   When I saw the bear, I knew <u>it</u>.

14.2b   Did you hear <u>it</u>?

Of course, information is lost, but the sentences are still grammatical.

14.2 Embedded questions: noun clauses beginning with a question word

Let's start with the biggest problem students have with noun clauses. To illustrate, I'll give you some examples of a very frequent error made by ESL students:

14.3a   I don't know where did he go.

14.4a   Do you know how much does this cost?

14.5a   Can you tell me when is the test?

Do you see what's going on? The students have questions on their mind:

14.3b   Where did he go?

14.4b   How much does this cost?

14.5b   When is the test?

but when they plug these questions into bigger sentences, they're no longer actual question—they're (jargon alert!) *embedded questions*. Question grammar is no longer necessary.

You may already be thinking "Yikes, how am I going to explain this?" Fortunately, there's a really handy trick that will help you teach this and help your students understand it. It's worked well for me, and it will for you too.

Here it is: The grammar that should be used in the noun clause is the same grammar that would be used to provide the information being discussed in a hypothetical answer. It's that simple. So imagining a possible answer will give you the grammar to use in the noun clause. Here are some examples:

14.6a   wrong noun clause grammar: I don't know <u>where did he go</u>.
   b   possible answer: <u>He went</u> to the mall.
   c   right noun clause grammar: I don't know <u>where he went</u>.

14.7a   wrong noun clause grammar: Do you know <u>how much does it cost</u>?

    b   possible answer: <u>It costs</u> $25.

    c   right noun clause grammar: Do you know <u>how much it costs</u>?

14.8a   wrong noun clause grammar: Can you tell me <u>when is the test</u>?

    b   possible answer: <u>The test is</u> next Monday.

    c   right noun clause grammar: Can you tell me <u>when the test is</u>?

Is that easy or what?

sample exercises 1: First, look at the possible answer to the questions. Then choose the correct question.

   ☐ A1: Do you know how many dogs does he have?

   ☑ A2: Do you know how many dogs he has?

       B: He has four dogs.

1. ☐ A1: Do you know when can she do it?

    ☐ A2: Do you know when she can do it?

       B: She can do it tomorrow.

2. ☐ A1: Is what the teacher said important?

    ☐ A2: Is what did the teacher say important?

       B: Yes, the teacher said there will be an exam tomorrow.

3. ☐ A1: I don't know where is John. Do you know?

    ☐ A2: I don't know where John is. Do you know?

       B: I think John is in the kitchen.

4. ☐ A1: Do you know when does the game start?

    ☐ A2: Do you know when the game starts?

       B: The game starts at 1:00.

5. ☐ A1: I don't know what I should say.

    ☐ A2: I don't know what should I say.

       B: You should say yes.

sample exercises 2: First, look at the answer to the questions. Then complete the noun clause in the question.

   A: Do you know where _____ *she works* _____?

   B: She works in a supermarket.

1. A: Do you remember how many children _____?

    B: I think she has three children.

2. A: Do you know when _____?

    B: The game starts at 1:00.

3. A: Do you know why _____?

    B: He was late because he had car problems.

4. A: I don't know where _____? Do you know?

    B: I think Noura lives in Abu Dhabi.

5. A: Did Sarah tell you why _____ on Sunday?

    B: She's got to work on Sunday because her company got a big order.

sample exercises 3: Change the questions to noun clauses. If you are not sure, remember to ask yourself, *How could I answer this question?* Because these are conversations, be sure to use the appropriate pronouns.

   A: Why was John upset with you?

   B: I don't know _____ *why he was upset with me* _____.

1. A: Where did Maria go?

    B: I'm not sure _____

2. A: What is Sofia's telephone number?

    B: I have no idea _____. Look in the phone book.

3. A: Where has your brother gone?

    B: I'm not sure _____

4. A: When does Mark's soccer game begin?

    B: I don't know. He didn't tell me _____.

5. A: Who did Alan go to the library with?

B: I don't know _____.

14.3 Noun clauses beginning with *if* or *whether (or not)*

In the previous section, we looked at noun clauses beginning with questions words. These noun clauses are based on information questions (minus the question grammar). Now we're going to look at noun clauses based on *yes/no* questions. I would start this lesson by first giving your students an example of an information question-based noun clause and then a *yes/no* question-based noun clause to show them the difference. Put these on the board:

> **When does the train arrive?**
> **I don't know when the train arrives.**
>
> **Does the train arrive at 4:30?**
> **I don't know if/whether the train arrives at 4:30.**

The main thing you want your students to see is that we can start the clause with either *if* or *whether.* If your students ask, or if you feel the need to explain *if,* which they may not be familiar with (and you really should), be careful not to befuddle them by straying into conditional sentence territory. This is not the conditional use of *if. Whether* will almost certainly be unfamiliar to your students. Make sure they don't confuse it with *weather. If* is more common than *whether,* but don't ignore *whether.*

But it's not as simple as that. It's optional to add *or not* to the sentence. *Or not* can be added right after *whether* or at the end of the noun clause:

14.9a   I don't know <u>whether or not</u> Paul came to the party.
   b   I don't know <u>whether</u> Paul came to the party <u>or not</u>.

With *if,* it can only be added to the end of the noun clause:

14.10   I don't know <u>if</u> Paul came to the party <u>or not</u>.

The main thing is for your students to understand the use of *if* and *whether.* Focus on that. *Or not,* I'd say, is of secondary importance.

This is an example of how there can sometimes be many variations of some grammar you're teaching which requires that you strike a balance between keeping it simple but taking the chance of oversimplifying and not teaching your students something they should know or the opposite—confusing them with too much information. We'll see some huge examples of that later. Personally, I tend to err on the side of being thorough and taking the risk of overdoing it. As always, though, you have to consider your students' needs and abilities. If you feel that you need to be thorough and cover variations but at the same time want to avoid overwhelming your students, you can do so by making it very clear in your presentation what the essential points are and what is of secondary importance. How do you do that? By telling them (duh) but also by repeating, repeating, repeating the essential point. Let students have no doubt what the main thing is that they need to get. Focus on it, and keep at it until they get it right, but be more tolerant of errors with what you consider secondary. Obviously, you want everybody to get everything down 100%, but you have to be realistic and know that that's a noble but generally unattainable goal.

sample exercises 4: Change the question to a noun clause. If you are not sure, remember to ask yourself *How could I answer the question?* Practice using *if, whether* or *whether or not.*

   A: Was Mary sick yesterday?
   B: I don't know _____ *if/whether she was sick yesterday* _____.

1. A: Does Tom have a car?
   B: I don't know _____.
2. A: Are cats smarter than dogs?
   B: I don't know. I'll ask my cat _____.
3. A: Has Linda done her homework?
   B: I don't know _____.
4. A: Does the show start at 9:00?
   B: I have no idea _____.
5. A: Would Michael like to go to the beach with us?
   B: I'll ask him _____.

sample exercises 5: Some of the sentences contain mistakes. Find the incorrect sentences and correct them.

1. I want to know will he come to the party.
2. Can you tell me is Paul going to be here tomorrow?
3. Whether you come to the party or not doesn't matter to me.
4. I don't remember we are supposed to read this book.
5. Does Michael speak French is not something I know.

14.4 Noun clauses with question words and infinitives

This is a short and not very difficult lesson that you could combine with one of the two previous lessons. When noun clauses begin with question words which contain a subject and the modals *can, could, ought to* or *should*, the subject and modal can be replaced with an infinitive:

14.11a   I don't know which book <u>I should read</u>.
    b   I don't know which book <u>to read</u>.

14.12a   Mary doesn't know where <u>she can buy</u> extra large baby shoes.
    b   Mary doesn't know where <u>to buy</u> extra large baby shoes.

14.13a   My mother isn't sure whether <u>she ought to say</u> yes or no.
    b   My mother isn't sure whether <u>to say</u> yes or no.

sample exercises 6: Change the sentences so that they have the same meaning by using infinitives.
       Please tell me what I should do.
       Please tell me what to do.

1. Mark told me what I should do.
2. Can you tell me where I can get my car fixed?
3. The recipe doesn't say how long I should cook it.
4. I've been thinking about what I should do about this problem for many days.
5. I told Carlos where he could cash a check.

sample exercises 7: Use your own words to complete the sentences with infinitives.

1. Everything in this restaurant looks so good. I don't know what _____.
2. Do you have any idea how _____ this problem?
3. I can't decide whether _____ a new car or _____ my old one.
4. Do you know how _____ to the mall from here?
5. Both of these books look very interesting. I don't know which one _____.

14.5 Object noun clauses beginning with *that*

Now we come to *that*-clauses. These are very important, but fortunately for you and your students, not terrible difficult. What we'll see here is how an independent clause can be the object of an entire sentence—in other words, a sentence inside a sentence. The way to present this is by first writing a couple of independent clauses on the board:

       Yesterday was my wife's birthday.
       Maria speaks German.

and then showing how those sentences can be the objects of another sentence:

       I forgot <u>(that) yesterday was my wife's birthday</u>.
       Nobody knows <u>(that) Maria speaks German</u>.

That is actually optional in *that*-clauses, which is why it's shown here in parentheses. It's important that your students understand this and understand that in everyday English, most native speakers omit *that*.

There isn't any mind-bogglingly challenging exercise that you can give your students to practice this grammar. What I like to do is give students some independent clauses—usually containing lame attempts at humor—and ask students to plug them into larger sentences. You might also ask students to complete sentences such as these in their own words.

sample exercises 8: Choose any sentence and use it as a noun clause to complete the sentences.
       ~~Cats are smarter than dogs~~.
       Ghosts are real.

Amsterdam is a beautiful city.
The USA will win the World Cup someday.
I am smart.
Our teacher is crazy.

1. Everybody knows (that) _____ *cats are smarter than dogs* _____.
2. I don't believe (that) _____.
3. Some people think (that) _____.
4. Do you agree (that) _____?
5. Most people don't think (that) _____.
6. Everyone agrees (that) _____.

14.6 Subject noun clauses beginning with *that*

That *that*-clauses can be the subjects of sentences is what we'll discuss next. Pretty clever, huh? I just used a *that*-clause as the subject of a sentence. Since a noun clause can do the same job as a noun, *that*-clauses can be subjects of sentences. In this case, however, *that* is not optional. Follow the same procedure as before. Write a couple of independent clauses on the board:

Mary failed the test.
Jim didn't tell his wife the truth.

and then show them how these sentences can be the subjects of a sentence:

<u>That Mary failed the test</u> was a big surprise.
<u>That Jim didn't tell his wife the truth</u> made her very angry.

Of course, sentences constructed in this way aren't terribly common. It's much more common to extrapose *that*-clauses and fill the spaces they leave behind with *it* as a (jargon alert!) *expletive* or *dummy subject* (so called because *it* has no meaning). It's only function is to fill a space. Unlike some languages, such as Spanish, English requires that the subject space in a sentence always be filled: (And do not waste your students' time by teaching them *extrapose, dummy subject* or *expletive*. They don't need to know that.)

<u>It</u> was a big surprise <u>that Mary failed the test</u>.
<u>It</u> made his wife very angry <u>that Jim didn't tell her the truth</u>.

Notice how the second sentence has to be rewritten slightly: *his wife* must precede *her*.

sample exercises 9: Choose any sentence and use it as a noun clause to complete the sentences.

~~Dogs are not as smart as cats.~~
There is life on other planets.
Smoking is bad for your health.
The Chicago Cubs will never win the World Series.
Professor Jones is a good teacher.
Americans eat only cheeseburgers.

a That _____ *dogs are not as smart as cats* _____ is obvious.
b It is obvious that _____ *dogs are not as smart as cats* _____.

1. a That _____ is believed by everyone.
   b It's believed by everyone _____.
2. a That _____ is a fact.
   b It is a fact that _____.
3. a That _____ is well known.
   b It's well known _____.
4. a That _____ is true.
   b It is true that _____.
5. a That _____ is not true.
   b It's not true that _____.

14.7 Noun clauses in reported speech

Yuk! That's how I feel about teaching *reported speech* (aka *indirect speech*). Why? Because a lot of grammar books would have you and your students believe something that isn't always true, but explaining why it isn't always true never fails to confuse students.

First of all, here is the oversimplified version: When we repeat something that someone said earlier, we can do so with either a direct quotation:

14.14a   Michael said, "I will help you."

or with an indirect quotation (aka reported speech):

14.15b   Michael said (that) he would help me.

And what happened with *will*? It turned into *would*. Why? Because, you may recall, in a weird way *would* is the past of *will*. That's the whole idea of this oversimplified reported speech lesson—that the verb form in the quoted speech steps back in time in reported speech. Put dialogs on the board to illustrate this to your students. Be sure to emphasize that the reported speech is about a conversation which took place in the past. Also, point out to your students that *that* is optional in noun clauses and that the pronouns may need to be changed as well. Here are two examples that you could put on the board:

1. last week
    Tom: I want to eat in the new Italian restaurant in the mall.
    John: OK, let's go someday.

    today
    John: Last week Tom said (that) he wanted to eat in the new Italian restaurant in the mall.
    Harry: I'd like to go there too.

2. yesterday
    Mary: I'm sick. I'm going to go to the doctor.
    Paul: OK, I hope you feel better.

    today
    Alan: Where's Mary? She's not in class today?
    Paul: She stayed home today. Yesterday she said (that) she was sick and (that) she was going
              to the doctor.

So why do I have a problem with all of this? Because in reality, when we're talking about a past discussion of something that <u>is still true</u>, we often <u>do not</u> change the verb to the past. Look at these two dialogs:

3. 5 minutes ago
    Sam: I work in a museum.
    Lucy: That's interesting.

    now
    Ali: What did Sam say? I didn't hear him.
    Lucy: He said (that) he works in a museum.

4. yesterday
    Noura: I live in a 300-year-old house.
    Gary: Really? That's very old.

    now
    Gary: Yesterday Noura told me (that) she lives in a 300-year-old house.
    Larry: Wow, that's very old.

In both of the dialogs above, it would have sounded odd to change to the past, and most native speakers would not.

So what to do? My advice is to explain this to your students, without making it seem like a big deal (because it isn't), and weasel out of having to teach them what they should <u>always</u> do in <u>every</u> situation by telling them to do what is logical. (When in doubt, obfuscate!)

Of course, we're not just talking about the present simple and past simple tenses. Here is a rather thorough table with a variety of tenses, modals and phrasal modals. Present it as a reference and in <u>no way</u> suggest that this is something that needs to be memorized. What you want to avoid, if possible, is getting into a huge discussion of modals and phrasal modals when you're supposed to be working on noun clauses. To avoid getting trapped in this grammatical quicksand, emphasize what I just said about this being a reference and zoom ahead to the exercises.

14.8 Quoted and reported speech

• quoted speech	• reported speech (past conversation/something that may or may not still be true)	• reported speech (recent past conversation/something that may still be true)
"I work in a bank."	He said (that) he worked in a bank.	He said (that) he works in a bank.
"I am studying."	He said (that) he was studying.	He said (that) he is studying.
"I ate lunch."	He said (that) he had eaten lunch.	He said (that) he ate lunch.
"I have finished."	He said (that) he had finished.	He said (that) he has finished.
"I had read that book."	He said (that) he had read that book.	same
"I will help you."	He said (that) he would help me.	He said (that) he will help me.
"I am going to do it."	He said (that) he was going to do it.	He said (that) he is going to do it.
"I can swim."	He said (that) he could swim.	He said (that) he can swim.
"I may go to the party."	He said (that) he might go to the party.	same
"I might sell my car."	He said (that) he might sell his car.	same
"I must lose weight."	He said (that) he had to lose weight.	He said (that) he has to lose weight.
"I have to leave."	He said (that) he had to leave.	He said (that) he has to leave.
"I should exercise."	He said (that) he should exercise.	same
"I ought to apologize."	He said (that) he ought to apologize.	same

sample exercises 10: Complete the sentences with reported speech. If two answers are possible, use the one that you think is best. Be ready to explain your answer.

    a   Noura: "I have to get a job."
    b   Last month Noura told me that _____ *she had to get a job* _____.

1. a   Paul: "I will be the next head of the sales department."
     b   Yesterday Paul said that _____.
2. a   Linda: "I have nine children."
     b   Linda told me that _____.
3. a   Alan: "I've bought a new car."
     b   I just talked to Alan, and he said that _____.
4. a   Mary: "I may call you tomorrow."
     b   Mary told me that _____.
5. a   Tom: "I have to read 100 pages tonight."
     b   Did you hear that? Tom said _____.

14.9 Plans: talking about past plans with noun clauses with *would* and *be going to*

Here's a bit of grammar about noun clauses and how they can be used with *would* and *be going to* to talk about past plans. Actually, this relates to reported speech (yuk) because we're going to compare direct speech in the form of independent clauses (which are therefore *not* noun clauses) to reported (indirect) speech which *is* in the form of a noun clause. Got that?

▸ **Direct speech about future plans**
Both *will* and *be going to* are possible:

   14.16   I <u>will/am going to</u> buy a new printer.

   14.17   They <u>will/are going to</u> complain to the manager.

▸ **Direct speech about past plans (which may have already happened or which may be unrealized or unconfirmed)**
Only *be going to* is possible. *Would* is <u>not</u> possible:

   14.18   I <u>was going to</u> buy a new printer.

   14.19   They <u>were going to</u> complain to the manager.

▸ **Reported (indirect) speech about past plans (which may already have happened or which may be unrealized or un-confirmed)**
Both *would* and *be going to* are possible:

   14.20   I said (that) I <u>would/was going to</u> buy a new printer.

14.21   Mary told me that they <u>would/were going to</u> complain to the manager.

Why isn't *would* possible in direct speech about past plans? My theory is that it's because it could be misunderstood as an implied conditional sentence (which it isn't). When you hear, for example, *I would…* or they *would…*, you expect if to follow as *if* it were a conditional situation:

14.22   I <u>would</u> buy a new printer <u>if</u>…

14.23   They <u>would</u> complain to the manager <u>if</u>…

But this isn't something to confuse your students with. The main thing is for them to get practice with using noun clauses to discuss past plans.

sample exercises 11: Complete the sentences with *would* and the correct form of *be going to*. Be sure to change pronouns when it is necessary.

      a   Nicholas: "I am going to support you."
      b   Nicholas lied when he told me that _____ *he would/was going to support me* _____.

1.   a   Rosa: "Tom is going to cook dinner."
     b   Rosa told me that _____.

2.   a   Carlos: "She'll arrive at 3:15."
     b   I think Carlos said _____, but I'm not sure.

3.   a   Alan: "Larry is going to take out the garbage."
     b   Alan said that _____.

4.   a   Michael: "I'll meet you at the library at 7:30."
     b   I'm pretty sure that Michael said _____.

5.   a   Lucy: "I'm going to call you later."
     b   Lucy told me that _____.

Chapter 15
The Passive

Could you...

- explain to a student why *a* can't be rewritten in the passive?

    a. His father died last week.

- explain why the passive is used in these sentences?

    b. Pearl Harbor was attacked by the Japanese on Dec. 7, 1941.
    c. My house was painted three years ago, and it already needs to be painted again.
    d. More emeralds are found in Colombia than in any other country.
    e. Portuguese is spoken in Brazil.
    f. A mistake was made in my project.

- explain whether *g* is passive?

    g. Michael got kicked out of high school.

15.1 The passive voice

The *passive* (aka *the passive voice*) is a way of putting sentences together which emphasizes the action of the verb rather than the doer of the verb. Grammarwise, it's quite straightforward, completely without complications and exceptions. It won't be easy at first, but once your students have learned the basic formula, they'll be able to apply it any time. The key, however, will be figuring out *why* the passive is used and *when* it is appropriate. Also, we'll discuss a very important way that *get* is used with the passive.

15.2 A lot of baloney is believed by some people about the passive.

A lot of baloney has been said by some people about how the passive should be avoided like the plague (along with clichés)—as if there were something profoundly sneaky, snooty, snobbish, sleazy, shady, suspicious, sly and other bad things that start with *s* about it. This is another example of mindless herd mentality: Other people who seem smart but don't know what they're talking about say something, so others say it too because if they don't, people might think they're not smart. If you encounter this nonsense, feel free to scoff at it because there is nothing inherently wrong with using the passive when it is appropriate. Obviously, however, the passive should not be used excessively by you because when it is used too much by people, their writing and speaking can be made by them to sound pompous, convoluted and crappy.

OK? Now that you know that the passive can be used without fear, let's talk about what it is, why we use it, when we use it and how to teach it.

15.3 Review past participles.

But before discussing the *why* and *when,* it's best to really focus on the *how*—the mechanics of the passive. That's what I do. But even before that, you need to be very sure your students are familiar with past participles. They must be in order to get anywhere with the passive. I always start my lesson on the passive with a review of just what a past participle is. Make sure they understand that the past participles of regular verbs are identical to the past simple form. Remember that some of your students might have learned the alternative terms *3rd form* or *verb 3* for the past participle.

15.4 Start with mechanics.

Now that you've done that, you're going to start with some very basic examples of active sentences and then show your students how they can be turned into passive sentences. Use only <u>irregular</u> verbs at first so that it's very clear that we're dealing with past participles and not past simple forms.

What you want your students to get is the basic subject/object switch, the use of *be* with the past participle and the *by*-phrase (Don't mention that the *by*-phrase isn't always necessary at first—that will come later.) Repeat the *be* + past participle business again and again and make sure that they understand that it is <u>not</u> the main verb which indicates the tense in a passive sentence but *be.*

Start by putting an active sentence like this on the board:

Alan   eats   cheeseburgers.
 subect   verb   object

Make sure they understand that *Alan* is the subject and that *cheeseburgers* is the object. How familiar they are with these terms and concepts will vary. As always, assume nothing. Review it more than you think is necessary. That's always a good policy. Remember, just because there aren't any questions doesn't mean there aren't any questions.

Point out that the tense of *eat* is present simple. Now show them this sentence:

Cheeseburgers   are eaten   by   Alan.
     subject   be + past participle   object

Emphasize that the tense is now contained within *be*. *Eat* was in the present simple tense in the active sentence, and now *be* is in the present simple tense in the passive sentence, which is why it has taken the form of *are*. Tell them that the main verb in the active sentence will always be in the form of the past participle in the passive sentence. In this case, *eat* has been replaced by the past participle *eaten*. (In perfect sentences, the main verb in the active sentence will already be in past participle form—don't mention that yet.)

One thing that you should discuss at some point is that the passive works only with transitive verbs. Some verbs (like *put*) are only transitive: they must have objects. Other (like *eat*) can be both transitive and intransitive: they can be used with or without objects. You can't make a passive sentence with an intransitive verb. (Try to make a passive sentence out of *Larry worked yesterday.*) I mention this transitive/intransitive business at some point when I discuss the passive, but I don't make a big deal out of because I've always found that students usually know the difference intuitively. Still, don't fail to mention it just in case there's some confusion.

Now give your students a few more examples with the present simple and then gradually expand to show them examples with the past simple, present continuous and past continuous. Keep using *by*-phrases. Leave the fact that *by*-phrases are often omitted from passive sentences, which is one of the reasons we use the passive, for later. Eventually get to some present perfect and past perfect examples and then sentences with the modal *will*. (You'll focus on other modals later.)

So still focusing on mechanics, it's time for some exercises. I suggest at first focusing on the whole idea of *be* containing the tense by having your students look at the tense of the active sentence main verb and then apply that tense to *be* in the passive sentence. This will also help familiarize them with the structure of passive sentences. Take your time with this because it won't be easy. In fact, you'll be surprised by how difficult it will be. You'll need to give them practice with negative sentences too, and that will be more difficult. This will really call on your students to use everything they know about tenses. Be sure to point out how subject pronouns in the active sentence become object pronouns in the passive sentence and vice versa.

sample exercises 1: Change these active sentences to passive by writing the correct form of *be*.
> A mouse ate the cheese.
> The cheese _____*was*_____ eaten by a mouse.

1. She is using the dictionary.
   The dictionary _____*is being*_____ used by her.
2. Larry drives the truck every day.
   The truck _____ driven by Larry every day.
3. I didn't do the work.
   The work _____ done by me.
4. They are taking the class now.
   The class _____ taken by them now.
5. He will go over the test results on Friday.
   The test results _____ gone over by him on Friday.
6. We have written the answers.
   The answers _____ written by us.

I suggest doing a lot more exercises like those above and then having your students practice changing active sentences to passives sentences. Do each tense thoroughly—one at a time with plenty of negative sentences.

sample exercises 2: Change these active sentences to passive. Be sure to change pronouns when it is necessary.
> He speaks Chinese.
> *Chinese is spoken by him.*

Mary doesn't eat meat.
Meat isn't eaten by Mary.

1. I teach English.
2. The boss didn't approve my request.
3. Many people take the bus.
4. We don't drink milk.
5. Carlos wrote a story.

sample exercises 3: Change these active sentences to passive. Be sure to change pronouns when it is necessary.
Sofia is riding a horse.
A horse is being ridden by Sofia.

They aren't doing the work.
The work isn't being done by them.

1. John is hiding the money.
2. The children are putting away the toys.
3. I'm not doing it.
4. The coach is choosing players.
5. Larry is doing nothing.

sample exercises 4: Change these active sentences to passive. Be sure to change pronouns when it is necessary.
Sam has paid the bill.
The bill has been paid by Sam.

She hasn't written the letter.
The letter hasn't been written by her.

1. We have started a new company.
2. A dog has bitten me.
3. I haven't seen that movie.
4. We haven't cleaned our rooms.
5. She has broken the window.

sample exercises 5: Change these active sentences to passive. Be sure to change pronouns when it is necessary.
Lucy saw the accident.
The accident was seen by Lucy.

She didn't ride the red bicycle.
The red bicycle wasn't ridden by her.

1. Jack stole my car last week.
2. She didn't make the sandwiches.
3. The pilot flew the airplane.
4. They didn't do it.
5. He didn't give the correct answer.

sample exercises 6: Change these active sentences to passive. Be sure to change pronouns when it is necessary.
Larry was cooking the hamburgers.
The hamburgers were being cooked by Larry.

We weren't listening to the music.
The music wasn't being listened to by us.

1. Francesca was riding a bicycle.
2. The people at the party were making a lot of noise.
3. The teacher wasn't grading the tests.
4. Noura and I weren't doing the dishes.
5. The judges were choosing the winner.

sample exercises 7: Change these active sentences to passive. Be sure to change pronouns when it is necessary.
The students had already read the book.

The book had already been read by the students.

He hadn't called her.
She hadn't been called by him.

We had never seen it.
It had never been seen by us.

1. Linda hadn't set up a meeting.
2. I'd done the work.
3. They had never seen a zebra.
4. John and I had never eaten Indian food.
5. We'd already ridden the motorcycle.

sample exercises 8: Change these active sentences to passive. Be sure to change pronouns when it is necessary.
Sarah will do all the work.
All the work will be done by Sarah.

They won't do it.
It won't be done by them.

1. The manager will explain the new plan at the meeting.
2. She won't cook dinner.
3. He'll change the light bulb.
4. John and he will give a speech.
5. He won't steal your money.

sample exercises 9: Change these active sentences to passive. Be sure to change pronouns when it is necessary.
Rosa is going to help me.
I'm going to be helped by Rosa.

They aren't going to do it.
It's not going to be done by them.

1. The news is going to surprise you.
2. I'm going to bring the hot dogs.
3. We're not going to pay for their wedding.
4. They're going to take the bus.
5. Carlos was going to fly the helicopter.

15.5 *why* and *when*

So now, finally, you're going to reveal to your students just why we do this crazy passive thing. We use the passive for the following reasons:

▶ **To emphasize the receiver of the action of the verb rather than the doer**

15.1a active: A bomb destroyed the building.
     b passive: The building was destroyed by a bomb.

We use the passive when we think that who or what is <u>receiving</u> the action of the verb is more important than who or what is <u>doing</u> the action of the verb (aka *the agent* or *the actor*). In the passive sentence above, we want to emphasize the destruction of the building and not that it was a bomb that destroyed it:

▶ **When the doer of the verb's action is unknown**

15.2a active: Somebody stole my car.
     b passive: My car was stolen.

Do you see a *by*-phrase here? No, you don't because one of the main reasons we use the passive is when we don't know who performed the action of the verb. Of course, we could say *by somebody*, but why? Obviously, it was somebody—a human— but if we don't know who, it's kind of dumb to say *by somebody*.

▶ **When the doer of the verb's action is obvious or not important**

15.3a active: Egyptians speak Arabic in Egypt.

b   passive: Arabic is spoken in Egypt.

Of course it's Egyptians who speak Arabic in Egypt, so the active sentence sounds goofy. The passive is better without *by Egyptians*:

15.4a   active: A delivery truck driver will deliver our new sofa between 2:00 and 5:00.
b   passive: Our new sofa will be delivered between 2:00 and 5:00.

Is it important to say *by a delivery truck driver* in the passive sentence? Nope.

▶ When we want to avoid revealing the doer of the action of the verb

15.5a   active: I made a mistake.
b   passive: A mistake was made.

Do you think that I enjoy telling people that I made a mistake? Do you? Does anyone? The passive is a way to avoid revealing who the doer of the verb is. It's a popular way for managers to deliver bad news or make snide comments to employees: *It was noticed that you didn't put a coversheet on the TPS report.*

Be careful with this because sometimes it can be pretty obvious that you're weaseling out of taking responsibility by using the passive. I recall several years ago watching a certain president of a certain country on television. He was discussing the fiasco which followed a certain invasion of another country—an invasion which he himself had ordered. "Mistakes were made," he admitted. "Yeah," I thought, "by you!"

sample exercises 10: Change these active sentences to passive. If you think there is a good reason for a *by*-phrase, include it in your answer. If you think there is not a good reason for a *by*-phrase, do not include it. Be ready to explain your answer.
> Mary Smith wrote this book in 1993.
> *This book was written by Mary Smith in 1993.*

> Somebody built my house in 1898.
> *My house was built in 1898.*

1. People invented gunpowder in China.
2. Teachers teach Spanish in my high school.
3. I'm sorry that I ran over your dog.
4. A man with red hair robbed the bank.
5. Somebody is going to open a new restaurant on Main Street.
6. Pirates buried the treasure.

15.6 Not always simple SVO

As is often the case, you have to choose between giving your students realistic and therefore more complicated examples which may confuse them and unrealistically easy examples which don't sufficiently strain their brains. My usual approach is to start simple and work toward the more complicated. In the case of the passive, obviously all sentences in English are not simple, short SVO (subject-verb-object) independent clauses. An SVO clause may be contained within a complex or compound sentence. There may be multiple subjects, objects or verbs. There may be adverbs and adverbial phrases. To put it in simpler terms, there may be stuff in the active sentence that doesn't move when the sentence is converted to a passive sentence. When you're just getting started with the passive, students may tend to think the object is always the last word in a sentence and may attempt to use adverbs and adverbial phrases as subjects of the passive sentence. For example, students may see the words underlined below as objects and try to move them to the front of a passive sentence:

15.6   She cooked dinner <u>yesterday</u>.

15.7   I did the work <u>carefully</u>.

15.8   Ali called his brother <u>in the morning</u>.

Make sure they don't think that. Have them look specifically for subjects, verbs and objects.

Also, it's important that your students understand that the mark of the passive is that a *by*-phrase is always <u>possible</u>—grammatically possible I mean. Whether it's needed or not, any passive sentence can have a *by*-phrase. That's the test to see if the passive is even possible. If no *by*-phrase is possible, then most likely the student is attempting to form a passive sentence with an intransitive verb. One interesting example you might want to work into your lesson is this:

15.9   I was born by my mother.

Of course, no one ever says this because it's rather obvious that it was your mother who *bore* you (from the verb *bear*: *bear/bore/born*), but it's an example of how a *by*-phrase is always possible even when it's not needed and also a good thing to mention because this is a very common error:

15.10   I borned in…

15.7 Passive modals

You've already given your students a little practice with the modal *will,* but now it's time to focus on modals and phrasal modals. There are two patterns: past and present/future. (This is an example of what is often true with modals and phrasal modals: there is no distinction between the present and future. When, after all, does the present end and the future begin? In a way, the future begins right now. We're all traveling into the future all the time.)

So anyway, past and present/future, OK? It's really just a matter of modal/semi-modal + *be* + past participle or modal/semi-modal + *have been* + past participle.

▶ **Present/future: modal/semi-modal + *be* + past participle**

Teach your students this pattern: modal/semi-modal + *be* + past participle:

15.11   This bill <u>must be paid</u> before the end of the month. (futurish, right?)

15.12   Something <u>has got to be done</u> about this problem right now. (definitely presentish, but remember, even one second from now is the future)

▶ **Past passive: modal/semi-modal + *have been* + past participle**

Teach your students this pattern: modal/semi-modal + *have been* + past participle:

15.13   The work <u>should have been done</u> three days ago.

15.14   This work <u>was supposed to have been finished</u> two weeks ago.

This will be a good time to review modals and phrasal modals. (You may want to review them before class yourself.) Students can never really be reminded enough about how common *have got (to)* is and how important it is to understand it (even if they never use it). It would also be a good idea to review *be supposed to, must* used for logical probability and *should* and *ought to* used for talking about expectations based on previous knowledge or experience.

Also, it's common to use *already* and *yet* with the modal/semi-modal + *have been* + past participle pattern, so try to work both into some of your examples:

15.15   Your homework should *already* have been done.

15.16   The information should not have been released to the public *yet*.

sample exercises 11: Change the active sentences to passive.
The kids must have eaten the chocolate cake.
The chocolate cake must have been eaten by the kids.

1. The plumber was supposed to fix the hot water heater.
2. The pilot had better check the fuel level.
3. The manager should already have contacted you.
4. A doctor has got to look at your leg.
5. Anyone could have done this.

sample exercises 12: Mixed tense review. Complete the sentences with the words in parentheses.
Who opened this letter? It (shouldn't, open) _____*shouldn't have been opened*_____ by anyone.

1. My red stapler is not on my desk. It (must, borrow) _____ by one of my kids.
2. I think I (may, transfer) _____ by my company to Vancouver soon.
3. These boxes (be supposed to, put on) _____ the truck tomorrow.
4. You (might, bite) _____ by the snake you were holding yesterday.
5. The teacher told us that the homework (had better, turn in) _____ on time.
6. I still haven't received my Tom's letter. I think it (may, send) _____ to the wrong address.
7. A new school (be going to, build) _____ on Oak Street next year.
8. The tires on your car are very worn. They (have got to, replace) _____ soon.

15.8 Passives with *get*

Did you think that the passive was all about *be* + past participle? Well, think again. The very common construction *get* + past participle is a form of the passive. Sometimes there's not much difference in meaning between *be* + past participle and *get* + past participle:

15.17a I <u>was</u> robbed yesterday.
     b I <u>got</u> robbed yesterday.

but sometimes there is a definite implication that the person who is the subject of the sentence is somehow responsible for what happened:

15.18 John <u>got</u> kicked out of school.

Grammarwise it's not terribly complicated. Everything I've said about *by*-phrases applies here as well.

Sometimes, when the speaker wants to make this idea of responsibility clear, reflexive pronouns are used. For example, in this sentence:

15.19 Jack <u>got himself</u> arrested by the police.

the use of *himself* makes it clear it was Jack's fault—he did something to make this happen.

This use of *get* is similar to the use of *get* discussed in the adjective chapter. There we saw that *get* is often used with adjectives—sometimes adjectives formed from past participles.

But what makes the use of *get* we're discussing here different is that a *by*-phrase is possible (but, of course, not always necessary). For that reason, the past participles used in this way are verbs and not adjectives. Also, only <u>past</u> participles can be used here. Yes, they also sometimes do double duty as participle adjectives, but they're not doing that here. Otherwise, present participle adjectives and garden variety adjectives would work here, and they definitely don't. (And no reason to confuse your students with this.)

sample exercises 13: Change the active sentences to passive sentences with *get*. Use a *by*-phrase only if you think there is a good reason for it. Be ready to explain your answer.

       A mosquito bit me.
       I got bitten by a mosquito.

1. The police said someone killed two guys last night.
2. A guy shot me.
3. A truck hit Paul.
4. Somebody hurt Mark in a fight.
5. A wolf ate David.

Chapter 16
Adverbs, Adverb Clauses, Adverb Phrases and More

Could you…

- answer this question: Which of these words are adverbs?

  slowly, about, back, well, fast, out, today, here, south

- answer this question: Are any of these sentences incorrect?

  a. I feel good.
  b. I feel well.
  c. I feel bad.
  d. I feel badly.

- explain the difference between a conjunctive adverb and a subordinating conjunction?
- explain why one of these sentences with an adverb clause could be reduced to an adverb phrase but the other could not?

  e. He drove all night while his wife slept in the back seat of his car.
  f. He drove all night while he thought about how to solve his problem.

16.1 Adverbs—an oddball grab bag

When you think of *adverb*, what comes to mind? Words like *quickly, slowly* and *carefully*, right? That's what your students would likely say. And yes, these are adverbs, but adverbs are a lot more than adjectives with an *-ly* stuck on the end. As you'll soon learn, all sorts of oddball words are adverbs that you never even thought of. Does *very* seem like an adverb? It is. Do *here* and *there* seem like adverbs? They are. Do *in* and *out* seem like adverbs? They are. Do *tonight* and *today* seem like adverbs? They are.

There are many types of adverbs which perform many functions. That's why this is an especially difficult aspect of English grammar to learn and to teach. It's important to understand that adverbs do not simply modify verbs. They can modify other adverbs, adjectives, phrases and clauses. Soon you'll understand why it has been said that when you don't know what part of speech a word is, say it's an adverb, and there's a good chance you'll be right.

Please note, however, that adverbs a murky business. There is no universally agreed-upon system for classifying adverbs nor what name to give those classifications. Look at several books and web sites, and you'll see a good deal of variation and overlap. I've tried to provide you with a good overview, but focus on concepts and meanings rather than terminolgy. Apply a big fat jargon alert! to the terminology we'll discuss for your own sake, but do not expect your students to memorize it.

And then we'll see that this adverbial function is performed not only by single-word adverbs but by adverb phrases and adverb clauses too. We'll talk about those later, but before we move on to the hard stuff, let's get the (relatively) easy stuff out of the way. Adverbs are generally classified as adverbs of degree, adverbs of manner, adverbs of place, adverbs of time, adverbs of frequency (sometimes included within adverbs of time, as I have done) and adverbs of purpose.

16.2 Adverbs of manner

Adverbs of manner means words that describe how people do things. The main thing you need to do at first is make sure your students don't confuse them with adjectives. Confusing them is easy since many adverbs are similar to adjectives (*slow/slowly*, for example) and some adverbs are identical to adjectives (*hard, fast* and *well*, for example). Keep it really simple at first. Problematic adverbs like *hard, fast* and *well* are discussed later. Use only *-ly* adverbs at first. I like to have students rewrite sentences so that they must change adjectives to adverbs. I don't recommend trying to come up with more exercises like these because, even though there are many more adjective/adverb pairs such as these, it's not easy to think of sentences that use them both without having to do a lot more rewriting than you want to get into at this point. You want to keep your focus on adverbs here without getting sidetracked by other grammar issues. However, the fact that adjectives modify nouns and adverbs modify verbs is something you really need to pound into your students heads. Keep reminding them of this!

sample exercises 1: Rewrite the sentences using adverbs instead of adjectives.

Larry is a slow runner.
Larry runs slowly.

1. I am a careful driver.
2. She is a bad singer.
3. Carlos is a deep thinker.
4. You are a quiet speaker.
5. It was a sudden change.

▶ **Comparative and superlative forms**

Like adjectives, adverbs have comparative and superlative forms. For most adverbs ending in *-ly*, it's a matter of using *more* and *the most*:

● **base form**	● **comparative form**	● **superlative form**
slowly	more slowly	the most slowly

▶ **Irregular adverbs**

No lesson would be complete without a bunch of exceptions:

● **base form**	● **comparative form**	● **superlative form**
hard	harder	the hardest
fast	faster	the fastest
late	later	the latest
far	farther/further	the farthest/furthest
well	better	the best
badly	worse	the worst

The adverbs *farther/further* are not 100% equal. When they are used to talk about distance, they are interchangeable, but for other meanings, *further* is used: *I drove farther* but *I explained further*. Remind your students that *far* is also an adjective.

▶ *well*

The fact that *well* is both an adjective and adverb is confusing to some native speakers, so you can be sure that it will be confusing to your students.

▷ **Adjectives: *well/bad***

Remind them that the adjective *well* means *in good health*. The opposite is *bad* (not *badly*). No matter how many times you hear people say *I feel badly about...*, it's wrong:

16.1 I am <u>well</u>.

16.2 She doesn't feel <u>well</u>.

16.3 I feel <u>bad</u>. I need to go to the doctor.

▷ **Adverbs: *well/badly***

The adverb *well* gives information about how somebody or something does something. The opposite is *badly* (not *bad*):

16.4 She sings <u>well</u>.

16.5 He doesn't speak Chinese <u>well</u>.

16.6 I play the piano <u>badly</u>.

This is also a good time to teach your students that it is common to use *not* + verb + (*very*) *well* instead of *badly*. The meaning is the same, but less strong, and for that reason, a little softer and more polite:

16.7 My husband doesn't dance very well.

sample exercises 2: Answer the questions. If the sentence is negative, write two possible answers.

Bob is a good football player. What can you say about him?
He plays football well.

Sarah is a bad tennis player. What can you say about her?
Sarah plays tennis badly.
Sarah doesn't play tennis well.

1. Mary is a good driver. What can you say about her?
2. Tom and Jerry are good singers. What can you say about them?

3. Larry was a bad dancer. What can you say about him?
4. Jim was a good swimmer. What can you say about him?
5. Michael is a bad cook. What can you say about him?

▶ *fast, hard* and *late*

Fast, hard and *late* are both adjectives and adverbs. This in itself isn't a big problem. The real problem is that students may naturally want to say, for example, *I worked hardly* or *The plane arrived lately*. That's discussed in the next section, but to get your students used to the idea that the adjective and adverb forms of *fast, hard* and *late* are identical, you may want to try the following exercise.

sample exercises 3: Write *adj* after the sentence if the word in italics is an adjective. Write *adv* after the sentence if the word in italics is an adverb.

> I got to work late yesterday. ___*adv*___
>
> My boss is angry because I was late yesterday. ___*adj*___

1. If you work *fast,* you will make more mistakes. _____
2. That airplane is really *fast.* _____
3. I told my daughter not to come home *late* from the party. _____
4. I might be *late* tomorrow. _____
5. My idea sounds *hard,* but I think it will be easy. _____
6. I tried *hard* to finish my work today, but I couldn't. _____

▶ *lately* and *hardly*

It's logical now to talk about what *lately* and *hardly* really mean. Explain to your students that in present perfect and past perfect questions and negative sentences, *lately* is often used instead of *recently*. They have the same meaning:

16.8a   Have you seen Alan <u>lately</u>?
   b   = Have you seen Alan <u>recently</u>?

Hardly is sometimes used with verbs and also with the modals *can* and *could* to mean *almost not*:

16.9   <u>I hardly know</u> Michael. I met him only one time.

16.10   Please turn up the volume. I <u>can hardly hear</u> anything.

Hardly is sometimes used with *any, anyone, anybody, anything* and *anywhere*. The meaning is the same as *almost no, almost no one, almost nobody, almost nothing* and *almost nowhere*:

16.11a   He has <u>hardly any</u> money.
    b   = He has <u>almost no</u> money.

16.12a   I talked to <u>hardly anyone</u> at the meeting.
    b   = I talked to <u>almost no one</u> at the meeting.

16.13a   We ate <u>hardly anything</u> at the party.
    b   = We ate <u>almost nothing</u> at the party.

sample exercises 4: Complete the sentences using the words in parentheses and *hardly*.

> My homework is very confusing. (understand) I ___*hardly understand*___ anything.

1. None of my friends is at this party. I (know) _____ anyone here.
2. My mother's eyes are very bad. She (can, see) _____ anything without her glasses.
3. I was very lazy yesterday. I (do) _____ anything all day except watch TV.
4. My husband is useless. He (ever, get off) _____ the sofa.
5. The music at the party was so loud that I (could, hear) _____ anything anyone said.

sample exercises 5: Rewrite the sentences with *hardly*. Use *any, anything* or *anybody* in your answers.

> I have almost no money.
> *I have hardly any money.*

1. Noura did almost nothing yesterday.
2. There's almost no time left.
3. Almost nothing was done about the problem.

Adverbs, Adverb Clauses, Adverb Phrases and More

4. I talked to almost no one.

5. Almost nobody goes there.

16.3 Adverbs of place

A really surprising collection of words are *adverbs of place*. Surprising because most of them don't really seem like adverbs. Many seem like adjectives, and if you didn't know better, that's what you might tell a student. And many—well, let's say that if you were asked by a student what part of speech they were, you'd squirm, obfuscate and change the subject. When I said earlier "…when you don't know what part of speech a word is, say it's an adverb, and there's a good chance you'll be right", these are the types of adverbs I was talking about. This is the sort of thing that, even though it's a grammar class, you teach more as a vocabulary exercise. Does that overlap with what might be done in a reading class? Yes. So what. By now students will already know many of these words anyway, so in no way do I recommend presenting them with this list as if it's something they need to memorize. All you really need to do is review the list and pick out a few that may be unfamiliar to your students to discuss or use as examples in sentences. I recommend, for each adverb of place that you choose, giving an example with *be* and an example with a main verb: (See the section on adverb placement which follows.)

16.14 The plane is <u>over</u> the city.

16.15 She walked <u>toward</u> the door.

16.16 We drove <u>south</u>.

16.17 He works <u>outdoors</u>.

- **adverbs of place**

about	above	abroad	anywhere	around
away	back	backward(s)	behind	below
down	downstairs	east	elsewhere	everywhere
far	here	in	indoors	inside
near	nearby	north	nowhere	off
on	out	outside	over	somewhere
south	there	toward(s)	under	up
upstairs	west	where		

I don't recommend trying to force these words into exercises. And remember, the fact that these are all adverbs of place is not anything your students need to totally understand. They're already using many, maybe most, of these words, anyway. Leave well enough alone and don't confuse them with grammar concepts that don't serve a purpose. This should seem more like a vocabulary lesson than a grammar lesson to your students. Remember that you're teaching them to use grammar, not teach it. But understanding adverbs of place will help you be a better grammar teacher.

16.4 Adverbs of time

An even bigger collection of words are adverbs of time. They fall into certain subcategories. Once again, by now your students will already know many of these words, and if they're using them right, that's all that matters. This too will be more of a vocabulary than grammar lesson. As with adverbs of place, I recommend just reviewing these and picking out a few to talk about more and use in examples. Whether your students know that these are adverbs of time isn't really important, so don't make a big deal about it. Knowing how to use these words is what's important. But you should know what they are, and if you do, you'll be a pretty smart ESL teacher. One subcategory that is a standard lesson in all grammar books is adverbs of frequency. We'll talk about those later.

- **definite points of time**

now	then	today	tomorrow	tonight
yesterday	next year, etc.	last week, etc.	the day after tomorrow/before yesterday	

- **indefinite frequency**

always	almost always	almost never	constantly	ever
frequently	generally	hardly ever	infrequently	never
normally	occasionally	often	rarely	regularly
seldom	sometimes	regularly	usually	

- **definite frequency**

annually	daily	fortnightly	hourly	monthly
nightly	quarterly	weekly	yearly	

- **indefinite time relationships**

already	before	early	earlier	eventually
finally	first	formerly	just	last
late	later	lately	next	previously
recently	since	soon	still	yet

▶ Adverbs of (indefinite) frequency

Adverbs of frequency, as these are generally called, are used to talk about *how often* we do something. (You may want to refer to the discussion of *how often* in Section 7.18.) They're important, so they are generally taught at a fairly low level in grammar books. For that reason, you should be prepared. First of all, I've already discussed my aversion to using percentages to teach adverbs of frequency, as is common. It just doesn't make sense nor does showing students a calendar showing how often somebody does something to illustrate the meaning of adverbs of frequency, as is also common. Why don't I think it makes sense? Because whether something is, for example *often* or *seldom* really depends on what we're talking about. If I do something five times a month, is that *often* or *seldom*? Well, it depends on what I'm doing—taking a shower or bashing myself in the head with a hammer. So how do I teach adverbs of frequency?

I have an amazingly clever system that works every time. Here it is: I have my students look in their bilingual dictionaries. That will save you from jumping through a lot of hoops, and besides, they're going to do it anyway. If I have a monolingual class, I may have a student write the meanings in his or her native language next to the adverbs of frequency on the board. Pretty cutting edge, huh?

▷ *almost never/hardly ever*

Grammar books usually teach *seldom* and *rarely,* which bugs me because in reality, we native speakers *seldom* say seldom and rarely say *rarely.* Instead we usually say *almost never* or *hardly ever,* which have the same meaning:

16.18a   I <u>hardly ever</u> watch TV.

    b   = I <u>almost never</u> watch TV.

▷ *almost always*

Like *almost never* and *hardly ever, almost always* absolutely should be taught along with other adverbs of frequency, and that's just what I do. You should too. I don't mean you should skip *rarely* and *seldom,* though. Teach them, but tell your students that *almost never* and *hardly ever* are more common. Put this on the board:

> always
>
> almost always
>
> usually
>
> often
>
> sometimes
>
> almost always = hardly ever = rarely = seldom
>
> never

As for exercises, it's hard to come up with exercises for what is more of a vocabulary lesson than a grammar lesson, especially when virtually all the answers would be grammatically correct. It makes sense to discuss these along with *how often* (as has already been done in Section 7.18), so what I often do to practice with adverbs of frequency is ask students questions about how often they do something—first two-way, with the student and me, then three-way, as we've discussed before, where I'll ask one student a question about another. (This is a great opportunity for some third person singular review.) The first student needs to ask the second, the second answers the first, and the first answers me. Coming up with things to ask your student is a perfect opportunity for some comic relief. After I've asked a few like these:

16.19   How often do you drink coffee?

16.20   How often do you go to (a nearby city)?

I'll ask a few like these:

16.21   How often do you ride a donkey?

16.22   How often do you go to (some weird or awful place your students would never want to go to)?

Without doubt, in answer to *How often do you…*?, you'll have students say things like *I always drink coffee* or *I always eat fish* or *I always ride a donkey,* which sounds as if they do these things 24 hours a day. You'll need to explain that we generally add

---

a time reference, some language to clarify, such as *in the morning, for dinner* or *when I visit my family in their remote mountain village high in Andes.*

Here are some exercises to give your students some practice with *hardly ever* and *almost never.*

sample exercises 6: Rewrite the sentences with *almost never* or *hardly ever.*

I hardly ever eat breakfast.
I almost never eat breakfast.

She almost never does her homework.
She hardly ever does her homework.

1. Alan hardly ever helps his mother.
2. We are almost never late.
3. Paul almost never calls me.
4. My boss is hardly ever in her office.
5. We almost never watch TV.

16.5 Adverbs of purpose

Adverbs of purpose describe why people do what they do. They supply the reason for an action or situation. By now your students will likely already know *because,* but the fact that *as* and *since* can mean *because* will likely be new. Especially emphasize *since.* Your students will recall *since* from the *for* and *since* lesson that's always part of perfect sentence lesson, but this meaning of *since* is something new and will confuse them, but hammer it home because this use of *since* is important.

- **adverbs of purpose**

as	because	in order to	now that	since
so	so that	to		

16.6 Adverbs modifying adjectives and other adverbs

That adverbs can modify not just verbs but adjectives and other adverbs is something your students should be aware of. Adjectives modified by adverbs was covered in our discussion of adjectives in Chapter 11, so rather than repeat everything, I encourage you to refer to Section 11.22. Here are some examples of adverbs modifying other adverbs:

16.23   He speaks Korean <u>extremely well</u>.

16.24   She sang <u>more beautifully</u> than ever.

16.25   He is absent <u>more often</u> that he is present.

16.26   I will <u>most definitely</u> call you.

16.27   I will <u>probably never</u> go to Antarctica.

16.28   My mother drives <u>quite slowly</u>.

16.29   I drive <u>really fast</u>.

16.30   We need to leave <u>right now</u>.

16.31   For a 90-year-old man, he plays rugby <u>surprisingly well</u>.

16.32   I woke up <u>unusually early</u>.

16.33   I stayed up <u>very late</u>.

I bring this up here as a kind of an introduction—something to familarize yourself and your students with—before wading into a more in-depth look at a potentially very confusing topic: adverbs of degree.

16.7 Adverbs of degree

Adverbs of degree (aka *qualifiers*) are words and phrases which in some way modify a quality of another word. If you value your sanity, I strongly discourage you from memorizing and God forbid teaching what follows as if it were etched in stone—unless that stone is pulverized and saturated with water (quicksand, get it?). Adverbs in general are a murky business, and this area is about as murky as it gets. A thorough review of books and web sites revealed an astonishing degree of disagreement—a hodgepodge of terminology, classifications and hierarchies. I challenge you to find any two books or websites that completely agree on any of this stuff. I'll do my best to synthesize and present this in a form that will help you help your students. Here goes:

▶ Intensifiers

Intensifiers are adverbs which *empasize, amplify* or *weaken* verbs (i.e. *qualify*), adverbs and adjectives. (Or at least that's one way of putting it. Some people group emphasizers and amplifiers together, some seperate downtoners from intensifiers, and some don't consider some of these to be adverbs at all! Should any of this worry you or your students? No!)

▶ Emphasizers

Emphasizer strengthen verbs, adverbs and adjectives.

- **emphasizers** (there are many more)

amazingly	certainly	definitely	entirely	extremely
fairly	fully	highly	incredibly	perfectly
pretty	quite	rather	really	thoroughly
unbelievably	unusually	very		

▷ Emphasizer + verb

16.34   She <u>really hates</u> me.

16.35   He <u>simply ignored</u> me.

▷ Emphasizer + gradable adjective

16.36   His explanation was <u>highly suspicious</u>.

16.37   This lasagna is <u>unbelievably good</u>.

▷ Emphasizer + adverb

16.38   Mary sings <u>pretty well</u>.

16.39   He drives <u>quite slowly</u>.

▶ Amplifiers

Amplifiers do to verbs and adjectives what they do to guitars—give them more impact, more power.

- **amplifiers**

completely	absolutely	totally	utterly

▷ Amplifier + absolute (aka non-gradable) adjective

16.40   It was <u>absolutely perfect</u>.

16.41   My project is <u>totally finished</u>.

▷ Amplifier + verb

16.42   My house was <u>completely destroyed</u> by the fire.

16.43   The vaccine utterly wiped out the disease.

▶ Downtoners

No, not the name of a blues band, *downtoners* weaken the meaning of verbs, adjectives and other adverbs.

- **downtoners**

a bit	almost	hardly	kind of	mildly
nearly	slightly	somewhat	sort of	to some extent

▷ Downtoner + adjective

16.44   I'm <u>a bit tired</u>.

16.45   She's <u>nearly ready</u>.

▷ Downtoner + verb

16.46   I think she <u>kind of likes</u> me.

16.47   I could <u>hardly understand</u> a word she said.

▷ Downtoner + adverb

16.48   Larry walks <u>sort of fast</u>.

16.49   David <u>somewhat foolishly</u> lent his brother-in-law $10,000.

In no way should you expect students to memorize anything more than the general idea. Focus on meanings and sentence patterns—keep it useful. OK, so how do you do that? My advice is to not teach your students the terminology we've just discussed as anything that needs to memorized (though *emphasize* is a good bit of vocabulary), and instead talk about "using adverbs with adjectives, verbs and other adverbs to make them stronger or weaker". Are the lists above definitive? Hardly, and there's a lot of overlap between *intensifiers* and *amplifiers*. Also, one problem is that giving students groups of words and phrasaes suggest that they are interchangable, which often is not the case, and that makes writing exercises difficult. But I'll try. Remember that the main thing to focus on is what these words mean and typical uses with adjectives, verbs and adverbs.

sample exercises 7:   Choose the word that has the same meaning as the word in italics.

1.   My old car breaks down all the time. I *certainly* need a new car.
     a.   very
     b.   highly
     c.   definitely
     d.   entirely

2.   I answered only 8 out of 100 questions on the final correctly. My score was *extremely* bad!
     a.   incredibly
     b.   pretty
     c.   rather
     d.   fairly

3.   Carlos is a pilot. He must work *very* carefully.
     a.   thoroughly
     b.   extremely
     c.   unusually
     d.   perfectly

sample exercises 8:

completely   absolutely   totally   utterly

1.   Write a sentence using one of these words and a verb.

2.   Write a sentence using one of these words and an adjective. (Review the idea of absolute adjectives and encourage your students to use them.)

sample exercises 9:   Choose the word that has the same meaning as the word in italics.

1.   I feel *sort of* sick.
     a.   hardly
     b.   almost
     c.   a bit
     d.   nearly

2.   I was so angry that I *almost* went crazy.
     a.   slightly
     b.   somewaht
     c.   nearly
     d.   slightly

3.   He makes mistakes because he works *kind of* carelessly.
     a.   almost
     b.   hardly
     c.   slightly
     d.   somewhat

16.8   placement of adverbs

Another maddening thing about adverbs is that they're shifty little devils. By that I mean they enjoy a lot more freedom to move around in a sentence than other parts of speech that pretty much must be anchored to one spot in a sentence. The flexibility that adverbs enjoy is something I occasionally mention to students. It's not random, of course, so there are some things you can teach your students, but be careful not to make too big a deal about strictly followed systems and rules with adverb placement. They're pretty slippery, and often how we use them has as much to do with what's customary as with what's correct.

16.9 Midsentence adverbs

A bunch of adverbs are called *midsentence adverbs* because, you guessed it, they're often found in the middle of a sentence.

- **midsentence adverbs**

almost always	almost never	already	always	ever
finally	frequently	generally	hardly ever	just
never	not ever	occasionally	often	probably
rarely	seldom	sometimes	usually	

But of course, it's not as simple as that. Although they're comfortable in the middle of a sentence, being adverbs, they like to move around. And where exactly they appear in the middle of a sentence depends on what verb it is they're modifying. Midsentence adverbs go before present simple and past simple verbs:

16.50   Larry <u>usually gets</u> to work on time.

16.51   She <u>probably went</u> to the library.

after present simple and past simple forms of *be*:

16.52   Carlos <u>was often</u> sick.

16.53   I'<u>m almost always</u> on time.

and between an auxiliary verb (aka helping verb) and a main verb:

16.54   You <u>should always wear</u> your seat belt.

16.55   I <u>have finally finished</u> my homework.

16.56   I <u>don't ever want</u> to talk to her again.

sample exercises 10: Rewrite the sentences so that they include the midsentence adverbs in parentheses.
　　　　My sister wakes up before 10:00 a.m. (hardly ever)
　　　　My sister hardly ever wakes up before 10:00 a.m.

1. We eat Mexican food. (almost always)
2. I have thought about quitting my job. (often)
3. English can be very difficult. (sometimes)
4. Maria has seen that movie. (never)
5. He is finished. (already)

sample exercises 11: Rewrite the questions so that they include the midsentence adverbs in parentheses.
　　　　Have you fallen off a turnip truck? (just)
　　　　Have you just fallen off a turnip truck?

1. Have you been to Hong Kong? (ever)
2. When does she eat dinner? (usually)
3. What did they do? (finally)
4. Why do you have to say that? (always)
5. Do you get headaches? (frequently)

16.10 Adverb phrases and adverb clauses

Now put on your thinking cap and get a double espresso. Beyond this point not much with *adverb* in its name is as easy as what we've already covered. We've talked primarily about single word adverbs before, but groups of words can do the job of adverbs too. These are called (jargon alert!) *adverb phrases* and *adverb clauses*. As we saw with adjectives and nouns, the idea that groups of words can perform the same function as single words is a fundamental concept of grammar that you should be familiar with.

16.11 Adverb phrases

First of all, adverb phrases (aka *adverbial phrases*) are words doing the job of an adverb which <u>do not</u> contain both a subject and a tensed verb. (i.e. a verb with time information—They might contain an infinitive like *to eat* or participle forms of a verb like *broken* and *driving*, but that's different. More on that later.) Here are some examples. The adverb phrases are underlined:

16.57   <u>When in Chicago</u>, I always visit my brother.

16.58   I always listen to the radio <u>while driving</u>.

16.59   <u>Before eating dinner</u>, I always wash my hands.

16.60   Mary has been unhappy <u>since losing her job</u>.

16.61   <u>After finishing your homework</u>, you can go out with your friends.

16.62   Mark finally saw the doctor <u>after having waited for two hours</u>.

16.63   <u>Not speaking Hungarian</u>, I had no idea what they were saying.

16.64   <u>Having lived in this city all my life</u>, I never get lost when I am driving.

The adverb phrases above are all reductions of adverb clauses. This will be explained later.

▶ **Prepositional phrase adverb phrases**

Prepositional phrases can function as adverb phrases. Did you know that? You do now. Just like ordinary run-of-the-mill adverbs, prepositional phrases can modify verbs:

16.65   Larry slipped <u>on a banana peel</u>.

16.66   <u>On Sunday</u>, she went to the beach.

and adjectives:

16.67   She was amazed <u>at my stupidity</u>.

and even adverbs:

16.68   I go to work early <u>in the morning</u>.

How much of this grammar are you going to explain to your students? Only as much as is helpful, and that probably won't be much. If you have some really bright, advanced students, maybe, but generally there's no need. How to use prepositional phrases is usually something students figure out pretty easily without being confused by deep grammar concepts like this. I wouldn't recommend any exercises for this.

▶ **Infinitive phrase adverb phrases**

As you know, *infinitive* means a verb with a *to* in front of it. Infinitive phases often function as adverbs of purpose—they answer the question *why*:

16.69   She's going to the store <u>to buy some milk</u>.

16.70   I called Larry <u>to ask him a question</u>.

A very common error is saying *for* or *for to* instead of *to*:

16.71   She's going to the store <u>for buy some milk</u>.

16.72   I called Larry <u>for to ask him a question</u>.

Be on the alert for this.

See also the discussion of *(in order) to* in Section 17.27.

sample exercises 12: Answer the questions with an infinitive phrase and the verb in parentheses.
   Alan needed milk. He went to the store.
   A: Why did Alan go to the store? (get)
   B: *He went to the store to get milk.*

   1.   Maria had a question for Sarah. Maria called Sarah.
        A: Why did Maria call Sarah? (ask)
        B:

2. Larry needs a new car. He is saving money.
   A: Why is Larry saving money? (buy)
   B:
3. Carlos is on an airplane now. He is going to Mexico. He will visit his mother
   A: Why is Carlos flying to Mexico? (see)
   B:
4. Rosa needs new shoes. She'll go to the shoe store tomorrow.
   A: Why will Rosa go to the shoe store tomorrow? (get)
   B:
5. Michael doesn't understand why he got an F on his essay. He is talking to his teacher.
   A: Why is Michael talking to his teacher? (ask)
   B:

16.12 Adverb clauses

Adverb clauses (aka *adverbial clauses*) are entire sentences—complete with (unlike adverb phrases) a subject and a tensed verb—which function as adverbs. The idea that an adverb clause could either be an independent clause or (depending on how you see it) could have started out life as an independent clause—meaning a simple sentence minding its own business before being stuck to another independent clause and turning into an adverb clause—is something you need to understand. Here are some examples. The adverb clauses are underlined:

16.73   My husband made dinner <u>while I watched TV</u>.

16.74   <u>As soon as the hiker saw the bear</u>, he climbed a tree.

16.75   My car is hard to start <u>every time it gets really cold outside</u>.

16.76   Larry didn't go to work <u>because he was sick</u>.

16.77   <u>Since you don't like my cooking</u>, you can do all the cooking from now on!

16.78   Sarah told Michael that she believes him <u>even though she knows he is lying</u>.

16.79   <u>Unless you apologize</u>, I'm never going to speak to you again.

16.80   <u>If we win this game</u>, we'll go to the semi-finals.

Notice that, lurking within each adverb clause, there is a sentence that would make sense if it were alone. For example,

16.81   As soon as the hiker saw the bear, he climbed a tree.

is really made up of two independent clauses:

16.82   The hiker saw the bear.

and

16.83   He climbed a tree.

When we turn an independent clause into an adverb phrase, it is no longer independent. That's a way of saying it wouldn't make sense alone. Now it isn't an independent clause but a (jargon alert!) *dependent clause*. For that reason,

16.84   The hiker saw the bear.
makes sense alone, but

16.85   As soon as the hiker saw the bear.

does not make sense alone.

All the underlined adverb clauses in examples 16.66-16.73 above are dependent clauses.

16.13 Conjunctions

As you may have noticed, words like *while, as soon as, every time, because, since, even though, unless* and *if* are used to create adverb clauses. These examples are just a few of a huge collection words we call (jargon alert!) *conjunctions*.

And there are <u>a lot</u> of conjunctions. They fall into various categories and subcategories, which we will soon discuss, but before that, here are some caveats: First of all, I remind you yet again that you are teaching your students to use English grammar, not teach it. They do not need to completely master all this grammar and terminology. Sure, it would be great if they did, but few can. Treat this as more of a vocabulary lesson than a grammar lesson. Some of the various conjunctions we'll discuss will be familiar to your students; many will not. We're going to be talking about sentence construction patterns and conjunctions. Your goal is to familiarize your students with those sentence construction patterns and teach them a lot of new conjunctions to plug into those sentences. Don't get too hung up on grammar. Remember, even if your students remain a bit shaky on putting sentences together, learning new and useful conjunctions will go a long way toward furthering their ability to understand and to be understood. Who will have an easier time communicating in English—a student with perfect grammar and a small vocabulary or a student who may make mistakes in grammar but has a wide-ranging knowledge of vocabulary? You know the answer.

Even though I recommend you emphasize vocabulary over grammar, don't ignore the grammar. Actually, it isn't that difficult anyway. And <u>you</u> should definitely know the grammar. As you have no doubt already realized by now, there is a lot more to adverbs than *slowly* and *quickly*. This whole subject is one of the hardest things you'll encounter on your quest to learn, and learn to teach, English grammar and one the easiest things to get totally confused by. (I'm totally confused right now.) But it's worth the effort.

And finally, once we get into conjunctions, you'll see that they really are an amazingly disparate bunch of words. Many of them are quite idiomatic—they're words or phrases that, despite often being superficially familiar to students, will be used in ways that are entirely new to them. To add to the confusion, many of the conjunctions we discuss actually have various other jobs in the English language—they are not just one part of speech but several.

16.14 Types of conjunctions

Conjunctions take their name from *conjoin*—join together—and you'll see that in one way or another, that's just what they all do. We'll look at the four types of conjunctions: *coordinating conjunctions, conjunctive adverbs, subordinating conjunctions* and *correlative conjunctions*. Here's a cool table to help you make sense of it all.

Figure 16.14

---

conjunctions

- connect words, phrases and clauses

coordinating conjunctions

- connect equal parts of a sentence: word to word, phrase to phrase, independent clause to independent clause

and	*or*
but	*so*
for	*yet*
nor	

conjunctive adverbs

- connect independent clauses (but some also function as ordinary adverbs)
- may also function as other parts of speech

(examples)

also	*if*
as a result	*nevertheless*
besides	*otherwise*
for example	*still*
finally	*then*
however	*therefore*

subordinating conjunctions

- connect two unequal parts of a sentence: independent clause to dependent clauses (aka main clause and subordinate clause)
- are used for adverb clauses, noun clauses and adjective clauses (aka relative clauses)
- may also function as other parts of speech

(examples)

after	*since*
although	*unless*
as long as	*until*
because	*where*
before	*while*

correlative conjunctions

- are pairs of conjunctions which require parallel (equal) structure after each one

either...or	*both...and*
not only...but (also)	*whether...or*
neither...nor	*just as...so*

This is the real thing—what separates the pros from the amateurs. The day you can explain to a befuddled student (or fellow teacher) the difference between a conjunctive adverb and a subordinating conjunction will be the day you'll know that you can call yourself a grammar teacher.

16.15 Coordinating conjunctions

These will be relatively easy, so don't squander a lot of time on it. Everything that comes after is a lot more difficult, so make sure you budget sufficient time for it.

The seven coordination conjunctions (aka *coordinators*) are *and, but, or, nor, for, so* and *yet*. These unassuming little guys connect independent clauses and do so quite efficiently and without drama, unlike some other high-maintenance conjunctions we'll meet later. Obviously, *and, but, or* and *so* are the ones you will focus on. *Nor* is less common, but you should talk about it a little. *Yet* and (especially) *for* are not often used nowadays as coordinating conjunctions, so spend very little on them.

When coordination conjunctions connect two independent clauses, they tell you something about how the clauses are related to each other.

To illustrate that and to liven up what might seem to your students at first to be a dull lesson, ask your students to explain the relationship between the clauses in the sentences below. To put it more simply, ask them what information the coordinating conjunction tells them. You'll have to help them with the last two:

16.86   I went to the store, <u>and</u> I bought some eggs and milk.

16.87   Alan looked for his lost keys, <u>but</u> he didn't find them.

16.88   I might go to London, <u>or</u> I might go to Paris.

16.89   Carlos has not read this book, <u>nor</u> does he want to.

16.90   She was lost, <u>so</u> she looked at a map.

16.91   I couldn't unlock the door, <u>for</u> I had forgotten my key.

16.92   Ali studied hard for the test, <u>yet</u> his score was very low.

The meanings of *and, but, or* and *so* are actually pretty easy, and besides, by the time you get to focusing on coordination conjunctions, your students will already know *and, but,* and *or,* though of course you never assume anything and cover them as if it were all brand new, but it'll go fast. *So* and *nor* will be less familiar to your students, so focus on them. At this point, I often emphasize the cause and effect meaning of *so* by rewriting sentences with *so* with *because*:

16.93   I was sick, so I went to the doctor.

has the same meaning as

16.94a   Because I was sick, I went to the doctor.

and

       b   I went to the doctor because I was sick.

This is a preview of the subordinating conjunctions that will soon follow, a can of grammatical worms up you don't want to just yet, but it's almost certain that your students already know *because* at this point.

Nor connects two negative independent clauses. It's not terribly common, so don't get too hung up on it:

16.95a   Carlos has not read this book. He does not want to.
       b   → Carlos has not read this book, <u>nor</u> does he want to.

When coordinating conjunctions connect independent clauses, a comma must be used after the first clause. I put something like this on the board to illustrate this:

   <u>Independent clause</u>, coordinating conjunction <u>independent clause</u>.

Make the comma as huge and as colorful as possible, then write an example or two underneath:

   <u>Independent clause</u>, coordinating conjunction <u>independent clause</u>.
           ↓   ↓   ↓
   I went to the store,   and   I bought some eggs.
   Noura was hungry,   but   she didn't eat.

Often, however, when the subject of both clauses is the same, it is not necessary to repeat the subject. When the subject is not repeated, no comma is necessary:

16.96a   <u>Larry</u> called Mary, and <u>he</u> invited her to his party.

    b   → <u>Larry</u> called Mary and invited her to his party.

When a modal verb and a main verb are repeated in the second clause, the modal verb is sometimes ellipted in addition to the subject. It isn't said because it is understood by both the speaker/writer and the listener/reader:

16.97a   <u>Larry</u> will call Mary, and <u>he will</u> invite her to his party.

    b   → <u>Larry</u> will call Mary and <u>will</u> invite her to his party.

    c   → <u>Larry</u> will call Mary and invite her to his party.

Remind your students that independent clauses have both a subject and a tensed verb, and that each could make sense alone, without being stuck to the other.

The rule about a comma having to be used after the first independent clause is often broken. The main reason, of course, is that most people don't know or don't care, but it is stylistically allowable in shorter, well-balanced sentences when a stronger, bolder effect is desired. Hemingwayesque, I suppose.

sample exercises 13: Use *and, but, or, nor* or *so* to complete the sentences.

    I don't like cold weather, _____*so*_____ I moved from Toronto to Miami.

1.   We can eat dinner at home, _____ we can go to a restaurant.
2.   I don't want to talk to him, _____ do I want to see him.
3.   Maria did her math homework before she left school, _____ she doesn't need to do it after dinner.
4.   He's been studying English for many years, _____ he can hardly speak English at all.
5.   Rosa graduated from college in June, _____ she got a good job right away.

sample exercises 14: If it is possible, rewrite the sentence as in the examples. Be careful about punctuation.

    I went to the store, but I didn't buy anything.
    I went to the store but didn't buy anything.

    Alan walked to the beach, but his sister rode her bicycle there.
    not possible

1.   John asked me a question, but I didn't know the answer.
2.   Sophia opened her book, and she began to read.
3.   We can have spaghetti for dinner, or we can go to a restaurant.
4.   Mark promised to help me fix my car, but he forgot all about it.
5.   My brother doesn't have a car, but he'll buy one soon.

16.16 Connecting sentences with *and* and *but*

Here are some examples that show you some typical sentence patterns:

16.98   Mary <u>is</u> late, <u>and</u> John <u>is too</u>.

16.99   Mary <u>is</u> late, <u>and so is</u> John.

16.100   Sam <u>won't</u> come to the party, <u>but</u> I <u>will</u>.

16.101   Ali <u>doesn't</u> drink coffee, <u>and</u> Noura <u>doesn't either</u>.

16.102   Ali <u>doesn't</u> drink coffee, <u>and neither does</u> Noura.

16.103   Carlos went to the beach, <u>but</u> Rosa <u>didn't</u>.

Notice that when both clauses are affirmative or both are negative, two patterns are possible. The way to teach this is to begin with sentences containing forms of *be* and sentences with modals. They're the easiest to start with because with both, an element in the first clause is being repeated. You can see that in 16.91, 16.92 and 16.93 above.

Only after you've done this should you give your students examples with main verbs (and no modal) because in this case, the main verb is not repeated. Instead, a form of *do* is used. You can see that in 16.96. *Have* is kind of a special case. Many students, you will find, have learned a rather old-fashioned way of using *have*. Nothing wrong with it, but I explain the modern way and encourage them to use it instead.

Here is kind of a thorough list of examples from *Rocket English Grammar* (shameless plug).

Figure 16.16

combining sentences with *and* and *but*				
sentences with *be*	**−** Paul ***isn't*** hungry,	*but*	**+** Lucy ***is***.	
	+ Paul ***is*** hungry,	*but*	**−** Lucy ***isn't***.	
	+ Paul ***is*** hungry,	*and*	**+** Lucy ***is*** too.	
	Paul ***is*** hungry,	*and*	so ***is*** Lucy.	
	− Paul ***isn't*** hungry,	*and*	**−** Lucy ***isn't*** either.	
	Paul ***isn't*** hungry,	*and*	neither ***is*** Lucy.	
sentences with modal verbs	**−** Paul ***can't*** swim,	*but*	**+** Lucy ***can***.	
	+ Paul ***can*** swim,	*but*	**+** Lucy ***can't***.	
	+ Paul ***can*** swim,	*and*	**+** Lucy ***can*** too.	
	Paul ***can*** swim,	*and*	so ***can*** Lucy.	
	− Paul ***can't*** swim,	*and*	**−** Lucy ***can't*** either.	
	Paul ***can't*** swim,	*and*	neither ***can*** Lucy.	
sentences with main verbs only and no modal verb	**−** Paul ***doesn't*** speak English,	*but*	**+** Lucy ***does***.	
	+ Paul speaks English,	*but*	**−** Lucy ***doesn't***.	
	+ Paul speaks English,	*and*	**+** Lucy ***does*** too.	
	Paul speaks English,	*and*	so ***does*** Lucy.	
	− Paul ***doesn't*** speak English,	*and*	**−** Lucy ***doesn't*** either.	
	Paul ***doesn't*** speak English,	*and*	neither ***does*** Lucy.	
sentences with the main verb *have* (The underlined forms are old-fashioned and less commom.)	**−** Paul ***doesn't*** have/***hasn't*** a car,	*but*	**+** Lucy ***does***/***has***.	
	+ Paul ***has*** a car,	*but*	**−** Lucy ***doesn't***/***hasn't***.	
	+ Paul ***has*** a car,	*and*	**+** Lucy ***does***/***has*** too.	
	Paul ***has*** a car,	*and*	so ***does***/***has*** Lucy.	
	− Paul ***doesn't*** have/***hasn't*** a car,	*and*	**−** Lucy ***doesn't***/***hasn't*** either.	
	Paul ***doesn't*** have/***hasn't*** a car,	*and*	neither ***does***/***has*** Lucy.	
sentences with present perfect verbs	**−** Paul ***hasn't*** eaten,	*but*	**+** Lucy ***has***.	
	+ Paul ***has*** eaten,	*but*	**−** Lucy ***hasn't***.	
	+ Paul ***has*** eaten,	*and*	**+** Lucy ***has*** too.	
	Paul ***has*** eaten,	*and*	so ***has*** Lucy.	
	− Paul ***hasn't*** eaten,	*and*	**−** Lucy ***hasn't*** either.	
	Paul ***hasn't*** eaten,	*and*	neither ***has*** Lucy.	

Look at the examples below and think about words which could be repeated in the second clause but which are ellipted. That's what makes this a challenge for students:

16.104a   Mary is late, and John is too.
     b   Mary is late, and so is John.

16.105   Sam won't come to the party, but I will.

16.106a   Ali doesn't drink coffee, and Noura doesn't either.
     b   Ali doesn't drink coffee, and neither does Noura.

16.107a   Larry has eaten, and Alan has too.
     b   Larry has eaten, and so has Alan.

16.108   Carlos went to the beach, but Rosa didn't.

I'll show you the same sentences with the ellipted words in brackets to show you what I mean:

16.109a   Mary is late, and John is [late] too.
     b   Mary is late, and so is John [late].

16.110   Sam won't come to the party, but I will [come to the party].

16.111a   Ali doesn't drink coffee, and Noura doesn't [drink coffee] either.
     b   Ali doesn't drink coffee, and neither does Noura [drink coffee].

16.112a   Larry has eaten, and Alan has [eaten] too.
     b   Larry has eaten, and so has Alan [eaten].

16.113   Carlos went to the beach, but Rosa didn't [go to the beach].

The meaning of *so* will be the hardest part of this. *So* has *so* many meanings that students can really get *so* confused by it. The one we're discussing here means something like *likewise* or *in the same way*. There are maddening times when, as a native speaker, you know exactly what something means, but it's *so* hard to say it another way *so* you can teach the meaning to your students. *So* do your best, and when that fails, have your students find this meaning of *so* in their bilingual dictionaries—with your help, if possible.

sample exercises 15: Complete the sentences. If the verb in the sentence is *have,* use the modern way. If there are two possible answers, write both answers.

He won't help her, but (I) _____*I will*_____.

Mary has a book, and (Tom) ____*Tom does too/so does Tom*____.

1.   Carlos doesn't know the answer, but (Alan) _____.
2.   Michael should study harder, and (you) _____.
3.   I'm not happy, and (Mark) _____.
4.   Sam didn't have any money, and (Sarah) _____.
5.   Mary has gone to bed, and (her brother) _____.
6.   Bill has a cat, but (his brother) _____.

sample exercises 16: Complete the conversations with answers which agree with the question. If the verb in the sentence is *have,* use the modern way. Write both possible answers.

A: John didn't do his homework. Did you?
B1:   – *I didn't either.*
B2:   – *Neither did I.*

A: Francesca can type. What about Michael?
B1:   + *He can too.*
B2:   + *So can he.*

1.   A: Lucy was in the lab. Was Maria?
     B1:   +
     B2:   +

2. A: Noura would like to leave work early. How about you?
    B1: +
    B2: +
3. A: Mark doesn't work on Saturday. Does his wife?
    B1: −
    B2: −
4. A: Alan doesn't have a soccer ball. What about his friends?
    B1: −
    B2: −
5. A: I've already been to that restaurant. How about you?
    B1: +
    B2: +
6. A: The children aren't going to the carnival. What about Larry?
    B1: −
    B2: −

16.17 Conjunctive adverbs

Conjunctive adverbs show relationships between independent clauses. An amazingly huge and varied bunch of words are conjunctive adverbs—all sorts of things that, if someone asked you what kind of a word it is—adjective, adverb or whatever, you'd really be on the spot. Just look at this list to see what I mean. And by no means is this THE complete list of conjunctive adverbs. There are more.

- **conjunctive adverbs**

accordingly	after all	afterward(s)	again	also
anyhow	as a result	at last	at once	at the same time
beforehand	besides	certainly	consequently	conversely
earlier	even so	eventually	finally	first, second, etc.
for	for example	for instance	further	furthermore
hence	however	immediately	in addition	in any case
in fact	in other words	in short	in the meantime	incidentally
indeed	later	likewise	meanwhile	moreover
namely	nevertheless	next	nonetheless	now
on the contrary	on the other hand	otherwise	perhaps	previously
similarly	so	still	subsequently	that is
then	therefore	thus	undoubtedly	

Even worse, many conjunctive adverbs play many roles. They're conjunctions sometimes and ordinary adverbs another; they might also be adjectives, prepositions, nouns, pronouns or interjections.

Many have tried to group conjunctive adverbs into categories, and as far as I can tell, no two classification systems agree. In just a half an hour on the internet, I found several, and I'm sure I could easily find more. Do conjunctive adverbs fall neatly into these categories?

example or illustration
similarity
contrast/concession
additional/order of importance
time sequence
emphasis
cause/effect
summary conclusion

Or maybe these categories?

illustrative
additive
cause/effect
adversative
temporal (having to do with time)

Or how about these categories?

> addition
> contrast
> time
> result
> another fact
> show a specific case
> comparison
> strengthen a point
> return to your point after conceding
> recognize a point off your main point

Or these?

> results
> general contrasts
> direct contrasts
> additional information
> stronger information
> unexpected results

Or these?

> result
> concession
> apposition (whatever that means)
> addition
> time
> contrast
> summary
> reinforcement

So which is correct? Good question. I'd say all of them are correct. Since there is no generally accepted system for classifying conjunctive adverbs, that's good news for you—no one can expect you to memorize one. But it's not all baloney. Looking at these attempts at classification will give you a pretty good idea of the kind of work conjunctive adverbs do.

Don't confuse your students with any this. For literally the umpteenth time, I remind you that you are teaching your students to use English grammar, not teach it. A student who understands the meaning of, for example, *meanwhile* or *however* or *therefore* (with the aid of his or her bilingual dictionary, if need be!) will intuitively know that they're used to show time sequence or contrast/concession or cause/effect without having to know and understand the terminology.

People who try to classify conjunctive adverbs are pathetic losers, and that explains why I have tried to do it myself. Here is a selection of conjunctive adverbs that I think are possibly unfamiliar to many students but are useful and common and a good place to start. I've tried to group them using language that would be understood easily by students to give them a general idea of what it's all about. Beyond that, focus on meaning.

Conjunctive adverbs can be used…

▶ **To talk about the reason for something—that something is the reason, or cause, of something else**

▷ *as a result* (= *because of that*)

16.114   I hurt my ankle. <u>As a result</u>, I cannot play basketball for two months.

▷ *consequently* (= *because of that*)
Consequently is usually used to talk about negative results:

16.115   Jack cheated on the test. <u>Consequently</u>, he was expelled from college.

▷ *therefore* (= *because of that*)

16.116   I forgot to pay my telephone bill. <u>Therefore</u>, my telephone was disconnected.

▷ *thus* (= *in this way, because of that, for example*)
Thus is very formal and more common in writing than in speaking:

16.117   The cook put poison in the spaghetti sauce. <u>Thus</u>, he lost her job and went to jail.

16.118   I was locked out of my house, but one of the windows was unlocked. <u>Thus</u>, I was able to get in.

▶ **To talk about the time relationship between two things—something happened before, at the same time or after something else**

▷ *in the meantime* (= *at the same time*)

16.119   At the mall I told my wife, "You go with the kids to buy new shoes. <u>In the meantime</u>, I'll wait here in the book store."

▷ *meanwhile* (= *at the same time*)

16.120   My wife will clean the kitchen. <u>Meanwhile</u>, I will do the laundry.

▷ *subsequently* (= *later*)

16.121   At first, the police believed that the man had been killed in the fire. <u>Subsequently</u>, they learned that he had been murdered.

▶ **To talk about things that happen in a different place**

▷ *elsewhere* (= *in another place/= in other places*)

16.122   This part of the city is very safe. <u>Elsewhere</u>, that's not true.

▶ **To help explain how we feel about something**

▷ *after all* (= *you need to understand/= the truth is*)

16.123   I was very upset when my dog died. <u>After all</u>, he was my only friend.

▶ **To help explain something further**

▷ *in other words*
In other words introduces simpler language that helps to clarify and explain what was said before:

16.124   Jack has difficulty telling the truth. <u>In other words</u>, he's a liar.

▶ **To give additional information that supports (makes stronger) what was just said**

▷ *besides* (= *also*)

16.125   I don't want to go to that restaurant. Their food is terrible and <u>besides</u>, I'm not hungry.

▷ *furthermore* (= *also*)

16.126   We don't have time to take a vacation. <u>Furthermore</u>, we need to save money.

▷ *in addition* (= *also*)

16.127   John works 60 hours a week at his job. <u>In addition</u>, he works at a second job on the weekend.

▷ *moreover* (= *also*)

16.128   That hotel is too expensive. <u>Moreover</u>, it's too far away from everything that we want to see.

▶ **To give additional information that does not support (makes weaker) something that was just said**

▷ *on the contrary* (= *the opposite is true*)

16.129   I wasn't upset when he didn't like my plan. <u>On the contrary</u>, I was glad to get his advice about how to improve it.

▶ **To give additional information that is opposite or different from what people expect**

▷ *however* (= *even though that is true*)

16.130   I eat only salads, and I run five kilometers every day. <u>However</u>, I cannot lose weight.

▷ *nevertheless* (= *even though that is true*)

16.131   Michael is not a good teacher. <u>Nevertheless</u>, he is very popular with his students.

▷ *nonetheless* (= *even though that is true*)
Nevertheless is more common than *nonetheless*:

16.132   The city hired 1,000 new police officers to fight crime last year. <u>Nonetheless</u>, crime is worse than before.

▷ *on the other hand* (= *but it is true that*)

16.133   I can't afford to buy a new computer. <u>On the other hand</u>, I really would like to have a new one.

▶ **To predict a different result**

▷ *otherwise* (= *if this is not done/= if this does not happen*)

16.134   You need to buy your ticket before Friday. <u>Otherwise</u>, it will be too late.

Since asking students in an exercise to choose the correct conjunctive adverb from a huge or even medium-sized list is unreasonable, I think it's better to ask them to try to figure out the meanings of conjunctive adverbs three at a time, as in the exercise below:

sample exercises 17:   Underline the best conjunctive adverb to finish the sentences.
  I don't want to go to the party. I'm tired. (Consequently/<u>Besides</u>/Nonetheless), Jack is going to be there, and I don't want to see him.

1.   It's 8:40 already? I need to be at work at 9:00. I have to leave now. (Meanwhile/Furthermore/Otherwise), I'll be late.
2.   I wasn't surprised when my son changed jobs. (Therefore/After all/Furthermore), the salary at his new job will be much higher than the salary at his old job.
3.   Smoking is bad for your health. (Furthermore/However/Otherwise), cigarettes are expensive.
4.   My boss is on vacation. (After all/In the meantime/On the other hand), I'm doing his job.
5.   The airplane had mechanical problems. (Therefore/Nevertheless/Furthermore), it was able to land safely.

16.18   punctuation and conjunctive adverbs
Now that you've thoroughly covered the meanings of these and other selected conjunctive adverbs that you feel are important, it's time for a boring but necessary discussion of punctuation.

Remember, we're always dealing with two independent clauses. But where the conjunctive adverb gets plugged into the second independent clause and how it's punctuated can vary.

▶ **Beginning of clause**
There are two ways:

▷ **With a semi-colon**

16.135   My cell phone battery was dead; therefore, I couldn't call you.

▷ **With a period**

16.136   My cell phone battery was dead. Therefore, I couldn't call you.

The second way, with a period, is more common. Remind your students that if they do use a semi-colon, the second clause does not begin with a capital letter.

▶ **Middle of a clause**
The conjunctive adverb can be inserted within the second clause between commas but where depends on the verb:

▷ **After *be***

16.137   Switzerland is a wonderful place to live. It is, <u>however</u>, very expensive.

▷ **Before main verbs**

16.138   Alan washed the outside of the car. Carlos, <u>meanwhile</u>, cleaned the inside.

▷ **After an auxiliary verb**

16.139   I don't want to live in Los Angeles. I would, <u>on the other hand</u>, like to live in San Francisco.

▶ **End of a sentence**

Conjunctive adverbs can follow independent clauses in which case a comma precedes the conjunctive adverb:

16.140   The man was very badly injured. The doctors tried to save him, <u>nevertheless</u>.

All of this seems rather straightforward, doesn't it? No, it isn't. It's a murky business. These punctuation patterns should all be presented with a big fat *usually*, a huge *sometimes* and a definite *maybe*. Conjunctive adverbs are slippery devils. Often what is, strictly speaking, correct sounds unnatural. There are patterns to how native speakers use their language—any language—that have much more to do with custom and convention than correctness.

Also, you can very easily see that a lot of the conjunctive adverbs in the list above wouldn't make any sense if used with these sentence and punctuation patterns. One factor to consider when sticking a conjunctive adverb into the middle of a sentence is just how much of an interruption it causes. In the case of *first, second,* etc., *next, then, finally, now, immediately, at once* and many others, not much, so commas are not used. Actually no comma is ever used with *then* even when it begins a sentence. My advice, therefore, is to definitely not get too hung up on punctuation, and do not, by any means, allow your students to think they can easily plug any of the conjunctive adverbs into any of the patterns we've discussed. Pick out several useful conjunctive adverbs that your students may not know or be comfortable using, and in case I haven't mentioned it before, focus on meaning!

16.19 Subordinating conjunctions and adverb clauses

You thought we were finished with conjunctions? Heh, heh, heh. Oh no, this long strange trip is far from over. So far we've talked about various ways to connect independent clauses, but now we're going to talk about how to stick two independent clauses together so that—wake up!, this is important—one of them is no longer independent. It is a dependent clause. (And naturally, there are plenty of akas involved. Independent clauses are also known as *main clauses,* and *dependent clauses* are also known as *subordinate clauses.*)

A few things will not change: we'll slog through a morass of conjunctions, we'll discuss various pathetic attempts to classify them, and I will remind you repeatedly not to overwhelm your students with theory and jargon but to focus on meaning. Remember that, while it may seem that I'm overwhelming *you* with theory and jargon, it's for your benefit so that you know what's going on, so that you can teach this in a simplified and accessible way *without* a lot of theory and jargon.

Here's what it's all about: As you know, independent clauses are called independent clauses because they can make sense alone without needing to be attached to anything in order to make sense. When we stuck two independent clauses together with a conjunctive adverb, we still had two independent clauses. Now, however, rather than using conjunctive adverbs to stick independent clauses together, we're going to be using words called (jargon alert!) *subordinating conjunctions* (aka *subordinate conjunctions*). When we do this, the clause with the subordinating conjunction no longer makes sense alone. It depends on the independent clause to make sense. It is a type of dependent clause, or more specifically, (jargon alert!) an *adverb clause* (remember that noun clauses and adjective clauses are also dependent clauses).

Figure 16.19

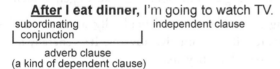

Let's take this sentence:

16.141   After I eat dinner, I'm going to watch TV.

If I say <u>only</u>

16.142   I'm going to watch TV.

it makes sense alone. But if I say <u>only</u>

16.143   After I eat dinner.

it doesn't make sense alone. It has to be attached to

16.144   I'm going to watch TV.

to make sense.

16.20 Adverb clauses and clause reversal

Make sure your students understand that the clauses can be reversed and that both patterns are equally common and have exactly the same meaning. The only difference is that one pattern requires a comma. Put something like this on the board and point out the comma:

My husband made dinner.	I watched TV.
independent clause	independent clause

My husband made dinner	while I watched TV.
independent clause	dependent clause

While I watched TV,	my husband made dinner.
dependent clause	independent clause

But before you do anything with your students, you want to be very sure that they understand how two clauses, one dependent and one independent, can be stuck together to make a sentence and to recognize which is which. They really need to get used to this sentence structure pattern because it is very common. Emphasize that one of the clauses would make sense alone and one would not.

Also, don't ever let students get the idea that the tense of one clause in any way requires a certain tense in another. Logic alone determines that. Keep that in mind when we get to conditional sentences.

sample exercises 18: Underline the adverb clauses and add commas where they are necessary.

<u>Before I go to bed</u>, I always take a bath.

I failed the test <u>even though I studied a lot</u>.

1. I took a shower before I jumped into the swimming pool.
2. Although I was very angry I didn't say anything.
3. You can go home when you are finished.
4. In case my ATM card doesn't work I always take cash when I travel.
5. I get angry every time I think about what Sam said about me.
6. The next time we go to that restaurant we should try the chicken curry.

16.21 What are subordinating conjunctions?

So what are subordinating conjunctions? Subordinating conjunctions are words and phrases used to attach dependent clauses to independent clauses which results in what's called a (jargon alert!) *complex sentence*. What's a complex sentence? A sentence with an independent clause and a dependent clause which may be an adverb clause, a noun clause or an adjective clause. (For more about sentence structure, complex sentences, compound sentences and all that, see Appendix E.)

Many will be familiar to your students already, but many useful ones that you and I use every day will not. Like conjunctive adverbs, many also function as other parts of speech. Getting the grammar down in terms of sentence structure will come pretty quickly. Learning the meanings of many new and useful subordinating conjunctions will take longer, so focus on that.

Subordinating conjunctions fall into different categories depending on their function. Thankfully, attempts at classifying subordinating conjunctions aren't quite as all-over-the-map as they are with conjunctive adverbs. It's generally agreed that there are five types, though what to name these groups is another matter. Here they are:

time (aka sequence)
cause (aka cause and effect, reason, causal, causality)
contrast (aka contrast/concession, concession and comparison, opposition)
place
condition

In case you're interested (and who wouldn't be?), sometimes contrast and concession are treated separately, and also manner is added to the list. Aren't conjunctions fun?

You definitely should be familiar with these function categories, but do not make a huge deal of them with your students. Discuss them? Yes. Insist that your students memorize them? No! Discussing these functions will help your students get a general understanding of what subordinating conjunctions are all about, but it's the subordinating conjunctions themselves that you want them to take away from this lesson, not how subordinating conjunction are classified. Your goal is that your students be able to use this language as accurately as possible, not teach it (in case I haven't mentioned that already).

I recommend you organize your subordinating conjunction lesson in the following way. You'll see that I've named them with language that should be easy for your students (so no *causal* or *concession*).

16.22 Adverb clauses about time

Several subordinating conjunctions are about time. Some will be familiar to your students, but many will not. One that likely won't be is *once,* so spend some time on that. Work on meaning by giving lots of examples and, if need be, unashamedly making use of bilingual dictionaries.

▶ *after*

16.145 <u>After</u> Larry saw the accident, he called the police.

16.146 The children should do their homework <u>after</u> they finish dinner.

▶ *as (= while)*

16.147 <u>As</u> Noura was sleeping, the burglar stole her jewelry.

16.148 I thought about what you said to me last night <u>as</u> I drove to work this morning.

▶ *as long as*

Avoid examples like *As long as you're going to the store for milk, get some orange juice too.* That's a different meaning of *as long as*—similar to *since* or *because*:

16.149 <u>As long as</u> I live, I will never forget this day.

16.150 You can stay here <u>as long as</u> you want to.

▶ *as soon as (= immediately after)*

16.151 <u>As soon as</u> the building started to shake, we ran outside.

16.152 I'll call you <u>as soon as</u> I arrive in New York.

▶ *before*

16.153 <u>Before</u> I ate breakfast, I took a shower.

16.154 Mary will finish her work <u>before</u> she goes home.

▶ *by the time (that) (= when)*

16.155 <u>By the time</u> that you graduate from college, you'll be 23 years old.

16.156 I hope dinner is ready <u>by the time</u> we get home.

▶ *every time (that)*

16.157 <u>Every time</u> that I hear that song, I remember my high school years.

16.158 My car is hard to start <u>every time</u> it gets really cold outside.

▶ *once (= when, after)*

16.159 <u>Once</u> you have completed Part A of your exam, begin Part B.

16.160 You can watch TV <u>once</u> you have finished your homework.

▶ *since (= from the time)*

16.161 <u>Since</u> I moved to Indiana, I have been very bored.

16.162 Alan has grown a lot <u>since</u> you were here before.

▶ *the first time (that)/the next time (that)/the last time (that),* etc.

16.163 <u>The first time</u> that I came to this city, I hated it.

16.164 I'll call you <u>the next time</u> I need some advice.

▶ *until/till*

16.165 <u>Until</u> I have enough money to buy a house, I'll have to rent an apartment.

16.166   We'll play football <u>till</u> it gets too dark to play.

▸ *when* (**sometimes = *while***)

16.167   <u>When</u> the TV show is over, I want you to go to bed.

16.168   I'm very busy now. I'll do it <u>when</u> I have time.

16.169   I never talk on my cell phone <u>when</u> I am driving. (= I never talk on my mobile phone while I am driving.)

▸ *whenever* (= ***any time***)

16.170   <u>Whenever</u> I feel sad, I call my mother.

16.171   I always visit my brother <u>whenever</u> I am in Toronto.

▸ *while*

16.172   <u>While</u> you are washing your car, I'll work in the garden.

16.173   The teacher watched the students <u>while</u> they were taking the test.

Since we're focusing on meaning, an excellent exercise is one that requires an understanding of the meanings of subordinating conjunctions:

sample exercises 19: Only one of the subordinating conjunctions makes sense. Underline the correct subordinating conjunction.

(<u>As soon as</u>/before) I saw the fire, I called the fire department.

1. The meeting is going to be almost over (by the time/every time) we get there.
2. (Whenever/Once) you have gotten your bachelor's degree, you should think about getting a master's degree.
3. (As/The last time) I was sitting in class this morning, I thought about what to cook for the party.
4. (As long as/Once) he lives, he won't forget the day he saw a ghost in the cemetery.
5. In my country, you cannot drive (since/until) you are 16.
6. I'm going to make dinner (when/while) I get home.

But, grammarwise, there is something very important you need to discuss. In future time clauses like these:

16.174   I will eat dinner after I get home.

16.175   Before I go to work tomorrow, I will stop for gas.

many students will want to say

16.176   I will eat dinner after I <u>will</u> get home.

16.177   Before I <u>will</u> go to work tomorrow, I will stop for gas.

Don't let them! This is a very common mistake. Make sure your students understand that the dependent clause should be in the present simple tense.

Now some sentence structure practice.

sample exercises 20: Use the sentences and the subordinating conjunction in parentheses to make sentences with adverb clauses. Write both possible sentence patterns. Be careful about punctuation, and be sure to change pronouns when it is necessary.

Mary finishes her homework. She can't watch TV. (until)
Until Mary finishes her homework, she can't watch TV.
Mary can't watch TV until she finishes her homework.

1. She says that. It makes me angry. (every time)
2. You take the test. You should review. (before)
3. You live in my house. You will follow my rules. (as long as)
4. I got to work. I started to feel sick. (after)
5. You need my car. You can borrow it. (whenever)
6. We bought this printer. We have been having problems with it. (since)

16.23 Adverb clauses about reasons (aka cause and effect)

Some subordinating conjunctions are about the cause, or reason, for something. *Because* will almost certainly be familiar.

(But remember, don't assume anything—explain it!) What will not be familiar is the use of *as* (which is not very common) and *since* (which is somewhat common) to mean *because,* so make a big deal about those (especially *since*).

▶ *as (= because)*

16.178   As my car was out of gas, I had to walk to work.

16.179   I took my umbrella with me this morning as I had heard that it might rain today.

▶ *because*

16.180   Because Mary was late for class, she didn't have enough time for the quiz.

16.181   Larry didn't go to work because he was sick.

▶ *now that (= because it is now true that)*

16.182   Now that you have finished your work, you can go home.

16.183   I feel much better now that I have lost 10 kilograms.

▶ *since (= because)*

16.184   Since you don't like my cooking, you can do all the cooking from now on!

16.185   The teacher gave me a zero since I cheated on the test.

▶ *so (that)*

So (that) is worth spending some time on. Several typical examples are given below. It's function is similar to *(in order) to,* which is discussed in Section 17.25 (where you will find an exercise requiring that students convert a sentence with *(in order) to* to one with *so (that).*

That is optional, and since native speakers do not use *that* more often than they do, be sure your students are aware of this and make sure to model these and other examples with *that* omitted.

▷ *so (that)* **somebody** *can/could*

16.186   She's calling David so she can ask him a question.

16.187   Mark took classes in the summer so that he could graduate in three years.

▷ *so (that)* **somebody** *will/would*

16.188   So that I'll be first in line, I'm going to leave early.

16.189   My brother bought a lot of food for the party so he would be sure to have enough.

16.190   Bill left took the bus to the concert so that he wouldn't have to park two miles away.

▷ *so (that)* **somebody** *don't/doesn't*

16.191   I've hidden a key outside my house so that I don't ever get locked out.

16.192   So that she doesn't miss the bus, she should leave now.

An exercise asking students to choose between two of the subordinating conjunctions in this group wouldn't work here since this is such a small group and three of these subordinating conjunctions have essentially the same meaning, but a sentence structure exercise will also reinforce your students' understanding of their meaning.

sample exercises 21: Use the sentences and the subordinating conjunction to make sentences with adverb clauses. Write both possible sentence patterns. Be careful about punctuation, and be sure to change pronouns when it is necessary.

    Michael forgot his key. He couldn't open the door. (since)
    Since Michael forgot his key, he couldn't open the door.
    Michael couldn't open the door since he forgot his key.

1.   I wasn't careful. I cut my hand. (because)
2.   I would not be late. I left two hours early. (so that)
3.   It was raining. The picnic was canceled. (as)
4.   The party is over. We have to clean up the house. (now that)

Adverbs, Adverb Clauses, Adverb Phrases and More

5. You asked me. I will tell you the truth. (since)

6. She would not forget my telephone number. She wrote it down. (so)

16.24 Adverb clauses about opposites (aka contrast/concession)

▶ *although*

16.193   <u>Although</u> I need a new car, I don't have enough money to buy one.

16.194   Mark gave me a ride to the airport <u>although</u> he wanted to stay home and watch the game on TV.

▶ *despite the fact that*

16.195   <u>Despite the fact</u> that Mark works three jobs, he finds time to spend with his family.

16.196   His sister lived a full and active life <u>despite the fact that</u> she was mentally challenged.

▶ *even though*

16.197   <u>Even though</u> I explained everything again and again, he still did it wrong.

16.198   Sarah told Michael that she believes him <u>even though</u> she knows he is lying.

▶ *in spite of the fact that*

16.199   <u>In spite of the fact that</u> cats are better than dogs, many people prefer dogs.

16.200   The Chicago Cubs have many loyal fans <u>in spite of the fact that</u> they hardly ever win a game.

▶ *though*

16.201   <u>Though</u> he studied very hard for the test, he failed.

16.202   I have to go now <u>though</u> I really would like to stay longer.

▶ *whereas* (= *even though it is true that*)

16.203   <u>Whereas</u> English is spoken in most areas of the USA, there are places where Spanish is the dominant language.

16.204   My son is very shy <u>whereas</u> my daughter is very outgoing.

▶ *while* (= *even though it is true that*)

16.205   <u>While</u> you have made some good points, I still disagree with you.

16.206   I have to say no to your invitation <u>while</u> I do appreciate your asking me.

I prefer to discuss these subordinating conjunctions with the term *opposite*, rather than *contrast* or *concession*. *Opposite* is a word your students will certainly understand at this point. *Contrast*, probably not. *Concession*, definitely not. Don't confuse your students with any of this terminology business—just teach the words.

And it's confusing to lump these words together as I have done above because they really should be handled as three separate topics. My advice to you is to do exactly that—treat these as three separate topics—two kind of important, one not so important.

The two important topics are *although, even though* and *though* and *despite the fact that* and *in spite of the fact that*:

16.25 *although, even though* and *though*
Make sure your students know that *although, even though* and *though* have the same meaning. Also, that *though* is less common than *although* and *even though*. And make sure they don't confuse *though* and *thought*, a common mistake.

sample exercises 22: Use the subordinating conjunction in parentheses to write sentences with adverb clauses. Write both possible sentence patterns. Be careful about punctuation.

My wife is still angry with me. I apologized to her 10 times. (even though)
Even though I apologized to my wife 10 times, she is still angry with me.
My wife is still angry with me even though I apologized to her 10 times.

1. I had a map. I got lost. (although)
2. She makes a lot of money. She's always broke. (even though)
3. I hate basketball. I promised to go to a game with my husband. (although)

4. You have a headache. Do you still want to go to the movie? (even though)
5. The doctors did everything they could. She didn't get better. (though)

16.26 *despite the fact that* and *in spite of the fact that*

Despite and *in spite of* are most commonly used as prepositions, not subordinating conjunctions (*Despite my fractured skull, I kept on playing rugby*), but don't let the fact that you're focusing on subordinating conjunctions stop you from teaching *despite* and *in spite of* properly. Just teach them and don't confuse your students with any grammar mumbo jumbo. Adding *the fact that* to these really results in a grotesque mouthful and is not especially common, but when we get to adverb phrases, you'll see that these aren't so grotesque or uncommon after all. For that reason, it's worth getting through this *the fact that* business.

sample exercises 23: Use the subordinating conjunction in parentheses to write sentences with adverb clauses. Write both possible sentence patterns. Be careful about punctuation.

> It was my idea. David got all the credit for it. (despite the fact that)
> *Despite the fact that it was my idea, David got all the credit for it.*
> *David got all the credit for it despite the fact that it was my idea.*

1. I study like crazy. I'm failing math. (despite the fact that)
2. He eats only fruit and salads. He can't lose weight. (in spite of the fact that)
3. Mark was innocent. He was convicted and sent to prison. (despite the fact that)
4. Everyone said it was a great movie. I hated it. (in spite of the fact that)
5. I followed the instructions exactly. It didn't work. (despite the fact that)

16.27 *while* and *whereas*

This meaning of *while* will very likely be new to your students. *Whereas* is of little importance unless you are teaching students in or destined for law or academia. I don't think it's worth the time to do any exercises with these. Just discuss some examples and move on.

16.28 Adverb clauses about place

There are only two subordinating conjunctions in this group, *where* and *wherever*.

▶ *where*

16.207 <u>Where</u> you go, I will follow.

16.208 I don't know <u>where</u> he went.

▶ *wherever*

16.209 <u>Wherever</u> you hide, I will find you.

16.210 You can go <u>wherever</u> you want.

16.29 Adverbs of condition

First of all, make sure your students understand the meaning of *condition* that concerns us here. They may know the word condition in the sense of a car being in good condition or bad condition, but they may not know it in the sense of one thing not happening/being true unless another thing happens/is true, etc. That may seem easy to explain, but since *if* is one of the subordinating conjunctions we use to discuss condition, you really need to explain the concept without using *if*. Good luck with that.

Be careful you don't get sucked too deeply into a discussion of adverb clauses of condition because this is just a preview of *conditional sentences,* a big, fat, massive, huge, gigantic, megalithic topic which will be discussed at enormous length in Chapter 18. First, second and third conditionals and all that is not a can of grammatical worms you want to open now.

▶ **Tense of the clauses**

Point out to your students that when a sentence is about something that always happens or is always true, both clauses are in the present tense:

16.211 Unless it rains, the children play outside after school. (The speaker is talking about something that is always true.)

but when a sentence is about something that might happen only one time, the independent clause is in the future tense, but the adverb clause is in the present tense:

16.212 Unless it rains, the children will play outside after school. (The speaker is talking about today only.)

This is true of all the subordinating conjunctions in this group.

Adverbs, Adverb Clauses, Adverb Phrases and More

▶ **even if** (= *in the unlikely event that, regardless of the fact that*)

16.213   <u>Even if</u> you ask me a million times, the answer will still be no.

16.214   We're going to the beach tomorrow <u>even if</u> it is snowing.

16.215   I'll finish my dissertation this year <u>even if</u> it kills me.

▷ **Meaning of *even if***

Even if emphasizes how absolutely certain the main clause is—there's no maybe about it regardless of whatever condition is met:

16.216   I always start my class on time <u>even if</u> some students are late.

Sometimes it's an extreme and unlikely condition:

16.217   <u>Even if</u> hell freezes over…,

16.218   <u>Even if</u> the Chicago Cubs win the World Series…, etc.

▶ *if*

16.219   <u>If</u> we win this game, we'll go to the semi-finals.

16.220   My mother worries <u>if</u> I am late.

▷ **A common student mistake with *if***

Students often make the mistake of putting the main clause in future tense as well as the adverb clause:

16.221   If you <u>will</u> have a problem, I will help you.

instead of:

16.222   If you have a problem, I will help you.

▶ *whether or not*

16.223   <u>Whether or not</u> you come with me, I am going to the party.

16.224   The teacher is going to start the test at 10:00 <u>whether or not</u> all the students are there.

▶ *unless*

16.225   <u>Unless</u> you apologize, I'm never going to speak to you again.

16.226   We eat dinner at 6:30 <u>unless</u> our father comes home late.

sample exercises 24: Only one of the subordinating conjunctions makes sense. Underline the correct subordinating conjunction.
(<u>If</u>/Unless) you are sick, you should go to the doctor.

1. (Unless/Whether or not) you pay the bill soon, your telephone will be disconnected.
2. (Unless/Whether or not) we win the game, we will still have fun playing.
3. I will lend you some money (if/unless) you don't have enough.
4. The school bus driver won't wait for you (even if/unless) he sees you running for the bus.
5. (Unless/If) my wife says I have to stay home, I'll go fishing with you on the weekend.

16.30 Adverb clauses reduced to adverb phrases

Get another double espresso because we still have to discuss how some adverb clauses can be reduced to adverb phrases. This definitely qualifies as advanced grammar. Most ESL students will never get to this level, but some do. Consider whether your students are ready for this, and if they are, then you definitely should be too.

Do you remember how clauses differ from phrases? You should. Clauses have a subject and a tensed verb. Phrases have no subject or tensed verb. Your students should understand the term tense by now, but if not, explain that tense = *time information*. That's what I do sometimes with lower-level students. In fact, in some languages, the word for tense and the word for *time* are the same.

Why the big deal about tensed verbs? Because phrases do have verbs, just not tensed verbs. They can be infinitive phrases, and you know that infinitives have no tense, or in the case of reduced adverb clauses, which we're looking at now, participles, and participles have no tense. Recall that there are two types of participles: past participles like *finished, eaten* and *been* and present participles like *finishing, eating* and *being*.

You might need to remind your students that regular verb past participles are identical to the past simple form. I generally don't use the term *present participle* with students, but if you do get into it with your students, remind them that *all* present participles end with *-ing*. (These aren't gerunds, so don't tell your students that they are.)

Three types of adverb clauses can be reduced to adverb phrases: time, reason (cause and effect) and opposites (contrast and concession).

As with all reductions of adverb clauses, the subject of both clauses *must* be the same. If not, the sentence won't make any sense, and could even be comical. In some cases, the subject of the main clause will seem to be mysteriously absent. That's because it's an imperative clause in which case the implied subject is always understood to be *you*:

16.227a When you are in Rome, [you] do as the Romans do.
    b   → When in Rome, do as the Romans do.

We saw before with independent clauses and dependent clauses (in this case adverb clauses) that the independent clause (aka main clause) and adverb phrase can be reversed. For clarity, I've chosen not to show that in the following examples. Also, in many cases, it seems to me, fronting the adverb phrase sounds more natural to me, more common. My advice is to remind students that they can be switched but leave it at that.

It may occur to you or some of your students that by reducing the adverb clause to an adverb phrase and thereby replacing the tensed verb with an untensed participle, we're losing some information—the tense, obviously, which is a handy way of telling people when stuff happened. Yep, that's true, but in reality it's not usually a problem—the meaning is generally clear anyway—but if the result is ambiguous or confusing, don't do it!

Throughout your discussion of adverb clause reduction, remind students of the occasional need to rewrite the main clause so that a pronoun becomes a proper noun. The reason is that when the subject is omitted from the adverb clause, the main clause must identify the subject. I've built that into a number of the following examples:

16.31 Time adverb clauses reduced to adverb phrases

▶ **Adverb clauses about time with *be* reduced to adverb phrases**
The subject of both clauses must be the same. The subject and verb (a form of *be*) are omitted. Use *while* and *when*:

16.228a While I was studying, I listened to the radio.
    b   → While studying, I listened to the radio.

16.229a When Mary is sick, she acts like a big baby.
    b   → When sick, Mary acts like a big baby.

16.230a While you're in Rome, be sure to see the Trevi Fountain.
    b   → While in Rome, be sure to see the Trevi Fountain.

16.231a When Bill wasn't working, he sat around drinking coffee.
    b   → When not working, Bill sat around drinking coffee.

sample exercises 25: If it is possible, change the adverb clauses to adverb phrases.
    When I am taking a shower, I like to sing.
    When taking a shower, I like to sing.

    I cooked dinner while Mary was studying.
    not possible

1. While I was in college, I worked as a waiter.
2. When you are taking a bath, don't use a hair dryer.
3. You should never smoke when you are putting gas in your car.
4. Larry read the newspaper while I was working in the garden.
5. While I am doing my homework, I like to listen to music.

▶ **Adverb clauses about time with other verbs reduced to adverb phrases**
The subject of both clauses must be the same. The subject is omitted. The verb is in present participle (*-ing*) form. Use *while, when, before* and *after*:

16.232a While I drove to work, I saw an accident.
    b   → While driving to work, I saw an accident.

16.233a When we lived there, we went to the beach every weekend.
b → When living there, we went to the beach every weekend.

16.234a Before Tom left, he told me what to do.
b → Before leaving, Tom told me what to do.

16.235a After Sarah got tired, she stopped playing tennis.
b → After getting tired, Sarah stopped playing tennis.

sample exercises 26: If it is possible, change the adverb clauses to adverb phrases.

Since Maria got sick, she hasn't been able to work.
Since getting sick, Maria hasn't been able to work.

Sofia did her homework while her brother was swimming.
not possible

1. You should always think twice before you send an angry email.
2. When you drive, don't forget to wear your seat belt.
3. My brother has slept on the sofa since his wife had a baby.
4. I lived in New Zealand before I moved to Australia.
5. Since Maria got married, she has gained 20 kilograms.

▶ **Past perfect or present perfect adverb clauses about time with *after* reduced to adverb phrases**
The subject of both clauses must be the same. The subject is omitted. The verb is in present participle (*-ing*) form or the auxiliary verb *have* is in present participle form with main verb in past participle form. Is that clear?

16.236a After Sofia had eaten, she took a nap.
b → After eating, Sofia took a nap.
c → After having eaten, Sofia took a nap.

16.237a After I've finished my homework, I'll call you.
b → After finishing my homework, I'll call you.
c → After having finished my homework, I'll call you.

The two versions shown of past perfect and present perfect adverb phrases are identical in meaning. I absolutely would not insist that my students learn the *having* + past participle version, but have your students practice with both versions just for fun.

sample exercises 27: If it is possible, change the adverb clauses to adverb phrases. Write both possible forms.

You can leave after you have done your work.
You can leave after doing your work.
You can leave after having done your work.

After my children had gone to school, I went to the mall.
not possible

1. After John had been sick for several weeks, he died.
2. We'll have a party after I've been promoted to assistant manager.
3. After Alan had eaten seven hot dogs, he got sick.
4. Sarah will graduate after she's taken her exams.
5. I finally went home after I'd waited for Maria for one hour.

16.32 Reason (cause and effect, etc.) adverb clauses reduced to adverb phrases
The subject of both clauses must be the same. The subject is omitted.

With past simple and present simple adverb clauses, the verb in the adverb phrase is in the present participle (*-ing*) form:

16.238a Because I spoke Spanish, I knew what they were saying.
b → Speaking Spanish, I knew what they were saying.

16.239a As I didn't want to see my ex-wife, I didn't go to the party.
b → Not wanting to see my ex-wife, I didn't go to the party.

16.240a Since it was a holiday, all the shops were closed.
b → Being a holiday, all the shops were closed.

16.241a Since John wasn't in a good mood, he didn't talk to anyone.
  b → Not being in a good mood, John didn't talk to anyone.

16.242a Because I live in Canada, I'm used to cold weather.
  b → Living in Canada, I'm used to cold weather.

16.243a Since you don't have a car, you'll have to take a taxi.
  b → Not having a car, you'll have to take a taxi.

16.244a Because Mary is a doctor, she knew exactly what to do.
  b → Being a doctor, Mary knew exactly what to do.

16.245a Since he's not a child, he should have known better.
  b → Not being a child, he should have known better.

With past perfect and present perfect adverb clauses, the auxiliary verb *have* is in present participle (*-ing*) form and the main verb is in past participle form:

16.246a As I've already seen that movie, I don't want to see it again.
  b → Having already seen that movie, I don't want to see it again.

16.247a Because he hasn't driven here before, he doesn't know the way.
  b → Not having driven here before, he doesn't know the way.

16.248a Since Larry had had lunch, he didn't want any pizza.
  b → Having had lunch, Larry didn't want any pizza.

16.249a Because Mary hadn't been there before, she got lost.
  b → Not having been there before, Mary got lost.

16.250a Since he's never done it before, he has no idea what to do.
  b → Never having done it before, he has no idea what to do.

16.251a As I'd never met her, I had no idea what she looked like.
  b → Never having met her, I had no idea what she looked like.

Remind your students that *since* (especially) and *as* can have the same meaning as *because*.

Expect your students to be puzzled by these adverb phrases. It will strike them as odd that you (imagine this in Homer Simpson's skeptical voice) *claaaaim* that these adverb phrases somehow still mean *because* even after you have gotten rid of *because* (or *since* or *as*). Assure them that despite this, we native speakers understand the cause and effect, meaning. (Or the *because idea,* as I would phrase it.)

sample exercises 28: Change the adverb clauses to adverb phrases.
  Because I know what John thinks, I wasn't surprised by his comments.
  Knowing what John thinks, I wasn't surprised by his comments.

  Since I didn't know the answer, I guessed.
  Not knowing the answer, I guessed.

1. Because Lucy didn't know who the man was, she didn't unlock the door.
2. Because I didn't want my wife to be angry, I didn't tell her what happened.
3. Since you lack experience, it will be difficult for you to get a job.
4. As I didn't have a car, I had to walk to work every day.
5. Since Mary and John have eight children, they need a larger house.

sample exercises 29: Change the adverb clauses to adverb phrases.
  Because Mary is very tall, she doesn't like to wear high heels.
  Being very tall, Mary doesn't like to wear high heels.

  Since I wasn't hungry, I didn't eat anything.
  Not being hungry, I didn't eat anything.

1. Because he was on a diet, he didn't want a piece of cake.
2. Since he isn't a member of the club, he can't come in.

---

3. Because Maria isn't a citizen of this country, she cannot get a job here.
4. Since I'm not married and don't have children, I don't need a big house.
5. Because Carl is an ESL teacher, he works long hours for low pay.

sample exercises 30: Change the adverb clauses to adverb phrases.

Because Carlos had grown up in Mexico, he could speak Spanish perfectly.
Having grown up in Mexico, Carlos could speak Spanish perfectly.

Because I had never been to Italy before, I was very excited about going.
Never having been to Italy before, I was very excited about going.

1. Because I've been to England many times before, I decided to go somewhere else for my vacation.
2. Because Michael had broken his leg, he had to cancel his trip to Puerto Rico.
3. Since I've never been to Los Angeles, I'm really looking forward to going there next week.
4. Because I had had dinner only an hour earlier, I didn't want to go out for dinner with my friends.
5. As I have had that disease before, I cannot get it again.

16.33 Adverb clauses about opposites (contrast/concession) with *despite the fact that* and *in spite of the fact that* reduced to adverb phrases

The subject of both clauses must be the same. The subject and *the fact that* are omitted. *Despite* and *in spite of* have the same meaning and are interchangeable.

With past simple and present simple adverb clauses, the verb in the adverb phrase is in the present participle (-*ing*) form:

16.252a   Despite the fact that Mary was very tired, she went to the party.
     b   → Despite being very tired, Mary went to the party.

16.253a   In spite of the fact that Larry's not very tall, he's an excellent basketball player.
     b   → In spite of not being very tall, Larry's an excellent basketball player.

16.254a   Despite the fact that my father was only 17 years old, he joined the Army.
     b   → Despite being only 17 years old, my father joined the Army.

16.255a   In spite of the fact that we weren't members of the club, they let us in anyway.
     b   → In spite of not being members of the club, they let us in anyway.

16.256a   In spite of the fact that I studied Chinese for several years, it's still very difficult for me.
     b   → In spite of studying Chinese for several years, it's still very difficult for me.

16.257a   Despite the fact that Mark doesn't study very much, he gets good grades.
     b   → Despite not studying very much, Mark gets good grades.

With past perfect and present perfect adverb clauses, the auxiliary verb *have* is in present participle (-*ing*) form and the main verb is in past participle form:

16.258a   Despite the fact that I have lived in New York City all my life, I've never been to Times Square.
     b   → Despite having lived in New York City all my life, I've never been to Times Square.

16.259a   In spite of the fact that Sofia has been to my house many times, she still can't remember how to get there.
     b   → In spite of having been to my house many times, Sofia still can't remember how to get there.

16.260a   Despite the fact that Joe left for the airport four hours before his flight, he still missed his plane.
     b   → Despite having left for the airport four hours before his flight, Joe still missed his plane.

16.261a   In spite of the fact that I hadn't been paying attention in class, I didn't have any trouble with the homework.
     b   → In spite of not having been paying attention in class, I didn't have any trouble with the homework.

16.262a   In spite of the fact that my brother has never worked a day in his life, he gets angry when people say he is lazy.
     b   → In spite of never having worked a day in his life, my brother gets angry when people say he is lazy.

16.263a   Despite the fact that I had never studied Arabic, it wasn't hard to get by when I went to Abu Dhabi.
     b   → Despite never having studied Arabic, it wasn't hard to get by when I went to Abu Dhabi.

Obviously, I went a bit overboard in coming up with examples of adverb clauses with *despite the fact that* and *in spite of the fact that* reduced to adverb phrases, but I wanted to include examples of *be* used in participle form, which is common but often overlooked by teachers and textbooks and also examples of *never* used in reduced present perfect and past perfect adverb clauses. This is a useful and handy little bit of grammar, so be sure to discuss it.

sample exercises 31: Change the adverb clauses to adverb phrases.
> In spite of the fact that I followed the instructions exactly, I still couldn't get it to work.
> *In spite of following the instructions exactly, I still couldn't get it to work.*

1. Despite the fact that I was very angry, I didn't say anything.
2. In spite of the fact that Mary wasn't in class, the teacher marked her present.
3. Despite the fact that John has lived in France for 10 years, he can't speak French.
4. In spite of the fact that we were never told of the change in plan, we figured out what to do anyway.
5. Despite the fact that I have a car, I usually walk to work.

sample exercises 32: Write sentences with adverb phrases using *despite* or *in spite of.*
> He makes good money. He is always broke.
> *Despite making good money, he is always broke.*

1. I have a backache. I'll help you move your sofa.
2. Tom doesn't know anything about the subject. He's full of advice.
3. The boys weren't old enough. They were able to buy alcohol.
4. I had never used that program before. I didn't have any problem with it.
5. Susan is 90 years old. She works 40 hours a week.

16.34 Present participle adverb phrases of manner with prepositional phrase time and place expressions

Present participles can serve as adverb phrases of manner, often with prepositional phrases relating to time and place (which are also adverbials). Here are some examples:

16.264   He sits around the house all day doing nothing.

16.265   We drove around the block looking for a parking space.

16.266   I lay on the sofa all afternoon reading.

Here's what it boils down to. In this sentence:

16.267   He sat thinking.

the present participle *thinking* is an adverb phrase of manner.

We can add all sorts of other stuff:

16.268   He sat on the sofa thinking.

16.269   He sat for three hours on the sofa thinking.

16.270   He sat for three hours on the sofa thinking about what a mess he had made of his life.

This is a pretty big blob of grammar for your students to make sense out of. I wouldn't overdo it with the grammar. Help them get the basic pattern down, and then have them practice forming sentences with verbs like these below that are often used in this way.

drive around	hang around	lie	lie around	run around
sit	sit around	stand	stand around	walk around

You could easily come up with many more. A couple of things you might want to mention, vocabularywise, are the difference between *lie* and *lay* (You *do* know the difference between *lie* and *lay*, don't you?) and that many phrasal verbs with *around* in American English would use *about* in British English:

16.271a   Mary and Larry <u>stood around</u> watching me while I did all the work. (AE)
   b   = Mary and Larry <u>stood about</u> watching me while I did all the work. (BE)

Also, remind your students that these little devils can be negative:

16.272   After Michael told me the truth, I stood there <u>not knowing</u> what to say.

sample exercises 33: Complete the sentences with adverb phrases.

> I sat at my desk for two hours. I did my math homework.

> I _____*sat at my desk for two hours doing*_____ my math homework.

1. Maria stood by the window. She listened to a bird sing.
   Maria _____ to a bird sing.

2. My lazy son-in-law hangs around the house all day. He does nothing.
   My lazy son-in-law _____ nothing.

3. Our boss was angry because she saw us standing around. We weren't doing anything.
   Our boss was angry because she saw us _____ anything.

4. My son just sat there, listened to me and didn't say anything.
   He just _____ anything.

5. Are you just going to sit around all night? Do you hope that she'll call you?
   Are you just going to _____ that she'll call you?

16.35 Correlative conjunctions

Don't give up now! The last group of subordinating conjunction we'll look at are (jargon alert!) *correlative conjunctions*.

Here's what it's all about: Correlative conjunctions are pairs of words that work together to show a relationship between two (or more) words, phrases or clauses. The words, phrases and clauses must be <u>equal</u>—each is a noun, each is a verb, each is an adjective, each is a prepositional phrases, etc.

Sounds simple enough, but in practice they can be tricky.

▶ *as/as*

The *as/as* correlative conjunction is used with adverbs and adjectives to show equality:

▷ Adjectives

> 16.273   Your house is <u>as big as</u> my house.

▷ Adverbs

> 16.274   My plan will work <u>as well as</u> hers.

sample exercises 34: Use *as/as* to write sentences with the same meaning.

> Mark is tall. Michael isn't shorter or taller than Mark.
> *Michael is as tall as Mark.*

> Sarah drives carefully. Mary drives less carefully than Sarah.
> *Mary doesn't drive as carefully as Sarah.*

1. My car is old. Your car isn't newer or older than my car.
2. Joe drives fast. Noura doesn't drive faster or slower than Joe.
3. Winter in Canada is cold. Winter in Mexico is less cold than winter in Canada.
4. Alan dances well. Carlos dances worse than Alan.
5. Maria speaks French badly. Rosa speaks French the same as Maria.

▶ *both/and*

Probably the easiest to teach is *both/and*. It's used to connect two pieces of information:

▷ Subjects

When *both/and* is used for subjects, the verb must be correct for a plural subject:

> 16.275   <u>Both Larry and I</u> are hungry.

> 16.276   <u>Both you and he</u> have to be at the meeting.

▷ Objects

> 16.277   I went to <u>both Spain and Portugal</u> last year.

▷ Verbs

> 16.278   You need to <u>both clean and paint</u> your house.

▷ Nouns

16.279   I am <u>both a husband and a father</u>.

▷ Adjectives

16.280   Jack is <u>both cruel and dishonest</u>.

▷ Adverbs

16.281   You have to do it <u>both slowly and carefully</u>.

▷ Prepositional phrases

16.282   There were birds <u>both on the ground and in the air</u>.

sample exercises 35: Use *both/and* to write sentences with the same meaning.
She spoke to you. She spoke to me.
She spoke to both you and [to] me.

1. Mark is married. I am married.
2. It's a printer. It's a scanner.
3. Mary has to be at the meeting. Her boss has to be at the meeting.
4. Linda lives in that building. Ali lives in that building.
5. My house has an indoor pool. My house has an outdoor pool.

▶ *either/or*

This is very useful to students—more useful than *neither/nor. Either/or* is used to connect two pieces of information which are options, but only one is possible:

▷ Subjects

When *either/or* is used to join two subjects, the verb agrees with the subject directly after *or*:

16.283   <u>Either Tom or Ali</u> is going to do it.

16.284   <u>Either Mary or John</u> will be the new manager.

▷ Objects

16.285   You can have <u>either coffee or tea</u>.

▷ Verbs

16.286   I'll <u>either fix</u> my old car <u>or buy</u> a new one.

▷ Nouns

16.287   All of the people at the party were <u>either doctors or nurses</u>.

▷ Adjectives

16.288   Seven students in my class were <u>either late or absent</u> today.

▷ Adverbs

16.289   You can do it <u>either quickly or carefully</u> but not both.

▷ Prepositional phrases

16.290   I'm going to hang this picture <u>either next to the window or over the sofa</u>.

▷ Independent clauses

16.291   <u>Either you stop making so much noise, or I will call the police</u>!

sample exercises 36: Use *either/or* to write sentences with the same meaning. There may be more than one good answer for some.
I should call my mother. I should write to my mother.
I should either call or write to my mother.
1. I'm going to stay home today. I'm going to go to the beach today.
2. John will give me a ride downtown. Mary will give me a ride downtown.

Adverbs, Adverb Clauses, Adverb Phrases and More

3. The children can play outside. The children can play upstairs.
4. We will play tennis. We will go swimming.
5. Do the work right. I will find someone else who can do it right!

▶ *neither/nor*

Neither/nor is used to connect two negative and equal pieces of information. It's a nice thing to drop into a conversation when you want to awe people with your grammatical magnificence. How important it is for your students depends, as is so often the case, on their needs, abilities and level. For the majority of students, it will not be terribly important:

▷ Subjects

When *neither/nor* is used to join two subjects, the verb agrees with the subject directly after *nor*:

16.292   <u>Neither my grandmother nor my grandfather</u> is alive.

16.293   <u>Neither my sister nor my brother</u> has children.

▷ Objects

16.294   I have <u>neither the time nor the right tools</u> to fix your car.

▷ Verbs

16.295   I <u>neither know nor care</u> what he thinks.

▷ Nouns

16.296   Jack is <u>neither a good man nor an honest man</u>.

▷ Adjectives

16.297   He is <u>neither rich nor handsome</u>.

▷ Adverbs

16.298   Michael works <u>neither hard nor well</u>.

▷ Prepositional phrases

16.299   My cell phone is <u>neither in my pocket nor on my desk</u>.

▷ Independent clauses

16.300   <u>I will neither write to him</u>, <u>nor will I speak to him</u>.

sample exercises 37: Use *neither/nor* to write sentences with the same meaning. There may be more than one good answer for some.

> I don't have the time to do it. I don't have the desire to do it.
> *I have neither the time nor the desire to do it.*

1. The movie wasn't funny. It wasn't interesting.
2. I would not eat them in a box. I would not eat them with a fox.
3. Larry wasn't a good singer. He wasn't a good dancer.
4. Mark doesn't like to exercise. Mark doesn't want to exercise.
5. My computer isn't working. Mary's computer isn't working.

▶ *not only/but*

The slipperiest of these is the most useful I think, so it's worth the effort to teach it. *Not only/but* is a good example of what a wise man (me) once said: When you're learning a language, sometimes it's the smallest words that are the biggest problem. Every student in your class certainly knows *not, only* and *but,* but putting sentences together with this correlative conjunction won't be easy.

This correlative conjunction is similar to *in addition*—one piece of interesting or surprising information is given, and then another piece of information that is *more* interesting or more surprising is given.

What's confusing is that one, *not only/but* can connect pairs of just about anything and two, there are a number of variations on *not only/but*. It is common but not necessary to use *also, too,* and *as well* (which is useful and very idiomatic—you should teach *as well* to your students) and *either* with *not only/but*. Sometimes *but* is omitted. Sometimes grammar similar to question grammar is used. In my obsessive compulsive determination to be thorough, I've tried to show these variations in the examples below.

In no way am I suggesting that you attempt to teach your students all of this. That would be wonderful, but it's not realistic. Your students would have a mental breakdown just like I almost did when I wrote this stuff. This is one of many areas where the best you can do is give your students a general familiarity with something.

Words in parentheses are optional and are shown as examples.

▷ **Subjects**

16.294   Not only the police but (also) the fire department came when I called 911.

▷ **Objects**

16.295   She cooked not only breakfast but lunch and dinner (too).

16.296   Not only did she cook breakfast but (also) lunch and dinner.

▷ **Verbs**

16.297   I not only saw a ghost but took a picture of it.

16.298   Not only did I see a ghost but took a picture of it.

▷ **Nouns**

16.299   Mark is not only a doctor but (also) a lawyer.

16.300   Not only is Mark a doctor but a lawyer (as well).

▷ **Adjectives**

16.301   Jack is not only lazy but crazy (too).

16.302   Not only is Jack lazy but crazy.

▷ **Adverbs**

16.303   You should drive not only slowly but (also) carefully.

16.304   Not only should you drive slowly but carefully (as well).

▷ **Prepositional phrases**

16.305   I looked for my lost keys not only in the bedroom but under the desk and behind the sofa.

16.306   Not only did I look for my lost keys in the bedroom but (also) under the desk and behind the sofa.

▷ **Independent clauses**

16.307   I not only don't have a TV, but I don't have a radio (either).

16.308   Mary not only has five cats, but she has seven dogs (too).

16.309   Not only does Mary have five cats, but she (also) has seven dogs.

Notice the punctuation in the independent clause examples. A comma is necessary only with independent clauses. Because the verb is the same in both clauses (in this case *have*), it would also be possible to write this sentence as a single independent clause with two objects (and no comma):

16.310   Mary not only has five cats but seven dogs (too).

16.311   Not only does Mary have five cats but (also) seven dogs.

When two independent clause are joined with *not only/but*, it is common to omit *but* and use a semi-colon:

16.312   Mary not only has five cats; she (also) has seven dogs.

16.313   Not only does Mary have five cats; she (also) has seven dogs.

Sometimes, when the first item of information has already been stated in a separate independent clause, it is replaced with that in a second independent clause:

16.314   Joe lived in Korea for many years. <u>Not only that</u>, <u>he</u> (also) <u>married a Korean woman</u>.

Don't demand perfection from your students in the exercises below. Be happy if they just get the basic idea.

sample exercises 38: Use *not only/but* (or one of the variations) to write sentences with the same meaning. There is more than one good answer for each.

> Michael saw the president. He shook his hand.
> *Not only did Michael see the president, but he also shook his hand.*

> The bus was late. It was full.
> *Not only was the bus late, it was also full.*

1. My daughter is beautiful. She is very intelligent.
2. I went to China last year. I went to Mongolia last year.
3. He bought 10 kilos of tomatoes. He bought 20 kilos of potatoes.
4. Alan washed the dishes. He cleaned the bathroom and did the laundry.
5. They will probably lose the battle. They might lose the war.

▷ *would rather/than*

Would rather/than is used to talk about preferences.

▷ **Objects**

16.315   I <u>would rather</u> have <u>pizza</u> for dinner than <u>tacos</u>.

▷ **Verbs**

16.316   I'<u>d rather watch</u> TV <u>than go shopping</u> with my wife.

▷ **Independent clauses**

16.317   I'<u>d rather you do this work</u> <u>than I do this work</u>.

sample exercises 39: Use *would rather/than* to write sentences with the same meaning.

> I like to listen to classical music more than I like to listen to rock music.
> *I'd rather listen to classical music than [listen to] rock music.*

1. I like to read books more than I like to watch TV.
2. Alan wants to have coffee more than he wants to have tea.
3. I prefer that you give this presentation than I give it.
4. He likes to work outside more than he likes to work in an office.
5. We like to camp more than we like to stay in a hotel.

Chapter 17
Gerunds, Gerund Phrases and Infinitives

Could you...

- explain how a verb can be a noun?
- explain *a* to a student?

    a. We are discussing going shopping.

- explain how *b* and *c* are different?

    b. Mary's favorite activity is playing tennis.
    c. Mary's favorite uncle is playing tennis.

- explain which of these sentences is better and why?

    d. The boss was angry about me being late, but she didn't say anything about Larry being late.
    e. The boss was angry about my being late, but she didn't say anything about Larry's being late.

- explain how *f* and *g* are different?

    f. I remembered to do it.
    g. I remembered doing it.

17.1 What is a gerund?

We already know what infinitives are—a verb with a *to* in front of it (except for bare infinitives—see Appendix F) that has no tense. So what's a *gerund*? The basic idea is pretty simple: A gerund is a verb in the *-ing* form that functions as a noun. In other words, a gerund *is* a noun. Gerunds are an essential aspect of English grammar that all students should be familiar with. But why combine gerunds and infinitives in one chapter? It's traditional to do so in grammar books because, as you'll see, they kind of overlap. There are a few cases where either a gerund or an infinitive could be used.

At first, gerunds will be confusing to your students—not because they are inherently very difficult—but because the idea that *-ing* means continuous (aka progressive) will be so ingrained by this point that it will be hard for them to let go of it. Make sure your students understand that gerunds are not continuous verbs (or verbs at all), that gerunds are nouns and that as nouns, they can do many of the jobs that regulars noun do.

This will strike your students as pretty odd. A verb can be a noun? Has our teacher completely lost it? To help my students get this through their heads, I give them several examples of ordinary nouns that are familiar to them and then replace them with gerunds to illustrate that gerunds can do the same job that ordinary nouns do (because they *are* nouns).

17.2 Gerunds as objects

First, illustrate gerunds as objects. At first, use only single word gerunds. Put something like this on the board:

> Mary likes <u>chocolate</u>.

After establishing that *chocolate* is most definitely a noun, show your students how an ordinary noun like *chocolate* can be replaced by the gerund *singing* and that *both* are nouns:

> Mary likes ~~chocolate~~.
> Mary likes <u>singing</u>.

Do a couple more like that. Then, to get them familiar with *gerund phrases* (before actually discussing them), try some like this:

> I like ~~pizza~~.
> I like <u>reading history books</u>.

Next, try some examples like this with a single word gerund and a gerund with modification—a gerund phrase:

> I like <u>basketball</u>. (noun object)
> I like <u>swimming</u>. (gerund object)
> I like <u>swimming in the sea</u>. (gerund phrase object)

Keep it simple though. By far the main thing you want to accomplish is getting your students to fully grasp the concept that a verb can function as a noun. That will take some doing, so don't rush into the complicated stuff.

17.3 Gerunds as subjects

Next, give your students some examples of gerunds as subjects. Do it in much the same way as you did with gerund objects—replacing nouns with gerunds and then gerund phrases:

> <u>Tennis</u> is fun. (noun subject)
> <u>Dancing</u> is fun. (gerund subject)
> <u>Dancing at the club</u> is fun. (gerund phrase subject)

17.4 Other things to point out

Don't overload your students, but early in your discussion of gerunds, you'll need to find the right time to mention these important points:

▶ **Negative gerunds**

Gerunds can be, and often are, negative:

> 17.1 I failed the test because I didn't study. That was stupid. <u>Not studying for the test</u> was stupid.

Tell your students that no form of *do, does* or *did* is used with negative gerunds. (Students are always happy to learn that any new grammar they're studying doesn't involve these troublemakers.)

▶ ***being* as a gerund**

Being can be a gerund too. Here we see a gerund phrase with *being* serving as the subject of a sentence:

> 17.2 <u>Being late for class</u> is bad.

▶ **Gerund objects of continuous verbs**

A gerund can be the object of a continuous verb, and that will look pretty odd to your students, so get them used to the idea:

> 17.3 Tom and his wife are <u>discussing buying</u> a new car.

sample exercises 1: Complete the sentences with the verb in parentheses. Some are negative.
> Noura finished (do) _____*doing*_____ her homework.

1. Larry quit (smoke) _____.
2. I need to lose weight, so my wife suggested (exercise) _____ more and (not, eat) _____ so much cake and ice cream.
3. Linda stopped (speak) _____ to me after I lied to her.
4. I am very sick, and I'm considering (go) _____ to the hospital.
5. I'm trying to study, so would you mind (not, make) _____ so much noise?

sample exercises 2: Complete the sentences with gerunds. Some are negative.
> Alan loves to play soccer. _____*Playing*_____ soccer is his favorite sport.

1. I have to wake up at 4:00 every morning. _____ at 4:00 every morning is very difficult.
2. I watched a show about Italian food. _____ a show about Italian food made me very hungry.
3. I don't speak Spanish, and that was a problem when I lived in Mexico. _____ Spanish was a problem when I lived in Mexico.
4. It's important to be on time for class. _____ on time for class is important.
5. John is not able to walk, and that makes life more difficult for him. _____ able to walk makes life more difficult for John.

sample exercises 3: Complete the sentences with gerund phrase subjects. Some are negative.
> Mary loves to play tennis. _____*Playing tennis*_____ is her favorite activity.

1. Gary lives in Los Angeles, but he doesn't have a car. _____ is a problem when you live in Los Angeles.
2. We live in Las Vegas, which is very exciting. _____ is very exciting.
3. My wife wants to go to Tahiti, but I think _____ would be too expensive.
4. My boss thinks we should do nothing, but I think _____ would be a big mistake.
5. My boss thinks we shouldn't do anything, but I think _____ would be a big mistake.

sample exercises 4: Complete the sentences with gerund phrase objects. Some are negative.

    I have to wake up a 4:30 every morning. I hate ___*having to wake up at 4:30*___ every morning.

1. We often try new restaurants. We love _____.
2. Mary didn't say good bye to Larry before he left. Mary was upset about _____.
3. Carlos has to go shopping for clothes with his mother. He hates _____.
4. My wife has to work on Sundays. She doesn't like _____.
5. He asked me to go to the funeral. I don't like funerals, and I considered _____, but I finally said I would.

17.5 Gerunds as subject complements

It's tempting to make a big deal out of no form of *be* being used with gerunds, since they are not continuous verbs, but don't do it. Here's why:

Be is indeed used for continuous verbs, and gerunds aren't continuous verbs or verbs at all, right? Well, then how, for example, would you explain these to your students?

    17.4   What I really love <u>is</u> <u>watching</u> old movies on TV.

    17.5   It <u>was</u> <u>punching</u> my boss in the nose that got me fired.

    17.6   What I hate about my new job <u>is</u> <u>having</u> to wake up so early.

This is potentially confusing to your students, so underline the entire gerund phrase rather than the gerunds only,

    17.7   What I really love <u>is</u> <u>watching old movies on TV</u>.

    17.8   It <u>was</u> <u>punching the boss in the nose</u> that got me fired.

    17.9   What I hate about my new job <u>is</u> <u>having to wake up so early</u>.

and demonstrate that the gerund phrases are nouns by replacing them ordinary nouns:

    17.10   What I really love <u>is</u> <u>pizza</u>.

    17.11   It <u>was</u> <u>my big mistake</u> that got me fired.

    17.12   What I hate about my new job <u>is</u> <u>the long hours</u>.

Gerunds used in this way are called (jargon alert!) *subject complements*. Do not confuse your students with this term—it'll just turn something easy into something difficult, and you'll be sorry you ever mentioned it. Between you and me, a subject complement is simply a way of renaming the subject with a linking verb—usually *be*—and saying that what's on one side of the linking verb and what's on the other are the same. That's why we can switch these sentences around:

    17.13a   Swimming is my favorite exercise.
        b   → My favorite exercise is swimming.

All of this blabbering is a lead up to an exercise meant to reinforce the idea of a gerund as subject complement.

sample exercises 5: Complete the sentences with gerunds and the correct form of *be*.

    What makes you really angry?
    What makes me really angry (listen) _____*is listening*_____ to my husband complain all the time.

1. What's your favorite way to relax?
   My favorite way to relax (play) _____ tennis.
2. What was your father's job?
   My father's job (drive) _____ a truck.
3. What was the problem in your class yesterday?
   The problem (get) _____ my students to wake up.
4. What's the best exercise?
   The best exercise (run) _____.
5. What was your biggest mistake?
   My biggest mistake (not, listen) _____ to my father's advice when I was young.

17.6 Gerunds as objects of prepositions

Just like ordinary nouns, gerunds can be objects of prepositions. That in itself won't be terribly difficult for your students, but it will lead up to a couple of common patterns of gerund use that, while not very difficult grammarwise, will be a bit challenging and very useful vocabularywise. These are perfect examples of the type of grammar lesson that I present more as a vocabulary lesson. What good is grammar if you don't know the words that native speakers plug into that grammar? Also, you may want to remind your students, if it comes up, that prepositions are wacky, unpredictable little creatures that come and go as they please. In other words, there is no rule students can learn about why a certain preposition is used here and another there. Prepositions are just something that has to be memorized. (They're not *entirely* random, but because there is a high degree of randomness, I just don't see any benefit to getting into it at all.)

Also, this isn't exclusively a gerund thing. The use of certain prepositions with certain verbs and adjectives is something that can be addressed without the focus on gerunds. There are many more such verbs and adjectives, and it can be a very useful to focus on them as a vocabulary lesson. (See Appendix B for long list of verb + preposition combinations and Appendix C for a list of adjective + preposition combinations.)

Before doing the following exercise, you might want to discuss how *apologize* can be used with two different prepositions:

17.14   I apologized <u>to</u> my sister <u>for</u> forgetting to pick her up at the airport.

sample exercises 6:   Use the correct form of the verb and a gerund to complete the sentences. Some must be negative.

My grandfather (talk about, fight) _____*talked about fighting*_____ in the war when he was in the army.

1. Tom's computer is old. Last night he (talk about, buy) _____ a new one.
2. I've never been to China. I'm (think about, go) _____ there next year.
3. Tom and Sarah were (think about, sell) _____ their house, but now they're (think about, not, sell) _____ it and renting it instead.
4. Oh no! Yesterday was my wife's birthday. I need to (apologize to, her, for, forget) _____ her birthday.
5. I was (think about, make) _____ hamburgers for dinner, but I (decide against, have) _____ hamburgers and made pizza instead.

17.7 Verb + noun/noun phrase + preposition + gerund/gerund phrase

blame (someone) for	criticize (someone) for	forgive (someone) for	keep (someone) from
prevent (someone) from	prohibit (someone) from	stop (someone) from	thank (someone) for

This is a common pattern of gerund use. Put a couple of examples like these on the board:

I <u>thanked</u>   <u>my math teacher</u>   <u>for</u>   <u>helping me</u>.
   verb +   noun/noun phrase + preposition + gerund/gerund phrase

My back problem   <u>keeps</u>   <u>me</u>   <u>from</u>   <u>playing golf</u>.
         verb + noun/noun phrase + preposition + gerund/gerund phrase

The grammar isn't terribly difficult, so spend time on the meanings of some of the unfamiliar vocabulary here.

Keep and its meaning of *remain, stay the same, don't change,* etc., is a handy thing for students. I always emphasize it.

Spend some time on *not blame someone for* to mean that you understand the reason why someone thinks something or does something. You could use these two examples to illustrate the two meanings:

17.15   After the accident, the police said it was the other driver's fault. They <u>did not blame me for causing</u> the accident.

17.16   I hate public speaking too, so I <u>do not blame you for being</u> nervous about your speech tomorrow.

Take some time for this. It'll be a bit difficult for your student, but because it's so common, it's worth the effort.

sample exercises 7:   Use the best verb from the list above and a gerund to complete the sentences. There may be more than one good answer for some. You can use a verb more than once.

Alan lied to me, and I will never forgive him. I will never _____*forgive him for lying*_____ to me.

1. My wife is very angry because I lost all our money gambling on sports. I think she will never _____ all our money gambling on sports.
2. He called you a big stupid idiot? I don't _____ angry with him. I'd be angry too.

3. The snow was very deep, so I couldn't go to work. The snow _____ to work.
4. My sister broke our father's favorite coffee mug, but she _____ it, so I got in trouble and not my sister.
5. My parents told me I'm not allowed to see my boyfriend. They _____ him.
6. When I was a boy, I was lazy. My father often _____ lazy.

17.8 *be* + adjective + preposition + gerund/gerund phrase

afraid of	angry about	bad at	excited about	good at
happy about	interested in	nervous about	proud of	responsible for
scared of	sick of	tired of	upset about	used to
worried about				

This is another common pattern of gerund use. Here are two examples to put on the board:

I	was sick	of	studying.
	be + adjective +	preposition +	gerund/gerund phrase

He	isn't happy	about	having to go to his mother-in-law's house for dinner.
	be + adjective +	preposition +	gerund/gerund phrase

Once again, the grammar won't be that terribly difficult, so treat this as a useful vocabulary lesson.

By far the biggest can of vocabulary worms that this will inevitably open is the difference between *used to,* as in *I used to live in New York, but now I live in Chicago,* and *be used to,* as in *My new shoes hurt my feet. I'm not used to them.* Whether you choose to bring this up or a pesky student asks you about it, it almost certainly will come up, and if it does, expect to spend 10 or 15 minutes more than you planned on this lesson.

sample exercises 8: Use the best adjective + preposition combination from the list above, the verb in parentheses and a gerund to complete the sentences. There may be more than one answer for some. You can use an adjective + preposition combination more than once. Be ready to explain your answer.

I hate this job. I am (work) _____*sick of working*_____ here.

Maria has to be at her new job at 6:00 in the morning. It's going to be difficult for her because she's not (wake up) _____*used to waking up*_____ so early.

1. Carlos is an excellent artist. He is very (draw) _____ pictures.
2. I love to study history. I am (learn) _____ more about ancient Greece.
3. I've had this boring job for 10 years, so I'm (work) _____ here.
4. I am afraid of flying, so I'm (fly) _____ to Tokyo next week.
5. Mark is very angry with me, so I'm (run into) _____ him at the party tonight.
6. Rosa was not (have) _____ to stay home Saturday night instead of going to the party with her friends.
7. My boss is crazy. She gets angry about everything, so I'm (make) _____ even one mistake on this project.

17.9 *have* + noun/noun phrase + (sometimes a preposition) gerund/gerund phrase

have a difficult time	have a good time	have a hard time	have a reason for
have a way of	have an excuse for	have difficulty	have fun
have no excuse for	have no reason for	have no way of	have trouble

There are a number of similar expressions involving *have,* a noun or noun phrase, sometimes a preposition and a gerund or gerund phrase. For example,

17.17   Jack has lied to me in the past, so I <u>have trouble believing his story</u>.

17.18   He <u>had a lot of difficulty understanding what I said</u>.

17.19   Do you <u>have an excuse for being late</u>?

Grammarwise, this gets a bit murky (as does much that follows). Are these even gerunds at all? It might surprise you, but there are aspects of English grammar that are not fully understood and agreed upon by experts. Do a bit of research, and you'll discover that there are about as many explanations for some things as there are experts explaining it. Much of it isn't even explanation at all but speculation and guesswork. The whole subject of gerunds used in the patterns we're discussing (beyond the easy stuff in Section 17.1 through Section 17.8) is a good example of this—are they gerunds at all?, are they present participles?, are they adverbial?, are they adjectival?, are they alien life forms? If the experts aren't sure, how can you make any sense of it all? Well, the good news is you don't need really need to because your students don't need to. They just need to learn these phrases and construction which, actually, aren't that difficult. But, against my better judgment, I'll put forth my own theory regarding just what these devilish things are.

My theory is that the *-ing* form which follows these phrases are part of adverbial prepositional phrases, but that sometimes the prepositions are omitted. Omitting prepositions in a prepositional phrase is kind of a radical idea, but all of the expressions below without prepositions can be rephrased with prepositions inserted. They don't sound natural, because they're not what we usually say, but I feel that they're all grammatical. For example,

17.20   Jack has lied to me in the past, so I have trouble <u>in believing</u> his story.

17.21   He had a lot of difficulty <u>in understanding</u> what I said.

17.22   She had a hard time <u>in helping</u> her son with his homework.

17.23   Mary had fun <u>by seeing</u> her friends at her high school reunion.

17.24   David had a good time <u>by spending</u> a month in Europe.

17.25   The mechanic had a difficult time <u>in figuring out</u> what was wrong with my car.

With prepositions in place, the *-ing* forms become objects of prepositions, and that makes them nouns and that makes them gerunds. Phew! I welcome comments of this theory.

If this discussion interests you, ~~get a life~~ great! But do not explain any of it to your students. It's far from generally accepted, and it will only confuse your students. By all means treat this and much that follows as a vocabulary exercise. As far as they're concerned, this is a collection of phrases with similar structure involving *have* and the *-ing* form. Leave it at that. It's knowing what these phrases mean and being able to use them that matters, not being able to discuss the deep grammar involved. Just teach them this formula:

> *have* + noun/noun phrase + (sometimes a preposition) gerund/gerund phrase

In the exercise below I think it's best to provide the phrase to be used because they depend on the context and because some of these are idiomatic, and students couldn't reasonably be expected to figure out which to use without help. Discuss the meanings of these various phrases and give them some exercises which reinforce their meaning and the use of gerunds (or whatever they are) with them.

sample exercises 9: Use the correct form of *have* and a gerund to complete the sentences.

I (have a hard time, believe) ____*have a hard time believing*____ his crazy story.

1.   I don't know what to think about his story. I (have no way of, know) _____ whether he's telling me the truth.
2.   Maria is (have fun, dance) _____ at this party, and she doesn't want to go now.
3.   My brother (have trouble, believe) _____ in ghosts until he saw one himself.
4.   You're an hour late! Do you (have an excuse for, be) _____ so late?
5.   We're going to (have a good time, play) _____ softball at the barbecue.
6.   You'll (have a difficult time, make) _____ this recipe. It's very complicated.
7.   I'm really sorry. I (have no excuse for, say) _____ those terrible things.

17.10 Verb + time or money expression + gerund/gerund phrase

This is a common construction which uses a very small group of verbs—*spend, waste* and *blow*. Can you think of any others? How about *squander*? How about *fritter away*? How about *donate*? Teach these if you want to, but the exercise below is based on *spend, waste* and *blow*. Make sure your students know that *spend* is neutral and means *using time or money productively or unproductively,* that *waste* is always an unproductive use of time or money and that *blow* means the same thing as *waste* but is very informal. Here are two examples that you could put on the board:

She	<u>spent</u>	<u>three hours</u>	<u>studying for her test</u>.
	verb +	time or money expression +	gerund/gerund phrase

Henry	blew	a million dollars	trying to build a flying bicycle.
verb	+	time or money expression	+	gerund/gerund phrase

The excruciatingly dull discussion in Section 17.9 regarding my theory of adverbial prepositional phrases with omitted prepositions applies equally here. All of these could be rephrased with the preposition *in* inserted:

17.26   She spent three hours *in* studying for the test.

17.27   David blew a million dollars *in* trying to build a flying bicycle.

so again, as objects of prepositions, that would make these *-ing* forms definitely gerunds.

As for your students (I almost forgot about them), all you need to do is teach them this formula:

> verb + time or money expression + gerund/gerund phrase

Do not say one word about prepositions.

sample exercises 10:   Use *spend, waste* or *blow* and a gerund to complete the sentences. There may be more than one good answer for some. Be ready to explain your answer.

> I went to the airport to pick up Mark. I waited two hours, but he didn't come. Later I learned that his flight had been canceled. I ____*wasted two hours waiting*____ for Mark at the airport.

1.   It cost $225 dollars to get my computer fixed, and it still doesn't work. I _____ my computer fixed, and it still doesn't work.
2.   Alan studied for three hours because he had a math test. He got an A on the test. Alan _____ for the test.
3.   David searched for ten years for a lost city in the jungle, and he didn't find it. David _____ for a lost city in the jungle, and he didn't find it.
4.   I had to get my roof repaired. It cost $3,000. I _____ my roof repaired.
5.   My mother is coming to visit me, so I needed to clean my house. My house was very dirty, so it took all day to clean it. I _____ my house.

17.11   *go* + gerund/gerund phrase

(bike) ride	(horseback) ride	(mountain) climb	(scuba) dive	boat
bowl	camp	dance	fish	golf
hike	jog	run	sail	shop
sightsee	skate	skateboard	ski	sky dive
surf	swim	trick-or-treat		

A number of enjoyable activities such as sports and shopping (enjoyable to some, anyway) are used in this common construction. Here are two examples to put on the board:

> My wife   went shopping.
> go + gerund/gerund phrase

> I'm going to go bowling with my friends tonight.
> go + gerund/gerund phrase

At least it's common to native speakers, but it will strike your students as a bit odd and for good reason—grammarwise, it is odd. My advice is not to attempt any explanation of the grammar involved. It's a bit murky and idiomatic and will only confuse them and you too. It's pretty hard to see how these *-ing* forms are nouns, which you have already told your students gerunds are, so conveniently fail to remind them of that here and just get on with teaching this as a vocabulary lesson. A far better use of your students' time will be discussing the meanings of these verbs, many of which will be unfamiliar to them. Provide them with a list of verbs, such as the one given here, that are used in this way (and there are more), and have them practice plugging them into this formula:

> *go* + gerund/gerund phrase

Make sure your students understand that *go* can be in any form including the continuous:

17.28   I hate going shopping with my wife.

Also, make sure that your students understand that all of these verbs can be used in the usual way, without *go*, but that it's less common. In other words, it's perfectly good English to say, for example, *I shopped yesterday* or *I swim every day*, but it would be much more common to say *I went shopping yesterday* or *I go swimming every day*.

sample exercises 11: Use *go* and a gerund to complete the sentences.

My wife and I love to dance. We _____*go dancing*_____ every weekend.

1. Alan often swims at the club. He _____ at the club last weekend.
2. My father and I love to fish. We used to _____ a lot when we lived in Minnesota.
3. Rosa is a good dancer. She _____ last night.
4. Sarah and her friends ski in Colorado every winter. They're going to _____ there next January.
5. I don't like to go camping, so I haven't _____ for a long time.
6. Michael and his wife needed some new clothes, so they're _____ tonight.

17.12 Other words and expressions used with gerunds

Here's a miscellaneous collection of other words and expressions used with gerunds—all common and all useful—so once again, treat this as more of a vocabulary lesson than a grammar lesson.

▶ *get used to*

17.29   After my husband died, it was difficult to <u>get used to</u> living alone.

17.30   We've lived above a disco for ten years, so we've <u>gotten used to</u> the noise.

▶ *in addition to*

17.31   <u>In addition to</u> having a car, I have a motorcycle.

17.32   <u>In addition to</u> not doing his work well, he also sleeps at his desk.

▶ *instead of*

17.33   I watched TV all night <u>instead of</u> studying.

17.34   <u>Instead of</u> being angry, you should say you're sorry.

▶ *look forward to*

17.35   I don't like Jack, so I'm not <u>looking forward to</u> seeing him at the party tonight.

17.36   My father's going to retire soon, and he's <u>looking forward to</u> not having to go to his office every day.

▶ *take advantage of*

17.37   Noura <u>took advantage</u> of having a day off from work to visit her mother.

17.38   There are many great museums in Washington DC. You should <u>take advantage of</u> being here to visit them.

▶ *take care of*

17.39   I *took care of* returning some books to the library this morning.

17.40   If you *take care of* making the drinks at the party, I'll take care of cooking the food.

sample exercises 12: Use one of the expressions from the list above and the verb in parentheses to complete the sentences with a gerund.

Francesca is studying Italian. She has an Italian neighbor. She should (have) _____*take advantage of having*_____ an Italian neighbor to practice speaking Italian.

1. I haven't seen my daughter for five years. She's coming to visit tomorrow. I'm (see) _____ her tomorrow.
2. Michael thought about buying a new car, but he decided to keep his old car. (buy) _____ a new car, Michael decided to keep his old car.
3. Sofia has a dog and a cat. (have) _____ a dog, Sofia also has a cat.
4. I don't have to work for a few days. I'm going to use the time to work on my car. I'm going to (not, have) _____ to work for a few days to work on my car.
5. (complain) _____ all the time, why don't you do something about your problems?

17.13 Possessives used with gerunds

Look at this sentence:

> 17.41   My wife was upset about being fired.

Who got fired? My wife, right? But what if I'm the one who got fired, and my wife is upset about that? How would we make that clear using a gerund? Would you say this?

> 17.42   My wife was upset about <u>me</u> getting fired.

That's what most native speakers would say, but strictly speaking, this is what they should really be saying:

> 17.43   My wife was upset about <u>my</u> getting fired.

Here are some more examples:

> 17.44a   formal: Michael was worried about <u>your</u> being sick.
>   b   informal: Michael was worried about <u>you</u> being sick.
>
> 17.45a   formal: <u>His</u> leaving the class early upset the teacher.
>   b   informal: <u>Him</u> leaving the class early upset the teacher.
>
> 17.46a   formal: The boss got angry about <u>my</u> being late, but he didn't say anything about <u>Sofia's</u> being late.
>   b   informal: The boss got angry about <u>me</u> being late, but he didn't say anything about <u>Sofia</u> being late.

You can see what the deal is. In the very best English, we use possessive adjectives (*my, his, your,* etc.) or possessive nouns (*my daughter's, Bob's, the manager's,* etc.) with gerunds as opposed to object pronouns (*me, him, you,* etc.) or nouns (*my daughter, Bob, the manager,* etc.)

Some people would say it's a matter of right and wrong, and sometimes I would be one of those people, but a more charitable way of explaining it would be in terms of formal and informal (or *careful* and *informal,* as I prefer).

Often, if the subject of the sentence is the same as the subject of the subject of the gerund phrase, the gerund phrase subject is deleted entirely. That's what we see in this example:

> 17.47   Michael was excited about going to Paris.

Anyone hearing this would assume that it's Michael who is going to Paris.

But when both subjects are not the same:

> 17.48   Linda wasn't happy about my telling everyone her big secret.

or even if they are the same, but there's a need to be extra clear:

> 17.49   Carlos was shocked at his being chosen to be the new regional manager.

use possessive adjectives or possessive nouns with gerunds if you want to use the very best English.

How important this is will depend on your students. If they're studying English for business or academic reasons, this is something worth covering. It's not terribly difficult, and if you can remember it yourself, it's a great way to awe people with your dazzling diction.

sample exercises 13:   Complete the sentences with gerunds and possessive adjectives or possessive nouns.
      We have ten cats. Some people think _____*our having*_____ ten cats is crazy.

1.   You lied to your father. _____ to your father is a very serious matter.
2.   Michael and Tom played the drums last night until 2:00 in the morning. Our neighbors were not happy about _____ the drums so late at night.
3.   He moved to California. My sister and I were surprised by _____ to California.
4.   You helped me. I appreciate _____ me.
5.   Linda laughed at my idea. I was very angry about _____ at my idea.

17.14 *by* + gerund/gerund phrase used for explaining how to do something

Gerunds with the preposition *by* are used to explain how to do something (or how it was done). You could easily give your students more practice with this by asking them how they did something, do something or will do something:

17.50   I lost weight <u>by eating only salads and running three miles every day</u>.

17.51   <u>By saving 25% or your salary every month</u>, you'll have $50,000 in five years.

sample exercises 14: Answer the questions by using *by* + gerund and the appropriate verb.

> cook   do   eat   sit   take   talk   ~~wash~~

1.   You might be able to get that ketchup stain out of your shirt ____*by washing*____ it with bleach.
2.   You can get to Maple Street _____ bus 42.
3.   _____ this in water instead of oil, it will have fewer calories.
4.   You'll save a lot of money _____ at home instead of in restaurants.
5.   _____ behind Carlos and looking at his test, I was able to get an A on my test.
6.   You won't solve your problems _____ about what you should do but _____ something about them!

17.15   Past forms of gerunds

When a gerund refers to something that <u>has happened</u>, it can take the form of a present perfect gerund: *having* + past participle. The best way to demonstrate this to your students is to work backward from an example of this to see how you arrived at this construction.

For example, compare these two sentences:

17.52   Tom and Mary <u>have climbed</u> Mount Everest.

17.53   Tom and Mary talked about <u>having climbed</u> Mount Everest.

You can see that the present perfect verb *have climbed* has turned in to the present perfect gerund *having climbed.*

Of course, most native speakers would say

17.54   Tom and Mary talked about <u>climbing</u> Mount Everest.

but there are two reasons why the present perfect gerund might be used: One, because sentences such as 17.54 aren't clear as to time. Maybe I know they've already climbed Mount Everest, so in this situation, I understand that they're talking about something that has already happened. But maybe I don't know that. Have Tom and Mary already climbed Mount Everest? Are they planning to climb Mount Everest? Are they simply talking about people in general climbing Mount Everest? You can see that the present perfect gerund, *having climbed,* adds clarity to the sentence. We understand that Tom and Mary are speaking of something that has happened in the past. The second reason to use present perfect gerunds is to show off your lofty lingo.

What if it were not clear that Tom and Mary are talking about something that they themselves did? Then this would be a way to clarify that:

17.55   Tom and Mary talked about <u>their having climbed</u> Mount Everest.

What if *I* were talking about Tom and Mary's climb up Mount Everest? How would I phrase the sentence then? You know:

17.56   I talked about <u>Tom and Mary's</u> having climbed Mount Everest.

With the possessive noun *Mary's* instead of *Mary,* the sentence is even loftier!

How important is this to your students? Only you can answer that question. It really depends on who they are and why they're learning English.

Here are two exercises to practice this. You might want to do a quick review of possessive adjectives and possessive nouns used with gerunds first. They are provided in some of the exercises in sample exercises 15, but the students will have to supply them in sample exercises 16.

sample exercises 15: Complete the sentences with present perfect gerunds. Some are negative.

> I didn't see Mary when she visited. I am sorry about _____*not having seen*_____ Mary when she visited.

1.   That was a terrible thing I did. I'm not proud of _____ that.
2.   Michael forgot to invite me. Michael apologized for his _____ to invite me.
3.   Michael didn't invite me. Michael apologized for his _____ me.
4.   I made a mistake. I was very embarrassed about my _____ a mistake.
5.   I couldn't be at the wedding. I apologized for _____ at the wedding.

sample exercises 16: Complete the sentences with present perfect gerunds. Use possessive adjectives and possessive nouns. Some are negative.

I told the woman who interviewed me for the job that I had worked for the ABC Company for several years. She was impressed by _____*my having worked*_____ for the ABC Company for several years.

1. I didn't know that she had been fired. I was surprised to hear about _____ fired.
2. Bill told Tom that Larry had quit his job. Bill told Tom about _____ his job.
3. You have a big mouth! You told everyone what happened! I'm really mad about _____ everyone what happened.
4. We didn't finish high school. We never tell anyone about _____ high school.
5. Because of _____ it before, it will be easy for you to do it again.

17.16 Verbs followed by gerunds and infinitives with the same meaning

| begin | can't stand | continue | hate | like |
| love | prefer | start | | |

A few verbs are used with infinitives or gerunds with no difference in meaning. It's a small group, but the verbs are very common, so you definitely need to cover this:

17.57a I <u>hate waking up</u> early.
   b = I <u>hate to wake up</u> early.

The only complication is that we <u>don't</u> use a gerund with a continuous main verb:

17.58 Michael is beginning doing his homework.

sample exercises 17: Complete the sentences with gerunds and infinitives.

Alan loves (play) _____*playing/to play*_____ soccer.

1. It started (snow) _____ about an hour ago.
2. I'm going to begin (study) _____ as soon as I get home.
3. Nobody likes (pay) _____ taxes.
4. When Ali was a boy, he hated (go) _____ to school.
5. I'm going to continue (work) _____ until I finish.

17.17 Gerunds and infinitives with a different meaning

An equally important but even smaller group of verbs can be used with either a gerund or an infinitive but with a difference in meaning. For example,

17.59 Please <u>remember to pay</u> the telephone bill tomorrow.

17.60 I <u>remember paying</u> the water bill. I paid it three days ago.

▶ *remember* and *forget*
A gerund is used for actions that have already happened:

17.61 Francesca <u>remembers going</u> to the White House when she was a girl.

17.62 She will never <u>forget seeing</u> the ghost of Abraham Lincoln when she was at the White House.

An infinitive is used to talk about needing to do something:

17.63 Did you <u>remember to turn off</u> the stove before you went to work?

17.64 I often <u>forget to lock</u> the door when I come home.

▶ *regret*
A gerund is used for actions that the speaker feels sorry about doing:

17.65 I <u>regret buying</u> this car. It's a piece of junk.

An infinitive is used when the speaker must inform another person of bad news:

17.66 I <u>regret to inform</u> you that there has been a tragic accident.

▶ *try*

A gerund is used to describe a way of doing something with the hope that it will be successful:

17.67   My computer wasn't working, so I <u>tried restarting</u> it, and it was OK after that.

An infinitive is used to describe an attempt to do something:

17.68   I <u>tried to fix</u> my printer, but I couldn't do it.

sample exercises 18: Use the verb in parentheses to complete the sentences with gerunds or infinitives.
        Have you tried (change) _____*changing*_____ the batteries? Maybe that's the problem.
        I tried (get) _____*to get*_____ there on time, but I couldn't because of the traffic.

1.   Larry wasn't at the meeting because I forgot (tell) _____ him that we changed it from 10:00 to 9:00.
2.   Ali tried (push) _____ the door instead of (pull) _____ it, and then it opened.
3.   The traffic was terrible on Highway 130 this morning, so I tried (take) _____ Highway 47, and it was a lot faster.
4.   Sometimes I forget (feed) _____ our dog.
5.   Who is that guy? I don't remember (meet) _____ him before.
6.   I regret (inform) _____ you that your parrot has died.

17.18   Subject gerund/gerund phrases = *it* + infinitives
Sentences with gerund subjects can be rephrased with *it* filling the place of the subject. In other words, the gerund is extraposed, moved to the end of the sentence. *It* used in this way is called a (jargon alert!) *expletive, filler subject* or *dummy subject*:

17.69a   <u>Dancing</u> is fun.
     b   → <u>It</u> is fun to <u>dance</u>.

17.70a   <u>Not being</u> late is important.
     b   → <u>It</u> is important <u>not to be</u> late.

sample exercises 19: Change the sentences as in the example.
        Growing up without a father was difficult.
        It was difficult to grow up without a father.

1.   Getting my car fixed is going to cost $450.
2.   Not studying for the test was stupid.
3.   Not forgetting your passport is important.
4.   Learning the truth was shocking.
5.   Being big or tall isn't necessary to be a good soccer player.

It's also possible for infinitives and infinitive phrases to be the subjects of sentences:

17.71   <u>To dance</u> is fun.

17.72   <u>To not be</u> late is important.

17.19   Verb + infinitive direct object
The most common use of infinitives is after verbs: *I like to read, He hates to wake up early, She refuses to give up, We want to eat lunch.* You get it. No terribly difficult grammar here, but the fact that infinitives (or infinitive phrases) are actually the objects of verbs such as these is something that might be of interest to you even if it isn't to your students. Much more important to them is, you guessed it, what some of these words mean. Here's a list that you might want to go over with your students. One of them, *manage,* is something useful that I like to teach students. By now they'll certainly know *manager* and possibly the verb *manage* (i.e. what a manager does), but probably not *manage to,* as in *My crazy ESL teacher gave me a ton of homework, but I managed to finish it all last night.* I'd emphasize *mean to* and *happen to* as well—both useful and different from the meanings of these words that the students may already know.

afford	agree	arrange	ask	care
claim	come	consent	decide	deserve
determine	fail	forget	happen	hate
hope	learn	like	love	manage
mean	need	offer	prepare	pretend
proceed	prove	refuse	remember	resolve

struggle	tend	threaten	volunteer	wait
want	wish			

sample exercises 20: Complete the sentences with a verb from the list above. Make sure the verbs are in the correct tense.

Mary was having a lot of trouble with her homework, so I _____*offered*_____ to help her.

1. The airport is 60 miles from Joe's house, and he had only one hour to get to the airport before his flight. By driving like a maniac, he _____ to get there in time for his flight.
2. I'm really angry. I've been _____ to see the doctor for two hours.
3. I had a big surprise today. I _____ to run into one of my best friends from high school at the mall today.
4. Mary's in big trouble. She _____ to send an email to her boyfriend, but she sent it to her husband instead.
5. I'd love to attend your wedding in Singapore, but I just can't _____

17.20 Verb + indirect object + infinitive direct object

Some verbs require an indirect object between the verb and the infinitive phrase. This isn't terribly difficult grammarwise and needless to say, it's focusing on what these verbs mean that will be the most useful to your students. *Get,* as in *I got my brother to do my do my project for me,* is common, useful and something you should discuss (and is discussed further in Section 17.26). There's a suggestion of coercion or trickery when we use *get* in this way. *Remind* is worth discussing too. Students often have difficulty understanding how *remind* is different from *remember.*

advise	allow	authorize	appoint	cause
challenge	command	convince	direct	encourage
forbid	force	get	hire	inspire
instruct	invite	motivate	order	permit
persuade	remind	require	teach	tell
urge	warn			

sample exercises 21: Complete the sentences with a verb from the list above and the appropriate indirect object. Make sure the verbs are in the correct tense. There may be more than one good answer.

My son forgets everything. If I didn't _____*remind him*_____ to put his shoes on in the morning, he'd go to school in his bare feet.

1. Larry didn't know how to ride a bicycle, but I _____ to do it.
2. I was very angry with my daughter for lying to me. I _____ to never do it again.
3. The policeman was going to give me a ticket, but I _____ to give me a warning instead.
4. Larry was afraid to talk to Mary, so I _____ to call her.
5. I was robbed yesterday. A guy with a gun _____ to give him my money.

17.21 Verb + (indirect object) + infinitive direct object

Yet another groups of verbs can be used with or without indirect objects. *Beg* is the word here that might be unfamiliar to your students.

ask	beg	choose	expect	like
need	prefer	prepare	want	wish

sample exercises 22: Complete the sentences with a verb from the list above and the appropriate indirect object if necessary. Make sure the verbs are in the correct tense.

Carlos told me that he _____*expects*_____ to pass the test.

Carlos is a good student, so I don't _____*expect him*_____ to fail the test.

1. I can't do all this work without your help. I _____ to help me.
2. I like coffee more than tea. I _____ to drink coffee.
3. When my wife said she wanted a divorce, I _____ to change her mind.
4. I have a dentist's appointment tomorrow at 3:00, so I _____ my boss if I can leave work early.
5. The manager thinks I'm the best person for the project, so she _____ to do it.

17.22 *be* + adjective + infinitive

Many adjectives can be followed by an infinitive or infinitive phrase:

17.73   I'm proud to say that my son graduated at the top of his class.

Gerunds, Gerund Phrases and Infinitives

17.74   Michael <u>is certain to be chosen</u> for the job.

Lots of good vocabulary here, and the grammar isn't terribly difficult, so I think you know what my advice is. Many of these adjectives your students will already know. I'd focus on *embarrassed, hesitant, likely, eager, proud, reluctant* and *naive.* (Make sure they know how *naive* is pronounced.) If you have any Spanish speakers in your class, it might be interesting, useful (and amusing) to discuss what *embarazada* means in Spanish. *Embarrassed/embarazada* is a good example of a (jargon alert!) *false friend* or *false cognate,* words in two languages—usually English and a (jargon alert!) *Romance language,* a language which evolved from Latin (the most widely spoken of which are Spanish, Portuguese, French, Italian and Romanian), that have a common origin and appear quite similar, and because they look quite similar, it's easy for students to assume the two words have the same meaning, and sometimes they do, but if the words have evolved to have different meanings, this assumption is wrong and can cause confusion.

amazed	angry	ashamed	careful	certain
delighted	determined	difficult	disappointed	disturbed
eager	easy	embarrassed	fortunate	glad
happy	hesitant	likely	lucky	naive
pleased	proud	ready	relieved	reluctant
right	sad	shocked	silly	sorry
stupid	sure	surprised	upset	wrong

Since, for many exercises like these, more than one answer would make sense, and obviously all would be grammatical, I like to give students a choice of three to make them focus on the meanings:

sample exercises 23: Underline the best adjective to complete the sentences.
   Tom's son dropped out of high school. He was (wrong, hesitant, <u>disappointed</u>) that his son dropped out of high school.

   1.   My wife believes that all people are good and honest. I think she's (happy, certain, naive) to believe this.
   2.   I love to go to new restaurants, and a new one opened last week in my town. I'm (eager, fortunate, glad) to go there.
   3.   Mark made a big mistake at work yesterday that will cost his company a lot of money. His boss doesn't know about it, and Mark is (relieved, reluctant, disturbed) to tell him.
   4.   I was worried that I might have cancer, so I was very (shocked, proud, relieved) to learn that I don't.
   5.   Tom hates his job and is looking for a new one. I think that he is (pleased, likely, lucky) to quit his job soon.

17.23 *be* + adjective + present perfect infinitive
In Section 17.22 we saw that many adjectives can be followed by an infinitive or infinitive phrase. Often they are followed by present perfect forms of those infinitive or infinitive phrases:

17.75   He <u>is lucky to have been</u> offered the job.

17.76   I <u>am sorry to have hurt</u> your feelings.

Are you surprised to have learned this? Embarrassed to have forgotten this? Ashamed not to have known this?

Remind your students that infinitives can be negative:

17.77   David <u>was lucky not to have been killed</u> when he fell into the piranha tank at the aquarium.

We haven't talked about reductions for a while, so it's likely you haven't talked about them with your students for a while. In sentences such as these, native speakers would typically barely pronounce or would even omit entirely the *h* in *have.* It's something you might want to model for your students (but remember to tell them not to try to imitate you).

sample exercises 24: Underline the best adjective to complete the sentences.
   I forgot his name. I was (hesitant, <u>embarrassed</u>, eager) to have forgotten his name.

   1.   You hurt my feelings. Are you (sorry, naive, shocked) to have hurt my feelings?
   2.   It was a terrible accident. I was (fortunate, upset, hesitant) not to have been killed.
   3.   John served his country. John is (determined, proud, ready) to have served his country.
   4.   She learned the truth. She's (careful, proud, sad) to have learned the truth.

sample exercises 25: Use a present perfect infinitive to complete the sentences. Some are negative.
   He didn't get the job. He was sorry _____*not to have gotten*_____ the job.

   1.   I saw my teacher at the party. I was surprised _____ my teacher at the party.

2. I wasn't able to help you. I'm sorry _____ able to help you.
3. You were in prison. Are you embarrassed _____ in prison?
4. I wasn't hurt in the accident. I'm lucky _____ in the accident.

17.24 Infinitives as adjectives

By now you should be used to how in grammar just about everything can be everything else in one way or another at one time or another. Maddening, isn't it? Well, infinitives can function as adjectives. Here are two examples you can put on the board:

> After the party, there were a lot of dishes <u>to wash</u>.
> Do you have a lot of work <u>to do</u> today?

I'm sure *to wash* and *to do* don't seem like adjectives to you. They don't to me either, and they won't to your students either, which is why you're not going focus on that but instead focus on practicing forming sentences with infinitives used in this way.

sample exercises 26: Arrange the words in parentheses to complete the sentences with infinitives used as adjectives.
(to, for, list, party, a, stuff, of, buy, long, the) I made _____*a long list of stuff to buy for the party*_____.

1. (gave, homework, do, to, us, a lot of) My teacher _____.
2. (a, to, big, by Wednesday, project, finish) I have _____.
3. (waiting, read, book, have, you're, while, to, a) Do you _____?
4. (Italy, many, in, see, places, to, beautiful) There are _____.
5. (a, say, thing, of, single, to, think) I can't _____.

17.25 Infinitives as adverbs of purpose, *(in order) to* and *so (that)*

Yes, infinitives can be adverbs too—adverbs of purpose. They answer the question *why*. For example,

17.78a Mary: Why are you saving money?
   b Noura: I'm saving money to buy a car.

Of course, the clauses in *I'm saving money to buy a car* could be reversed as *To buy a car, I'm saving money*. That sentence pattern isn't as common, so you might feel it's not worth mentioning. If you do, you could ask your students to rewrite the answers below in the same way. Also, *in order to* could be used in sentences such as these in place of *to*. Also, they could be rephrased with adverb clauses and the subordinating conjunction *so (that)*. All of these sentences have the same meaning:

17.79a I'm saving money <u>to buy</u> a car.
   b = I'm saving money <u>in order to buy</u> a car.
   c = I'm saving money <u>so I can buy</u> a car.
   d = I'm saving money <u>so that I can buy</u> a car.

And of course, they could also be written as:

17.80a <u>To buy</u> a car, I'm saving money.
   b – <u>In order to buy</u> a car, I'm saving money.
   c = <u>So I can buy a car</u>. I'm saving money.
   d = <u>So that I can buy</u> a car. I'm saving money.

but my advice is to focus on the nonfronted patterns. (See Section 16.24 for more about *so (that)*).

sample exercises 27: Answer the questions using complete sentences with infinitives as adverbs of purpose. Use *to* or *in order to*.
Why did you go to the supermarket?
(milk, buy) *I went to the supermarket (in order) to buy milk.*

1. Why did you fly to Oregon?
(my mother, see)
2. Why did Alan call you?
(question, ask)
3. Why did he go to the library?
(book, get)
4. Why did you stop at the gas station?
(gas, buy)
5. Why did she go to the bank?
(a check, cash)

sample exercises 28: Rewrite the sentences using *so* or *so (that)*. Use the word in parentheses.

Lucy is looking for John in order to return his calculator. (can)
Lucy is looking for John so that she can return his calculator.

I'm setting my alarm clock in order not to oversleep. (don't)
I'm setting my alarm clock so I don't oversleep.

1. We are hurrying in order not to miss the bus. (don't)
2. Alan is studying in order to get a good grade on his exam. (will)
3. He's buying a map in order not to get lost when he goes to Istanbul. (doesn't)
4. Mary woke up at 4:30 this morning in order to get to work early. (could)
5. I didn't go to the party in order not to see Michael. (wouldn't)
6. We waited for three hours in order to get tickets for the game. (could)

17.26 Causative verbs

Causative verbs are verbs used to say that the subject of a sentence is the reason, or cause, that somebody did something or that something happened.

There aren't many of them, and all causative verbs are used in ways that are not causative, so this is not about learning new verbs but about learning new ways to use a handful of verbs that are already quite familiar to students:

| get | have | help | let | make |

17.81   I got my hair cut.

17.82   Alan got me to buy him a new computer.

17.83   I had the driver take me to the airport.

17.84   Larry helped me cook dinner.

17.85   My teacher let me leave class.

17.86   My boss made me work on Saturday.

All of these are very common, so definitely spend time on them. The grammar is not terribly difficult. *Get* is a bit tricky, but no big deal.

Anyway, here are causative verbs doing their thing:

▶ *make*
Make means to use power or authority to cause people to do things:

17.87   The robber <u>made</u> me give him my money.

17.88   Sometimes my boss <u>makes</u> me work on Saturday.

▶ *have*
Have means to arrange for someone to do something or to pay someone to do something:

17.89   I <u>had</u> my secretary make a doctor's appointment for me.

17.90   Carlos <u>had</u> a tailor shorten his new pants.

▶ *help*
Help means to help someone do something (duh). It can also be used with either an infinitive with *to* or a (jargon alert!) *bare infinitive*, but don't worry your students with that:

17.91   My son <u>helped</u> us (to) clean the basement.

17.92   Are you going to <u>help</u> me (to) wash these dishes?

(A bare infinitive isn't anything you need to discuss with your students, but because you're dying to know, bare infinitives are basically infinitives used without *to*. Main verbs used with auxiliary verbs are bare infinitives. In *He can swim, swim* is a bare infinitive.)

▶ *let*
Let means to give someone permission for something or to allow something to happen:

17.93   I let my daughter go to the party.

17.94   John lets his clothes get really dirty before he washes them.

▶ **get (someone) to**

Get (someone) to means to persuade someone to do something. Notice that *to* must be used with the verb after *get*:

17.95   The price for the computer was $900, but I got the sales guy to lower the price to $800.

17.96   Mary wanted to stay home and watch TV, but I got her to give me a ride to the store.

Have and *get* are often passive. In the passive, *have* and *get* have the same meaning, but *get* is more common:

17.97a   I talked to a dentist about having my teeth whitened.
     b   = I talked to a dentist about getting my teeth whitened.

17.98a   Carlos had his hair cut.
     b   = Carlos got his hair cut.

I like to explain to my students that the sound of *make* is sometimes too strong. Even when people actually have the power or authority to make other people do things, they often use *have* for a softer and more polite sound:

17.99   The teacher had his students write a three-page essay.

17.100   My daughter made a lot of mistakes in her homework, so I had her do it over.

sample exercises 29: Use *make, have, help, let* or *get* to complete the sentences. There may be more than one good answer for some. Be sure to use the correct verb tense and form.

My sister's car is at the mechanic, so I ____*let*____ her use mine.

1.   I wasn't going to pay more than $25,000 for this car, but the salesperson _____ me to pay $29,000.
2.   I don't want to do it, and there is no way you can _____ me do it!
3.   My boss wasn't happy with my work. I think she's going to _____ me do it over.
4.   I said I was sorry. Now will you please unlock the door and _____ me come inside?
5.   My soup was cold. I _____ the waiter bring me another bowl.
6.   I'm having a problem with my computer. Would you _____ me figure out what the problem is?

sample exercises 30: Change the sentences to passive.
     Gary had somebody fix his flat tire.
     Gary had his flat tire fixed.

1.   Why did you have somebody cut your hair so short?
2.   I need to have somebody take a passport picture.
3.   Do you know where I can get somebody to cash a check?
4.   You have to get somebody to dry clean this sweater.
5.   I'm going to get somebody to repair this watch.

17.27 *too* and *enough* used with infinitives

It's very common to use *too* and *enough* with infinitives. It's also very common for students to confuse *too* and *very*, and it's about time you put a stop to it! Explain to your students that *very* is neutral. It's not good or bad. *Too* is always bad, always a problem. I like to use scenarios like this when I explain this to my students: I'm looking at a huge diamond ring in a jewelry store. The ring costs a million dollars. Is it *too* expensive? Many students might say yes, but then I'll tell them that I'm rich, and that I have a million dollars cash right here in my pocket. I can buy the ring no problem. Yes, the ring is *very* expensive, but for me, it's not *too* expensive. You can also use examples where *too* makes no sense at all. It's impossible to be (philosophical discussions aside) too happy, too beautiful, too rich, etc.

▶ **too**

Too and infinitives are used in these patterns:

▷ **be + too + adjective + (for someone) + infinitive**

17.101   He is too short to play basketball.

17.102   My homework is too difficult for me to figure out.

Gerunds, Gerund Phrases and Infinitives   245

▷ **Verb + *too* + adverb + (*for* someone) + infinitive**

17.103 I <u>drove too slowly to get away</u> from the police.

17.104 She <u>speaks too fast for me to understand</u>.

▶ *enough*
Enough and infinitives are used in these patterns:

▷ **Verb + *enough* + noun + infinitive**

17.105 I <u>saved enough money to buy</u> a car.

17.106 She didn't have <u>enough gas to drive</u> to the beach.

▷ ***be* + adjective + *enough* + infinitive**

17.107 She <u>is tall enough to touch</u> the ceiling.

17.108 The suitcase <u>wasn't big enough to hold</u> all my stuff.

▷ **Verb + adverb + *enough* + (*for* someone) + infinitive**

17.109 Did David <u>run fast enough to get away</u> from the tiger?

17.110 Carlos doesn't <u>speak loudly enough for me to understand</u>.

sample exercises 31: Some of the sentences contain mistakes. Find the incorrect sentences and correct them.

1. This coffee is too hot, but I like hot coffee, so no problem.
2. I don't make money enough to buy a house.
3. She arrived too late to hear the beginning of the speech.
4. Do you have enough chocolate to make a cake?
5. Put on a coat. It's very cold to go outside without a coat on.

sample exercises 32: Use the words in parentheses, *enough* and an infinitive to complete the sentences.
(sick/stay) Sarah wasn't _____*sick enough to stay*_____ home from work.

1. (have/money/buy) Are you sure you _____ this watch? It costs $2,000.
2. (work/hard/graduate) Do you think Mary will _____ from college?
3. (early/say) I didn't get to the airport _____ good bye to her before she left.
4. (big/for everyone/have) The wedding cake wasn't _____ a piece.
5. (tall/be) Linda isn't _____ a model.

sample exercises 33: Use the words in parentheses, *too* and an infinitive to complete the sentences.
(tired/keep) Let's take a break. I'm _____*too tired to keep*_____ working.

1. (busy/talk) Please call me later. I'm _____ to you right now.
2. (badly/stay) The coach told me that I play football _____ on the team.
3. (hot/drink) Be careful. That tea is _____.
4. (long/read) This book is _____ in one week.
5. (tough/cut) This cheap steak is _____.

Chapter 18
Conditionals

Could you...

- explain to a student why the past tense is (seemingly) being used in these sentence about the future?

    a.   I could take you to the mall after dinner if I had a car.

    b.   If I didn't have to work tomorrow, I would go with you to the picnic.

- explain to a student which of these sentences is better?

    c.   If I was you, I'd apologize to her right now.

    d.   If I were you, I'd apologize to her right now.

- explain to a student what's wrong with this sentence?

    e.   If you would have left earlier, you wouldn't have been late for class.

18.1 Introduction

Conditional sentences are an absolutely essential aspect of everyday spoken and written English, yet many ESL students—even advanced ESL students—never really come close to mastering them. Even though, in terms of sentence structure, they're much less difficult than much of what we've discussed already, many students (and maybe their teachers too), are flummoxed because they don't understand some basic concepts that are essential to understanding conditional sentences. It's absolutely worth the effort for your students and worth budgeting time for.

18.2 Important concepts

So before we plunge into conditionals, it would be very helpful to focus on some basic concepts first. These are for your benefit. I'm not recommending that you go over all of this with your students—just things for you to be aware of that will make your job easier.

▶ Important concept 1: possible, etc. vs. impossible, etc.

A concept that is essential for your students to understand is the difference between talking about something that is really <u>possible</u>—maybe not certain or even probable—but at least possible as opposed to something that is <u>impossible</u>, hypothetical or at least very unlikely. This idea is absolutely vital to understanding conditional sentences. You don't need to make a big deal out of this right off before you even begin, but it'll come up soon, so get ready. (Of course, opinions regarding whether something is possible, etc., or impossible, etc., can vary from person to person.)

▶ Important concept 2: present = future

Another concept to be aware of is that grammarwise, no distinction is made between the present and the future.
One second from now is the future, after all, so we'll talk about the past and we'll talk about the present/future.

▶ Important concept 3: the past is not the past

Something that will strike your students as pretty weird is that with conditional sentences we seem to use the past tense when we're not talking about the past. In fact, they will think, sometimes we seem to use the past tense to talk about the future. How weird is that? What you must understand, and what your students need to accept and be comfortable with even if they don't really understand, is that what appears to be the past tense is not the past tense at all. It's the (jargon alert!) *past subjunctive*. The past subjunctive, though it's entirely different from the past tense, is identical in form to the (jargon alert!) *past indicative*. The past subjunctive is used when the speaker or writer believes something is contrary to fact, impossible, very unlikely, etc. We'll talk more about that later (and the *past perfect subjunctive* too!), but the main thing you need to keep in mind to help your students understand is that what may look like the past tense that you and your students are familiar with isn't—it's something different, and as long as your students can do it, they don't need to understand it. What I usually do is tell students that it's not the past tense but another way to use *the form of* the past tense. That works just fine. I never speak of the subjunctive with my students.

▶ Important concept 4: familiar sentence structure

We'll be focusing primarily on sentences that follow these patterns:

> If <u>blah, blah, blah</u>, yada, yada, yada.

> Yada, yada, yada <u>if blah, blah, blah</u>.

Do they look familiar? They should because they're what we saw when we studied adverb clauses—a dependent clause and a main clause following this pattern (notice the comma):

> dependent clause, + independent clause

or this pattern:

> independent clause + dependent clause

The conditional sentences that we'll be focusing on in this chapter are made up of an *if*-clause and a result clause. Well, guess what. An if-clause is a type of adverb clause. *If* is a subordinating conjunction, and the *if*-clause is a dependent adverb clause. The result clause is an independent clause—it could make sense alone without the *if*-clause stuck to it. You might want to review Figure 16.20 and Appendix E.

▶ **Important concept 5: one clause tense doesn't determine the tense of another**
We'll be discussing both *if*-clauses and result clauses at great length (and other stuff at medium length), and a lot of it will involve the tense of those clauses. Do not get the idea that the tense of one clause determines the tense of the other clause. All that matters is what's logical, and as you'll see, that will allow for a lot of freedom for clauses to wander around all over the place tensewise.

▶ **Important concept 6: meanings of *condition* and *conditional***
And finally, you need to make very sure your students understand the meanings of *condition* and *conditional,* which they'll be hearing again and again. Tell them that *conditional* is the adjective form of the noun *condition,* and then ask them what condition means. I guarantee you, most of your students will answer something like *My car is in good condition.* That's not wrong, but you'll need to teach them the meaning of condition that we're going to be discussing in this chapter and do so without a conditional sentence, which they haven't studied yet. (Though by now they'll likely already have some idea what it's all about. They can't have gotten this far without having heard plenty of conditional sentences already, but don't assume anything!) It's not difficult to get the basic idea across. What I do is pick a student and say something like this:

> I asked Linda here to give me a ride to the airport, and she said, "Sure, but the airport is very far. You have to give me $5.00 for gas. No $5.00, no ride. Give me $5.00, no problem, let's go."

That, I tell my students, is a condition—then we get out the bilingual dictionaries.

18.3 Zero conditionals: always true
What's called the zero conditional is used to talk about something that's <u>always</u> true—not just one time but always:

18.1a   If I have a question, I ask my teacher.

18.2a   Sarah gets sleepy whenever she eats a big lunch.

18.3a   When my wife drinks coffee, she has trouble sleeping.

In fact, *always* could be inserted into all of these sentences:

18.1b   If I have a question, I <u>always</u> ask my teacher.

18.2b   Sarah <u>always</u> gets sleepy whenever she eats a big lunch.

18.3b   When my wife drinks coffee, she <u>always</u> has trouble sleeping.

Zero conditional sentences are used with *if, when, whenever* and *every time.* There is no difference in meaning:

18.4a   <u>If</u> I eat shrimp, I get sick.

   b   = <u>When</u> I eat shrimp, I get sick.

   c   = <u>Whenever</u> I eat shrimp, I get sick.

   d   = <u>Every time</u> I eat shrimp, I get sick.

In zero conditional sentences, the tense of <u>both</u> clauses is present. That might not seem particularly noteworthy now, but you'll soon see that it is, so emphasize this to your students. Put something like this on the board:

> If I <u>eat</u> shrimp,   I <u>get</u> sick.
> present tense   present tense

You can't remind your students enough that the clauses can be reversed. You might want to give them an example or two of this:

> <u>If I have a question</u>, I ask my teacher.
> = I ask my teacher <u>if I have a question</u>.

sample exercises 1: Make zero conditional sentences with the words in parentheses. Be careful about punctuation.

> I have a car problem. I call my brother-in-law. (if)
> *If I have a car problem, I call my brother-in-law.*
>
> Her boss gets mad. She is late for work. (when)
> *Her boss gets mad when she is late for work.*

1. I don't drink coffee in the morning. I get a headache. (if)
2. My brother visits. He sleeps on the sofa. (whenever)
3. I don't get enough sleep. I feel awful the next day. (when)
4. I make a lot of noise. My neighbors get mad. (if)
5. The baby wakes up. The phone rings. (every time)

18.4 First conditional: true in the present or in the future

First conditional sentences are about something that is true, real or possible now or in the future (Remember that we make no distinction grammarwise between the two in conditional sentences.) What makes this different from the zero conditional is that we are <u>not</u> talking about <u>always</u> but rather a specific time (maybe stated or maybe understood but not stated):

18.5   If you give me a 10% discount, I will buy it.

18.6   You might not pass your English test next week if you don't study.

Only *if* is used—no *when, whenever* or *every time*.

In first conditional sentences, the tense of the *if*-clause is present and the result clause contains a modal. The modal is usually *will*, but *should, ought to, must, may, might, can, have to, have got to* and *be going to* are also possible:

18.7   If he <u>needs</u> help with his homework, my sister <u>will help</u> him.
       present tense   modal + verb

A very common mistake is to use *will* in the *if*-clause:

18.8   If he <u>will need</u> help with his homework, my sister <u>will help</u> him.

so be on guard for that.

Don't confuse your students by making a big deal out of there not being any difference between the present and future. It's intuitive and not a problem. It's clear from the context and from time reference language what is meant.

Give your students examples of some negative conditionals (zero and first). Either clause or both clauses can be negative:

18.9   When I <u>don't get</u> enough sleep, I <u>can't stay</u> awake in class.

18.10   If he <u>doesn't pass</u> the chemistry final exam, he <u>won't graduate</u> from high school.

sample exercises 2: Make first conditional sentences with *will* and the words in parentheses.

> Michael (visit) _____*will visit*_____ his sister if he (go) _____*goes*_____ to Chicago.
>
> If he (not, apologize) _*doesn't apologize*_, I (not, speak) _____*won't speak*_____ to him again.
>
> I (not, be) _____*won't be*_____ happy if you (be) _____*are late*_____.

1. Paris (be) _____ very crowded if you (go) _____ there in July.
2. I (not, buy) _____ the house if they (not, lower) _____ the price.
3. If I (have) _____ time, I (help) _____ you after dinner.
4. I (not, make) _____ a cake tonight if I (not, have) _____ enough eggs.
5. If she (not, be) _____ here tomorrow, we (cancel) _____ the meeting.

sample exercises 3: Make first conditional sentences with the words in parentheses.

> If my boss (tell) _____*tells*_____ me to work late, I (might, be) _____*might be*_____ late for dinner.
>
> This is a very small project. It (should, not, take) _*shouldn't take*_ too long if you (not, make) _____*don't make*_____ any mistakes.

1. Francesca (ought to, get) _____ all of her math homework done in the afternoon if she (want) _____ to go to the mall with her friends tonight.
2. If you (visit) _____ New York City, you (should, not, miss) _____ the Metropolitan Museum of Art.
3. If I (be) _____ too busy, I (may, not, be) _____ able to come to your party.
4. I feel sick. I (might, not, go) _____ to work tomorrow if I (not, feel) _____ better.
5. Mark's house (should, be) _____ right around the next corner if I (be) _____ reading this map correctly.

18.5 Second conditional: not true in the present or in the future

Second conditionals is when we get into the whole subjunctive/not the past for unreal, imaginary, hypothetical situations thing I talked about in the introduction to this chapter. I like to introduce the second conditional by choosing a student and then describing two scenarios—the first where, let's say Mary, tells me that she wants to ask me a question. I look at Mary and say "OK, what's your question Mary? If I know the answer, I will tell you," and then I write this on the board:

> If I <u>know</u> the answer, I <u>will</u> tell you.

Next, in the second scenario, I explain that Mary has already asked me her question and that, unbelievably, I don't know the answer. Looking at Mary, I say "That's a difficult question, Mary. I want to tell you the answer, but I don't know the answer. If I knew the answer, I would tell you," and then I write this on the board:

> If I <u>knew</u> the answer, I <u>would</u> tell you.

Now I ask the students to look at the two sentences on the board, and I ask them to tell me what's different about them. They'll easily see what's different, of course, but why are they different? I'll ask them "Why has the second sentence changed? Am I talking about the past?" If you do the same, make sure your students know that the answer is <u>no</u>, you are <u>not</u> talking about the past, and then make a BIG GIANT DEAL of explaining that in conditional sentences, when we are talking about something that is not true, that is not real, that is (probably) not possible or that is only imaginary, we use the <u>form</u> of the past. Keep repeating that it is the <u>form</u> of the past, but it <u>is not</u> the past—it's a <u>different way</u> to use the <u>form</u> of the past. That's what I do. I never use the term *subjunctive,* and I don't suggest that you do, but if you have students who are really bright and can handle it, go for it.

Explain that second conditionals are used with *if* and a verb in the form of the past, and a result clause with a modal—usually *would* or *could* but *might* is common too. There are exceptions, as we'll see later, but keep it simple for now—*would, could* or *might*.

Before getting into exercises, you'll want to give your students a number of examples, including several negative examples, and discuss some things: why we seemingly violate the rules of basic grammar and say *If were you…* instead of *If I was you…* and just what exactly is the difference between *would* and *could.* I would do them in just that order: one, examples—some negative and some with *be* in the result clause; two, a *was/were* discussion and finally, a *would/could* discussion. Here are some examples. Remind them again that the clauses can be reversed. Also, remind them that *would* is often contracted to *'d.* Here are some good examples to put on the board and discuss with your students:

> I could buy a new car if I had enough money.
> If I knew her telephone number, I would call her.
> He'd go with us to the movie if he didn't have to work.
> If Carlos asked me for help, I'd be happy to help him.
> Sarah wouldn't be sick all the time if she exercised more and didn't eat so much junk food.

Now, ask them to look at these examples and underline as shown:

> I'd make a lot of changes if <u>I were</u> the president of this country.
> He'd help me if <u>he weren't</u> so busy.
> If <u>I were</u> you, I would study more and watch TV less.

Now, ask your students if we normally say *I were* or *he weren't*? Would we native speakers say, for example, *I were sick yesterday*? or *He were working*? Of course we wouldn't. Explain to your students that in <u>conditional</u> sentences, however, in the very best English, we use <u>only</u> were and <u>never</u> was. Leave it at that. Resist the temptation to teach them what the subjunctive is all about—there's no need, but mention that a lot of native speakers don't understand any of this, so they will hear *was.* They should try to remember to say *were,* but if they don't, it's not the worst mistake in the world. (And what is the worst mistake in the world?)

And make sure your students don't say *If I would be…*, *If I would go*, etc. This is a common mistake.

Also, make sure your students understand that *could* is about <u>possibilities</u> only but that *would* is about <u>intention</u>, what you would <u>actually</u> do. And good luck trying to define *would* without using *would*. I illustrate the difference with something like this, emphasizing *could* and *would*: "If I won a million dollars in the lottery, I <u>could</u> buy a million candy bars, but I <u>would</u> put the money in the bank."

sample exercises 4: Make second conditional sentences with the words in parentheses. Decide which is better—*would* or *could*. Sometimes both *would* and *could* are possible. Be ready to explain your answer.

I want to answer your question, but I don't know the answer. If I (know) _____*knew*_____ the answer, I (tell) _____*would tell*_____ you.

He speaks English. If he (not, speak) _____*didn't speak*_____ English, he (not, be) _____*couldn't be*_____ an English teacher.

1. I don't have a car. I (get to) _____ work faster if I (have) _____ one.
2. Alan isn't here. I (ask) _____ him to help me if he (be) _____ here.
3. I want to go to the picnic with you, but I have to work today. If I (not, have) _____ to work today, I (go) _____ to the picnic with you.
4. I'm really busy. If I (not, be) _____ so busy, I (help) _____ you.
5. Sarah and Mary have visas. If they (not, have) _____ visas, they (not, enter) _____ this country.
6. Rosa is very tired. If she (not, be) _____ so tired, I'm sure she (be) _____ happy to help you.

sample exercises 5: Make zero, first or second conditional sentences with the words in parentheses. If you think a modal verb is necessary, use the one you think is best. Be ready to explain your answer.

1. My best friend lives in Los Angeles, and I visit her every time I travel there. If I (be) _____ in L.A., I always (visit) _____ her.
2. Sam might come for dinner tonight. If he (come) _____, we (have) _____ fried chicken for dinner.
3. Francesca usually doesn't have any problem with her homework, but when she (have) _____ a problem, she (ask) _____ her father for help.
4. Linda has a lot of homework. She says she (stay) _____ home tonight if she (not, finish) _____ it.
5. John is tall, so he can reach the books on the top shelf of the bookcase. He (not, reach) _____ them if he (not, be) _____ so tall.
6. You are not rich, so you have to work, but if you (be) _____ rich and (not, have) _____ to work, what (do) _____ you _____ with your time?

18.6 Second conditional with past result clauses

Second conditional sentences can have past result clauses. The basic idea is that if something were true, possible, probable, etc., now (as well as in the past), something about the past would have been different or would have happened differently. The result clause is usually formed with *would have* or *could have*, but other modals are possible—especially *might have*. (But not *may have*! See Section 12.21 if you're wondering why.) Compare these two sentences:

18.11　My Chinese neighbors are talking now. If I spoke Chinese, I <u>could understand</u> them.

18.12　My German neighbors were talking yesterday. If I spoke German, I <u>could have understood</u> them.

Here are some more examples. Always remember to include some negative examples and examples with *be*. Remind your students that the contraction *mightn't* is almost never used:

18.13　I <u>would have gone</u> to the Japanese restaurant with you if I didn't hate sushi.

18.14　If Mary didn't have rich parents, she <u>couldn't have gone</u> to Stanford.

18.15　She <u>wouldn't have</u> said those crazy things if she didn't have mental problems.

18.16　If I liked country music, I <u>would have gone</u> with them to the concert last weekend.

18.17　If I didn't have car problems, I <u>wouldn't have taken</u> a taxi to work, and I <u>would have saved</u> a lot of money.

18.18　She <u>might not have had</u> an accident if she weren't always talking on her cell phone when she drives.

18.19   If you weren't such a doofus, you <u>wouldn't have made</u> such a complete idiot of yourself at the party last night and everyone wouldn't be mad as hell at you now!

It would also be a very good idea to remind your students that native speakers reduce *would have, could have* and *might have* to *woulda, coulda* and *mighta*. Be sure they understand that you're telling them this to help them with their listening and not their speaking—better to speak clearly than to try to imitate native speakers which will only result in their being less clear.

sample exercises 6: Complete the sentences with the verbs in parentheses. Use the modals *would, could* and *might*. There may be more than one good answer for some. Be ready to explain your answer.

If I didn't have financial problems myself, I (give) _____*would have given*_____ you enough money to pay your medical bills last year, and I (give) _____*would give*_____ Linda the money she needs now.

1. If I were you, I (not, be) _____ happy about getting an F in English last semester, and
2. I (not, be) _____ happy about the D you got on the exam today.
3. We (go) _____ to our daughter's wedding last month if it weren't so expensive to fly to Australia from here.
4. Mark (not, be) _____ able to communicate so easily with people in Korea last year if he didn't speak Korean so well.
5. If Lucy weren't a doctor, _____ she (know) _____ what to do when her husband had a heart attack?
6. I already told you I really want to have dinner at your mother's house! If I didn't want to have dinner at your mother's, I (not, say) _____ that I do.

18.7 *were to* used for hypothetical future events

If I were to tell you that you will someday find your way out of this maze we call English grammar, would you believe me?

If I were to tell you that

18.20   If I told…

can be rephrased as

18.21   If I were to tell…

would you be absolutely fascinated? Yes? Good, then I'll continue. Second conditionals can sometimes be rephrased using the *were to* + infinitive pattern. It doesn't make sense for every second conditional. It's generally used for hypothetical future events. Here are some examples:

18.22a   If I <u>won</u> the lottery, I would pay off my mortgage.
    b   = If I <u>were to win</u> the lottery, I would pay off my mortgage.

18.23a   If we <u>sold</u> this house, I wonder how much we could get for it.
    b   = If we <u>were to sell</u> this house, I wonder how much we could get for it.

18.24a   If you <u>went</u> back to school, what would you study?
    b   = If you <u>were to go</u> back to school, what would you study?

In case you're wondering, although this might look like a conditional form of the phrasal modal *be to* that we talked about in Section 12.27, it isn't. That was about real plans, arrangements, requirements, expectations, etc. This is about unreal, hypothetical future events or situations.

And once again, we come to this question: are you going to teach this to your students?, and once again, my answer is a definite maybe. It depends on their level and their needs. (But never what's on the test. No good teacher EVER thinks about that.)

sample exercises 7: Change these sentences as in the example.

If I told my boss what I really think of him, do you think he'd fire me?
If I were to tell my boss what I really think of him, do you think he'd fire me?

1. If this machine broke down, I wouldn't know how to fix it.
2. If she had quintuplets, her husband would have a heart attack.
3. If I offered you a 15% discount, would you say yes?
4. If you touched that wire, you'd be killed instantly.
5. If we raised our prices, how much do you think our sales would fall?

18.8 Third conditional: not true in the past

Now we're getting to the good stuff—really useful grammar that we native speakers use every day but that, unfortunately, few ESL students ever get to or if they do, never come close to mastering. I've always thought of the third conditional as being an accurate gauge of an advanced ESL student's true level—a goal that, if attained, is a sign of a high level of fluency and an achievement to be proud of. I'm not sure it really makes sense to place so much importance on it, but I do because of its being very common, essential and fairly difficult. With much of the grammar that we've studied so far, an ESL student could actually find various ways to get his or her meaning across in some other way—without using that grammar, but for the meaning conveyed by the third conditional, there really is no other good way to do it.

Here's what it's all about: third conditional sentences are about something that was not true, that was not real, that was not possible or that was only imaginary <u>in the past</u>. The *if*-clause is formed with the (jargon alert!) *past perfect subjunctive* (not that you're going to confuse your students with that term) which boils down to *had* + past participle. The result clause is usually made up of *would, could* or *might* + *have* + past participle (but we'll see some exceptions later—leave it at that for now).

But before putting the formula on the board, which you definitely should do, I recommend doing what I do to demonstrate the third conditional. Remember the scenario I described in Section 18.5 where Mary asked me a question that I didn't know the answer to? What I'll do is remind the students of this conversation. I'll repeat it but with a few reminders inserted that this is the present. Looking at Mary, I'll say "Oh, that's a difficult question, Mary. I want to tell you the answer now, but I don't know the answer. If I knew the answer, I would tell you," and then I write this on the board:

> If I <u>knew</u> the answer, I <u>would</u> tell you.

Then I make a BIG GIANT DEAL of telling the students that it's now one day later, that this same conversation I had with Mary was yesterday, in the past. Now I'm talking to Mary about the conversation I had with her yesterday. I look at Mary say "Yesterday, you asked me a difficult question, but I didn't know the answer. I wanted to tell you the answer, but I didn't know the answer. If I had known the answer, I would have told you," and then I write this on the board:

> If I <u>had known</u> the answer, I <u>would have</u> told you.

Now I ask students to look at the two sentences on the board, and I ask them to tell me what's different about these sentences. Of course they'll easily see what, but why? I'll ask them "Why has the second sentence changed?" Unlike before, we really are talking about the past, so the main thing is to teach them that the reason the second sentence has changed is for that reason: we *are* talking about the past—an unreal, untrue, etc., situation in the past. Now it's formula time.

Write the formula for the third conditional under the example so that it looks like this:

> If   I   <u>had known</u>   the answer,   I   <u>would have told</u>   you.
> *had* + past participle   +   *would/could/might* + *have* + past participle

Here are some more examples to write on the board:

> If we <u>had left</u> his house 15 minutes earlier, we <u>wouldn't have missed</u> the start of the movie.
> If he <u>hadn't spent</u> all his time watching TV, he <u>could have gotten</u> better grades.
> If I <u>had had</u> more money, I <u>would have bought</u> a new car instead of a used car.

Had had is going to look pretty odd to your students. You'll have to explain it sooner or later, so why not now?

You should give them an example with *be* too:

> If Carlos <u>had been</u> there, he <u>might have been</u> able to help.

Be careful you don't inadvertently teach your students a very common mistake made by native speakers. Many native speakers make a grammatical error when forming third conditional *if*-clauses. They say *would have* instead of *had*. This is common, but it is not correct. Be careful! This is one of the secret ways we grammarians can spot a person who is not one of us. Don't let it happen to you!

> 18.25a   wrong: If you <u>would have left</u> earlier, you wouldn't have been late for class.
> b   right: If you <u>had left</u> earlier, you wouldn't have been late for class.

In addition to reminding your students about *woulda, coulda* and *mighta,* you should also model how *had* is often contracted to *'d* and tell your students that when we native speakers talk fast, *'d* is almost inaudible (impossible to hear). Here are some examples that you could use. Remember the technique I recommended several hundred pages ago—repeat the sentences slowly, then moderately fast then just as a native speaker would without any concession to the listener—full reduced. Do this a few times to give your students a lot of listening practice:

18.26   If he'd known you were coming, he <u>woulda</u> ordered pizza.

18.27   If we'd studied more, we <u>mighta</u> passed the test.

18.28   If I'd had enough money, I <u>coulda</u> bought it.

sample exercises 8: Change the second conditional sentences to third conditional sentences.

If my sister were here, I would show her my new car.

If my sister had been here, I would have shown her my new car.

We couldn't figure out these math problems if we didn't have this calculator.

We couldn't have figured out these math problems if we hadn't had this calculator.

1. If we went to Beijing, we might go to the Forbidden City.
2. Sarah could make some cookies if she had enough chocolate.
3. I would help her if she asked me.
4. If I saw another student cheating on the test, I wouldn't tell the teacher.
5. I couldn't see anything if I didn't have my glasses.
6. If you were sick, would you stay home from work?

sample exercises 9: Make first, second or third conditional sentences with the words in parentheses and modals that you think are correct.

If the supermarket (not, be) _____*hadn't been*_____ closed when we got there, we could have gotten something to make for dinner tonight.

I can't ask Rosa because she isn't here. If she were here, I (ask) _____*could ask*_____ her.

1. If I (need) _____ a ride to the mall, I'd ask my neighbor.
2. If you (not, waste) _____ your time goofing around, you could have gotten all your work done.
3. You (not, be) _____ late to the meeting yesterday if you'd left earlier.
4. Noura might come over tonight if she (have) _____ enough time.
5. If your car (be) _____ stolen, would your insurance company pay for a new one?
6. I'd go with you to the soccer game tomorrow if I (not, have) _____ to work.
7. Carlos wouldn't have burned dinner if he (not, fall) _____ asleep on the sofa after he put it in the oven.
8. Ali might visit tomorrow. If he (be) _____ here, ask him for some advice about your problem.
9. The movie we saw last night was terrible. You (not, like) _____ it if you had gone with us.

18.9 Third conditional with present result clauses

In the previous section we focused on third conditionals with a past result clause. Now, how about third conditionals with present result clauses? How exciting is that? The idea is that if something about the past had been different or happened differently, something *would, could* or *might* be different in the present. Compare these two sentences:

18.29a   Mark didn't finish high school. If he had finished high school, he <u>could have gotten</u> a better job.
    b   Mark didn't finish high school. If he had finished high school, he <u>could get</u> a better job now.

Here are some more examples:

18.30   If you hadn't spent all your money yesterday, you <u>would have</u> enough money now.

18.31   She <u>might believe</u> you if you hadn't lied to her before.

18.32   If you'd done what I told you, you <u>wouldn't be</u> in this mess now.

18.33   We'd be lying on the beach in Cancun now if my husband <u>hadn't lost</u> our passports.

18.34   Mark <u>would still have</u> his job if he hadn't been so rude to his boss.

18.35   If you had taken Maple Street like I told you, we <u>wouldn't be</u> stuck in this traffic.

sample exercises 10: Complete the sentences with the verbs in parentheses. Use the modals *would, could* and *might.* There may be more than one good answer for some. Be ready to explain your answer.

If Sarah hadn't gone to Canada last week, she (be) _____*would have been*_____ at the meeting yesterday, and she (be) _____*would be*_____ at the meeting tomorrow.

1. If Maria could speak English better, she (understand) _____ what everybody at the party was

saying last night, and she (understand) _____ what we are talking about now.

2. If I'd studied more last week, I (know) _____ the answers to yesterday's quiz, and I (know) _____ the answers to the homework I'm doing now.

3. If Sam had read my email last week, he (not, done) _____ everything wrong, and the boss (not, be) _____ angry now.

4. Ali wanted to be here. He (come) _____ if he didn't have to pick up Noura at the airport today.

5. If you had gotten gas yesterday as I suggested, you (not, run out of) _____ gas, and we (not, be) _____ sitting here now in this car on the side of the road.

6. If Linda had been paying attention yesterday, she (understand) _____ what we were talking about at the meeting, and she (not, be) _____ totally confused about what to do now.

7. Somebody stole my car. If I hadn't left it unlocked, it (not, be) _____ stolen, and I (not, be) _____ standing here on the corner right now waiting for the bus.

18.10 Implied conditionals

Often, especially in conversation, conditionals are *implied*: the result clause is stated, but the *if*-clause is not. We native speakers do this all the time without realizing it. Could this be explained as ellipsis at work? Yep. *I would like…* is an example of an implied conditional. The best way to illustrate this to students is to give them examples of conversations:

| 18.36a | Sam: | Was Mark at the game yesterday? |
| b | Dave: | Mark would have been there, but he had to work. |

| 18.37a | John: | I'm thinking about quitting my job. |
| b | Alan: | Are you crazy? That's not a good idea. I wouldn't do that. |

| 18.38a | Sarah: | Let's go the beach. |
| b | Noura: | What a great idea! I'd love to go to the beach. |

| 18.39a | Ali: | Do you understand now? |
| b | Lucy: | Thanks, I couldn't have done it without you. |

| 18.40a | Waiter: | May I take your order? |
| b | Tom: | Yes, I'd like a cheeseburger and a cup of coffee. |

| 18.41a | Rosa: | Mary was at my house yesterday, and now I can't find my gold necklace. I think she stole it. |
| b | Larry: | That's impossible. I know Mary. She would never have done that. |

Ask the students to supply the implied *if*-clause. Do them one at a time. They probably will be confused at first, so you'll likely have to help them with the first one—maybe all of them. Here are the same conversations with the implied *if*-clauses:

18.42a	Sam:	Was Mark at the game yesterday?
b	Dave:	Mark would have been there, but he had to work.
c		= Mark would have been there [if he hadn't had to work].

18.43a	John:	I'm thinking about quitting my job.
b	Alan:	Are you crazy? That's not a good idea. I wouldn't do that.
c		= Are you crazy? That's not a good idea. I wouldn't do that [if I were you].

18.44a	Sarah:	Let's go the beach.
b	Noura:	What a great idea! I'd love to go to the beach.
c		= What a great idea! I'd love to go to the beach [if we went to the beach].

18.45a	Ali:	OK, do you understand now?
b	Lucy:	Thanks, I couldn't have done it without you.
c		= Thanks, I couldn't have done it without you [if you hadn't helped me].

18.46a	Waiter:	May I take your order?
b	Tom:	Yes, I'd like a cheeseburger and a cup of coffee.
c		= Yes, I'd like a cheeseburger and a cup of coffee [if I had a cheeseburger and a cup of coffee].

18.47a	Rosa:	Mary was at my house yesterday, and now I can't find my gold necklace. I think Mary stole it.
b	Larry:	That's impossible. I know Mary. She would never have done that.
c		= That's impossible. I know Mary. She would never have done that [if she had had the chance to do that].

This may seem somewhat artificial because no one ever has to actually supply an implied conditional. The idea is that becoming familiar with the concept of implied conditionals will help you to teach conditionals and help your students to understand them.

sample exercises 11: Rewrite the sentences to complete the *if*-clauses.

1. A: Can I borrow some money?
   B: I'd be happy to, but I'm totally broke.
   = I'd be happy to, if _____ *I weren't totally broke* _____.

2. A: Larry's not here. He was a little sick yesterday. Do you think he's going to stay home?
   B: No, he'd have called by now. He should be here soon.
   = No, he'd have called by now if _____. He should be here soon.

3. A: Is Sofia going to the movie?
   B: Sofia would go, but she has a lot of homework to do.
   = Sofia would go if _____.

   A: Have you called Carlos?
   B: I would have called him, but my cell phone battery's dead.
   = I would have called him if _____.

4. A: I have to go to school now, but Sarah might come while I'm gone. She left her book here last night.
   B: No problem. I'll give it to her.
   = I'll give it to her if _____.

5. A: We're going camping next week. Do you want to come with us?
   B: I would, but I promised my mother I'd visit her.
   = I would if _____.

6. A: You could have seen Michael, but you weren't here. What happened?
   B: Yes, I know. I could have, but I forgot he was coming.
   = Yes, I know. I could have if _____.

7. A: Are you going to have lunch with us?
   B: I would, but I have a doctor's appointment.
   = I would if _____.

18.11 Conditional sentence pattern practice

OK, we've covered all the basic uses of the conditional that use the dependent clause, + independent clause and independent + dependent clause patterns (almost—we'll talk about a few grandiloquent variations in a few pages). Now would be a good time to give your students a little more practice with those patterns—practice with continuous, passive, interrogative (questions), imperative and negative conditional sentences. All of these patterns are very common, as you will see. We native speakers use them every day. They're second nature to us, but beyond the abilities of most ESL students. Well, what are you gonna do about it!

My rationale here is that ESL grammar books and ESL teachers tend to focus on simple, uncomplicated grammar patterns because they're easy to teach. That's OK for starters, but grammar, like life (as you may have noticed), gets complicated. I think it's a good idea to give your students practice with those complications.

▶ Continuous, passive, interrogative, imperative conditional sentences

Here are examples of each. No new grammar here, but big chunks of grammar that we've talked about in previous lessons plugged into conditional sentences. Your students will already have seen some examples of some of these, but it's a good idea to give them more practice.

▷ Continuous

18.48 If I hadn't been taking a shower when you called, I could have heard the telephone ring.

18.49 If my husband made more money, we wouldn't be living in this dump.

▷ Passive

18.50 If I were chosen to be the new manager, I would have to work longer hours.

18.51 If you leave your keys in your car, it might be stolen.

▷ **Interrogative**

18.52 If I asked you to lend me $5,000, would you give it to me?

18.53 If you were rich, what would you buy?

▷ **Imperative**

18.54 If you go out, don't forget to close the door.

18.55 If you need help, tell me.

sample exercises 12: Complete the sentences.

You were not listening. You don't know what's going on.

If you _____*had been listening*_____, you'd _____*know what's going on*_____.

1. You might see Mary today. I want you to give her this bag of cookies.
    If you _____, _____.
2. Because I was studying, I wasn't listening to the radio.
    If I _____, I _____.
3. You might go to Mexico City. Go to the museum there.
    If you _____, _____.
4. We don't have to be quiet because the baby isn't sleeping.
    If the baby _____, we _____.
5. Sarah might be fired. She can easily find another job.
    If Sarah _____, she _____.
6. It didn't snow a lot yesterday. School wasn't canceled.
    If it _____, school _____.

sample exercises 13: Complete the questions.

A: If you could live anywhere in the world, _____*where would you live*_____?
B: *I would live in Paris.*

1. A: If you knew the answer, _____?
    B: Yes, I would tell you.
2. A: If Mary had accepted the job offer, _____?
    B: Her salary would have been $70,000.
3. A: If Lucy had been looking out the window, _____?
    B: No, she couldn't have seen the accident.
4. A: If you get married someday, _____?
    B: I'd like to have three children.
5. A: If you had had a problem, _____, right?
    B: Yes, you're right. I wouldn't have known what to do.

▶ **Negative conditional sentence practice**

The whole using-the-past-when-we're-not-talking-about-the-past idea is hard enough for students, and when we add negative to that, it's even harder. Either or both clauses in a conditional sentence can be negative. Your students have already seen that, but it's a good idea for them to get some additional practice:

▷ **Negative zero conditional**

18.56 Whenever our father isn't in a good mood, we don't talk to him.

18.57 When my boss doesn't let me leave at 2:30, I'm not home when my kids get home from school.

▷ **Negative first conditional**

18.58 If she isn't there when I get there, I won't wait for her.

18.59 If you don't hurry, you won't be there when your class starts.

▷ **Negative second conditional**

18.60 If he weren't so sick, he wouldn't take so much medicine.

Conditionals   257

18.61   If I didn't speak Swedish, I wouldn't be able to talk to Uncle Erik.

▷ **Negative third conditional**

18.62   If Jack hadn't been driving so fast, he wouldn't have run into that tree.

18.63   If Rosa hadn't forgotten her keys, she wouldn't have been locked out of her house.

sample exercises 14: Complete the zero conditional sentences with the words in parentheses.
If Mary's favorite stylist (not, be) _____*isn't*_____ working when she goes to the salon, she (not, let) _____*doesn't let*_____ anyone else cut her hair.

1.   When the kids (not, have) _____ a lot of homework, they play in the backyard or watch TV.
2.   If Mary (not, be) _____ studying, we (not, have to) _____ worry about making noise.
3.   Whenever Alan (not, call) _____ his mother to tell her where he is, she gets worried.
4.   If people (not, be) _____ on the guest list, we (not, allow) _____ them to enter the club.
5.   If my car (not, start) _____, there (not, be) _____ any other way for me to get to work.

sample exercises 15: Complete the first conditional sentences with the words in parentheses. Use *will* if it is necessary.
If you (not, follow) _____*don't follow*_____ my instructions, I (not, be) _____*won't be*_____ responsible if you're hurt.

1.   If you (not, be) _____ careful, you'll make a mistake.
2.   If Larry's at the party, I (not, talk) _____ to him.
3.   If they (not, have) _____ enough money, I'll lend it to them.
4.   We (not, go) _____ to the beach if it (not, be) _____ warm tomorrow.
5.   If you (not, buy) _____ at least 10 pizzas, there (not, be) _____ enough for everybody.

sample exercises 16: Complete the second conditional sentences with the words in parentheses. Use *would* if it is necessary.
If Jack (not, cheat on) _____*didn't cheat on*_____ his exams, he (not, be) _____*didn't cheat on*_____ able to pass any of his college classes.

1.   If you (not, be) _____ a teacher, what would you like to be?
2.   That's a bad idea. I (not, do) _____ that if I were you.
3.   If you (not, eat) _____ so much, you (not, be) _____ overweight.
4.   If the teacher (not, be) _____ so boring, the students (not, fall) _____ asleep in class.
5.   If she (not, stay out) _____ all night partying, she (not, be) _____ so sleepy at work.

sample exercises 17: Complete the third conditional sentences with the words in parentheses. Use *would have* if it is necessary.
If Jack (not, cheat on) _____*hadn't cheated on*_____ his exams, he (not, be) _____*wouldn't have been*_____ able to pass any of his high school classes.

1.   If I (not, be) _____ hiding in the closet, her husband would have found me.
2.   If she'd been more polite, I (not, get) _____ so angry.
3.   If my car (not, be) _____ at the mechanic, I (not, be) _____ driving my wife's car.
4.   If Francesca (not, be) _____ looking up at just the right moment, she (not, see) _____ the supernova.
5.   If Sam (not, screw around) _____ all semester, he (not, have to) _____ do his final project in one day.

18.12 *wish*

The conditional is more than zero, first, second and third conditional sentences. When you wish for something, you're wishing for something that didn't happen, isn't happening or hasn't happened yet and might not happen at all. In every case, it isn't real, isn't possible (or, at the very least, is not at all certain), and for that we use the past subjunctive or past perfect subjunctive.

Here are examples of how *wish* is used for the past, present and future. A few contain examples of ellipsis:

▶ *wish* **in the past**
Wish in the past uses the past perfect subjunctive:

18.64   That math exam was really hard. I didn't study, and that was a mistake. I wish I <u>had studied</u> for the exam.

18.65   Our teacher reviewed for the exam yesterday, and I was absent. I wish I <u>hadn't been</u> absent.

18.66   My friends went to a nice restaurant for lunch yesterday, but I couldn't go. I wish I <u>could have gone</u> with them.

18.67   I'm having a lot of problems with my new car. I wish I <u>hadn't bought</u> it.

18.68   I failed the test. I didn't study, but I wish I <u>had</u>.

▶ *wish* **in the present**

Wish in the present uses the past subjunctive of a main verb:

18.69   I can't go bike riding with my friends because I don't have a bicycle. I wish I <u>had</u> a bicycle.

18.70   We can't go shopping because today's a holiday, and the stores are closed. I wish today <u>weren't</u> a holiday.

18.71   I'm sorry. I want to help you, but I don't know the answer. I wish I <u>knew</u> the answer, but I don't.

18.72   I don't speak Italian, but I wish I <u>did</u>.

18.73   I need to ask Ali a question, but he's not here. I wish he <u>were</u>.

▶ *wish* **in the future**

Wish in the future uses the past subjunctive of a modal or phrasal modal: (Notice the ellipsis in 18.75 and 18.76)

18.74   I'm trying to sleep, and my neighbors keep making noise. I wish they <u>would shut up</u>.

18.75   Sarah can't come with us to the movie tonight. I wish she <u>could</u>.

18.76   Mary and Tom are going to bring their dog to our wedding. I wish they <u>weren't</u>.

18.77   It hasn't rained in a long time. I wish it <u>would rain</u>.

18.78   My sister is going to Hawaii. I've always wanted to go to there. I wish I <u>could go</u> with her.

▶ *wish* **with** *would* **and** *could*

Here are more examples of how *wish* is frequently used with *would* and *could*:

18.79   I wish you <u>would be</u> quiet. I'm trying to study.

18.80   I hate this hot weather. I wish it <u>would cool off</u>.

18.81   I wish you <u>wouldn't smoke</u> in the house.

18.82   What you're doing is really bothering me. I wish you <u>would quit</u> doing that.

This will likely be a challenge to your students. Only you can decide whether your students are ready for this, but don't dismiss this as formal or rare. It is neither. This is how we native speakers speak every day yet is a perfect example of grammar that few if any ESL students ever get to, and if they do, ever come close to mastering.

sample exercises 18: Complete the sentences with the correct form of the verb. There may be more than one good answer for some.

I get angry every time she says that. I wish she _____*wouldn't say*_____ that.

You shouldn't have bought that car. I wish you _____*had bought*_____ a different car.

1. Mary never stops calling me. I don't have time to talk to her sometimes, so I wish she _____ me so much.
2. We live in a small house. I wish we _____ a bigger house.
3. Are you ever going to quit asking me? You keep asking me and asking me, and the answer is still no. I wish you _____ me.
4. I told my daughter not to quit school, but she did it anyway. I wish she _____ school.
5. My plane leaves at 5:25 a.m. tomorrow morning. I wish it _____ so early.
6. I'm really hungry, and we're not eating until 8:00. I wish we _____ sooner.
7. Sarah isn't going to make my favorite cookies for my birthday. I wish she _____ them.
8. My sister has a big mouth. I told her a secret, and now everyone knows. I wish she _____ such a big mouth.
9. It's too bad you aren't going to be at my graduation next week. I wish you _____ there.
10. Carlos goes to a school far away. I wish he _____ to a school that was closer to home.
11. It's too bad you couldn't go with us last night. I wish you _____ with us.

18.13 Canceling *if* in conditional sentences

Now we'll look at three ways that the *if*-clause can be altered. All three of these are rather formal and fairly uncommon, so depending on your students, you may not feel these are worth the time or effort. If you decide to do this with your students, be very sure that they understand that it is never necessary to use any of these. All are entirely optional variations. What follows are three sets of examples and an exercise for each:

▶ *had*

If is canceled, and *had* is put in front of the subject:

18.83a   If I had known you were coming, I would have baked a cake.
   b   = Had I known you were coming, I would have baked a cake.

18.84a   You would have passed the test if you had studied.
   b   = You would have passed the test had you studied.

▶ *were*

If is canceled, and *were* is put in front of the subject:

18.85a   If I were you, I would go to a doctor.
   b   = Were I you, I would go to a doctor.

18.86a   If she were here, we could ask her.
   b   = Were she here, we could ask her.

18.87a   If you saw a ghost, would you freak out?
   b   = If you were to see a ghost, would you freak out? (This is the pattern we saw in Section 18.7.)
   c   = Were you to see a ghost, would you freak out?

▶ *should*

There are two ways that first conditional sentences can be made with should. One of them also cancels if. Both of them are formal and not common.

▷ *should* before the verb

In one way, *should* can be put before the verb in the *if*-clause (notice how *has* changes to *have* and *comes* changes to *come*):

18.88a   If he has a problem, I will help him.
   b   = If he should have a problem, I will help him.

18.89a   If Mary comes while I am at work, please give her this book.
   b   = If Mary should come while I am at work, please give her this book.

▷ *should* before the subject

In the other way, *should* can be put before the subject, and *if* canceled:

18.90a   If he has a problem, I will help him.
   b   = Should he have a problem, I will help him.

18.91a   If Mary comes while I am at work, please give her this book.
   b   = Should Mary come while I am work, please give her this book.

sample exercises 19: Complete the sentences without using *if.*

   If you had put on sunscreen as I suggested, you would not be sunburned now.
   _____*Had you put on*_____ sunscreen as I suggested, you would not be sunburned now.

   I would have flown to Madrid if I hadn't taken the train.
   I would have flown to Madrid _____*had I not taken*_____ the train.

1. I would have visited you if I had known you were in the hospital.
   I would have visited you _____ you were in the hospital.
2. If you had gotten up earlier, you wouldn't have been late for work.
   _____ earlier, you wouldn't have been late for work.
3. I would never have believed it if I hadn't seen it with my own eyes.
   I would never have believed it _____ it with my own eyes.
4. If she had been caught by the police, she might have been put in jail.

_____ by the police, she might have been put in jail.

5. If it hadn't started raining, the fire would have continued burning for a long time.

_____ raining, the fire would have continued burning for a long time.

sample exercises 20: Complete the sentences without using *if.*

If Sarah were here, what would you say to her?

_____*Were Sarah*_____ here, what would you say to her?

We would already be there if the traffic weren't so bad.

We would already be there _____*were the traffic not*_____ so bad.

If you went to Hawaii, which island would you stay on?

If you _____*were to go*_____ to Hawaii, which island would you stay on?

_____*Were you to go*_____ to Hawaii, which island would you stay on?

1. If John were here, he might know what to do.

_____ here, he might know what to do.

2. If I weren't a teacher, I'd like to be an engineer.

_____ a teacher, I'd like to be an engineer.

3. If you were rich, where would you live?

_____ rich, where would you live?

4. Do you think he would still be vice-president of the company if he weren't the boss's son?

Do you think he would still be vice-president of the company _____ the boss's son?

5. We could go to the beach today if it weren't so cold.

We could go to the beach today _____ so cold.

6. If you lost your job, how would you support yourself?

If _____ your job, how would you support yourself?

_____ your job, how would you support yourself?

7. If I fell in love with you, would you promise to be true?

If _____ in love with you, would you promise to be true?

_____ in love with you, would you promise to be true?

sample exercises 21: Complete the sentences without using *if.*

You might miss your connecting flight if the plane arrives late.

You might miss your connecting flight if _____*the plane should arrive*_____ late.

You might miss your connecting flight _____*should the plane arrive*_____ late.

1. Can he exchange this shirt for a larger one if this one is too small?

Can he exchange this shirt for a larger one if _____ too small?

Can he exchange this shirt for a larger one _____ too small?

2. You can see me after class if you have any questions.

You can see me after class if _____ any questions.

You can see me after class _____ any questions.

3. Will you cancel the barbecue if it rains tomorrow?

Will you cancel the barbecue if _____ tomorrow?

Will you cancel the barbecue _____ tomorrow?

4. If Mary needs some advice, I'd be happy to talk to her.

If _____ some advice, I'd be happy to talk to her.

_____ some advice, I'd be happy to talk to her.

18.14 *would rather* in conditional sentences

Another way to use the subjunctive in a contrary-to-reality situation is with *would rather.* It's used when we talk about what we wish had been different from reality in the past, what we wish were different from reality in the present or what we wish were different from what is planned or expected in the future. Got that? Here are several examples. (The last two use present continuous for future, which we looked at in Section 5.13.) Notice how the verb in the initial statement changes when it is repeated in the second statement with *wish.* Also, once again, ellipsis is at work. I've supplied the elliptical words in brackets (but they don't have to be elliptical—it's optional):

18.92   Alan <u>wasn't</u> at the meeting. I'd rather <u>he had been</u> [at the meeting].

18.93   Maria _told_ everybody what happened. Would you rather she <u>had kept</u> her mouth shut?

18.94   Maria _told_ everybody what happened. Would you rather <u>she hadn't [told</u> everybody what happened]?

18.95   You father _is_ very strict. Would you rather he <u>weren't</u> [very strict]?

18.96   My daughter <u>works</u> in a circus. I'd rather she <u>worked</u> in an office.

18.97   My daughter <u>works</u> in a circus. I'd rather she <u>didn't</u> [work in a circus].

18.98   Larry <u>is going to quit</u> school. I wish he <u>were going to stay</u> in school.

18.99   Larry <u>is going to quit</u> school. I wish he <u>weren't [going to quit</u> school].

18.100 Michael <u>isn't going to be</u> there. I'd rather he <u>were [going to be</u> there].

18.101 The game<u>'s starting</u> at 7:00 in the morning. I'd rather it <u>were starting</u> later.

18.102 The game<u>'s starting</u> at 7:00 in the morning. I'd rather it <u>weren't [starting</u> at 7:00 in the morning].

sample exercises 22:   Complete the sentences.

My son goes to a college far away. I'd rather he _____*went*_____ to a college that was closer.

Our neighbor has 12 dogs. I'd rather she _____*didn't have*_____ so many dogs.

1. Mary lives in a dangerous neighborhood. I'd rather she _____ in a safe neighborhood.
2. Mary lives in a dangerous neighborhood. I'd rather she _____ in a dangerous neighborhood.
3. Sam is taking the bus downtown. I think this is a bad idea. I'd rather he _____ a taxi.
4. Don't do it that way. I'd rather you _____ it this way.
5. We're leaving at 10:00. Would you rather we _____ leaving later?
6. I'm not happy that you're going to do it. I'd rather you _____.

sample exercises 23:   Complete the sentences with the verb in parentheses.

Alan is a teacher. I'd rather he (be) _____*Were you to go*_____.

My daughter got married when she was very young. I'd rather she (wait) _____*had waited*_____.

1. We bought a new car last month. What a mistake. I'd rather we (keep) _____ our old car.
2. We rent an apartment. I'd rather we (own) _____ a house.
3. My husband wants to paint our house green, but I'd rather he (leave) _____ it the color it is now.
4. We went out last night, and today I'm really tired. I'd rather we (stay) _____ home.
5. You want to walk all the way to the mall? It's two miles! I'd rather you (drive) _____.
6. Larry loves fried chicken and pizza. I'd rather he (eat) _____ more fruit and vegetables.

18.15 _would you mind_ in conditional sentences

When we ask if somebody _would mind,_ what we're asking about isn't real yet, it hasn't happened yet, it's imaginary, hypothetical—and for that reason, we use the past subjunctive. We can also ask about a hypothetical alternative to what happened in the past. You may want to refer to Section 12.6 where _would you mind_ was discussed from a modal point of view. And don't forget to review just what the verb _mind_ means. It's always a bit confusing to students that we, in effect, say yes by saying no. In other words, I might say that _Yes, you may smoke in my house_ by saying _No, I wouldn't mind if you smoked._

▶ _would you mind_ **in the present/future**

For present/future (remembering that we make no distinction because the future starts right now), we use the past subjunctive. Some have examples of ellipsis:

18.103 My car won't start. Would you mind if I <u>borrowed</u> yours?

18.104 Teacher, would you mind if I <u>were</u> late for class tomorrow?

18.105 I might not be at the meeting tomorrow. Would you mind if I <u>weren't</u> [at the meeting tomorrow]?

18.106 My house is being painted. Would you mind if I <u>stayed</u> with you for a few days?

▶ _would you mind_ **in the past**

For the past, we use the past perfect subjunctive:

18.107 Larry went to his sister's wedding. Would she have minded if he <u>hadn't [gone</u> to her wedding]?

18.108   Maria helped you with your problem. If she <u>hadn't [helped</u> you with your problem], would you have minded?

18.109   I was at the meeting, but would you have minded if I <u>hadn't been</u> [at the meeting]?

sample exercises 24:   Complete the sentences with the words in parentheses.

I don't want to see that movie. Would you mind if we (go) _____*went*_____ to a different movie?

Would you mind if I (not, help) _____*didn't help*_____ you with your homework tonight? I'm very busy.

1.   I'd rather stay home and relax, so would you mind if I (not, go) _____ shopping with you?
2.   I'd like to get there earlier, but it's so far away. Would you mind if I (not, get) _____ there until later?
3.   I don't feel like cooking tonight, so would you mind if we (go) _____ out for dinner?
4.   Would you mind if I (listen) _____ to the radio while you are studying?
5.   We need to save money. Would you mind if we (not, take) _____ a vacation this summer?
6.   That taxi last night cost me $75! Would you have minded if we (walk) _____ there?

sample exercises 25:   Use *would you mind* to make conditional sentences. Change only the second sentence.

I have a doctor's appointment. I want to leave early today.
Would you mind if I left early today?

1.   It's cold. I want to close the window.
2.   We have something important to do. We want to go home at 3:30.
3.   I had a lot of work to do last night. I didn't want to go shopping with you.
4.   We have to stop at the bank on the way. We want to be late to your party.
5.   I don't have time to do it today. I want to do it tomorrow.

18.16 *it's (about) time* in conditional sentences

It's about time we got to the end of this book, don't you think? I do. When we use this expression, we're suggesting or demanding (depending on the speaker's tone of voice, which you should discuss with your students) a change from the current reality. Because the change hasn't happened, it's not yet real, it's hypothetical—you know what I mean. Let your students know that *about* is optional, but native speakers use it more often than not:

18.110   Sarah's been sick for a week. It's time she <u>went</u> to a doctor.

18.111   You haven't taken out the garbage yet? Well, it's about time you <u>did [take</u> out the garbage].

18.112   Our son is 36 years old, and he still lives with us. It's about time he <u>moved out</u>.

sample exercises 26:   Complete the sentences with the words in parentheses.

You've been screwing around all night! It's time you (do) _____*did*_____ your homework.

1.   We need to be there in 15 minutes. It's time we (get) _____ moving.
2.   What I told you before was a lie. It's about time you (know) _____ the truth.
3.   Look at our ugly old sofa. It's time we (buy) _____ a new one.
4.   It's 3:00 in the morning, and my son hasn't come home yet. It's time he (come) _____ home.
5.   You're 40 years old. It's about time you (get) _____ married.
6.   I haven't been to the dentist in ten years. It's about time I (go) _____.

18.17 Ellipsis with the conditional

It is extremely common to use ellipsis with the conditional. Because of this, because there are various ways ellipsis is used with the conditional and possibly because I have OCD, I will now deluge you with examples and exercises. This may seem excessive, but I really think this is important. This is how native speakers speak. This isn't for every student, of course, but if you're lucky to have some serious minded advanced students, this will keep them busy for hours (allowing you to check your email, get a cup of coffee and maybe take a nap), and they'll really benefit by it:

18.113a   Rosa: When your husband isn't working, what does he do?
       b   Lucy: He loves to go fishing. Whenever he can, he does.
       c   = He loves to go fishing. Whenever he can [go fishing], he [goes fishing].

18.114a   Mary: Are you going to figure out what's wrong with the car?
       b   Sofia: I will if I can.
       c   = I will [figure out what's wrong with the car] if I can [figure out what's wrong with the car].

18.115a Ali: You should leave now if you want to get there on time.
    b Bill: You're right. If I don't, I won't.
    c = You're right. If I don't [leave now], I won't [get there on time].

18.116a John: Do you have a swimming pool? Swimming is great exercise. You should do it.
    b Mark: No, but if I did, I would.
    c = No, but if I [had a swimming pool], I would [swim].

18.117a Noura: Are you going to buy a new car?
    b Sarah: I would if I could, but I can't, so I won't.
    c = I would [buy a new car] if I could [buy a new car], but I can't [buy a new car], so I won't [buy a new car].

18.118a Alan: Are you the manager of this office?
    b Paul: I wish I were, but I'm not.
    c = I wish I were [the manager of this office], but I'm not [the manager of this office].

18.119a Joe: Are you sure you want to go shopping? You don't have to if you don't want to.
    b = Are you sure you want to go [shopping]? You don't have to [go] if you don't want to [go].
    c Rosa: Yes, I want to. If I didn't, I wouldn't.
    d = Yes, I want to [go shopping]. If I didn't [want to go shopping], I wouldn't [go shopping].

18.120a Lucy: Why didn't you call the fire department? Didn't you smell the smoke?
    b Sofia: No, but if I had, I would have.
    c = No, but if I had [smelled smoke], I would have [called the fire department].

18.121a Joe: Were you invited to Tom's wedding?
    b Gary: No, and even if I had been, I still wouldn't go.
    c = No, and even if I had been [invited to Tom's wedding], I still wouldn't go [to Tom's wedding].

18.122a Mary: Hi Sarah.
    b Sarah: Mary! What a surprise. I didn't know you were coming. If I had, I would have cleaned the house.
    c = Mary! What a surprise. I didn't know you were coming. If I had [known you were coming], I would have cleaned the house.

18.123a Ali: Did you visit your son last summer.
    b Mark: No, he lives far away. If he didn't, I might have.
    c = No, he lives far away. If he didn't [live far away], I might have [visited my son last summer].

sample exercises 27: Underline the correct words.
    A: I'm sure you know the answer to this homework question. Will you please tell me?
    B: Sorry, but I don't know the answer. I can't tell you. If I (do/did), I (would/will), but I (don't/didn't).

1. A: Is the mechanic going to finish your car today?
    B: I hope so. If she (won't/doesn't), I'm going to have a problem getting to work tomorrow.
2. A: If you have to work on Saturday, will you still be able to come to our picnic?
    B: I want to come, but I may have to work Saturday. If I (didn't/don't), I (will/would).
3. A: If your company transferred you to Arizona, would you go?
    B: I hate hot weather, but I (will/would) if I had to.
4. A: Are you going to go to the museum exhibit tomorrow?
    B: I don't want to go alone, but Linda might go. If she (did/does), I (will/would) too.
5. A: Are you going with your family on their trip to China?
    B: No, I (will/would) if I (could/can), but I (can't/couldn't) because I have to stay here and work.
6. A: Do you really believe me?
    B: I already said I believe you. If I (don't/didn't), I wouldn't say I do.
7. A: Do you know how to fly a plane?
    B: I sure do. I'm a pilot, so if I (don't/didn't), it would be difficult for me to do my job.
8. A: Why are you wearing a tie?
    B: I'm wearing a tie because I'm going to a job interview. I (won't be/wouldn't be) if I (weren't/am not).
9. A: You should have studied for the exam. You failed it.
    B: Yes, I (should have/should), but I (don't/didn't). If I (hadn't/had), I (wouldn't/wouldn't have).

10. A: Is it true that David was eaten by hyenas?
     B: Yes, it's true. I wish he (hadn't been/wouldn't have been) because it certainly ruined our vacation.

sample exercises 28: Complete the conditional sentences using ellipsis. There may be more than one good answer for some.
     A: Do you want to go to a Japanese restaurant with us?
     B: I'm not hungry, and even if I _____*were*_____, I don't like Japanese food.

     A: How did you finish that big project so fast?
     B: By working all night. If I _____*hadn't*_____, I couldn't have.

1. A: Can you translate this letter in Spanish for me?
    B: Sorry, I can't speak Spanish, but if I _____, I would.
2. A: Did Sofia go to the doctor yesterday?
    B: No, she didn't because if she _____, she would have been late for work.
3. A: Can you give me a ride to the airport tomorrow?
    B: I want to help you, but I have to work. I _____ if I _____, but I _____.
4. A: Do you always eat breakfast?
    B: Yes, I do. If I _____, I get really hungry at work.
5. A: Are you married?
    B: Yes, I am. If I _____, why would I be wearing this wedding ring?
6. A: Does Mary smoke?
    B: I'm not sure. If she _____, I have never seen her.
7. A: Wow! How did you get such a good grade on the calculus exam?
    B: I studied like crazy. If I _____, I couldn't have done so well.
8. A: You lost your keys? How did you get inside your house?
    B: I got in through a window that was open. I don't know how else I _____ if it _____.

sample exercises 29: Complete the sentences so that the speaker is wishing for the opposite for what is real or true. Use ellipsis.
     I don't know the answer. I wish I _____*did*_____, but I don't.

     Gary started smoking when he was in high school, but he wishes he _____*hadn't*_____.

1. John bothers me. He's here now, but I wish he _____.
2. Sam bothers me too. He was here yesterday, but I wish he _____.
3. Larry found out what happened. I wish he _____, but he did.
4. I couldn't go to the concert last night, but I wish I _____.
5. I'm not taking a vacation next summer. I wish I _____, but I'm not.
6. Rosa can't help me. I wish she _____, but she can't.
7. Michael isn't going to be there. I wish he _____, but he isn't.
8. Noura won't go with us, but I wish she _____.
9. I don't live in Canada. I wish I _____, but I don't.
10. My husband doesn't know how to dance, but I wish he _____.

sample exercises 30: Complete the sentences. Use ellipsis.
     Sam talks too much. I'd rather he _____*didn't*_____.

     Are you going to paint the house purple? I'd rather you _____*weren't*_____.

1. You have a gun? They're dangerous. I'd rather you _____.
2. My wife got her hair cut really short. I'd rather she _____.
3. Larry isn't going to be there, but I'd rather he _____.
4. Linda didn't follow the plan. I'd rather she _____.
5. John won't take my advice. I'd rather he _____.
6. Why did you do that? I'd rather you _____.
7. My son doesn't have a job. I'd rather he _____.
8. Michael is planning to go skydiving, but I'd rather he _____.
9. He didn't listen to me. I'd rather he _____.
10. I don't exercise. My wife would rather I _____.

Irregular Verbs

infinitive	past simple	past participle	infinitive	past simple	past participle
be	was, were	been	hide	hid	hidden
bear	bore	borne/born	hit	hit	hit
beat	beat	beat/beaten	hold	held	held
begin	began	begun	hurt	hurt	hurt
bend	bent	bent	keep	kept	kept
bet	bet	bet	know	knew	knew
bid	bid	bid	lay	laid	laid
bind	bound	bound	lead	led	led
bite	bit	bitten	learn	learned/learnt	learned/learnt
bleed	bled	bled	leave	left	left
blow	blew	blown	lend	lent	lent
break	broke	broken	lie	lay	lain
bring	brought	brought	light	lighted/lit	lighted/lit
build	built	built	lose	lost	lost
burn	burned/burnt	burned/burnt	make	made	made
buy	bought	bought	mean	meant	meant
catch	caught	caught	meet	met	met
choose	chose	chosen	mistake	mistook	mistaken
come	came	come	pay	paid	paid
cost	cost	cost	put	put	put
creep	crept	crept	quit	quit	quit
cut	cut	cut	read	read	read
deal	dealt	dealt	rid	rid	rid
dig	dug	dug	ride	rode	ridden
dive	dived/dove	dived/dove	ring	rang	rung
do	did	done	rise	rose	risen
draw	drew	drawn	run	ran	run
dream	dreamed/dreamt	dreamed/dreamt	say	said	said
drink	drank	drunk	see	saw	seen
drive	drove	driven	seek	sought	sought
eat	ate	eaten	sell	sold	sold
fall	fell	fallen	send	sent	sent
feed	fed	fed	set	set	set
feel	felt	felt	shake	shook	shaken
fight	fought	fought	shine	shone/shined	shone/shined
find	found	found	shoot	shot	shot
fit	fit/fitted	fit/fitted	show	showed	shown/showed
flee	fled	fled	shrink	shrank	shrunk
fly	flew	flown	shut	shut	shut
forbid	forbade	forbidden	sing	sang	sung
forget	forgot	forgotten	sink	sank	sunk
forgive	forgave	forgiven	sit	sit	sit
freeze	froze	frozen	sleep	slept	slept
get	got	gotten/got[1]	slide	slid	slid
give	gave	given	smell	smelled/smelt	smelled/smelt
go	went	gone	speak	spoke	spoken
grow	grew	grown	speed	sped/speeded	sped/speeded
hang	hung/hanged[2]	hung/hanged[2]	spell	spelled/spelt	spelled/spelt
have	had	had	spit	spit/spat	spit/spat
hear	heard	heard	split	split	split

infinitive	past simple	past participle	infinitive	past simple	past participle
spoil	spoiled/spoilt	spoiled/spoilt	tear	tore	torn
spread	spread	spread	tell	told	told
spring	sprang/sprung	sprang/sprung	think	thought	thought
stand	stood	stood	throw	threw	thrown
steal	stole	stolen	understand	understood	understood
stick	stuck	stuck	undertake	undertook	undertaken
sting	stung	stung	upset	upset	upset
stink	stank/stunk	stank/stunk	wake	woke	woken
strike	struck	struck/stricken	wear	wore	worn
string	strung	strung	weave	wove	woven
swear	swore	sworn	weep	wept	wept
sweep	swept	swept	win	won	won
swim	swam	swum	wind	wound	wound
swing	swung	swung	withdraw	withdrew	withdrawn
take	took	taken	write	wrote	written
teach	taught	taught			

In English, the infinitive form (also called the *base form* or *simple form*) and the present form of all verbs (except *be*) are always the same. Only the *-s* form (also called the *third person singular*) is different. For example, *go.* The infinitive form is *go,* and the present form is also *go.* Only *goes* is different. See Section 4.4 for more about this.

[1]*Gotten* is used in America English. *Got* is used in British English.

[2]*Hung* is used for pictures, clothes, etc. *Hanged* is used for criminals:

> I <u>hung</u> my coat in the closet.
> They <u>hanged</u> the murderer.

Verb + Preposition Combinations

A

accuse *(someone)* of
add *(something)* to
adjust to
admit *(something)* to
agree with *(someone)* about
apologize to *(someone)* for
apply for/to
approve of
argue about/over *(something)* with *or* argue with *(someone)* about/over
arrange for
arrest *(someone)* for
arrive at *(a room or a building)*/in *(a city or a country)*
ask *(someone)* for/about

B

base *(something)* on
beg *(someone)* for
begin with
believe *(something)* about/in
belong to
blame *(someone)* for *or* blame *(something)* on
boast of/about
borrow *(something)* from
brag about

C

care for/about
choose between/from
collide with
combine *(something)* with
comment on
communicate with
compare (somebody *or something)* with/to
compete with
complain to *(someone)* about *or* complain about *(something)* to
concentrate on
confess to
confuse *(something)* with
congratulate *(someone)* on/for
consist of
contribute *(something)* to
convince *(someone)* of
correspond with
count on
cover *(something)* with
crash *(something)* into
cure *(someone)* of

D

decide on/against
demand *(something)* from

depend on
die from/of
disagree with *(someone)* about
disapprove of
discourage *(someone)* from
discuss *(something)* with
dream of/about

E

escape from
exchange *(something)* for
exclude *(someone or something)* from
excuse *(someone)* for
expel *(someone)* from
experiment on
explain *(something)* to

F

fail at
feel about
feel like
fight against/with *(someone or something)* for
fill *(something)* with
focus on
forget about
forgive *(someone)* for

G

get married to
get rid of
get sick of
get tired of
graduate from

H

happen to
hear of/about
help *(someone)* with
hide *(something)* from
hope for

I

insist on
interfere with *(someone or something)*/in
introduce *(someone)* to
invest in
involve *(someone)* in

J

joke about

K

know *(something)* about

L

laugh at/about
leave for
lend *(something)* to
listen to
look at
look for
look forward to
look like

M

matter to
meet with

O

object to
participate in

P

pay *(someone)* for
play with
point at
pray for *(something)*/to
prepare *(someone or something)* for
prevent *(someone or something)* from
prohibit *(someone)* from
protect *(someone or something)* from
provide *(someone)* with *(something)*
or provide *(something)* for
punish *(someone)* for

R

react to *(something)*
read about *(someone or something)*
recover from
refer to
rely on
remind *(someone)* of
reply to
resign from
respond to

result in
retire from
rob *(someone or something)* of
run into

S

save *(someone)* from/*(something)* for
search for
share *(something)* with
shout at
smile at
speak to/with *(someone)* about
specialize in
stand for
stare at
substitute *(someone or something)* for
succeed in
suffer from
suspect *(someone)* of

T

take care of
talk to/with *(someone)* about
tell *(someone)* about
thank *(someone)* for
think of/about
trust *(someone)* with

U

use *(something)* for

V

vote for

W

wait for
wait on
warn *(someone)* about
wonder about
work on
worry about
write to *(someone)* about

Adjective + Preposition Combinations

A
absent from
accused of
accustomed to
acquainted with
addicted to
afraid of
   unafraid of
allergic to
amazed at/by
angry at/with *(someone)* about
annoyed with/at *(someone)* about
anxious about
appreciated for
ashamed of
associated with
astonished at/by
attached to
aware of
   unaware of

B
bad at *(doing something)*
bad for *(your health)*
based on
beneficial to
boastful for
bored with
brilliant at
busy with

C
capable of
   incapable of
careful with/about/of
certain about
characteristic of
clever at
confused about
connected with
conscious of
content with
crazy about
crowded with
curious about

D
delighted at/about
dependent on
derived from
different from
disappointed in/with
disgusted with/by

divorced from
doubtful about

E
eligible for
ineligible for
engaged to
enthusiastic about
   unenthusiastic about
envious of
equal to
excellent at
excited about
   unexcited about
experienced at/in
   inexperienced at/in
exposed to

F
faithful to
   unfaithful to
familiar with
   unfamiliar with
famous for
fed up with
finished with
fond of
free of/from
friendly to/with
   unfriendly to/with
frightened of/by
full of
furious at/with *(someone)* about
furnished with

G
generous with/about
gentle with
good at *(doing something)*
good for *(your health)*
grateful to *(someone)* for
   ungrateful to *(someone)* for
guilty of/about

H
happy about
   unhappy about
hopeful of/about
hungry for

I
identical with/to
immune to
impressed with/by

unimpressed with/by
indifferent to
inferior to
innocent of
interested in
   uninterested in
involved in/with

J
jealous of

K
kind to
unkind to

L
late for
limited to
lucky at

M
mad about (something) *(mad = crazy* in BE)
mad at *(someone)* about *(something)* *(mad = angry* in AE)
made of
married to

N
nervous of/about
nice to
notorious for

O
opposed to
   unopposed to
optimistic about

P
patient with
impatient with
pessimistic about
pleased with
polite to
   impolite to
popular with
   unpopular with
prepared for
   unprepared for
present at
proud of
punished for
puzzled about

Q

qualified for
   unqualified for

R

ready for
related to
   unrelated to
relevant to
respectful to
   disrespectful to
responsible for
rid of
right about

S

sad about
safe from
satisfied with
   unsatisfied with
dissatisfied with

scared of/by
sensitive to
separate from
serious about
shocked by
sick of
similar to
skilful at
slow at
sorry for/about
successful in/at
   unsuccessful in/at
suitable for
   unsuitable for
superior to
sure of/about
   unsure of/about
surprised at
suspicious of

T

terrible at
terrified of/by
thankful to/for
thirsty for
thrilled with
tired of/from
troubled with
typical of

U

upset about
used to

W

worried about
wrong about

Noun + Preposition Combinations

A
access to
advantage of
admiration for
alternative to
attack on
attitude to/towards
associate (somebody or something) with

C
commend (somebody) on
comparison between
connection between
contrast (somebody or something) with
credit for
characteristic of
cure for

D
decrease in
delay in
desire for
difference betweendifficulty in/with
disadvantage of

E
effect on
exception to
expert on/at/in
experience in/with

H
hope for

I
increase in
influence on
information about
intention of

K
knowledge of

L
lack of
link with

M
matter with

N
need for
notice of

O
opinion of/about

P
pleasure in
preference for
protection from

R
reaction to
reason for
recipe for
reduction in
relationship with
report on
responsibility for
result of
respect (somebody) for
rise in
room for

S
solution to
smell of
sympathy for

T
tax on
taste of
threat to
trouble with

U
use of

V
victim of

Sentence Structure

A brief lesson in sentence structure—three basic patterns

As a professional ESL teacher, you should know this stuff. It's pretty basic and would make you look dumb if you didn't know it. So learn it!

▶ Simple sentence (aka independent clause)

A simple sentence contains, at the very least, a subject and a verb. It expresses a complete thought.

> He   ate.
> subject   verb

> He   ate a pizza.
> subject   verb

> He   ate a pepperoni pizza in the living room with his wife last night.
> subject   verb

You're not limited to one subject or one verb.

▷ Compound subject

> Mary and Sarah will go to the beach.
> subject   subject   verb

▷ Compound verb

> Alan   washed the car and cut the grass.
> subject   verb   verb

▶ Compound sentence

A compound sentence contains two independent clauses joined by a coordinating conjunction.

> Rosa was hungry,   but   she didn't eat anything.
> independent clause   coordinating conjunction   independent clause

> Tom's car wouldn't start,   so   he had to take the bus to work.
> independent clause   coordinating conjunction   independent clause

▶ Complex sentence

Complex sentences are more complex. That must be why they're called complex sentences. They consist of an independent clause and one or more dependent clauses. A dependent clause begins with a subordinating conjunction. Many subordinating conjunctions are used to form dependent clauses.

> I failed my chemistry test   because   I didn't study for it.
> independent clause   subordinating conjunction
>   dependent clause

When the dependent clause is placed before the independent clause, a comma must follow the dependent clause.

> Because   I didn't study for my chemistry test,   I failed it.
> subordinating conjunction   independent clause
>   dependent clause

Adjective clauses (aka relative clauses) covered in Chapter 12 are also a type of dependent clause. They begin with a set of subordinating conjunctions called (jargon alert!) *relative pronouns: who, whom, which, that, whose* or (jargon alert!) *relative adverbs: when, where* and *why.*

Noun clauses covered in Chapter 14 are a type of dependent clause too. They are introduced by a set of subordinating conjunctions called (jargon alert!) *noun clause markers: if, whether, how, what, when, where, which, who, whom, whose, why, however, whatever, whenever, wherever, whichever, whoever* and *whomever.*

Appendix F
Main Verb Forms

main verbs (aka lexical verbs)							
indicative						subjunctive	
verb 1 (V1) aka 1ˢᵗ form			**verb 2 (V2) aka 2ⁿᵈ form**	**verb 3(V3) aka 3ʳᵈ form**			
infinitive	present simple = base	present simple + s	past simple	past participle	present participle	present	past
(to) talk	talk	talks	talked	talked	talking	talk	talked
(to) go	go	goes	went	went	going	go	went
(to) eat	eat	eats	ate	eaten	eating	eat	ate
(to) have	have	has	had	had	having	have	had
(to) do	do	does	did	done	doing	do	did
infinitive	**present simple = base**		**past simple**	**past participle**	**present participle**		
(to) be	as/is/are		was/were	been	being	be	were

▸ **Form overlap**

It's likely you've studied a foreign language, and if so, you might have been confused by the fact that the various categories that roughly coincide with what we see above required an entirely different form for each. That was difficult, but at least once you got it down, you could always tell what role the verb was playing by looking at it. English confuses students and teachers alike in a different way: the fact that identical forms of verbs are used for several purposes. Look at *talk*, for example. The form *talk* and the form *talked* both appear three times in this table.

Here are some key points to keep in mind:

- The term *main verb* (aka *lexical verb*) simply means a verb that is not an *auxiliary verb* (aka *helping verb*). The term is not common because the default term for *main verb* is simply *verb*. When you say *verb*, main verbs are what come to mind. It's only when we need to discuss auxiliary verbs that we make a distinction by using a more specific term, *auxiliary verb* (or *modal auxiliary verbs,* a subset of *auxiliary verbs*).

- *Indicative* is a term that is also seldom used because, again, it's the default. It boils down to what we use when we're talking about what is real or what is possible as opposed to what is not real, what is not possible, what is imaginary or hypothetical. There is never a time when you will need to confuse your students with the term *indicative,* but you should know what it means.

- *Subjunctive* is what we use when we talk about what is not real, what is not possible, what is imaginary or hypothetical. The subjunctive is used in conditional sentences which are not discussed until Chapter 18 of this book. There is never a time when you will need to confuse your students with the term *subjunctive,* but you should know what it means.

- The fact that the infinitive and the base form of the present simple are identical in English is potentially very confusing to your students. I recommend NOT making a big deal out of getting your students to understand the difference. It would be counterproductive—better to oversimplify—but you should understand the difference.

- *Do, have* and *be* are both main verbs <u>and</u> auxiliary verbs. Did you know that? You do now. This will at times lead to some confusion, but the main way to address this is not by going nuts trying to get your students to understand the deep grammar involved but by getting them used to *patterns*. With *do* and *have,* you will at some point need to discuss the fact that they're both main and auxiliary verbs. With *be,* never. Get into the deep grammar at your peril.

- Although *be* is main verb and an auxiliary verb, I never discuss *be* in terms of its being either of those. Because *be* is such a special case—very important but very different from other verbs, I generally treat it as unique (a good vocabulary item to teach your students): There are main verbs, there are auxiliary verbs and there is *be,* all alone in a group of one. If you go beyond this and get into the deep grammar with your students, you'll wish you hadn't.

- We normally think of the infinitive as always following *to.* Strictly speaking, that's not always true. The form of the verb that follows a modal auxiliary verb, for example, in *He can play the piano,* is what's called a *bare infinitive*—the infinitive form without *to.* Is there ever a time when you need to confuse your students with the term *bare infinitive*? What do you think?

- The terms *verb 1, verb 2* and *verb 3* are common, may already be familiar to some of your students, and are a handy way of avoiding the more difficult terminology, *present simple, past simple* and *past participle.* The term *verb 1* is additionally handy for reasons which I will discuss below.

▶ **Infinitives, the present simple and verb 1: an easy way to sidestep grammatical quicksand**

Let's talk about the infinitive vs. present simple form in more detail. You should definitely understand the difference, and in a perfect world your students would understand the difference too, but we don't live in a perfect world. Again and again, the grammar you're teaching will involve the use of either the infinitive or the present simple or perhaps a switch from one to the other. The fact that the infinitive and the present simple (with the exception of *be*—a special case—and the 3rd person singular *-s* form) are identical is potentially very confusing to your students. Do they really need to know the difference? No, they don't, and trying to get them to understand the difference will give both you and your students a big headache.

The good news is that with the handy little term *verb 1,* you can make everything easier—easier for you and easier for your students. With *verb 1* and a bit of oversimplification, you can sidestep this grammatical quicksand and speed your students on the way to their goal—understanding how to use English (if not necessarily understanding it well enough to teach it)—faster than if you needlessly confuse them with things that don't matter.

Here's what it boils down to: The terms *verb 1, verb 2* and *verb 3* (or *V1, V2* and *V3*) are common in some parts of the world. Verb 1 refers to the present simple, verb 2 refers to the past simple and verb 3 refers to the past participle. Your students, with rare exception, are going to see infinitives as verb 1. Grammarwise, that's wrong. Infinitives are different from the present simple/verb 1. Are you going to make a BIG GIANT DEAL of explaining the difference? No! You're going to get on with your lesson. They'll learn to use the right <u>form</u>, which is all that matters surface grammarwise, without understanding the deep grammar involved—which they don't need to understand!

▶ **Oversimplification for a good cause**

Students will tend to see main verbs has having some sort of basic form—the form they learn first— and then all the variations: either extra bits stuck on the end or different forms. They'll learn, for example, *work,* and know that various things are stuck onto it: *-s, -ed* and *-ing.* With irregular verbs they'll be aware that sometimes, instead of extra bits, we change the form entirely. That's plenty to figure out, and to add to their burden, they'll need to learn that there are times when, for reasons they may not fully understand, verbs don't have any extra bits or alternative forms—we use the basic form. To help them know when to use that basic form, regardless of whether it's the infinitive or the present simple, I strongly encourage you to strongly encourage your students to memorize two things:

▷ **One, use verb 1 any time a verb is used with any auxiliary verb**

can
could
do/does/did
may
might
must
shall
should
will
would

Is it really verb 1? No! It's the *bare infinitive*—the infinitive used without *to*. Are you going to explain bare infinitives to your students. Don't even think about it. It's verb 1, and get on with it! Of course you'll do this in stages. First, you'll discuss this in terms of *do, does* and *did.* Later, when you discuss the future, with *will.* Only when you get to modal auxiliaries will you discuss it in terms of the entire list above. You'll be amazed at how much grief it will save you and how much easier it will be for your students if you can get them to memorize this.

▷ **Two, use verb 1 any time a verb follows *to*.**

Examples of this will come in stages. At first, you'll likely have a discussion regarding some or all of these:

> hate to
> like to
> love to
> need to
> want to

Later, you'll discuss this again when you get to

> be going to

and (if you teach these as a separate lesson before actually getting to phrasal modals, as I like to do)

> have to
> have got to

Only when you get to phrasal modals will you discuss this with the entire list of phrasal modals (where you'll revisit *have to* and *have got to*):

> be able to
> be going to
> be supposed to
> be to
> had better
> have got to
> have to
> ought to
> used to

Is it really verb 1? No! Does it matter? No!

Answer Key

CHAPTER 2

sample exercises 1, page 15
1. am
2. are
3. is
4. are
5. is

sample exercises 2, page 16
1. She's angry.
2. I'm on the phone.
3. They're watching TV.
4. The door's open.
5. We're here.

sample exercises 3, page 16
1. The children are playing in the park.
2. Francesca's doing her homework.
3. Dinner's served at 7:00.
4. I'm listening to the radio.
5. The students are studying.

sample exercises 4, page 17
1. They're not outside.
2. They aren't outside.
3. The doctor's not at the clinic.
4. The doctor isn't at the clinic.
5. You're not listening.
6. You aren't listening.
7. He's not an engineer.
8. He isn't an engineer.
9. I'm not hungry.

sample exercises 5, page 17
1. John's not a student.
2. John isn't a student.
3. We're not in front of the supermarket.
4. We aren't in front of the supermarket.
5. I'm not finished.
6. He's not in bed.
7. He isn't in bed.
8. They're not here.
9. They aren't here.

sample exercises 6, page 17
1. I'm not eating breakfast.
2. Mark's not reading a book.
3. Mark isn't reading a book.
4. The projects aren't finished.
5. He and I aren't mechanics.
6. You're not washing the car.
7. You aren't washing the car.

sample exercises 7, page 17
1. the pilot's sleeping
2. Ali's not in the library
   or Ali isn't in the library
3. the soldiers are fighting
4. Toyotas are made in Japan
5. her sister's not here
   or her sister isn't here

sample exercises 8, page 18
1. Are the cats under the sofa?
2. Is Carlos tired?
3. Are Tom and his wife in the gym?
4. Are you and John working hard?
5. Is the house dirty?

sample exercises 9, page 18
1. was
2. were
3. was
4. was
5. were

sample exercises 10, page 18
1. Noura was dancing.
2. The coffee was hot.
3. The men were truck drivers.
4. The house was sold.
5. My parents were there.

sample exercises 11, page 19
1. I wasn't upstairs.
2. The women weren't at the party.
3. She and I weren't angry.
4. My house wasn't clean.
5. Maria wasn't a secretary.

sample exercises 12, page 19
1. John and Mark weren't in the bank.
2. The keys weren't in my pocket.
3. I wasn't talking on the telephone.
4. Her cell phone wasn't stolen.
5. Our father wasn't cutting the grass.

sample exercises 13, page 19
1. My friends weren't at the game.
2. John wasn't taking a test.
3. The door wasn't locked.
4. The show wasn't over.
5. We weren't done.

sample exercises 14, page 19
1. the party was fun
2. John and Michael weren't at the meeting
3. the students were listening to the teacher
4. the doctor wasn't in the clinic
5. the movie wasn't good

sample exercises 15, page 19
1. Was the calculator was on the table?
2. Was his father was a police officer?
3. Were the men were late?
4. Were the cookies were eaten by the children?
5. Was the mechanic was fixing the car?

sample exercises 16, page 19
1. Michael was washing the dishes.
2. Were the girls in the classroom?
3. They weren't there.
4. I wasn't doing my homework.
5. Was Noura talking to her friend?

sample exercises 17, page 20
1. Linda isn't in the hospital.
2. Three boys are outside.
3. Is the bird flying?
4. Are Tom and Lucy married?
5. She isn't reading in the library.

sample exercises 18, page 20
1. I am
2. we weren't
3. it was
4. she's not
   or she isn't
5. he was

CHAPTER 3
sample exercises 1, page 24
1. The birds are flying.
2. I'm reading a book.
3. The pilot's sleeping.
4. Mark's using his computer.
5. The teachers are talking.

sample exercises 2, page 24
1. The printer's not working.
2. The printer isn't working.
3. The children aren't being bad.
4. He's not doing his homework.
5. He isn't doing his homework.
6. Alan's not helping his mother.
7. Alan isn't helping his mother.
8. John and his brother aren't talking to their friends.

sample exercises 3, page 24
1. Is the cat looking out the window?
2. Am I doing this the right way?
3. Is the mechanic fixing the truck?
4. Is your father cooking dinner?
5. Are the children being noisy?

sample exercises 4, page 25
1. John is not working now.
2. The baby's sleeping.
3. Is Mark studying?
4. I'm not listening to you.
5. Michael is eating breakfast.

sample exercises 5, page 25
1. I was driving my car.
2. Alan and I were talking.
3. They were trying to answer the question.
4. The students were doing their homework.
5. My mother was writing a letter.

sample exercises 6, page 25
1. Maria and her son weren't washing the dishes.
2. The pilot wasn't talking on the radio.
3. I wasn't flying to Poland.
4. Tom and I weren't making dinner.
5. Her husband wasn't looking for a job.

sample exercises 7, page 25
1. Were the managers having a meeting?
2. Was Rosa planting flowers?
3. Were Alan and his friends going to the mall?
4. Were you lying on the sofa?
5. Was the airplane landing?

sample exercises 8, page 25
1. Were you doing your homework?
2. She was not listening.
3. The bird was not singing.
4. John wasn't sleeping.

5. Were you studying?

sample exercises 9, page 25
1. are fighting
2. weren't being
3. was working
4. Were...listening
5. aren't playing

sample exercises 10, page 26
1. was reading
2. are sleeping
3. Were...playing
4. is being
5. was watching/am doing

CHAPTER 4
sample exercises 1, page 29
1. go
2. am talking
3. are fixing
4. work
5. am teaching

sample exercises 2, page 30
1. Do they speak English?
2. Do Mary and Larry live in Mexico?
3. Do the teachers eat lunch at 12:30?
4. Do they have a new car?
5. Do your friends know the answer?

sample exercises 3, page 30
1. They do not have a cat.
2. We do not speak French.
3. You do not study in the library.
4. Tom and Alan do not work in an office.
5. My parents do not live in Florida.

sample exercises 4, page 31
1. You don't have a big house.
2. The boys don't listen to the radio.
3. They don't like pizza.
4. My children don't play soccer.
5. I don't live in Spain.

sample exercises 5, page 31
1. Yes, they sit in the back of the classroom.
   Yes, they do.
2. No, they don't play tennis.
   No, they don't.
3. Yes, I have a red car.
   Yes, I do.
4. No, they don't speak English.
   No, they don't.
5. No, I don't want to eat dinner.
   No, I don't.

sample exercises 6, page 32
1. speak
2. lives
3. eats
4. eat
5. work

sample exercises 7, page 32
1. Does Maria swim in the lake?
2. Does Larry sleep all day?
3. Does he go to work at 8:00?
4. Does John watch TV?
5. Does the doctor play tennis?

sample exercises 8, page 32
1. Sarah does not have a computer.
2. His father does not go to work at 7:30.

3. My husband does not wash the dishes.
4. The dog does not eat potato chips.
5. Mary does not leave at 7:00.

sample exercises 9, page 32
1. Rosa doesn't sleep in class.
2. He doesn't leave at 7:30 every day.
3. My brother doesn't live in a big house.
4. The teacher doesn't have a big nose.
5. John doesn't watch TV.

sample exercises 10, page 33
1. No, she doesn't listen to the teacher.
   No, she doesn't.
2. Yes, he lives in Montana.
   Yes, he does.
3. No, he doesn't know him.
   No, he doesn't.
4. Yes, he has a truck.
   Yes, he does.
5. No, she doesn't work at the library.
   No, she doesn't.

sample exercises 11, page 34
1. Did Ali finish his homework?
2. Did Linda see Larry?
3. Did he write a letter?
4. Did Carlos sleep late?
5. Did the students read their books?

sample exercises 12, page 34
1. Alan didn't think about the answer.
2. Michael didn't talk to his sister.
3. Mary didn't put the baby on the bed.
4. Your dog didn't eat my dinner.
5. Bill didn't fly to Ecuador.

sample exercises 13, page 34
1. Yes, he took the bus.
   Yes, he did.
2. No, she didn't eat the apple.
   No, she didn't.
3. Yes, they saw the accident.
   Yes, they did.
4. Yes, I drank the milk.
   Yes, I did.
5. Yes, he worked yesterday.
   Yes, he did.

sample exercises 14, page 35
1. A: Does
   B: doesn't
2. A: didn't
   B: Did
   A: did
3. A: Does
   B: does
4. A: Does
   B: doesn't
5. A: Do
   B: don't
   A: don't
   B: don't

sample exercises 15, page 35
1. Does he know the answer?
2. Did she go to the bank?
3. Does Tom have a cat?
4. Do you want to go to the mall?
5. Did Mary and Larry take the bus downtown?

sample exercises 16, page 35
1. Does he speak Korean?
2. Are you hungry?
3. Did she read the book?
4. Are you studying?
5. Did she have breakfast?

sample exercises 17, page 36
1. Mary followed the plan, but Michael didn't ~~follow the plan~~.
2. I feel sick. Does he ~~feel sick~~ too?
3. My mother likes to eat fish, but my father doesn't ~~like to eat fish~~.
4. We agree with you, but they don't ~~agree with you~~.
5. Sarah went to the party. Did her brother ~~go to the party~~?

sample exercises 18, page 36
1. go to the library
2. do it
3. want to eat
4. drink coffee
5. do it

sample exercises 19, page 36
1. The library closes at 8:30, and the supermarket does too.
2. Susan bought a TV last week, and I did too.
3. Mary read that book, and Michael did too.
4. I know how to swim, and my brother does too.
5. John thinks it's a good idea, and Sam does too.

sample exercises 20, page 37
1. I did go to Mars in a UFO.
2. She does have 14 children.
3. I do believe you.
4. I did do my homework yesterday.
5. I do do my homework every day.

sample exercises 21, page 38
1. Lucy doesn't do everything well.
2. We don't do all our shopping on Saturday.
3. I don't do my homework in the library.
4. She doesn't do it carefully.
5. Mark doesn't do the dishes after dinner.

sample exercises 22, page 38
1. Does he do his work slowly?
2. Do they always do it the wrong way?
3. Does Sarah do her homework at school?
4. Do they do their exercises before dinner?
5. Does he do his work in his office?

sample exercises 23, page 38
1. I didn't do it.
2. He didn't do the laundry.
3. You didn't do the right thing.
4. Tom didn't do everything wrong.
5. Larry didn't do a lot of work.

sample exercises 24, page 39
1. Did she do the best she could?
2. Did Carlos do a good job?
3. Did they do the wrong thing?
4. Did he do it yesterday?
5. Did she do it right?

CHAPTER 5
sample exercises 1, page 42
1. I'll make you a sandwich.
2. They'll be working.
3. He'll write a book.
4. Larry and Carlos will go to the mall.
5. He'll be angry.

sample exercises 2, page 43
1. Will they come after dinner?
2. Will he give Mark $1,000?

3. Will you help me?
4. Will Noura be at the party?
5. Will the girls watch a movie?

sample exercises 3, page 43
1. Will you go to work tomorrow?
2. Will Sofia take a shower this evening?
3. Will you be here next Friday night?
4. Will the students have homework today?
5. Will Alan be studying later?

sample exercises 4, page 43
1. They won't help her.
2. I won't go.
3. He won't change his mind.
4. Alan won't be there.
5. She won't do it.

sample exercises 5, page 44
1. I won't wake up early next Saturday.
2. The teacher won't have a class tomorrow afternoon.
3. Maria won't do her homework tomorrow evening.
4. I won't be working later.
5. They won't eat meat next Friday.
6. They won't be here next week.

sample exercises 6, page 44
1. My mother's going to make dinner.
2. The doctor's going to call me.
3. We're going to be at the mall.
4. They're going to buy a new car.
5. Larry's going to be late.

sample exercises 7, page 44
1. Is Sofia going to have chicken for dinner?
2. Are you going to wash your car?
3. Are your friends going to go to Taiwan?
4. Is he going to work in the garden?
5. Are you and she going to be here next Sunday?

sample exercises 8, page 44
1. He's not going to be here later.
2. I'm not going to do it.
3. We're not going to eat in that restaurant again.
4. He's not going to read this book.
5. They're not going to have dinner after the movie.

sample exercises 9, page 48
1. Mary's calling me at 8:00.
2. We're eating dinner soon. We're having spaghetti.
3. When are you doing your homework?
4. How many people are coming to the party?
5. Why are you going there?

sample exercises 10, page 48
1. The show starts at 8:00.
2. When does the game begin?
3. The store opens at 10:00.
4. When is the test?
5. The test is next Tuesday.

sample exercises 11, page 50
1. a Rosa isn't going to be here today, but she is going to be ~~here~~ tomorrow.
   b Rosa isn't going to be here today, but she is ~~going to be here~~ tomorrow.
2. a I'm not going to ride my bike before dinner, but I am going to ~~ride my bike~~ after dinner.
   b I'm not ~~going to ride my bike~~ before dinner, but I am going to ride my bike after dinner.
3. a Paul is going to ~~speak at the conference~~. Is Sam going to speak at the conference?
   b Paul is ~~going to speak at the conference~~. Is Sam going to

speak at the conference?
4. a They're going to go, and I am going to ~~go~~ too.
   b They're going to go, and I am ~~going to go~~ too.
5. a I'm going to leave early today. Are you going to ~~leave early today~~ too?
   b I'm going to leave early today. Are you ~~going to leave early today~~ too?

sample exercises 12, page 50
1. I didn't say anything, but I was about to ~~say something~~.
2. We'll get to the meeting around 9:00, but Carlos won't ~~get to the meeting~~ until later.
3. I'm not going to be on time for the meeting, but Noura is going to be ~~on time for the meeting~~.
   I'm not going to be on time for the meeting, but Noura is ~~going to be on time for the meeting~~.
4. Linda won't be working when we get there, but Mark will be ~~working when we get there~~.
   Linda won't be working when we get there, but Mark will ~~be working when we get there~~.
5. I won't be at work tomorrow. Will you be ~~at work tomorrow~~?
   I won't be at work tomorrow. Will you ~~be at work tomorrow~~?

sample exercises 13, page 50
1. B1: 'm not going to
   B2: 'm not
2. B: will
3. B1: 's not going to
      or isn't going to
   B2: 's not
      or isn't
4. B1: 'm going to
   B2: am
5. B: was about to

CHAPTER 6
sample exercises 1, page 54
1. I/them
2. He/us
3. They/her
4. We/him
5. I/her

sample exercises 2, page 56
1. ours/theirs
2. My/hers
3. Your/ours
4. my/yours
5. hers/mine

sample exercises 3, page 57
1. boys'/girls'
2. Larry's
3. company's
4. children's
5. friend's parents'

sample exercises 4, page 58
1. I won't give him money.
2. My mother will bake me a birthday cake.
3. John bought his son a car.
4. Noura didn't send Rosa an email.
5. Do you teach them English?

sample exercises 5, page 58
1. Are you sending a letter to Michael?
2. Your teacher left a message for you.
3. I'm going to get a new computer for my daughter.
4. Maria gave some cookies to her friends.
5. Did they show the picture to you?

sample exercises 6, page 59
1. a

2. the
3. the
4. the
5. a
6. the
7. a

sample exercises 7, page 60
1. Ø
2. The
3. Ø
4. the
5. Ø

sample exercises 8, page 60
1. any *or* some
2. any
3. any
4. any/some
5. any *or* some

sample exercises 9, page 61
1. Nobody went to the meeting.
2. I don't have anything.
   or I have nothing.
3. Is everyone here?
4. Everyone in the office hates the new manager.
5. I didn't go anywhere.
   or I went nowhere.

sample exercises 10, page 62
1. Michael spoke to nobody.
2. She didn't say anything.
3. He has no money.
4. I don't have any idea.
5. She went nowhere.
6. Don't say anything to anybody.
7. Tell no one what happened.
8. Don't let anyone in this room.

sample exercises 11, page 63
1. My friend gave me some bad advice.
2. This book has a lot of interesting information in it.
3. I was late for work because there was a lot of traffic.
4. We need lots of new furniture for our new house.
5. The history of my country is very interesting.

sample exercises 12, page 65
1. The hunter shot himself in the foot.
2. Sam and Dave did the work themselves.
3. We did all the work ourselves. Nobody helped us.
4. Larry and I will meet with you tomorrow at 10:00.
5. The boss asked Sarah and me to come to her office.

sample exercises 13, page 65
1. himself
2. yourselves
3. myself
4. themselves
5. herself

CHAPTER 7
sample exercises 1, page 70
1. Was his mother sleeping?
2. Is it finished?
3. Are you sure?
4. Is it written in pencil?
5. Is Linda being helped by the police officer?

sample exercises 2, page 70
1. Should Noura take her medicine?
2. Can Carlos ride a bicycle?
3. Will you help me later?

4. Would Maria like to help?
5. Will we be there soon?

sample exercises 3, page 70
1. Do the children make a lot of noise?
2. Does her sister live in San Francisco?
3. Do her brothers live in Los Angeles?
4. Do you play basketball?
5. Do you and he play basketball?

sample exercises 4, page 70
1. Was Lucy driving?
2. Will Mary go to Japan?
3. Does Sam have three children?
4. Did Tom go to Ireland?
5. Did Ali have fun at the party?
6. Does Maria goes to work very early?
7. Will he do it tomorrow?

sample exercises 5, page 71
1. Who will she talk to?
2. Who does Tom hate?
3. Who are you going to stay with?

sample exercises 6, page 71
1. What did you buy?
2. What can Jim play?
3. What is John making?

sample exercises 7, page 71
1. When did Alan call Sarah?
2. When does the class start?
3. When can you do it?

sample exercises 8, page 72
1. What time will she come?
2. What time does Francesca get home?
3. What time is the test?

sample exercises 9, page 72
1. Where was John?
2. Where will Alan go?
3. Where do you live?

sample exercises 10, page 72
1. Why does Mary walk to work?
2. Why is the student absent?
3. Why are you going to the library tomorrow?
4. Why did Sofia call her friend?

sample exercises 11, page 73
1. What kind of store is it?
2. What kind of books does he read?
3. What kind of courses will you take?

sample exercises 12, page 73
1. Which shirt did you buy?
2. Which one does she want?
3. Which one is yours?

sample exercises 13, page 73
1. Whose pen is it?
2. Whose is it?
3. Whose house did she go to?

sample exercises 14, page 74
1. How much money do you have?
2. How much orange juice is (there) in the refrigerator?
3. How much coffee did you buy?
4. How much money was stolen?

sample exercises 15, page 74
1. How many books are (there) on the table?
2. How many cookies did they eat?
3. How many people will come to the wedding?

sample exercises 16, page 74
1. How often does he go shopping?
2. How often does he work on Saturday?
3. How often was Alan late?

sample exercises 17, page 75
1. How far is it to the park?
2. How far was it from your house to Larry's house?
3. How far is it from here to the beach?

sample exercises 18, page 75
1. How do you get to work?
2. How did she fix it?
3. How can I lose weight?

sample exercises 19, page 75
1. How does she play tennis?
2. How well does she play tennis?
3. How does he walk?
4. How late did they come home?

sample exercises 20, page 76
1. How long is the book?
2. How hard is it?
3. How old are you?
4. How are you?

sample exercises 21, page 76
1. How long will you be in Australia?
2. How long were your students sleeping?
3. How long did she work?

sample exercises 22, page 77
1. How long does it take her to drive to work?
2. How long did it take you to do your homework?
3. How long will it take to install this program?
4. How long did it take you to get there?

sample exercises 23, page 77
1. What did you do last night?
2. What are you doing?
3. What will he do on Saturday?
4. What is she going to do tonight?
5. What are you doing tomorrow?

sample exercises 24, page 78
1. Who is John helping?
2. Who is helping Carlos?
3. What damaged the museum?
4. What did the fire damage?

sample exercises 25, page 79
1. Who(m) does John sit next to?
   Next to whom does John sit?
2. Who(m) is Ali dancing with?
   With whom is Ali dancing?
3. Who(m) did he look at?
   At whom did he look?
4. Who(m) will Sam make dinner for?
   For whom will Sam make dinner?

sample exercises 26, page 80
1. Aren't you listening to me?
2. Didn't you do your homework?
3. Isn't this painting beautiful?
4. Don't you know anything?
5. Isn't your name Carl?

sample exercises 27, page 81
1. had she
2. aren't there
3. would he
4. am I not
5. is she

CHAPTER 8
sample exercises 1, page 84
1. I made up a story.
   I made a story up.
   I made it up.
2. The teacher will call off the test.
   The teacher will call the test off.
   The teacher will call it off.
3. He called back his friend.
   He called his friend back.
   He called him back.
4. Please clean up this mess.
   Please clean this mess up.
   Please clean it up.
5. They're tearing down the building.
   They're tearing the building down.
   They're tearing it down.

sample exercises 2, page 84
1. Jack cheats on the tests.
   Jack cheats on them.
2. She looked for her son.
   She looked for him.
3. I'll get on the horse.
   I'll get on it.
4. I'm counting on John.
   I'm counting on him.
5. Don't fall for his lie.
   Don't fall for it.
6. I dealt with the problem.
   I dealt with it.

sample exercises 3, page 84
1. follow-up
2. back up
3. lay off
4. get-together

sample exercises 4, page 85
1. adj
2. v
3. adj
4. adj
5. adj
6. v

CHAPTER 9
sample exercises 1, page 88
1. I've got brown hair.
2. He's got brown hair too.
3. We've got a small house.
4. Paul's got a broken arm.
5. You've got a big mouth.

sample exercises 2, page 89
1. Our house hasn't got a garage.
2. We haven't got enough time.
3. Carlos hasn't got a calculator.
4. Tom and Linda haven't got any children.
5. The children haven't got their homework.

sample exercises 3, page 89
1. Have you got enough money?
2. Has Lucy got a problem?
3. Has her house got a basement?
4. Have I got food in my teeth?
5. Has Mark got brown hair?

sample exercises 4, page 90
1. I've got to take my son to soccer practice.
2. The pilot's got to fly to Norway.
3. They've got to take a test.

4. Michael's got to clean his house.
5. I've got to get to work early tomorrow.

sample exercises 5, page 91
1. I haven't got to go to the meeting.
2. Carlos hasn't got to go to school on Thursday.
3. You haven't got to do it.
4. The store hasn't got to return your money.
5. They haven't got to get there until 11:00.

sample exercises 6, page 91
1. Have they got to fly to Beijing?
2. Has she got to be here early tomorrow?
3. Have I got to wear a suit?
4. Has Mary got to pick up her friend at the airport?
5. Has Alan got have to wash the car?

sample exercises 7, page 92
1. No, she hasn't.
2. Yes, it has.
3. I haven't, but my wife has.
4. I have, but he hasn't.

sample exercises 8, page 92
1. Yes, I've got to.
2. No, he hasn't got to.
3. Carlos and Alan have got to, but John hasn't got to.
4. Yes, he's got to.

CHAPTER 10
sample exercises 1, page 97
1. have eaten
2. ate
3. have been
4. has been
5. was

sample exercises 2, page 98
1. Rosa has been here for 30 minutes.
2. I have been sick for one week.
3. Maria has been cleaning for three hours.
4. We have had this car for five years.
5. The baby has been sleeping for two hours.

sample exercises 3, page 98
1. 's reading/'s been reading
2. are studying/'ve been studying
3. 'm driving/'ve been driving
4. 's watching/'s been watching
5. 're looking/'ve been looking

sample exercises 4, page 99
1. Have you ridden a donkey?
2. Have they gone home?
3. Has she fallen asleep?
4. Have Sarah and her sister seen that movie?
5. Has Francesca painted her room pink?

sample exercises 5, page 99
1. They haven't been there before.
2. She hasn't met him.
3. Jim hasn't worn his new shoes.
4. We haven't had dinner.
5. I haven't taught this class.

sample exercises 6, page 99
1. She's thrown the ball.
2. Sofia's written a letter.
3. We've done our work.
4. The show's begun.
5. They've taken a taxi.

sample exercises 7, page 99
1. Have…you
2. has fallen

3. haven't done
4. has…been
5. has…gone

sample exercises 8, page 101
1. She hadn't left yet.
2. He'd lived in Chicago since 1985.
3. They'd already had dinner.
4. I'd never been to Timbuktu before.
5. We'd never driven on that road.

sample exercises 9, page 101
1. Had they had breakfast?
2. Had he given her some money?
3. Had you been reading?
4. Had Tom already arrived?
5. Had Sofia just gone to bed?

sample exercises 10, page 101
1. Maria hadn't spoken with her sister.
2. I hadn't told her the answer.
3. They hadn't been watching TV.
4. We hadn't taken the bus.
5. They hadn't done it already.
6. Paul hadn't gone home.

sample exercises 11, page 102
1. hadn't seen
2. had ridden
3. hadn't done
4. Had…been
5. hadn't…told

sample exercises 12, page 102
1. Larry was late for work because his car had broken down.
2. I didn't talk to Sofia when I called because she'd gone to bed.
3. Bill failed the test because he hadn't studied for it.
4. I was hungry all day because I'd forgotten to bring my lunch to work.
5. I didn't know what to do because I hadn't paid attention to the teacher.
6. They wouldn't let her in the bar because she hadn't brought her ID.

sample exercises 13, page 103
1. will have been
2. will not have finished
3. will have been waiting
4. will not have gotten
5. will have been

sample exercises 14, page 105
1. for
2. since
3. since
4. for
5. since
6. for
7. for

sample exercises 15, page 106
1. already
2. yet
3. just
   or already

sample exercises 16, page 106
1. Has John ever written a book?
2. Has your father ever driven a truck?
3. Have you ever been to Japan?
4. Has Carlos ever read this book?
5. Have you ever had a broken heart?

sample exercises 17, page 107
1. am
2. reading

3. Have
4. been
5. have
6. did
7. go
8. went
9. Have
10. been
11. have
12. been

sample exercises 18, page 108
1. there
2. been there
3. finished dinner
4. studying
5. been studying
6. heard about it

CHAPTER 11
sample exercises 1, page 110
1. nice perfume
2. good idea
3. wrong answer
4. fantastic house
5. angry man

sample exercises 2, page 110
1. He seems upset.
2. It feels soft.
3. It looks beautiful.
4. They smell stinky.
5. He got tired.

sample exercises 3, page 112
1. taller
2. more dangerous
3. easier
4. better
5. farther

sample exercises 4, page 112
1. Your house is small. My house is bigger.
2. Is Beijing smaller than Shanghai?
3. Emeralds are more expensive than diamonds.
4. French food tastes better than English food.
5. I got a bad grade on the Spanish test, but Mary's grade was worse.

sample exercises 5, page 113
1. most modern
2. simplest
3. most expensive
4. worst
5. best

sample exercises 6, page 113
1. Is the Amazon River the longest river in the world?
2. Sam is the craziest guy I know.
3. I got a 99 on my quiz. That was the best score in my class.
4. My youngest child is eight years old.
5. Yesterday was the worst day of my life.

sample exercises 7, page 113
1. b
2. d
3. d
4. b

sample exercises 8, page 114
1. hardest
2. stupidest
3. most expensive
4. largest

5. least interesting

sample exercises 9, page 115
1. worried/adj
2. married/adj
3. hidden/v
4. done/adj
5. lost/v

sample exercises 10, page 115
1. absent from
2. ready to
3. angry with
   or mad at
4. made of
5. ready for

sample exercises 11, page 116
1. getting
2. gotten
3. got
4. get
5. getting

sample exercises 12, page 117
1. used to
2. get used to/getting used to
3. get used to
4. used to
5. get used to

sample exercises 13, page 118
1. confusing
2. embarrassed
3. embarrassing
4. exciting…excited
5. irritated

sample exercises 14, page 119
1. football stadium
2. apple juice
3. can opener
4. school teacher
5. bus driver

sample exercises 15, page 121
1. $50,000-a-year
2. four-bedroom
3. 100-meter
4. 20-minute
5. four-day-a-week

sample exercises 16, page 123
1. My house is the same as your house.
2. This book is different from that book.
3. My house and your house are not the same.
4. Paul's bicycle is similar to my bicycle.
5. These shoes are like those shoes.

sample exercises 17, page 123
1. New York City and Los Angeles are different.
   New York City is different from Los Angeles.
2. My tie and your tie are alike.
   My tie is like your tie.
3. Larry and his twin brother are the same.
   Larry is the same as his twin brother.
4. My car and your car are similar.
   My car is similar to your car.
5. These tires and those tires are the same.
   These tires are the same as those tires.

sample exercises 18, page 124
1. pretty
2. a bit

3. terribly
4. totally
5. extremely
6. a little
7. absolutely

CHAPTER 12
sample exercises 1, page 129
1. May I open the window?
   or Could I open the window?
   or Can I open the window?
2. May we go home early?
   or Could we go home early?
   or Can we go home early?
3. May I have a glass of water?
   or Could I have a glass of water?
   or Can I have a glass of water?
4. May my sister use your car?
   or Could my sister use your car?
   or Can my sister use your car?
5. May I have more time to finish my project?
   or Could I have more time to finish my project?
   or Can I have more time to finish my project?

sample exercises 2, page 130
1. Would you mind if I closed the door?
   Do you mind if I close the door?
2. Would you mind if my son swam in your pool?
   Do you mind if my son swims in your pool?
3. Would you mind if I turned up the heat?
   Do you mind if I turn up the heat?
4. Would you mind if I spoke with your manager?
   Do you mind if I speak with your manager?
5. Would you mind if I didn't go shopping with you tonight?
   Do you mind I don't go shopping with you tonight?

sample exercises 3, page 130
1. Would you fix my bicycle?
   or Could you fix my bicycle?
   or Will you fix my bicycle?
   or Can you fix my bicycle?
2. Would you help me with my homework?
   or Could you help me with my homework?
   or Will you help me with my homework?
   or Can you help me with my homework?
3. Would you open the window?
   or Could you open the window?
   or Will you open the window?
   or Can you open the window?
4. Would you turn off the TV?
   or Could you turn off the TV?
   or Will you turn off the TV?
   or Can you turn off the TV?
5. Would you pick me up at the train station?
   or Could you pick me up at the train station?
   or Will you pick me up at the train station?
   or Can you pick me up at the train station?

sample exercises 4, page 131
1. Would you mind moving this sofa for me?
2. Would you mind taking us to the library?
3. Would you mind going shopping with me tomorrow?
4. Would you mind being here at 7:00?
5. Would you mind not walking so fast?

sample exercises 5, page 132
1. c
2. a
3. b
4. d

5. c

sample exercises 6, page 133
1. Can I borrow your bicycle?
   Would you mind lending me your bicycle?
2. Would you mind lending me your football?
   May I borrow your football?
3. Would you mind if I borrowed your dictionary?
   Will you lend me your dictionary?
4. Could I borrow your snow shovel?
   Will you lend me your snow shovel?
5. Would you mind if I borrowed your grill?
   Would you mind lending me your grill?

sample exercises 7, page 133
1. Mark had to do his homework.
2. I had to go to the airport.
3. He had to help his father.
4. Did you have to wake up early?
5. Did you have to make dinner?

sample exercises 8, page 134
1. NN
2. NA
3. NN
4. NA
5. NA

sample exercises 9, page 135
1. had better
2. should
   or ought to
3. had better
4. should
5. had better

sample exercises 10, page 136
1. You should have eaten breakfast.
2. You shouldn't have tried to start a fire with gasoline.
3. She should have kept her big mouth shut.
4. He should have called his father.
5. He shouldn't have forgotten to bring his glasses to the movie theater.
   or He should have brought his glasses to the movie theater.

sample exercises 11, page 137
1. could walk
2. Could...understand
3. can't come
4. couldn't call
5. could...figure out
   or can...figure out
6. Can...tell/can't read
   or Could...tell/can't read

sample exercises 12, page 137
1. I'm not able to sleep on airplanes.
2. Was the tech guy able to figure out what was wrong with your computer?
3. Mark's able to see a lot better with his new glasses.
4. The doctors weren't able to save him.
5. I wasn't able to get my car started.

sample exercises 13, page 138
1. used to/both
2. used to/both
3. used to
4. both
5. both

sample exercises 14, page 138
1. won't be able to come
2. may not have to pay/might be able to get
3. will have to rewrite

4. should be able to pass
5. might be able to see

sample exercises 15, page 139
1. would you rather do—stay home or go to the library
2. you rather leave tomorrow than today
3. he rather drive all night or stop at a motel
4. would he rather go—to Munich or [to] Berlin
5. she rather be married than be single

sample exercises 16, page 140
1. rather go to London than [go to] Paris
   rather go to London
2. rather play tennis than go swimming
   rather play tennis
3. rather walk to the beach than drive [to the beach]
   rather walk
4. rather stay home than go shopping with you
   rather stay home
5. rather take a taxi than go in your car
   rather take a taxi

sample exercises 17, page 141
1. has to be
2. must not know
3. may be
4. must be
5. can't be/have got to be

sample exercises 18, page 143
1. must have arrived
2. might have arrived
3. cannot have arrived
4. may not have gotten
5. may not have seen
6. might not have heard

sample exercises 19, page 144
1. might
   or may
   or could
2. may not
   or might not
3. will (probably) not
   or am (probably) not going to
4. will (probably)
   or am (probably) going to
5. (probably) will not
   or am (probably) not going to

sample exercises 20, page 147
1. should come
   or ought to come
2. shouldn't have taken
3. should love
   or ought to love
4. shouldn't have cost
5. should have come
6. shouldn't take

sample exercises 21, page 148
1. B: were going to
2. A: were going to
   B: wasn't going to/was going to
3. A: were...going to
   B: was going to
4. B: were...going to
   A: was going to/were going to

sample exercises 22, page 149
1. I am supposed to finish this work before I go home.
2. You're not supposed to talk in a library.

3. John is supposed to give a presentation next week.
4. Are we supposed to read Chapter 5 or Chapter 6 for our homework?
5. The show is supposed to start at 9:00.

sample exercises 23, page 149
1. B: is supposed to
2. B: was supposed to
3. B: are supposed to
4. B: aren't supposed to
5. A: am...supposed to
   B: are supposed to

sample exercises 24, page 150
1. are to
2. are not to
3. was to have/is to
4. were to have
5. was to have
6. is to/are to/was to have

sample exercises 25, page 152
1. Two People Were Killed in a Crash
2. The Pope is Going to Visit the White House
3. A Hurricane Has Destroyed Miami
4. A Bank Robber Was Arrested
   or A Bank Robber Has Been Arrested
5. ESL Teachers Are Demanding a Pay Raise
6. The Mayor is Going to Declare the City Bankrupt

sample exercises 26, page 153
1. Medford is only 15 miles from here. He must have by now.
2. It's got to be. It looks exactly like his car.
3. I don't know. They might have.
4. They ought to be, but they're not.
5. It's after 5:00, so he should have by now, but I don't know if he has yet.
6. I wanted to, I was going to, and I should have, but I didn't.
7. I was going to, but I was busy, so I didn't.
8. I was supposed to, but I didn't.
9. Yes, she was to have, but she didn't.
10. She should be. She never goes anywhere in the evening.
11. He may. He's not sure.
12. Yes, the judges were to have, but they postponed their decision.

CHAPTER 13
sample exercises 1, page 157
1. ~~He~~ works in my office.
2. ~~It~~ cost $25,000.
3. ~~They~~ live next to me.
4. ~~He~~ called you.
5. ~~She~~ is from Milan.

sample exercises 2, page 157
1. (who/that live near me)
2. (which/that was 450 pages long)
3. (which/that was really funny)
4. (who/that waited on us)
5. (which/that didn't make any sense at all)

sample exercises 3, page 157
1. She told me a story that was interesting.
2. My wife bought some shoes that cost $70.
3. The people who sat behind us at the movie theater talked a lot.
4. How many people who live in Florida speak Spanish?
5. The teacher asked me a question that was very difficult.

sample exercises 4, page 158
1. We ate ~~it~~ at the picnic.
2. I live next to ~~him~~.
3. I had never met ~~her~~ before.
4. You were talking to ~~them~~.
5. I bought ~~them~~ yesterday.

sample exercises 5, page 158
1. (which/that we had last night)
2. (which/that she wore to the party)
3. (who(m)/that I talked to)
4. (which/that he made)
5. (who(m)/that I sat next to on the plane)

sample exercises 6, page 159
1. The mechanic whom I talked to said it would cost $1,000 to fix my car.

   The mechanic who I talked to said it would cost $1,000 to fix my car.

   The mechanic that I talked to said it would cost $1,000 to fix my car.

   The mechanic I talked to said it would cost $1,000 to fix my car.
2. We don't understand the language which she speaks.

   We don't understand the language that she speaks.

   We don't understand the language she speaks.
3. Some people whom I know never take a bath.

   Some people who I know never take a bath.

   Some people that I know never take a bath.

   Some people I know never take a bath.
4. The guy whom I live next to is interesting.

   The guy who I live next to is interesting.

   The guy that I live next to is interesting.

   The guy I live next to is interesting.
5. The man whom I saw was very tall.

   The man who I saw was very tall.

   The man that I saw was very tall.

   The man I saw was very tall.

sample exercises 7, page 160
1. The boy behind whom I sat in grammar school is a lawyer now.
2. I didn't get the job for which I applied.
3. The woman with whom I work is from Lebanon.
4. The subject about which she gave a presentation was interesting.
5. The opera during which I slept was by Wagner.

sample exercises 8, page 160
1. I don't know the man to whom you were talking.
2. The student in front of whom I sit is from Germany.
3. I saw a movie with some friends with whom I work.
4. The woman under whom we live plays loud music all night.
5. It is an amazing story about which many books have been written.

sample exercises 9, page 161
1. I talked to a man whose wife is an artist.
2. Did the woman whose arm was broken go to the hospital?
3. The airplane whose wing fell off crashed.
4. Where is the man whose wallet was stolen?
5. The actor whose show was canceled was working as a waiter.

sample exercises 10, page 161
1. That's the park where we play soccer sometimes.
2. I still remember the day when my son was born.
3. Is there a day when I can meet with you?
4. Did he tell you the restaurant where he was going?
5. The day when my parachute didn't open was the worst day of my life.

sample exercises 11, page 162
1. Did Larry tell you the reason why Mary went to the hospital?
2. That was the reason why David was arrested by the police.
3. Does anyone know the reason why the ESL teacher jumped out the window?
4. Nobody knows the reason why she was so angry.
5. I wonder if we will ever know the reason we are put on this Earth.

sample exercises 12, page 163
1. no change
2. Elephants, which are native to Africa and Asia, are very intelligent.
3. no change
4. Coffee, which originally came from the Middle East, is now grown in many countries.
5. no change

sample exercises 13, page 164
1. The deserts, most of which were made by Sofia, were fantastic.
2. We checked in 11 pieces of luggage, all of which British Airways lost.
3. Almost 40 people, few of whom were qualified, applied for the job.
4. At the conference, I spoke to 300 people, hardly any of whom were interested in what I had to say.
5. Every year, Canada produces 27 million liters of maple syrup, most of which comes from the province of Quebec.

sample exercises 14, page 164
1. Larry caught five fish, the largest of which weighed five pounds.
2. Twenty girls skated in the competition, the youngest of whom was only 15.
3. Alan took five courses last semester, the hardest of which was calculus.
4. We looked at seven houses in San Francisco, the least expensive of which cost more than a million bucks.
5. My mother has three brothers, the oldest of whom is 47 years old.

sample exercises 15, page 166
1. I don't like the girl ~~who is~~ dancing with my brother.
2. What's the name of the cat ~~which is~~ sleeping on the sofa?
3. The loud music ~~which was~~ playing outside kept me awake all night.
4. Some of the people ~~who are~~ coming to our party are really weird.
5. The lions ate a man ~~which was~~ bothering them at the zoo.

sample exercises 16, page 166
1. The teacher noticed a boy who was cheating on the test.

   The teacher noticed a boy cheating on the test.
2. I saw an elephant which was riding a bicycle at the circus.

   I saw an elephant riding a bicycle at the circus.
3. A bus which was carrying 39 passengers plunged into the valley below.

   A bus carrying 39 passengers plunged into the valley below.
4. Look! There's a guy who is trying to break into that house.

   Look! There's a guy trying to break into that house.
5. A woman who was asking about the painting you're selling left a message for you.

   A woman asking about the painting you're selling left a message for you.

sample exercises 17, page 167
1. I can't eat food containing a lot of salt.
2. Anyone visiting that country must have a visa.
3. The family living next to us has a swimming pool.
4. People living in glass houses shouldn't throw stones.
5. Kids going to that school have to wear uniforms.

sample exercises 18, page 168
1. Some buildings which were destroyed by the tornado were never rebuilt.

   Some buildings destroyed by the tornado were never rebuilt.
2. The desk which was used by Homer when he wrote *The Odyssey* was sold for $1,000,000.

   The desk used by Homer when he wrote *The Odyssey* was sold for $1,000,000.
3. The money which was stolen by the bank manager was returned to the bank.

   The money stolen by the bank manager was returned to the bank.
4. Did you hear about the explorer who was eaten by cannibals?

   Did you hear about the explorer eaten by cannibals?
5. The jewels which were taken by the thieves were valued at $65,000.

   The jewels taken by the thieves were valued at $65,000.

sample exercises 19, page 168
1. People who are afraid of flying take the train or just stay home.

   People afraid of flying take the train or just stay home.

2. She has a heart that is as cold as ice.
   She has a heart as cold as ice.
3. Mark has a dog that is bigger than a horse.
   Mark has a dog bigger than a horse.
4. A man who was bent with age sat down beside me.
   A man bent with age sat down beside me.
5. We saw mountains which were white with snow.
   We saw mountains white with snow.

sample exercises 20, page 168
1. The teacher said the words that were on the board might be on the test.
   The teacher said the words on the board might be on the test.
2. A Chinese family moved into the house that is next to us.
   A Chinese family moved into the house next to us.
3. The car that is in the garage belongs to my uncle.
   The car in the garage belongs to my uncle.
4. I grew up in a town that is near Chicago.
   I grew up in a town near Chicago.
5. What's the name of that guy who is by the door?
   What's the name of that guy by the door?

sample exercises 21, page 169
1. Rosa, not having any cash, had to use her credit card.
   Not having any cash Rosa, had to use her credit card.
2. I, getting angrier and angrier, waited for him to come home.
   Getting angrier and angrier, I waited for him to come home.
3. Alan, wearing his only suit, left for his job interview.
   Wearing his only suit, Alan left for his job interview.
4. Maria, lying on the beach with her sunglasses on, didn't see the alligator.
   Lying on the beach with her sunglasses on, Maria didn't see the alligator.
5. Larry, wishing he could fly, watched the birds for hours.
   Wishing he could fly, Larry watched the birds for hours.

sample exercises 22, page 170
1. Maria, wondering why he didn't call, sat for hours by the phone.
   Maria sat for hours by the phone, wondering why he didn't call.
2. I, knowing she would think I was nuts, told her the whole story.
   I told her the whole story, knowing she would think I was nuts.
3. Frank, not noticing that the light was red, ran into the truck.
   Frank ran into the truck, not noticing that the light was red.
4. Alan, not having the nerve to tell his father the truth, lied to him for months.
   Alan lied to his father for months, not having the nerve to tell him the truth.
5. John and Mary, having heard that the movie was terrible, didn't want to go to it with us.
   John and Mary didn't want to go to the movie with us, having heard that it was terrible.

sample exercises 23, page 170
1. Bill, hot and dirty from working in the garden all day, went inside and took a shower.
   Hot and dirty from working in the garden all day, Bill went inside and took a shower.
2. Baffin Island, more than twice the size of Great Britain, has a population of only 11,000.
   More than twice the size of Great Britain, Baffin Island has a population of only 11,000.
3. Michael, angry about his manager's criticism, sat quietly at his desk.
   Angry about his manager's criticism, Michael sat quietly at his desk.
4. The girls, not interested in hearing Bob's dumb jokes, left the room.
   Not interested in hearing Bob's dumb jokes, the girls left the room.
5. I, mad as hell, felt like punching him in the nose.
   Mad as hell, I felt like punching him in the nose.

sample exercises 24, page 170
1. John, nervous about running into his ex-wife, arrived at the party.

John arrived at the party, nervous about running into his ex-wife.
2. Bill, afraid to say a word, kept his mouth shut.
   Bill kept his mouth shut, afraid to say a word.
3. Larry, sick with worry, lay awake all night.
   Larry lay awake all night, sick with worry.
4. Linda, sad and lonely, walked along the beach.
   Linda walked along the beach, sad and lonely.
5. The children, terrified of the monster they knew was in the closet, went to bed.
   The children went to bed, terrified of the monster they knew was in the closet.

sample exercises 25, page 172
1. We saw Michael eating lunch with Bob Jackson, the man who wants to buy Michael's business.
2. I asked Rosa, my sister-in-law, to bake a cake for the party.
3. Her husband lost $85,000, their life's savings, in Las Vegas.
4. I ran into Steve Barkley, my high school English teacher, at the supermarket.
5. My ex-brother-in-law, a complete lunatic, shocked everyone with his rudeness.
6. A complete lunatic, my ex-brother-in-law shocked everyone with his crazy ideas.

sample exercises 26, page 172
1. Have you read the novel *War and Peace*?
2. The discovery that Frank was the murderer shocked everyone.
3. We ESL teachers aren't paid enough.
4. I went to the party with my friend Sarah.
5. The fact that I had a broken leg prevented me from going on the trip.

sample exercises 27, page 173
1. Carlos, an excellent student, always gets good grades.
2. An excellent student, Carlos always gets good grades.
3. Nicholas, a liar and a bully, is hated by many who have worked for him.
4. A liar and a bully, Nicholas is hated by many who have worked for him.
5. Greenland, the largest island in the world, has a population of only 57,000 people.
6. The largest island in the world, Greenland has a population of only 57,000 people.
7. Sarah, a book lover, can never pass a used book store without going in for a look.
8. A book lover, Sarah can never pass a used book store without going in for a look.
9. Yosemite, one of the USA's most popular national parks, is 140 miles east of Los Angeles.
10. One of the USA's most popular national parks, Yosemite is 140 miles east of Los Angeles.

sample exercises 28, page 173
1. The police suspected his wife, a woman with a history of poisoning husbands, of the crime.
   The police suspected his wife of the crime, a woman with a history of poisoning husbands.
2. David lives in Kempton, a small town in the middle of nowhere.
3. I had to pay $2,000, a lot more than I expected, to get my car fixed.
   I had to pay $2,000 to get my car fixed, a lot more than I expected.
4. We ate lunch at El Taco Loco, a Mexican restaurant near our house.
5. I hired Mary Jones, a woman with an excellent resume, for the job.
   I hired Mary Jones for the job, a woman with an excellent resume.

sample exercises 29, page 173
1. A man helped me fix my bicycle, which was very nice of him.
2. Sarah is very sick, which makes me worry.
3. Joe crashed his car, which didn't surprise me because he always drives too fast.
4. The doctor said my friend doesn't have cancer anymore, which

was great news.

5. Last year we went to Venice, which, in my opinion, is the most beautiful city in the world.

CHAPTER 14

sample exercises 1, page 176
1. A2
2. A1
3. A2
4. A2
5. A1

sample exercises 2, page 176
1. she has
2. the game starts
3. he was late
4. Noura lives
5. she's got to work

sample exercises 3, page 176
1. where she went
2. what it is
3. where he has gone
4. when it begins
5. who he went to the library with

sample exercises 4, page 177
1. if he has a car
   or if he has a car or not
   or whether he has a car
   or whether or not he has a car
   or whether he has a car or not
2. if cats are smarter than dogs
   or if cats are smarter than dogs or not
   or whether cats are smarter than dogs
   or whether or not cats are smarter than dogs
   or whether cats are smarter than dogs or not
3. if she has done her homework
   or if she has done her homework or not
   or whether she has done her homework
   or whether or not she has done her homework
   or whether she has done her homework or not
4. if the show starts at 9:00
   or if the show starts at 9:00 or not
   or whether the show starts at 9:00
   or whether or not the show starts at 9:00
   or whether the show starts at 9:00 or not
5. if he'd like to go to the beach with us
   or if he'd like to go to the beach with us or not
   or whether he'd like to go to the beach with us
   or whether or not he'd like to go to the beach with us
   or whether he'd like to go to the beach with us or not

sample exercises 5, page 178
1. I want to know if he will come to the party.
   or I want to know if he will come to the party or not.
   or I want to know whether he will come to the party.
   or I want to know whether or not he will come to the party.
   or I want to know whether he will come to the party or not.
2. Can you tell me if Paul is going to be here tomorrow?
   or Can you tell me if Paul is going to be here tomorrow or not?
   or Can you tell me whether Paul is going to be here tomorrow?
   or Can you tell me whether or not Paul is going to be here tomorrow?
   or Can you tell me whether Paul is going to be here tomorrow or not?
3. correct
4. I don't remember if we are supposed to read this book.
   or I don't remember if we are supposed to read this book or not.
   or I don't remember whether we are supposed to read this book.
   or I don't remember whether or not we are supposed to read this book.
   or I don't remember whether we are supposed to read this book.
5. Whether Michael speaks French is not something I know.
   or Whether or not Michael speaks French is not something I know.
   or Whether Michael speaks French or not is not something I know.

sample exercises 6, page 178
1. Mark told me what to do.
2. Can you tell me where to get my car fixed?
3. The recipe doesn't say how long to cook it.
4. I've been thinking about what to do about this problem for many days.
5. I told Carlos where to cash a check.

sample exercises 7, page 178
(answers will vary)

sample exercises 8, page 178
(answers will vary)

sample exercises 9, page 179
(answers will vary)

sample exercises 10, page 181
1. he would be the next head of the sales department
   or he will be the next head of the sales department
2. she had nine children
   or she has nine children
3. he had bought a new car
   or he has bought a new car
4. she might call me tomorrow
   or she may call me tomorrow
5. he had to read 100 pages tonight
   or he has to read 100 pages tonight

sample exercises 11, page 182
1. Tom would/was going to cook dinner
2. she would/was going to arrive at 3:15
3. Larry would/was going to take out the garbage
4. he would/was going to meet me at the library at 7:30
5. she would/was going to call me later

CHAPTER 15

sample exercises 1, page 184
1. is
2. wasn't
3. is being
4. will be
5. have been

sample exercises 2, page 184
1. English is taught by me.
2. My request wasn't approved by the boss.
3. The bus is taken by many people.
4. Milk isn't drunk by us.
5. A story was written by Carlos.

sample exercises 3, page 185
1. The money is being hidden by John.
2. The toys are being put away by the children.
3. It's not being done by me.
4. Players are being chosen by the coach.
5. Nothing is being done by Larry.

sample exercises 4, page 185
1. A new company has been started by us.
2. I've been bitten by a dog.
3. That movie hasn't been seen by me.
4. Our rooms haven't been cleaned by us.
5. The window has been broken by her.

sample exercises 5, page 185
1. My car was stolen by Jack last week.
   or My car was stolen last week by Jack.
2. The sandwiches weren't made by her.
3. The airplane was flown by the pilot.

4. It wasn't done by them.
5. The correct answer wasn't given by him.

sample exercises 6, page 185
1. A bicycle was being ridden by Francesca.
2. A lot of noise was being made by the people at the party.
3. The tests weren't being graded by the teacher.
4. The dishes weren't being done by Noura and me.
5. The winner was being chosen by the judges.

sample exercises 7, page 185
1. A meeting hadn't been set up by Linda.
2. The work had been done by me.
3. A zebra had never been seen by them.
4. Indian food had never been eaten by John and me.
5. The motorcycle had already been ridden by us.

sample exercises 8, page 186
1. The new plan will be explained by the manager at the meeting.
   or The new plan will be explained at the meeting by the manager.
2. Dinner won't be cooked by her.
3. The light bulb will be changed by him.
4. A speech will be given by John and him.
5. Your money won't be stolen by him.

sample exercises 9, page 186
1. You're going to be surprised by the news.
2. The hot dogs are going to be brought by me.
3. Their wedding isn't going to be paid for by us.
4. The bus is going to be taken by them.
5. The helicopter was going to be flown by Carlos.

sample exercises 10, page 187
1. Gunpowder was invented in China.
2. Spanish is taught in my high school.
3. I'm sorry that your dog was run over.
4. The bank was robbed by a man with red hair.
5. A new restaurant is going to be opened on Main Street.
6. The treasure was buried by pirates.

sample exercises 11, page 188
1. The hot water heater was supposed to be fixed by the plumber.
2. The fuel level had better be checked by the pilot.
3. You should already have been contacted by the manager.
4. Your leg has got to be looked at by a doctor.
5. This could have been done by anyone.

sample exercises 12, page 188
1. must have been borrowed
2. may be transferred
3. are supposed to be put on
4. might have been bitten
5. had better be turned in
6. may have been sent
7. is going to be built
8. have got to be replaced

sample exercises 13, page 189
1. The police said two guys got killed last night.
2. I got shot.
3. Paul got hit by a truck.
4. Mark got hurt in a fight.
5. David got eaten by a wolf.

CHAPTER 16
sample exercises 1, page 191
1. I drive carefully.
2. She sings badly.
3. Carlos thinks deeply.
4. You speak quietly.
5. It changed suddenly.

sample exercises 2, page 192
1. Mary drives well.

2. Tom and Jerry sings well.
3. Larry danced badly.
   Larry didn't dance well.
4. Jim swam well.
5. Michael cooks badly.
   Michael doesn't cook well.

sample exercises 3, page 193
1. adv
2. adj
3. adv
4. adj
5. adj
6. adv

sample exercises 4, page 193
1. hardly know
2. can hardly see
3. hardly did
4. hardly ever gets off
5. could hardly hear

sample exercises 5, page 193
1. Noura did hardly anything yesterday.
2. There's hardly any time left.
3. Hardly anything was done about the problem.
4. I talked to hardly anyone.
5. Hardly anybody goes there.

sample exercises 6, page 196
1. Alan almost never helps his mother.
2. We are hardly ever late.
3. Paul hardly ever calls me.
4. My boss is almost always in her office.
5. We hardly ever watch TV.

sample exercises 7, page 198
1. c
2. a
3. b

sample exercises 8, page 198
(answers will vary)

sample exercises 9, page 198
1. c
2. c
3. d

sample exercises 10, page 199
1. We almost always eat Mexican food.
2. I have often thought about quitting my job.
3. English can sometimes be very difficult.
4. Maria has never seen that movie.
5. He is already finished.

sample exercises 11, page 199
1. Have you ever been to Hong Kong?
2. When does she usually eat dinner?
3. What did they finally do?
4. Why do you always have to say that?
5. Do you frequently get headaches?

sample exercises 12, page 200
1. She called Sarah to ask her a question.
2. He's saving money to buy a new car.
3. He's flying to Mexico to see his mother.
4. She'll go to the shoe store tomorrow to get new shoes.
5. He is talking to his teacher to ask why he got an F on his essay.

sample exercises 13, page 204
1. or
2. nor
3. so
4. yet

5. and

sample exercises 14, page 204
1. not possible
2. Sophia opened her book and began to read.
3. We can have spaghetti for dinner or go to a restaurant.
4. Mark promised to help me fix my car but forgot all about it.
5. My brother doesn't have a car but will buy one soon.

sample exercises 15, page 206
1. Alan does
2. you should too/so should you
3. Mark isn't either/neither is Mark
4. Sarah didn't either/neither did Sarah
5. her brother has too/so has her brother
6. his brother doesn't

sample exercises 16, page 206
1. She was too.
   So was she.
2. I would too.
   So would I.
3. She doesn't either.
   Neither does she.
4. They don't either.
   Neither do they.
5. I have too.
   So have I.
6. He isn't either.
   Neither is he.

sample exercises 17, page 210
1. Otherwise
2. After all
3. Furthermore
4. In the meantime
5. Nevertheless

sample exercises 18, page 212
1. I took a shower before I jumped into the swimming pool.
2. Although I was very angry, I didn't say anything.
3. You can go home when you are finished.
4. In case my ATM card doesn't work, I always take cash when I travel.
5. I get angry every time I think about what Sam said about me.
6. The next time we go to that restaurant, we should try the chicken curry.

sample exercises 19, page 214
1. by the time
2. Once
3. As
4. As long as
5. until
6. when

sample exercises 20, page 214
1. Every time she does that, it makes me angry.
   It makes me angry every time she does that.
2. Before you take the test, you should review.
   You should review before you take the test.
3. As long as you live in my house, you will follow my rules.
   You will follow my rules as long as you live in my house.
4. After I got to work, I started to feel sick.
   I started to feel sick after I got to work.
5. Whenever you need my car, you can borrow it.
   You can borrow my car whenever you need it.
6. Since we bought this printer, we have been having problems with it.
   We have been having problems with this printer since we bought it.

sample exercises 21, page 215
1. Because I wasn't careful, I cut my hand.
   I cut my hand because I wasn't careful.
2. So that I would not be late, I left two hours early.

I left two hours early so that I would not be late.
3. As it was raining, the picnic was canceled.
   The picnic was canceled as it was raining.
4. Now that the party is over, we have to clean up the house.
   We have to clean up the house now that the party is over.
5. Since you asked me, I will tell you the truth.
   I will tell you the truth since you asked me.
6. So she would not forget my telephone number, she wrote it down.
   She wrote my telephone number down so she would not forget it.

sample exercises 22, page 216
1. Although I had a map, I got lost.
   I got lost although I had a map.
2. Even though she makes a lot of money, she's always broke.
   She's always broke even though she makes a lot of money.
3. Although I hate basketball, I promised to go to a game with my husband.
   I promised to go to a game with my husband although I hate basketball.
4. Even though you have a headache, do you still want to go to the movie?
   Do you still want to go to the movie even though you have a headache?
5. Though the doctors did everything they could, she didn't get better.
   She didn't get better though the doctors did everything they could.

sample exercises 23, page 217
1. Despite the fact that I study like crazy, I'm failing math.
   I'm failing math despite the fact that I study like crazy.
2. In spite of the fact that he eats only fruit and salads, he can't lose weight.
   He can't lose weight in spite of the fact that he eats only fruit and salads.
3. Despite the fact that Mark was innocent, he was convicted and sent to prison.
   Mark was convicted and sent to prison despite the fact that he was innocent.
4. In spite of the fact that everyone said it was a great movie, I hated it.
   I hated the movie in spite of the fact that everyone said it was great.
5. Despite the fact that I followed the instructions exactly, it didn't work.
   It didn't work despite the fact that I followed the instructions exactly.

sample exercises 24, page 218
1. Unless
2. Whether or not
3. if
4. even if
5. Unless

sample exercises 25, page 219
1. While in college, I worked as a waiter.
2. When taking a bath, don't use a hair dryer.
3. You should never smoke when putting gas in your car.
4. not possible
5. While doing my homework, I like to listen to music.

sample exercises 26, page 220
1. You should always think twice before sending an angry email.
2. When driving, don't forget to wear your seat belt.
3. not possible
4. I lived in New Zealand before moving to Australia.
5. Since getting married, Maria has gained 20 kilograms.

sample exercises 27, page 220
1. After being sick for several weeks, John died.
   After having been sick for several weeks, John died.
2. not possible
3. After eating seven hot dogs, Alan got sick.
   After having eaten seven hot dogs, Alan got sick.
4. Sarah will graduate after taking her exams.
   Sarah will graduate after having taken her exams.

5. I finally went home after waiting for Maria for one hour.
   I finally went home after having waited for Maria for one hour.

sample exercises 28, page 221
1. Not knowing who the man was, Lucy didn't unlock the door.
2. Not wanting my wife to be angry, I didn't tell her what happened.
3. Lacking experience, it will be difficult for you to get a job.
4. Not having a car, I had to walk to work every day.
5. Having eight children, Mary and John need a larger house.

sample exercises 29, page 221
1. Being on a diet, he didn't want a piece of cake.
2. Not being a member of the club, he can't come in.
3. Not being a citizen of this country, Maria cannot get a job here.
4. Not being married and not having any children, I don't need a big house.
5. Being an ESL teacher, Carl works long hours for low pay.

sample exercises 30, page 222
1. Having been to England many times before, I decided to go somewhere else for my vacation.
2. Having broken his leg, Michael had to cancel his trip to Puerto Rico.
3. Never having been to Los Angeles, I'm really looking forward to going there next week.
4. Having had dinner only an hour earlier, I didn't want to go out for dinner with my friends.
5. Having had that disease before, I cannot get it again.

sample exercises 31, page 223
1. Despite being very angry, I didn't say anything.
2. In spite of not being in class, the teacher marked Mary present.
3. Despite having lived in France for 10 years, John can't speak French.
4. In spite of never having been told of the change in plan, we figured out what to do anyway.
5. Despite having a car, I usually walk to work.

sample exercises 32, page 223
1. Despite having a backache, I'll help you move your sofa.
   or In spite of having a backache, I'll help you move your sofa.
2. Despite not knowing anything about the subject, Tom's full of advice.
   or In spite of not knowing anything about the subject, Tom's full of advice.
3. Despite not being old enough, the boys were able to buy alcohol.
   or In spite of not being old enough, the boys were able to buy alcohol.
4. Despite never having used that program before, I didn't have any problem with it.
   or In spite of never having used that program before, I didn't have any problem with it.
5. Despite being 90 years old, Susan works 40 hours a week.
   or In spite of being 90 years old, Susan works 40 hours a week.

sample exercises 33, page 224
1. stood by the window listening
2. hangs around the house doing
3. standing around not doing
4. sat there listening to me not saying
5. sit around all night hoping

sample exercises 34, page 224
1. My car is as old as your car.
2. Joe drives as fast as Noura.
3. Winter in Canada isn't as cold as winter in Mexico.
4. Carlos doesn't dance as well as Alan.
5. Maria speaks French as badly as Rosa.

sample exercises 35, page 225
(Words that would probably be ellipted by native speakers are shown in brackets.)
1. Both Mark and I are married.

2. It's both a printer and [a] scanner.
3. Both Mary and her boss have to be at the meeting.
4. Both Linda and Ali live in that building.
5. My house has both an indoor [pool] and outdoor pool.

sample exercises 36, page 225
(Answers may vary. More than one possible answer is given for some, and there may be other possible correct answers. Words that would probably be ellipted by native speakers are shown in brackets.)
1. I'm going to either stay home today or go to the beach.
   or I'm either going to stay home today, or I'm going to go to the beach.
2. Either John or Mary will give me a ride downtown.
   or Either John will give me a ride downtown, or Mary will [give me a ride downtown].
3. The children can either play outside or [can play] upstairs.
   or The children can play either outside or upstairs.
   or The children can either play outside, or they can play upstairs.
4. We will either play tennis, or we will go swimming.
   or We will either play tennis or [will] go swimming.
5. Either do the work right, or I will find someone who can [do it right]!

sample exercises 37, page 226
(Answers may vary. More than one possible answer is given for some, and there may be other possible correct answers. Words that would probably be ellipted by native speakers are shown in brackets.)
1. The movie was neither funny nor interesting.
   or The movie was neither funny, nor was it interesting.
2. I would neither eat them in a box nor with a fox.
   or I would neither eat them in a box, nor would I eat them with a fox.
3. Larry was neither a good singer nor a good dancer.
   or Larry was neither a good singer, nor was he a good dancer.
4. Mark neither likes to exercise nor wants to [exercise].
   or Mark neither likes to exercise, nor does he want to [exercise].
5. Neither my computer nor Mary's [computer] is working.

sample exercises 38, page 228
(Answers may vary. More than one possible answer is given for each, and there are other possible correct answers. Words in parentheses are optional and are shown as examples. Words that would probably be ellipted by native speakers are shown in brackets.)
1. My daughter is not only beautiful, but she is (also) very intelligent.
   or Not only is Francesca beautiful; she is very intelligent (too).
   or Francesca is not only beautiful but (also) very intelligent.
   or Not only is Francesca beautiful but very intelligent (too).
2. I not only went to China last year, but I went to Mongolia (as well).
   or I not only went to China last year but [to] Mongolia (as well).
   or Not only did I go to China last year, but I went to Mongolia (too).
3. He bought not only 10 kilos of tomatoes but (also) 20 kilos of potatoes.
   or Not only did he buy 10 kilos of potatoes; he bought 20 kilos of potatoes (too).
   or He bought 10 kilos of tomatoes. Not only that, he bought 20 kilos of potatoes (too).
4. Alan not only washed the dishes, but he cleaned the bathroom and did the laundry (as well).
   or Alan not only washed the dishes but (also) cleaned the bathroom and did the laundry.
   or Not only did Alan wash the dishes, he cleaned the bathroom and did the laundry (too).
5. They will not only probably lose the battle but might lose the war (too).
   or They will not only probably lose the battle, but they might lose the war (as well).
   or They will probably lose the battle, and not only that, they might lose the war (too).
   or Not only will they probably lose the battle; they might lose the war (too).

sample exercises 39, page 228
(Words that would probably be ellipted by native speakers are shown in brackets.)
1. I'd rather read books than watch TV.
2. Alan would rather have coffee than [have] tea.
3. I'd rather you give this presentation than I [give it].
4. He'd rather work outside than [work] in an office.
5. We'd rather camp than stay in a hotel.

CHAPTER 17
sample exercises 1, page 230
1. smoking
2. exercising/not eating
3. speaking
4. going
5. not making

sample exercises 2, page 230
1. Waking up
2. Watching
3. Not speaking
4. Being
5. Not being

sample exercises 3, page 230
1. Not having a car
2. Living in Las Vegas
3. going to Tahiti
4. doing nothing
5. not doing anything

sample exercises 4, page 231
1. trying new restaurants
2. not saying good bye to Larry
3. going shopping for clothes with his mother
4. having to work on Sundays
   or working on Sundays
5. not going [to the funeral]

sample exercises 5, page 231
1. is playing
2. is driving
3. was getting
4. is running
5. was not listening

sample exercises 6, page 232
1. talked about buying
2. thinking about going
3. thinking about selling/thinking about not selling
4. apologize to her for forgetting
5. thinking about making/decided against having

sample exercises 7, page 232
1. forgive me for losing
2. blame you for being
3. stopped me from going
   or prevented me from going
   or kept me from going
4. blamed me for breaking
5. prohibited me from seeing
   or stopped me from seeing
   or prevented me from seeing
   or kept me from seeing

sample exercises 8, page 233
1. good at drawing
2. interested in learning
3. sick of working
   or tired of working
4. nervous about flying
   or scared of flying

5. afraid of running into
   or nervous about running into
   or scared of running into
   or worried about running into
6. happy about having
7. afraid of making
   or nervous about making
   or scared of making
   or worried about making

sample exercises 9, page 234
1. have no way of knowing
2. having fun dancing
3. had trouble believing
4. have an excuse for being
5. have a good time playing
6. have a difficult time making
7. have no excuse for saying

sample exercises 10, page 235
1. spent $225 getting
   or wasted $225 getting
   or blew $225 getting
2. spent three hours studying
3. spent ten years searching
   or wasted ten years searching
   or blew ten years searching
4. spent $3,000 getting
5. spent all day cleaning

sample exercises 11, page 236
1. went swimming
2. go fishing
3. went dancing
4. go skiing
5. gone camping
6. going shopping

sample exercises 12, page 236
1. looking forward to seeing
2. Instead of buying
3. In addition to having
4. take advantage of not having
5. Instead of complaining

sample exercises 13, page 237
1. Your lying
2. their playing
   or Michael and Tom's playing
3. his moving
4. your helping
5. her laughing
   or Linda's laughing

sample exercises 14, page 238
1. by taking
2. By cooking
3. by eating
4. By sitting
5. by talking/by doing

sample exercises 15, page 238
1. having done
2. having forgotten
3. not having invited
4. having made
5. not having been

sample exercises 16, page 239
1. her having been
2. Larry's having quit
3. your having told

4. our not having finished
5. your having done

sample exercises 17, page 239
1. snowing/to snow
2. studying/to study
3. paying/to pay
4. going/to go
5. working/to work

sample exercises 18, page 240
1. to tell
2. pushing/pulling
3. taking
4. to feed
5. meeting
6. to inform

sample exercises 19, page 240
1. It's going to cost $450 to get my car fixed.
2. It was stupid not to study for the test.
3. It's important not to forget your passport.
4. It was shocking to learn the truth.
5. It isn't necessary to be big or tall to be a good soccer player.

sample exercises 20, page 240
1. managed
2. waiting
3. happened
4. meant
5. afford

sample exercises 21, page 240
1. taught him
2. told her
   or warned her
3. persuaded him
   or got him
4. urged him
   or encouraged him
5. forced me

sample exercises 22, page 240
1. expect you
2. prefer
3. begged her
4. asked
5. chose me

sample exercises 23, page 242
1. naive
2. eager
3. reluctant
4. relieved
5. likely

sample exercises 24, page 242
1. sorry
2. fortunate
3. proud
4. sad

sample exercises 25, page 242
1. to have seen
2. not to have been
3. to have been
4. not to have been hurt

sample exercises 26, page 243
1. gave us a lot of homework to do
2. a big project to finish by Wednesday
3. have a book to read while you're waiting
4. many beautiful places to see in Italy
5. think of a single thing to say

sample exercises 27, page 243
1. I flew to Oregon (in order) to see my mother.
2. He called me (in order) to ask a question.
3. He went to the library (in order) to get a book.
4. I stopped at the gas station (in order) to buy gas.
5. She went to the bank (in order) to cash a check.

sample exercises 28, page 28
1. We are hurrying so (that) we don't miss the bus.
2. Alan is studying so (that) he will get a good grade on his exam.
3. He's buying a map so (that) he doesn't get lost when he goes to Istanbul.
4. Mary woke up at 4:30 this morning so (that) she could get to work early.
5. I didn't go to the party so (that) I wouldn't see Michael.
6. We waited for three hours so that we could get tickets for the game.

sample exercises 29, page 245
1. got
2. make
3. have
   or make
4. let
5. had
   or made
6. help

sample exercises 30, page 245
1. Why did you get your hair cut so short?
2. I need to have a passport picture taken.
3. Do you know where I can get a check cashed?
4. You have to get this sweater dry cleaned.
5. I'm going to get this watch repaired.

sample exercises 31, page 246
1. This coffee is very hot, but I like hot coffee, so no problem.
2. I don't make enough money to buy a house.
3. correct
4. correct
5. Put on a coat. It's too cold to go outside without a coat on.

sample exercises 32, page 246
1. have enough money to buy
2. work hard enough to graduate
3. early enough to say
4. big enough for everyone to have
5. tall enough to be

sample exercises 33, page 246
1. too busy to talk
2. too badly to stay
3. too hot to drink
4. too long to read
5. too tough to cut

CHAPTER 18
sample exercises 1, page 249
1. If I don't drink coffee in the morning, I get a headache.
2. Whenever my brother visits, he sleeps on the sofa.
3. I feel awful the next day when I don't get enough sleep.
4. My neighbors get mad if I make a lot of noise.
5. Every time the phone rings, the baby wakes up.

sample exercises 2, page 249
1. will be/go
2. won't buy/don't lower
3. have/will help
4. won't make/don't have
5. isn't here/will cancel

sample exercises 3, page 249
1. ought to finish/wants
2. visit/shouldn't miss

3. am/may not be
4. might not go/don't feel
5. should be/am

sample exercises 4, page 251
1. would get to/had
   or could get to/had
2. would ask/were
   or could ask/were
3. didn't have/would go
4. weren't/would help
   or weren't/could help
5. didn't have/couldn't enter
6. weren't/would be

sample exercises 5, page 251
1. am/visit
2. comes/will have
3. has/asks
4. will stay/doesn't finish
5. couldn't reach/weren't
6. were/didn't have/would...do

sample exercises 6, page 252
1. wouldn't have been/wouldn't be
2. would have gone
   or could have gone
   or might have gone
3. wouldn't have been
4. would...have known
5. wouldn't have said

sample exercises 7, page 252
1. If this machine were to break down, I wouldn't know how to fix it.
2. If she were to have quintuplets, her husband would have a heart attack.
3. If I were to offer you a 15% discount, would you say yes?
4. If you were to touch that wire, you'd be killed instantly.
5. If we were to raise our prices, how much do you think our sales would fall?

sample exercises 8, page 254
1. If we had gone to Beijing, we might have gone to the Forbidden City.
2. Sarah could have made some cookies if she had had enough chocolate.
3. I would have helped her if she had asked me.
4. If I had seen another student cheating on the test, I wouldn't have told the teacher.
5. I couldn't have seen anything if I hadn't had my glasses.
6. If you had been sick, would you have stayed home from work?

sample exercises 9, page 254
1. needed
2. hadn't wasted
3. wouldn't have been
4. has
5. were
6. didn't have
7. hadn't fallen
8. is
9. wouldn't have liked

sample exercises 10, page 254
1. would have understood/would understand
   or could have understood/could understand
   or might have understood/might understand
2. would have known/would know
   or would have known/might know
   or might have known/would know
   or might have known/might know
3. wouldn't have done/wouldn't be
   or might not have done/wouldn't be

4. would have come
5. wouldn't have run out of/wouldn't be
6. would have understood/wouldn't be
   or might have understood/might not be
7. wouldn't have been/wouldn't be

sample exercises 11, page 256
1. he were going to stay home
2. she didn't have so much work to do
3. my cell phone battery weren't dead
4. she comes
5. I hadn't promised my mother I'd visit her
6. I hadn't forgotten he was coming
7. I didn't have a doctor's appointment

sample exercises 12, page 257
1. see Mary today/give her this bag of cookies
2. hadn't been studying/would have been listening to the radio
3. go to Mexico City/go to the museum there
4. were sleeping/would have to be quiet
5. is fired/can easily find another job
6. had snowed a lot yesterday/would have been canceled

sample exercises 13, page 257
1. would you tell me
2. what would her salary have been
   or how much would her salary have been
3. could she have seen the accident
4. how many children would you like to have
5. you wouldn't have known what to do

sample exercises 14, page 258
1. don't have
2. isn't/don't have to
3. doesn't call
4. aren't/don't allow
5. doesn't start/isn't

sample exercises 15, page 258
1. aren't
2. won't talk
3. don't have
4. won't go/isn't
5. don't buy/won't be

sample exercises 16, page 258
1. weren't
2. wouldn't do
3. didn't eat/wouldn't be
4. weren't/wouldn't fall
5. didn't stay out/wouldn't be

sample exercises 17, page 258
1. hadn't been
2. wouldn't have gotten
3. hadn't been/wouldn't have been
4. hadn't been/wouldn't have seen
5. hadn't screwed around/wouldn't have had to

sample exercises 18, page 259
1. would stop calling
   or wouldn't call
2. lived in
3. would quit asking
4. hadn't quit
5. didn't leave
6. were eating
7. were going to make
8. didn't have
9. were going to be
10. went
11. could have gone

sample exercises 19, page 260

1. had I known
2. Had you gotten up
3. had I not seen
4. Had she been caught
5. Had it not started

sample exercises 20, page 261

1. Were John
2. Were I not
3. Were you
4. were he not
5. were it not
6. you were to lose
   Were you to
7. I were to fall
   Were I to fall

sample exercises 21, page 261

1. this one should be
   should this one be
2. you should have
   should you have
3. it should rain
   should it rain
4. Mary should need
   Should Mary need

sample exercises 22, page 262

1. lived
2. didn't live
3. were taking
4. did
5. were
6. weren't

sample exercises 23, page 262

1. had kept
2. owned
3. left
4. had stayed
5. drove
6. ate

sample exercises 24, page 263

1. didn't go
2. didn't get
3. went
4. listened
5. didn't take
6. had walked

sample exercises 25, page 263

1. Would you mind if I closed the window?
2. Would you mind if we went home at 3:30?
3. Would you have minded if I hadn't gone shopping with you?
4. Would you mind if we were late to your party?
5. Would you mind if I did it tomorrow?

sample exercises 26, page 263

1. got
2. knew
3. bought
4. came
5. got
6. went

sample exercises 27, page 264

1. doesn't
2. don't/will
3. would
4. does/will

5. would/could/can't
6. didn't
7. didn't
8. wouldn't be/weren't
9. should have/didn't/had/wouldn't have
10. hadn't been

sample exercises 28, page 265

1. could
2. had
   or had gone
3. would/could/can't
4. don't
5. weren't
6. does
7. hadn't
8. could have/hadn't been

sample exercises 29, page 265

1. weren't
2. hadn't been
3. hadn't
4. had
   or could have
5. were
6. could
7. were
8. would
9. did
10. did

sample exercises 30, page 265

1. didn't
2. hadn't
3. were
4. had
5. would
6. hadn't
7. did
8. weren't
9. had
10. did

Index

A

adjective clauses, 155
  reduced to adverb phrases, 218
adjective phrases, 155
adjectives
  adjective preposition combinations, 115, 117
  adverbs used with compound adjectives, 121
  comparative forms, 110
  comparisons with *same, similar, different, like* and *alike,* 122
  compound adjectives, 119
  get used with, 115
  gradable vs. non-gradable adjectives, 124
  modified by adverbs, 123
  nouns used with, 118
  participle adjectives, 114
  possessive adjectives, 54
  superlative forms, 112
adverb clauses, 191, 199, 201
  nonrestrictive (aka nonessential), 162
  object clauses, 157
  restrictive (aka essential), 162
  subject adjective clauses, 156
adverb phrases, 191, 199, 218
adverbs, 14
  adverbs of (indefinite) frequency, 194
  adverbs of degree, 196
  adverbs of place, 194
  adverbs of purpose, 196
  adverbs of time, 194
  indefinite adverbs, 60, 191
  non-grading, 124
  relative adverbs, 161
  used to modify adjectives, 123
  used to modify non-gradable adjectives, 124
  used with compound adjectives, 121
American English, 10, 45, 58, 88, 115, 223, 268
amplifiers, 197
appositives, 171
articles, 59
aspect, 13

B

bare infinitives, 244
be going to, 41, 44
be, 13, 277
  in *yes/no* questions, 17
  infinitive form, 13
  past contractions, 18
  past negative, 18
  past, 18
  present contractions, 16
  present negative, 16
  present, 15

  short answers, 20
  six uses of, 13
been to, 107
British English, 10, 45, 58, 88, 115, 223, 268

C

causality, 102
chunks (aka lexical phrases), 9
cloze exercises, 65
cognates, 116
  fasle cognates (aka false friends), 242
collocations, 9
  fixed collocations, 9
  strong collocations, 9
  weak collocations, 9
complex sentences, 212
compound sentences, 35
conditionals, 247
  first conational, 249
  implied conditionals, 255
  second conditional, 250
  third conditional, 254
  zero conditional, 248
conjunctions, 202
  conjunctive adverbs, 202, 207
  coordinating conjunctions, 202, 203
  correlative conjunctions, 202, 224
  subordinating conjunctions, 202, 211
continuous (aka progressive), 23
  -ing form, 23
  present used for future plans, 47
  present, 24
contractions
  importance of emphasizing use of, 2
  with *will,* 43
  with present perfect, 98
  with past perfect, 101
  with future perfect, 103
  with *be,* 16, 18
crash blossoms, 152

D

deductive teaching, 8, 88
dependent clauses, 7, 23, 24, 72, 100, 102, 103, 105, 175, 201, 211, 212, 214, 248, 256, 275
did, 29, 33
direct objects, 57
distractors, 132
ditransitive objects, 57
do, 29, 69
  auxiliary verb and main verb, 38
  emphatic *do,* 37, 69, 78
  negative, 30

present simple, 29
   -*s* form, 31
   short answers, 31
does, 29, 32
downtoners, 197
dummy subject, 75, 175, 240

E
ellipsis, 35
   with *do, does* and *did,* 35
   with future, 49
   with *have got to,* 92
   with modals and phrasal modals, 152
   with perfect tenses, 107
   with the conditional, 263
embedded questions, 175
emphasizers, 197
emphatic *do,* 37, 69, 78
error correction, 8
   fossilized errors, 8
   global errors, 8
   local errors, 8
ESL vs. EFL, 10
expletives, 75, 175, 240
extraposition, 169

F
false beginners, xviii
false cognates (aka false friends), 242
filler subject, 240
fronting, 78
functions, 127
future continuous, 26
future perfect, 102
   continuous, 104
   contractions with 103
future, 41
   be about to, 49
   be going to, 41, 44
   present continuous used for future plans, 47
   present simple used for future plans, 48
   shall, 45
   will, 41

G
games, 7
gerund phrases, 229
gerunds, 229

H
have
   auxiliary verb and main verb, 95
have got to, 87
   = *have to,* 90
   negatives with *have got to,* 91
   questions with *have got to,* 91
have got, 87
   negatives with *have got,* 89
   questions with *have got,* 89
headlinese, 151

I
i+1, 9
idioms, 6, 9
indefinite adverbs, 60, 62
indefinite pronouns, 60, 61, 62
independent clauses, 7, 23, 35, 72, 100, 105, 178, 187, 201, 202, 203, 207, 210, 211, 212, 217, 225, 227, 248, 256, 275
indirect objects, 57
inductive teaching, 8, 88
indicative, 13, 247, 277
infinitives, 229, 278
intensifiers, 197
interference, 9
intonation, 81
inversion, 67-71, 74, 77, 98

K
Krashen, 9

L
lesson plans, 3
lexical phrases (aka chunks), 9
lexicon, 83
listening, 81
   important in a grammar class, 1, 21
   with *have got* and *have got to,* 88
   with past perfect and present perfect, 107
   with reduced pronouns, 65

M
metalanguage, 6
mood, 13
motivation, 5

N
noun clauses, 175, 275
   noun clause markers, 275
nouns, 53
   adverbial nouns, 14
   compound nouns, 118
   count nouns, 62
   noncount nouns, 62
   possessive nouns, 56

O
object pronouns, 53

P
passive voice, 183
past participles, 96
past perfect, 100
   continuous, 104
   contractions with, 101
   used to show causality, 102
perfect tenses, 95
   future perfect, 102
   past perfect, 100
   present perfect, 96
phrasal verbs, 9, 83
pitch, 81
possessive adjectives, 54
possessive nouns, 56
prepositions, 2

adjective preposition combinations, 115
    phrasal prepositions, 159
present participle phrases, 165
present participles, 23
present perfect, 96
    continuous, 104
    contractions with, 98
    short answers with, 98
present simple, 29
productive skills, 1
pronouns, 53
    indefinite pronouns, 60, 61, 62
    object pronouns, 53
    reflexive pronouns, 64
    relative pronouns, 157, 275
    subject pronouns, 53

Q

quantifiers, 62
questions, 67
    embedded questions, 175
    importance of focusing on, 2
    information questions, 70, 82
    negative questions, 79
    tag questions, 80
    with *have got to*, 91
    with *have got*, 89
    yes/no questions, 70, 82

R

receptive skills, 1
reductions, 1, 2, 46
    in questions, 82
    reduced pronouns, 65
reflexive pronouns, 64
reported speech, 181
Romance languages, 242

S

short answers
    with *be*, 20, 26
    with present perfect, 98
speaking
    continuous practice, 26
    practice with *did*, 34
    practice with *do*, 30, 34
    practice with *does*, 33, 34
    practice with possessive adjectives and possessive nouns, 57
    practice with possessive adjectives, 55
    practice with subject pronouns and object pronouns, 54
    three-way speaking exercise with *be*, 21
student-centered teaching, 1, 88
    vs. teacher centered, 8
subject complements, 231
subject pronouns, 53
subject-verb agreement, 31
subjunctive, 247, 253, 277

T

tense, 13
textbooks, 4

V

verbs
    auxiliary verbs, 24, 31, 38, 67, 69, 77, 95, 210
    causative, 244
    ditransitive verbs, 57
    intransitive verbs, 184, 187
    irregular, 33
    main verbs, 36
    main verbs, 67, 277
    modal (and phrasal modal) auxiliary verbs, 67, 69, 77, 87, 127
    phrasal verbs, 83, 160
    regular, 33
    transitive verbs, 159, 184
    verb 1, 33, 34, 42, 277, 278
    verb 2, 33, 277, 278
    verb 3, 33, 114, 183, 277, 278
vocabulary
    when to avoid and when to focus on, 2

W

will, 41
    negative contractions of, 43
    plans, 45
    predictions, 45
    questions, with *will*, 42
word stock, 83

CPSIA information can be obtained at www.ICGtesting.com
Printed in the USA
LVOW01s1509250215

428334LV00016B/489/P